GUINNESS Book of
SQUASH

MICHAEL PALMER

GUINNESS SUPERLATIVES LIMITED
2 Cecil Court, London Road, Enfield, Middlesex

Editor: Anne Marshall
Design and layout: Jean Whitcombe

© Michael Palmer and Guinness Superlatives Ltd, 1984

Published in Great Britain by
Guinness Superlatives Ltd, 2 Cecil Court, London Road,
Enfield, Middlesex

Set in Plantin 10/12 pt
Filmset by Fakenham Photosetting Ltd, Fakenham, Norfolk
Printed and bound in Spain by TONSA, San Sebastian

British Library Cataloguing in Publication Data
Palmer, Michael
    The Guinness book of squash.
    1. Squash rackets (Game)
    I. Title
    796.34'3   GV1004

ISBN 0-85112-270-1

Qamar Zaman of Pakistan and Hiddy Jahan of England.
'Excuse me', Jahan appears to be saying to his former
countryman as he attempts to reach the ball. Two of the
greatest players of modern-day squash. *Tim Pike*

CONTENTS

FOREWORD

When accepting the commission to compile *The Guinness Book of Squash* no one mentioned that in addition to a need for modest literary skills there was also a requirement to be something of super sleuth and explorer rolled into one. I should have known better. My own association with the sport and some knowledge of the painstaking research that went into Rex Bellamy's admirable *The Story of Squash* and John Horry's *The History of Squash Rackets* should have warned me of the problems ahead. Squash may be expanding and growing in many countries, but its communications are still very basic and information hard to obtain.

This book is not intended to be a history of the game. That subject is well covered by the two volumes mentioned. This is an attempt to document the sport as it stands today, to look at its past, to feature some of the heroes and more importantly to detail the world-wide development of squash and some of the attendant sectors such as the professional player, spectator squash and the competitive scene. Additionally I have unearthed some, but by no means all, of the fascinating facts and feats of squash, which perhaps will settle arguments about the longest, shortest, youngest, oldest, most, etc.

How well I have succeeded you can judge for yourself. If there are gaps in various sections then I plead that the most likely reason is that the information has either not been received or is currently not available. Squash, it seems, has taken a perverse delight in hiding much of its early beginnings and the formative years of the 1920s and 1930s. And modern day squash records suffer frequently from the neglect inherent in social systems whereby the priorities of squash administrators are to raise cash and keep things running. The writing down for posterity what actually happens comes a poor third. The latter comment, of course, is a generalisation, but I do feel there is a danger that squash in its headlong rush for mass recognition may be repeating the mistakes that left us with such a sketchy impression of its formation. It is my sincere hope that publication of this book will go some way to help avert this threat and prompt the memories of many squash enthusiasts around the world who could make a fascinating and valuable

---

Dean Williams of Australia (*left*) and Stuart Davenport of New Zealand (*right*). Extrovert Williams who livens the world squash scene both on and off the court seen in action against New Zealand number 1, Davenport, who despite his youthfulness has already made his mark on the world scene. *Tim Pike*

---

contribution to the documentation of the sport in future editions, either with a photograph or editorial information.

Fortunately, there do exist such people as Ian Wright, secretary of the European Squash Rackets Federation, who has made it his business to assemble a most valuable collection of books on squash. These date back to the turn of this century and must form the basis for any serious research into the history of squash. I am much indebted to Ian's assistance, advice and help in making available the unpublished notes of former SRA secretary Henry Hayman. Mr Hayman's accounts of meetings of the Tennis and Rackets Association concerning the court, the ball and the racket were most helpful in piecing together what information exists on these subjects.

The selection of the 'Champions of Squash' may earn criticism if only for those who have been left out, but there is simply not space to portray the career of every player who has won an international title of significance.

The sections on squash-playing nations and championship results will, I hope, help everyone to appreciate how widely the game has developed, firstly by noting the different countries involved and secondly by becoming aware that other areas of the world, namely Asia and the Caribbean, have now initiated important championships that may eventually rival some traditional events.

'Who Runs Squash', as the title suggests, outlines how the game is governed and may give a better understanding of the respective roles of the various federations and associations.

The 'Tournament Players' feature many of the top men and women professionals whose activities form the sport's shop window. Their future is intimately linked to the subject of spectator squash, a further section which takes a look at the modern phenomena of glass and plastic courts and television.

Facts and Feats is unfortunately only a small section. Very few nations have taken the trouble to detail their own record makers but again I express the hope that publication of those who have bothered will stir others into action.

Squash's biggest battles ahead may lie with the media, how the sport tackles the vexed question of television; and with itself. Is the sport susceptible to the changes of rule and format that may be necessary if squash is ever to achieve even modest exposure via television? And if anyone is wondering why squash should pursue television in such an apparent slavish manner they have only to look around at the changing patterns of leisure. Much of this change has come about with the public having a better understanding and knowledge, via television, of the different sport opportunities that are available. Since squash has to compete in the market place, just like other sports, for a person's time and money, the sport cannot sit back and hope that its own inherent appeal will continue to win followers in the next decade in the same way that it has done over the last ten years.

Finally, I would like to thank that amiable Irishman, Larry Halpin, editor of the *Squash Player* magazine, for his substantial contribution to this book by way of research and compiling information and background material for many of the sections. Without Larry's help I should never have been able to beat the printer's :adline.

Acknowledgements

The author would like to thank the following for all their help and assistance in the preparation of this book.

Larry Halpin, Editor of *Squash Player* magazine, for editorial and research assistance.

Ian Wright, custodian of the SRA library, for advice, help and making available his unique collection of squash books and memorabilia.

Andrew Shelley, tournament secretary of the SRA, for being so patient in answering so many queries.

Dunlop Sports Company, for co-operation and help with the feature on the manufacture of squash balls and rackets.

Secretaries and members of national associations who answered letters and provided information.

Robin Eley Jones, for his photographs and use of his library.

Rex Bellamy, author of *The Story of Squash* (Cassell), for a brief extract from his book, used in the article on Roshan Khan.

Country abbreviations

Aus	Australia
Bah	Bahamas
Bar	Barbados
Bel	Belgium
Ber	Bermuda
Can	Canada
Egy	Egypt
Eng	England
Fin	Finland
GB	Great Britain and N. Ireland
Guy	Guyana
HK	Hong Kong
Ind	India
Ire	Ireland
Jam	Jamaica
Jap	Japan
Ken	Kenya
Mal	Malaysia
Mex	Mexico
Net	Netherlands
NZ	New Zealand
Pak	Pakistan
Phi	Philippines
PNG	Papua New Guinea
St. Vin	St. Vincent
Rho	Rhodesia
SA	South Africa
Sco	Scotland
Sin	Singapore
Swe	Sweden
Swz	Switzerland
USA	United States of America
Wal	Wales
Zim	Zimbabwe

1 History of the game

Tracing the exact origins of any sport is far from easy, and squash is no exception, but there is no doubt that the game developed from rackets which appears to have been first played in the walled yards of London taverns and prisons in the early 19th century.

Inexplicably, in the 1820s, rackets travelled the few miles north-west to the infinitely more sedate surroundings of Harrow school. Sometime in the next decade, almost certainly by accident, a softer ball than that used normally in rackets found its way on to the courts at Harrow. Thus two slightly different variations of the same theme known as 'harder' and 'squash' – depending on the ball used – began to develop. In 1850 two roofless rackets courts were built at the school and when, in 1864, a covered court was erected and four squash courts appeared on the site of one of the earlier roofless versions the two games took on entirely separate identities.

Squash doubtless grew in popularity in the years that followed but, apart from the building of the first-ever privately owned court by former Harrow pupil Vernon Harcourt in Oxford in 1883, little or nothing of its progress is charted. Indeed, the first known published reference to the game is a mention in *The Badminton Library of Sports and Pastimes* in 1890: 'There are now in existence in England several private houses with a more elaborate "squash" court attached, built indeed like a smaller hard-ball court.'

The first in-depth explanation of the game and its rules appeared in *The Boys' Own Paper* in 1893. Author Somerville Gilbey introduced the game with these words: 'Squash, a corruption of squash racquets, is a familiar name to all Harrow boys and might be so with advantage to other boys as well because it designates a capital game which, without requiring any large expenditure of pocket-money or amount of apparatus, can be played anywhere there are walls. Give a Harrow boy a wall – if a blank one so much the better – and two others, or even one other, at right angles to it, with a clear space between, and the probability is it won't be long before he is busy at squash rackets.' It is interesting to note that Gilbey sometimes referred to the game as 'rugby squash' because he believed it had its origins in the rugby fives courts at Harrow.

The early days of squash. Boys at Harrow School waiting to play rackets practise with a softer ball in a courtyard

The first book on squash, entitled *The Game of Squash*, written by world champion rackets and tennis player Eustace Miles, was published in 1901. Miles wrote that even though there had not yet been an official championship, very few competitions and no professionals devoted solely to the game, thousands of people throughout the world played and enjoyed squash.

Meanwhile the game was already establishing itself in America. In 1891 the Philadelphia Racket Club had built a squash court and when, in 1907, the United States Squash Racquets Association (USSRA) was formed and held the world's first national championship, the club provided the winner, John A. Miskey. A year later a USSRA national team championship was held.

The Americans preferred the use of a harder ball and longer narrower courts and, because of lack of standardisation of courts and equipment, the American game rapidly developed its own identity. This rift has never been healed and today the Americans still play predominantly the 'hardball' game while in the rest of the world the 'softball' or 'international' game is unchallenged.

In England in 1907 the Tennis and Rackets Association was formed with a special committee to look after the interests of squash. This was followed by the forming of two other national associations, one in South Africa in 1910 which decided to conform to the rules as being played in Britain and the other in 1911 in Canada.

By 1920 Britain still had no squash association of its own but there was plenty of activity. The first two match challenges for the professional championship of the British Isles took place between Charles Read and Oke Johnson and this was the forerunner of the two main British events – the Amateur and Open Championships. Over in America the 'hardball' game was developing apace and the donation of a cup by Mr Henry G. Lapham of Boston stimulated a match in 1922 between the USA and Canada – an occurrence which makes the Lapham Cup the oldest international fixture.

In February 1922 Mrs Joyce Cave became Britain's first-ever Amateur champion when she beat her sister Nancy and it was not until the following year that the men's event was inaugurated and Tommy Jameson crowned champion.

In 1923 the Tennis and Rackets Association formalised standards for the court and the ball. In the following year the playing rules were standardised and in 1925 the dimensions for the racket were laid down.

The year 1926 saw the scoring system changed in Britain from a 15-point game to the 9-point game and as the Americans had already standardised their rules on play and equipment, this further cemented the rift between the American and British games.

By the mid-twenties long flannel trousers were giving way to shorts, court walls were being plastered and team events were proving popular. England and America were competing in international competition (England joined in the Lapham Cup) which posed problems for players attempting to adapt from one ball to another. Charles Arnold, Britain's first squash professional, was quoted at the time: 'the ball is a very vexed question in squash' . . . some things never change!

The Squash Rackets Association was founded on 13 December 1928 in the Royal Automobile Club in Pall Mall, London. Although affiliated to the Tennis and Rackets Association, it took over complete responsi-

The formation of the Women's Squash Rackets Association in 1934 helped to popularise the game among women and this meant more work for professionals such as Charles Arnold, pictured here in 1938 giving lessons at the Kensington Country Club. *Keystone Press/Fox Photos*

bility for the British game throughout the world. Its first executive committee was formed on 1 April 1929 and the first SRA Handbook appeared in the 1929/30 season.

1930 was a year of many firsts, heralding the English Inter-County Championship, the Inter-Services Championship, and most important of all, the first British Open. Charles Read, professional at the Queen's Club in London was designated 'Open champion' but lost both legs of a challenge match against Don Butcher of London's Conservative Club who thus became the first winner of the event that was to be regarded as the unofficial world championship until 1976 and is still rated by many of the top players as *the* title to win. Butcher retained the title the following year when he defeated Charles Arnold but the 1930s really belonged to the man who beat him in 1932 – Abdel Fattah Amr (better known as Amr Bey). With that victory the stylish Egyptian, who played his squash at the Royal Automobile Club in Pall Mall, became the first man to win the British Amateur and British Open titles in the same season. In all he held six Amateur and six Open titles during the thirties including the 1933 Open in which he was unchallenged.

Manufacturers of squash balls had to ensure that their products met certain conditions and specifications. These were drawn up by the Tennis and Rackets Association and when the SRA was formed in December 1928, the authority to grant approval passed to that body. Six months later the TRA 'Standard' mark (shown left) was still being used although this was eventually replaced by the SRA's own mark

SPECIFICATION of THE STANDARD SQUASH RACKET BALL as
laid down by the TENNIS & RACKETS ASSOCIATION.

JULY 1929.

1. <u>Size</u> $1\frac{9}{16}$ - $1\frac{10}{16}$ Outside diameter.

2. <u>Weight</u> 360 - 380 grains - Apothecaries or Troy Weight.
                 Balls must be weighed in temperature of 68°.F.
                 (approximately)

3. <u>Bounce</u> When dropped from 100 inches on to concrete bounce of ball must not
be less than 36 inches, not more than 38 inches.
                The bottom of ball must be resting at 100
                inches.
                The bounce measurement is taken to bottom of
                ball at top of its bounce.
                Balls must be kept in an even temperature of 68°F.
                for 12 hours prior to testing and must be tested
                in temperature of 68°F. (approximately)
                Balls must be dropped five or six times to
                secure accurate bounce test.
                Balls can be handled before and during test but
                not warmed.

4. <u>Inflation</u> Finger with light pressure on ball must almost touch opposite wall.
                Balls should have as low inflation as possible
                consistent with their regaining their shape
                after hard impact.

5. <u>Play</u> Balls must have been tested in play and approved by the Testing
Committee of the Squash Rackets Association.

6. <u>Miscellaneous</u>.
        Balls must have matt finish.
        Balls must be round.
        Balls must not be liable to break.
        The walls of balls should be even and seams should not affect play of
        ball.
        It is found that bounce tests of balls are unsatisfactory if carried
        out within one week of their manufacture.

Applicants who wish their balls to be authorised for stamping with
the "Standard" mark should submit same for testing either to Colonel
Basset, 19 Denbigh Street, S.W.1. or to W.D. Macpherson Esq., 21
Buckingham Gate, S.W.1. to whom all enquiries concerning balls
should be sent.

Until Authority is granted by the Squash Rackets Association balls
must not be stamped with the Standard mark. Once granted the
Applicant is responsible for seeing that all balls stamped by him
conform to the Standard specification. Failure to comply with this
condition will render an Applicant liable to have his right to use
the Standard mark withdrawn.

Manufacturers to whom a permit to use the Standard mark has been
granted will be responsible for stamping balls made by them to the
Standard specification with the Standard mark.

TO AMERICA FOR SQUASH: THE BRITISH LADY TOURISTS.

MRS. G. DU BOULAY.

THE HON. ANNE LYTTON MILBANKE.

MRS. V. S. DANIELL.

MRS. G. BRYANS WOLFE (CAPTAIN).

(TOP) MISS NANCY CAVE (EX-CHAMPION).
(CENTRE) MISS SUSAN NOEL (CHAMPION).
(BOTTOM) MISS C. FENWICK (EX-CHAMPION).

The Women's Squash Rackets Association are sending a team to the States to meet the American women players. Despite the absence of at least two notable players, the team is a strong one. The tour will include participation in the American championships at Philadelphia and a series of international matches. In the past the women's British squash championship has been held three times each by Miss Nancy Cave, her sister, Miss Joyce Cave, and Miss C. Fenwick, the only other winners being Miss S. Huntsman and Miss Susan Noel, the present holder.

First televised squash? Not quite, but an old picture just the same. It was taken on 16 February 1939 at the Alexandra Palace studios, London, during the early days of British television. The occasion was an interview with the visiting American women's squash team. Mrs I. McKechnie of the British team is far right of the back row and seated are Susan Noel (*left*) and Ann Page, the USA champion

The years 1932 to 1934 were particularly important to the development of women's squash in Britain. In 1932 the SRA appointed a committee to manage the women's game in this country and the following year a British women's team toured overseas for the first time when they visited North America where they won the Wolfe–Noel Cup, an event run intermittently until 1968. In 1934 the Women's Squash Rackets Association was founded and, like the SRA, not only took charge of the game in England but unofficially acted as governing body for the international game.

By 1932 62 clubs and organisations were affiliated to the SRA, together with 50 individuals, and Devonshire had formed the first county association. In that year a squash ball cost 1/6d (7½p), a racket about £1 and a brick and cement court could be built for less than £600. A court with a gallery and changing facilities would have been as much as £800!

In 1933 a British women's team went to America to play their counterparts under American rules. The team was led by Mrs G. Bryans Wolfe, the non-playing captain, and Susan Noel, the then British women's champion. Together they donated a trophy – the Wolfe–Noel Cup – to be competed for annually by the two countries. The British team also contained former Open champions in Nancy Cave and Ciceley Fenwick and the Americans were beaten 4–1 at the Sleepy Hollow club near New York. The Cup was contested 16 times, between 1933 and 1968, with Britain winning 11 and the USA 5.
Illustrated London News

The game made great strides in England during the middle and later thirties with many competitions being started, and in 1937 the seeds were sown for the formation of a home international tournament when Scotland played both England and Ireland.

Following a dispute with the SRA over the standard ball, the professionals formed a breakaway association but the argument was resolved just before the war and the two bodies merged.

The growth of the game in the 1930s is best illustrated by the SRA's membership figures in 1939. The first county association had only been formed in 1931, but at the outbreak of war the SRA had 32 counties within its membership, divided into 10 areas with a combined total of 320 clubs. Countries affiliated had risen from four in 1931 to include organisations from Ireland, Scotland, Wales, Australia, Egypt, India, New Zealand, South Africa, Hong Kong, Federated Malay States and China.

However, not everything was rosy in the squash garden. Towards the end of the decade there were strong but unsuccessful moves, at various times, to

K. C. Gandar Dower, the British Amateur champion in 1938–39 (pictured here with Susan Noel), had the novel idea of introducing a 'hazard' into the court to alleviate the problem of long, boring rallies. This was an angled block of wood 18 in (46 cm) and 6 in (15 cm) wide which fitted into the backhand corner of the court. *Illustrated London News*

introduce a faster ball, lower the tin by two inches, put holes or marks just above the tin which, if hit, would give a player a bonus point, and place obstacles in certain places around the court – particularly in the back corners. Why were such radical changes being suggested? Many people felt that rallies were becoming too long and saw these as possible ways of shortening them. As was suggested by criticism in the 1920s . . . some things *really* don't change, bearing in mind the arguments that have raged from the mid seventies onwards concerning the ball and long, boring matches.

Gray's, one of the most famous manufacturing names in squash and their advert from the 1929–30 SRA handbook

After the growth of the 1930s, squash, like every other sport, suffered harshly from the rigours of the Second World War. Many buildings in London had been damaged or destroyed and squash balls were in very short supply and/or poor quality.

The Bath Club was one of those damaged and the 1946 British Amateur had to move to the Lansdowne Club. It was this competition more than most that brought home the stark reality of what had gone on in the previous six years. Missing from the field of 90 were the only three men other than the great Amr to win the championship in the thirties – Victor Cazalet, Cyril Hamilton and Kenneth Gandar Dower, the last champion before the war. All had been killed in action. As the game got under way again, Norman Borrett, currently president of the English SRA, registered the first of his five successive victories, while Jim Dear, who had finally won the Open title in the 1938/9 season after being runner-up three times, lost the first post-war championship to Mahmoud

Karim. This was the last British Open played on the challenge system but the new knock-out format seemed to make little difference as the same two fought out the next year's final with the same result.

Although building restrictions were still in force in the late forties which prevented the growth of the game, it was estimated that some 200 000 people were visiting the 300 clubs still in use throughout Britain. It seemed certain that a boom would come as soon as restrictions were lifted.

But the boom was not destined to arrive, in England at any rate, until the late 1960s by which time squash had already become an overwhelmingly popular public sport in Australia. Curtain raisers to the squash growth were undoubtedly the Khans with their dominance of the world's major events in the 1950s. Their skills inspired many to the sport and the eventual arrival of a home-grown hero in the form of Jonah Barrington in the mid sixties was just the catalyst that British squash needed.

Barrington's feats, his ability to 'sell' himself and the game and his rivalry with the Australian Geoff Hunt ushered in the era of professionalism as court building in Britain got under way and at a speed that no one would have believed possible in the depressing post-war years. The success of commercial squash court operations in Australia was mirrored in Britain as land and money became available and the sport's inherent appeal of brisk exercise in pleasant surroundings triggered a surge of court development that was to last from the late sixties to the end of the next decade.

This in turn fuelled interest in the continent of Europe where the sport is steadily gaining a foothold in many countries, particularly in Germany where the expansion rate has been phenomenal. Elsewhere in the world, squash continues to expand, notably in south-east Asia where Singapore leads the way with an almost fanatical enthusiasm.

Not surprisingly, membership of the International Squash Rackets Federation, founded in 1967, has grown from a handful of countries to the present state of more than 50 members. The ISRF took over control of the sport from the SRA in the year of their formation and is now the body responsible for implementing and changing the rules.

The professional game has prospered too with the International Squash Players Association being formed in 1973 and now looking after the interests of more than 100 members. A Women's Players Association was formed in April 1984.

The men's squash game did not go 'Open' until 1980, but by the mid seventies the amateur who could survive with the pro's at the highest level was a dying breed. The Women's Squash Rackets Association had

DOUBLES

Doubles has long been played in North America – their first national championship began in 1933 and its popularity there has been aided by specially built courts. In England, however, the game barely survives, owing existence to its appeal as a 'fun event' rather than a competition of a serious nature, although having said that, the women's SRA have run a 'Doubles Cup' since 1957, and in February 1984 a

Prince's Club, London was believed to be the first club to build a court specifically for doubles and in 1935, when the court was opened, Jim Dear, the professional at Prince's, and the Hon. Anne Lytton-Milbanke were beaten in a special exhibition match by Mrs. I. McKechnie and Amr Bey, the British Open champion.
Illustrated London News

British national doubles championship for both men and women was played at the South Marston Country Club, Swindon in Wiltshire. This was the first time there had been a British men's doubles championship at either national or international level. The men's event was won by Christy Willstrop and Bob Forde and the women by Karen Butterworth and Nicola Spurgeon.

Squash differs from other court games in that it has developed almost exclusively as a singles game, and looking at the size of the singles court it is easy to see why. The lack of space for four active players prevents a fluid game developing and there is also the high probability that unless extreme caution is exercised someone will be struck with either a ball or racket or both.

The standard dimensions of a doubles court (45 ft (13·7 m) long by 25 ft (7·6 m) wide, as opposed to singles court dimensions (32 ft (9·7 m) × 21 ft (6·4 m), are the same as those accepted by the United States SRA so any effort to eventually draw together the two codes (American and international) could find immediate common ground in doubles.

The first doubles court in England is believed to have been at the Prince's Club and this was not of standard size. Susan Noel, British women's Open champion 1932–34, writing in her book *Sports Women's Manual* (1950), thinks the Prince's court had been improvised from an old rackets court or some similar disused playing area. However, she recalls that the members treated the game seriously and frequently arranged tournaments. This use continued until the club closed down in 1939. Miss Noel thinks that the doubles game in Britain owed more to the taste for doubles acquired by English women's teams touring America during the 1930s.

In 1935 Miss Lytton Millbanke (Lady Anne Lytton) and Mrs McKechnie won the women's national doubles title in the United States and in 1936 the same partnership proved successful in a women's Open event held at Prince's. Other women who toured abroad also became interested and Susan Noel has no doubt that it was the influence of these players which resulted in the construction of standard doubles courts, built to American specifications, at the Ladies Carlton Club, the St. Johns Wood Squash Rackets Club and the Edinburgh Sports Club. These three standard courts, together with the non-standard Prince's were the only courts in Britain and unhappily the only one now remaining is at Edinburgh since after the closure of Prince's, the other two courts were lost as a result of the Second World War.

already approved Open competition in 1973, so in many ways they were more far-sighted than the men in anticipating future trends in squash.

In 1977 plans were revealed in England for a four wall glass squash court and although it took several years before such a court appeared, the announcement sparked the movement towards spectator squash. This development could possibly bring about radical changes within squash since spectator squash is not merely about people watching but about providing entertainment and this could mean permanent rule changes, new scoring and a different ball.

Squash is feeling the effect of the need to sell itself via television and as the sport approaches the year 2000 there could be spectacular developments in store.

MILESTONES

1830s Softer ball introduced to game of rackets at Harrow school.

1850 Two roofless rackets courts built at Harrow.

1853 First covered rackets courts erected at Prince's Club, London.

1864 Four squash courts built on the site of one of the roofless rackets courts at Harrow.

1883 First private court built by Vernon Harcourt at Oxford.

1890 First recorded reference to squash in *Badminton Library of Sports and Pastimes*.

1891 Philadelphia Racquet Club build a squash court.

1893 First in depth article on game in *The Boys' Own Paper*.

1899 First press reports and results are published.

1901 First book on squash published, *The Game of Squash*, written by Eustace Miles.

1907 United States Squash Racquets Association is formed and holds world's first national championship. Tennis and Rackets Association set up committee to look after squash.

1910 South Africa set up national association and championship.

1911 Canada follows South Africa's lead.

1912 Charles Arnold, who taught the Prince of Wales to play and produced first coaching manual, becomes Britain's first professional.

1918 What is believed to be Australia's first court is erected in Sydney.

1920 Charles Read beats A. W. B. Oke Johnson over two legs to become first British professional champion.

1922 Mrs Joyce Cave wins first British Women's Championship. Bath Club Cup is inaugurated and won by Royal Automobile Club. Henry Lapham from Boston presents trophy for annual international competition.

1923 First British Men's Amateur Championship is played. Tennis and Rackets Association formalise standards for the court and ball.

1924 First British touring team goes to North America and finishes runner-up to US in Lapham Cup. Playing rules are standardised by Tennis and Rackets Association.

1926 British game changes scoring system from 15-point game to 9-point game.

1928 Squash Rackets Association (SRA) is founded. Jesters Club founded by Jock Burnet to spread sportsmanship in squash, court tennis, Eton fives, rackets and rugby fives.

1929 SRA produce first handbook.

1930 Charles Read is designated 'Open champion' but loses first British Open Championship to Don Butcher. Yorkshire become first Inter-County champions. Army wins inaugural Inter-Services event.

1931 F. R. S. Strickland wins first ever Australian Amateur Championship. F. D. Amr Bey wins first of six British Amateur titles. Devonshire form England's first county association.

1932 New Zealand's first Amateur Championship is played. Amr becomes first man to win British Amateur and Open titles in same season. SRA appoint committee to manage women's game in Britain.

1933 British women's team tours overseas for the first time.

1934 Women's Squash Rackets Association (WSRA) is formed. Londonderry Cup comes into existence. Susan Noel completes four British Open wins.

1935 Australian Squash Rackets Association is founded.

1936 Cumberland Cup is inaugurated.

1937 Amr wins his sixth British Open and sixth British Amateur titles. First England v. Scotland and Ireland v. Scotland international matches.

1938 Jim Dear wins British Open after being runner-up in three previous years. Margot Lumb wins fifth British Open title in succession.

1946 In the last British Open played on the challenge format, Mahmoud Karim beats Jim Dear. Norman Borrett wins the first of five British Amateurs. Joan Curry beat Alice Teague to become the first post-war women's champion.

1947 The British Open is played for the first time on knock-out basis and Karim beats Dear 10–8 in the fifth.

1948 Fluorescent lighting introduced to squash. Aberdeen SRC, apparently the first club founded specifically for squash, celebrates its 40th birthday. First post-war book on game written by Don Butcher – *Introducing Squash*.

1949 Lt. Cdr. L. Bourke devises scoresheet for purpose of marking games and it is produced by Dunlop. Danes are first European team to visit England. SRA celebrate 21st birthday by producing 200 copies of handbook – they had published 450 in inaugural year.

1950 Sussex win first of four successive Inter-County titles.

1951 First radio commentary on 7 April 1950/1 British Open semi-final between Karim and Wilson is broadcast on Home Service – overseas listeners hear part of final as Hashim Khan wins first of seven titles.

Curtain raisers to the era of modern-day professional squash were the Khans, notably Hashim Khan (*left*) seen here being congratulated by his brother Azam after winning the 1955 Professional Championship of the British Isles (now discontinued) for the fifth time.
Illustrated London News

1952 HRH The Duke of Edinburgh becomes patron of SRA. English county associations now number 28.

1953 Abdul Bari scratches from British Open semi-finals through illness and tragically dies soon after aged 33 from thrombosis of the brain. All four British Open semi-finalists were related for only time in history – Abdul Bari, Hashim Khan, Azam Khan and Roshan Khan.

1954 One in four English clubs experiment with American scoring system but vote 7 to 1 against change.

1955 First English touring team since 1927 as SRA side visit South Africa, Rhodesia and Kenya – they go down 1–3 in Test Series v. South Africa but are to gain revenge in 1957 when South Africa are beaten 3–0 in Britain.

1956 First overseas squash books are published – *An Introduction to Squash Techniques* by W. Mattick, *Squash Techniques* by H. Napier (both Australian) and Ibrahim Safwat produces rules in Arabic.

1957 In March, Roshan Khan beats Hashim in British Open final – the great man's first defeat in Britain since arriving early in 1952.

1958 Janet Morgan retires after winning 10 British women's championships in succession. Hashim wins his seventh British Open title.

1959 England team visits Australia and New Zealand, winning each international match and both national titles.

1960 Brian Phillips' book *Tackle Squash Rackets This Way* is first to include refereeing and marking guidelines. Butyl ball is experimented with – mixture of synthetic and natural rubber.

1961 Surrey win Inter-County title – they will go on to achieve 13 in a row. President of SRA since 1947, Capt. J. E. Palmer-Tomkinson dies – he had played in four British Amateur finals and won title in 1926.

1962 Heather Blundell (later McKay) is beaten for last time in career as she loses 2–3 to Fran Marshall in Scottish Open. In February she wins first of 16 consecutive British women's championships. Mohibullah Khan wins British Open to complete 13 years of Khan rule.

1963 Ken Hiscoe becomes the first Australian to win British Amateur title. Hiscoe joins Dick Carter and Owen Parmenter in Australian team that beats Pakistan, England and Great Britain – all 3–0. Heather Blundell has already won her second British Open – Australian squash has arrived. Michael Oddy beats Mohibullah Khan in British Open semi-final to end Khan clan's run and becomes first British finalist for 11 years. Aboutaleb wins title – the first Egyptian to do so since 1949.

1964 As Pakistan grip loosens on the British Open, it closes on the British Amateur – Aftab Jawaid wins first of three consecutive titles by beating Egypt's Tewfik Shafik. Heather Blundell wins third British Open and Australia beats GB 3–2 in first women's international between the two. Aboutaleb beats Ibrahim Amin in the only all-Egyptian final in the history of the men's British Open.

1965 Mohibullah Khan beats Hashim Khan in last US Open – hereafter US and Canadian Opens are combined as North American Open. Jawaid beats Geoff Hunt to retain British Amateur. GB beat New Zealand 3–0 in first women's international between the countries. Aboutaleb completes hattrick of British Open wins by beating Aftab Jawaid. Michael Oddy retires after 12 months of ill-health.

1966 Mohibullah Khan wins first North American Open. Aftab Jawaid takes third British Amateur by beating Dick Carter. Geoff Hunt reaches semi-finals for second successive year and Ken Hiscoe for the fifth. Heather McKay (née Blundell) wins fifth British Open and in men's event there is the first British success since the challenge system was abolished as Jonah Barrington beats Aboutaleb, Amin and Jawaid.

1967 Jonah Barrington wins British Amateur to become the first since Amr to win Amateur and Open in same season. Hiscoe reaches the last four for the sixth year in a row. GB women record first win over Australia. Heather McKay is British women's champion for the sixth time. First World Amateur Championships held in Australia in August. Host country win team title by beating GB, New Zealand, South Africa, India and Pakistan without conceding a rubber. Pakistan finish last, recording only victory against New Zealand. Geoff Hunt beats fellow-Australian Cam Nancarrow in individual final. Hiscoe and Barrington are losing semi-finalists. Barrington retains British Open as Aboutaleb wins just nine points in the final. International Squash Rackets Federation is established.

1968 January: Jonah Barrington beats Mike Corby to win British Amateur – Adam Hill and Jeremy Lyon complete all-British last four. Heather McKay beats Bev Johnson 9–0, 9–0, 9–0 in first all-Australian women's British Open final. December: Barrington again beats Corby in Amateur final and Lyon and Paul Millman ensure all-British semi-finals for second consecutive time.

1969 January: Geoff Hunt wins British Open at first attempt – he and losing finalist Cam Nancarrow are first Australians to reach last four of the event. Heather McKay wins eighth British women's title as Fran Marshall gets just two points in the final. Australia retains World Amateur Team event and Hunt beats Barrington in individual final. December: Barrington avenges that defeat by beating Hunt 3–2 to win his third British Open.

1970 Aftab Jawaid finishes runner-up in British Amateur and Open Championships – to Hunt and Barrington, respectively. Marcia Roche becomes South Africa's first major women's tournament finalist by reaching British Open final but secures only two points as Heather McKay wins her ninth title. Mohibullah Khan Jnr wins Drysdale Cup (unofficial world Under-19 title) at 15.

1971 Pakistan's Gogi Alauddin wins two British Amateur titles – beating Bill Reedman in January and Mo Asran in December. Heather McKay equals Janet Morgan's record of ten consecutive British Opens. Australia and Geoff Hunt complete hat-tricks in World Amateur team and individual events. In December Sheila Speight plays for England v. Wales – she first played an international against the same opposition in April 1949! Geoff Hunt turns professional. World's first all glass backwall installed on the championship court at the Abbeydale Club, Sheffield.

1972 Jonah Barrington wins fifth British Open by beating Hunt 3–2 after losing opening game 0–9. Gogi Alauddin and Hiddy Jahan herald arrival of new Pakistani force by reaching last eight. In February, Lawrence Verney represents Wales having first played for the country in the same month 22 years earlier. Heather McKay sets new record with eleventh British Open win. Cam Nancarrow beats Bill Reedman in first all-Australian British Amateur final.

1973 Barrington beats Alauddin to win sixth British

Open. McKay wins her 12th in succession, takes her 14th consecutive Australian title and turns professional as WSRA approves 'Open' competition in Britain. England finish top of ten teams in first European Championships. GB women are beaten three times in internationals v. South Africa. Australia again win world team title and Cam Nancarrow wins individual. Mohibullah Khan (18) is youngest-ever winner of British Amateur – Qamar Zaman is losing finalist and Hiddy Jahan and Mohammed Saleem complete first-ever all-Pakistani semi-finals line-up. England's Phil Kenyon wins Drysdale Cup. International Squash Players Association and European Squash Rackets Federation founded. Women's SRA approve Open competition.

1974 Jonah Barrington, aiming to equal Hashim Khan's record of seven British Open wins, is beaten in quarter-finals by Mohammed Yasin; Yasin goes on to final but has to withdraw through injury giving Geoff Hunt the only final walkover in the history of the event. England's Sue Cogswell reaches women's final but is beaten by Heather McKay – the Australian's 13th triumph. Hunt wins first South African Open. Mohibullah repeats win over Zaman in British Amateur. Jonny Leslie is first British Closed champion. First televised squash in England as BBC's *Grandstand* features British Open. SRA adopt official scoresheet designed by Ian Wright.

1975 Qamar Zaman wins his only British Open as he beats Gogi Alauddin in the first all-Pakistani final since Azam v. Mohibullah in 1962. Heather McKay wins 14th women's British Open. Australia's Kevin Shawcross wins British Amateur. GB win just three games as they lose 0–5 to Pakistan in first 'Open' international match at Wembley. Phil Kenyon wins first British Under-23 title as Gawain Briars succeeds him as Drysdale Cup champion. Qamar Zaman and Mohibullah Khan turn professional.

1976 February: first World Open is incorporated with British Open at Wembley – Hunt beats Mohibullah Khan in final. Gogi Alauddin and Qamar Zaman are losing semi-finalists – Hunt v. Pakistan as it will be many times in the future. Heather McKay wins 15th British Open and first women's world championship in Brisbane. GB become first country other than Australia to win men's world team title, Pakistan finish second. Kevin Shawcross wins individual event to add world title to British. Bruce Brownlee is first New Zealander to win major title by beating Jonny Leslie in final of British Amateur. Murray Lilley beats Barry O'Connor 9–3, 10–8, 2–9, 7–9, 10–8 in 2

The rivalry between Britain's Jonah Barrington and Australia's Geoff Hunt was an ever-present stimulus to the professional squash scene, particularly during the first half of the 1970s. Here Barrington (*right*) has just lost to Hunt in the quarter-finals of the 1977/8 British Open at Wembley. *All Sports*

hours 35 minutes in the British Amateur Championship at Wembley – the longest recorded match at that time (the record is to stand until 1983). Sue Cogswell wins first British Women's Closed and Angela Smith is Under-23 champion.

1977 Geoff Hunt wins fourth British Open as he beats Cam Nancarrow in repeat of 1968/9 final. Hashim Khan wins first of his vintage titles. Heather McKay wins 16th British Open by beating Australian compatriot Barbara Wall in first all-professional final – then announces retirement from the event. Hunt wins his fourth South African Open. Pakistan win World Amateur team title and provide both individual finalists as Maqsood

Ahmed beats Mohammed Saleem. Hunt retains World Open title and Egypt's Gamal Awad is British Amateur champion. Angela Smith becomes first British girl to turn professional. Plans for glass wall court announced.

1978 Hunt wins fifth British Open by beating Zaman in repeat of World Open final and takes his fifth South African Open. Sue Newman succeeds Heather McKay as women's British Open champion. Awad retains British Amateur by beating Atlas Khan. First demountable court promotion in Sweden giving an audience of 600.

1979 Sharif Khan wins tenth North American Open. Hunt wins sixth South African Open – since 1973 he has played 165 matches in 32 tournaments in South Africa without loss; since turning pro in 1971 he has played 164 tournaments throughout the world, appeared in 155 finals, won 139 and lost just 25 times in 637 matches. GB win World Amateur team title beating Pakistan in final but new star is born in individual event – 15-year-old Jahangir

Khan, not in Pakistan team and asked to qualify, wins title with final victory over Phil Kenyon. Deanna Murray needs just 9½ minutes on court to beat Christine Rees in Welsh Championships – the shortest recorded match in history. Hunt retains World and British Open titles with wins over Qamar Zaman. Torsam Khan, elder brother of Jahangir, ranked 13 in the world and newly-elected president of ISPA, collapses and dies on 28 November during Australian Championships. Barbara Wall continues Australian dominance in women's British Open with victory over Sue Cogswell. Heather McKay retains world individual title but Australia are beaten by GB in final of first world team competition.

1980 Jonny Leslie beats Ross Norman in last British Amateur. Hunt wins fourth World, seventh British and seventh South African Opens. Jonah Barrington wins British Closed at the age of 39 beating Gawain Briars who is 17 years his junior. Vicki Hoffman wins first of four British Opens. Squash goes 'Open' with distinction between amateurs and professionals being abolished.

1981 Hunt wins record eighth British Open at expense of young Jahangir Khan who had beaten him weeks earlier at Chichester. Both matches last over two hours and the Open defeat is Jahangir's last as we go to press. First four-wall transparent Plexiglass court used in Cologne for German Masters and first glass frontwall used for World Open in Toronto where Jahangir beats Hunt to become youngest-ever champion at 17 years 354 days. Sue Cogswell wins her fifth British Closed. Rhonda Thorne beats Vicki Hoffman to succeed Heather McKay as world champion. England are runners-up to Australia in team event and Lisa

Opie beats Martine Le Moignan in all-English World Junior final. First ISRF World Championships since game went 'Open' held in Sweden – Pakistan wins team title and Steve Bowditch is individual champion from severely depleted field.

1982 Jahangir Khan beats Hiddy Jahan to win first British Open title. Geoff Hunt is forced to retire from the game through injury. Lisa Opie wins British Closed and reaches final of Open where she is beaten by Vicki Cardwell (née Hoffman) who records her third successive victory. Women's and men's British Opens are played as combined event for first time. Final stages of World Open played on three transparent walled court at National Exhibition Centre in Birmingham, 1600 spectators attend each session, earlier rounds are played at various venues throughout England. Jahangir Khan retains title but Australia's Dean Williams defeats Hiddy Jahan and Qamar Zaman to reach final. Ahmed Safwat of Egypt beats Jonah Barrington in first World Over-35 final.

1983 Alison Cumings causes major upset by beating Lisa Opie and Martine Le Moignan to win British Closed. Jahangir Khan and Gamal Awad play longest match on record – two hours 46 minutes in final at Chichester, Jahangir wins 3–1. Jahangir retains British Open title by beating Awad – Vicki Cardwell again beats Lisa Opie in women's final to record fourth win and then announces her retirement from the international circuit. ISPA decide not to grade South African Open. Hiddy Jahan becomes British citizen and plays number 1 for England in ISRF World Team Championships in New Zealand. First use of four-wall glass court in France and England.

2 Elements of the game

HISTORY OF THE COURT

The modern squash player is able to play and enjoy a game of squash using a racket and ball which have been manufactured to a high standard and which utilise all the benefits of life in a technological age. The same description could be applied to the court in which the game is played since a club, if it is to stay in business these days, will ensure that members have courts with wooden, well-sprung floors, white plastered walls, efficient lighting, good ventilation and temperature control. Some courts, and increasingly this is becoming a norm, will have glass backwalls to improve the general ambience of the club. Yet the luxury of the modern court, and luxury is not overstating the case, must be considered a far cry from the courts of the 1920s and earlier. The truth is that when squash began it was played on rackets courts or even in *ad hoc* conditions utilising two or three walls with floors of asphalt. In the latter half of the 19th century the squash courts that were constructed were often in singles or pairs at country houses and schools, and were usually built with wooden planks for floors and walls.

Part of squash's popularity was that the courts were cheaper to build and took up less space than those of rackets. The dimensions were slightly wider and considerably longer than present-day sizes, as demonstrated by the known measurements of three courts from those early days which were 23 ft 4 in (7·1 m) wide, 40 ft (12·2 m) long and 18 ft (5·5 m) high.

With so much building going on, both in England and in America, and no official guidelines to follow, it is little wonder that there were courts of all shapes and sizes. Possibly if there had been some attempt at standardisation then North American and international squash would not be divided as it is by the two different codes and two different courts.

It was not until 1909 that the Tennis and Rackets Association in England sat down to discuss the subject and by then they were faced with a number of problems apart from size; notably which materials should be used in construction, and the size and quality of the squash ball to be used on a particular court.

Eventually they came up with some suggested dimensions: length 30 ft (9·1 m), breadth 21 ft (6·4 m), height of the front wall 14 ft (4·3 m) and height of the backwall 8 ft 6 in (2·6 m). They felt that a cement or stone floor was preferable to wood but a wood block floor laid on cement was almost as good. The side walls could be wood, although this was not considered as good as cement, but the front and back walls should definitely be stone or cement. The playline (tin) was recommended to be 19 in (48 cm) from the floor, although there could be flexibility – a relaxation the Association also decided was proper in relation to all court dimensions. If builders wished to stray from the T & RA suggestion they could do so but dimensions had to be proportionate and in no cases should a court be longer than 36 ft (10·9 m) or shorter than 26 ft (7·9 m). These somewhat vague specifications may seem peculiar by modern standards of precision, but they were considered adequate at the time and sufficient as a guide for those wishing to build.

The T & RA no doubt at that stage had in mind encouraging expansion of the game and they knew that vast expense would be involved in changing existing courts. Therefore they could not take too strict an attitude which might deter people.

Even in 1910 the cost of a court was £250 to £300, not inconsiderable at the time, and developers would not wish to invest in squash unless they thought they were doing it correctly.

If the T & RA failed to grasp the nettle on that occasion it was not long before they were forced to do so, the Association being pushed into the situation by the popularity of squash. The growth of the game meant that visits were exchanged by players of one court to another and the differences in court sizes quickly became apparent. For example, one Yorkshire touring side early in the 1920s usually found themselves playing four or five matches on different sized courts with a different ball for each.

Clearly something had to be done and in April 1923 the T & RA, after considering proposals and canvassing opinion from leading players of the time, opted for the following dimensions: length 32 ft (9·7 m), breadth 21 ft (6·4 m), height of the tin 19 in (48 cm), height of front wall 15 ft (4·6 m), and back wall 7 ft (2·1 m). These differed from the 1909 specifications with the court being longer, the front wall higher and backwall lower. The new sizes were accepted immediately although it is extraordinary to think that at the time of acceptance a court of those dimensions did not exist. The measurements were based purely on the opinion of experienced players and officials and were totally experimental. However, since they have stood the test of time it must be said that the people who drew up the sizes obviously knew their sport.

From the building point of view the recommendation was that the front wall in all cases should be cement or composition, the side and back walls to be cement, composition or wood, the walls to be white, all lines to be red, and the floors whitewood for indoor courts and cement for open air. No variation from this schedule was to be permitted although it was known that most courts would be adjudged 'non-standard'. This led in 1925 to a relaxation in the specification to allow an error of 1 per cent in all round measurements, which permitted courts as small as 31 ft 8¼ in × 20 ft 9½ in or as large as 32 ft 3¾ in × 21 ft 2½ in. This 1 per cent margin was to prove beneficial for an English club in 1955, 30 years later. Some non-standard courts were being reconstructed and it was found that the space available meant they would still be slightly short. Accordingly, the club approached the SRA to see if the courts could be used for inter-county matches and the SRA sticking to the rules, replied that if the building came within the 1 per cent error allowed in 1925, then they could be used, providing that standard courts were not available for play.

These days it is rare to find a non-standard court, a benefit from the standardisation achieved in the twenties and the fact that the SRA in 1930 appointed their own advisory architect, Mr A. W. D. Reid, who drew up plans for types of approved courts, including estimates of costs, to assist builders. These moves brought order to squash court building and it is interesting to look briefly at how the costs of construction have risen in the last 50 years.

Initial SRA approval schemes in 1930 included a wood side walled court with small gallery at £200, an all brick cement court for £400 and a de luxe version of (b) being better ventilated with additional gallery and changing accommodation for £750.

In 1931/2 these costs appear in the SRA handbook as £250/300, £590 and £850, respectively, and remained at this level until 1937/8 when court (b), now with a maple floor, actually went down in price to £550. By 1938/9 costs had risen to £360, £600 and £900. The first post-war club court to be built in England cost between £2900 and £3000, a tremendous increase but still comparatively cheap when compared to prices in the 1980s when a court can be 10 or 12 times as much depending on the location and what services are already on site.

The boom in squash court building in the 1960s and 1970s was fuelled by system building with pre-cast

concrete blocks enabling speedy erection of batteries of courts. Other materials, such as laminates are now also utilised and glass has come along to play a major role, not only as part of the court construction itself but in helping to improve the general design of clubs.

The would-be club developer has a wide choice of systems to use when it comes to selection of courts, ranging from the prefabricated concrete, traditional brick to various laminates of which the main constituent is particle board. Various finishes are also available. The cost of a single court to be added to an existing complex at 1984 prices might be between £9000 and £10 000 yet it could be anywhere between £30 000 and £40 000 per court if the complex is being

Towards the end of the 1930s a number of companies were offering their services as squash court constructors – one of the better known being 'En-Tout-Cas'. The photographs show examples of courts built for private clubs (Leicestershire Squash Club) and private individuals (Lady Howard de Walden). This advertisement appeared in the 1939 WSRA handbook

started from scratch and all other facilities have to be built as well. With land costs also rising, the price of squash club development will now deter all but the serious investor and gone are the days when the euphoria of a squash boom would tempt many people into the market without proper consideration to the project.

HISTORY OF THE SQUASH RACKET

The squash racket, unlike the ball, does not have a turbulent history, and little is recorded as to how the Tennis and Rackets Association (T & RA) in 1925 reached their decision to standardise the dimensions of the racket.

What is known is that from the time of deciding to take action and to approving a proposal to make the standard length of a squash racket 27 in (68 cm) and the head no larger than a rackets racket it took the Association just over two months of deliberation. Compared to the arguments that have raged over the ball, almost for as long as the game has been played, it is quite extraordinary that a specification for the game's other vital piece of equipment should be settled in such speedy and apparently arbitrary fashion. As many squash players used a shortened rackets racket presumably the thinking was that the smaller squash court needed a smaller racket and all that was required was to decide on a standard length. Certainly the decision appears to have been accepted without dispute so most people must have considered the T & RA ruling as being satisfactory.

The Squash Rackets Association (SRA) had taken control by the time the subject was discussed again and in the SRA handbook of 1930/1 there is considerable amplification of the dimensions. The item stated that the racket head should be circular in shape and its internal length should not exceed $8\frac{1}{2}$ in (22 cm) nor its internal breadth 7 in (18 cm). The maximum thickness of the frame was set at $\frac{9}{16}$ in (1·4 cm). The framework and handle had to be of wood, while the grip could be of any material. The requirement about the head being circular in shape was removed in 1936 since some Australian manufacturers had produced a flat-headed variety and the SRA felt there was no need to raise an objection.

No further recorded change took place except that the words 'and handle' were dropped, it presumably being assumed that the specification for a wooden framework was embracing enough. However, a minute reference from 1938 refers to rackets with steel shafts being permitted but there is no indication of how this permission came about.

Eventually, after the Second World War the racket dimensions, like those of the court and ball, were

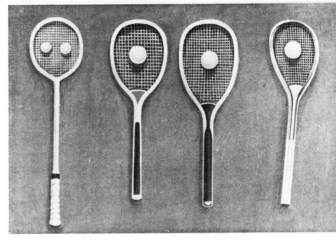

At the turn of the century squash enthusiasts used various types of rackets and balls to pursue their sporting interest as this photograph from E. H. Miles' *The Game of Squash*, 1901, shows

added as an appendix to the rules of the game, ensuring that no change could be made without official approval. The racket therefore has changed little over the years, although today's purchaser is faced with a bewildering array of different coloured rackets with highly sophisticated cosmetics, differing weights, veneers and stringing. Technology has introduced new materials into racket construction, making them lighter and more durable.

The subject of rackets made from light metal or other materials has been bubbling away in the background for many years and this came to a head in September 1983 when the ISRF relaxed the rule that racket heads should be made of wood. Also the maximum weight permitted for a racket was reduced to 9 ounces (255 grammes). However, the basic design and shape formulated more than 100 years ago has stood the test of time.

The Racket
How the Dunlop Maxply Light squash racket is made

The strength, durability, weight and balance of a squash racket depend on the expert arrangement of wooden veneers. When blended together these thin pieces of timber give exceptional strength to the racket head which is vital in a robust game like squash.

Rackets such as the Maxply Fort and International use peeled veneers of hickory, beech and ash in the head. But, when Dunlop researchers started to design the new Maxply Light racket, they decided that a combination of sliced and sawn veneers could give the required qualities of lightness of feel and balance without affecting strength. The woods used are cane (or bamboo) and ash together with a very thin fibre

THE RACKET How the Dunlop Maxply Light squash racket is made

The balance of a squash racket is vital to good play. Obtaining the right balance begins early in the production process. Dunlop carefully weigh every veneer and ensure that only those of uniform weight and thickness are used in a particular racket. Sensitive weighing and measuring machines help but the experience and judgement of the operator is still important.

The wedge, or throat, of a squash racket bears a tremendous strain during play. It is therefore important to use a strong and reliable wood for this component which, after all, links the handle with the head. Here mahogany is being machined into the required triangular shape with concave curves on each side.

Early in the production process the veneers are worked in a width which is twice that of a finished racket. These

'doubles' are later split in two. Here, the glued veneers are being placed on the outside of the veneers and pulled tight. The veneers then take up the shape of the head and the glued mahogany wedge can be positioned. Also positioned at this time is a special ash and fibre insert which gives added strength to the head. A lateral pressure of about $1\frac{1}{2}$ tons is applied so that the wedge is squeezed into position against the head formed by the action of the handle veneers coming together. The assembly is clamped together and cured in an oven at 230 °F (110 °C) for an hour. The metal former is then removed and the 'bend', as it is known at this stage, is split in two.

Each frame is sanded to a pre-determined thickness on an automatic sanding machine and then sixty-four holes are automatically drilled into the racket head. These will later accommodate the racket's strings.

Left
Pairs of these holes are joined together by machining a groove between them. This allows the strings to lie in the grooves and be protected from wear and tear during play.

Right
A leatheroid overlay is added to the shoulders of the racket to give extra strength.

When the overlay has been shaped to the contours of the racket, the handle is fitted. Here obeche wood is being glued and clamped in position.

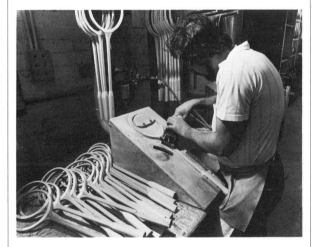

Now complete with handle the racket is sanded by hand to ensure a smooth surface for painting and decoration.

Before painting each racket has to be carefully masked. When the racket has been through the sophisticated

electrostatic paint conveyor the masking is removed and transfers are carefully applied by hand.

Gripping is carried out by hand and is a skilled operation.

Left
The all important strings are inserted. With the Maxply Light Dunlop customers have a choice of natural gut or synthetic stringing.

Right
The famous Flying D symbol has been applied to the strings and all that remains is one final inspection and polish.

inlay. This combination was the result of much research and testing. The racket is designed to weigh between 7·5 and 8 oz (213–227 g) with the balance of +5 to −5 (338–348 mms). In addition to the woods used to make the racket head, others, notably mahogany and obeche, are used to make other components of the racket such as the throat and handle. All the woods and veneers for use in this racket are kiln dried at the Dunlop factory to a uniform moisture content of 12 per cent. This ensures that there is enough moisture to produce a strong bond during gluing and to aid the final painting process.

HISTORY OF THE SQUASH BALL

'No implement at any game has more to answer for than the ball at squash rackets. All its life it has been subject to constant change and men have grown short in temper when its merits or demerits have been discussed. No doubt in attempting to make the squash ball fit the court and at the same time the skill of both expert and beginner an impossible task was being undertaken.'

This quotation from *Squash Rackets and Fives*, published in 1937 could quite easily have been written four years ago instead of more than 40 because discussion, argument and debate still follow the humble squash ball, that vital yet much abused piece of sporting equipment without which the game of squash would not have evolved.

In view of the controversies that continually seem to surround the ball it seems strange that there is no mention of the ball in the minutes of the Tennis and Rackets Association before 1923 nor is there any definite information as to when a ball specifically for squash use was first made. The leading names of ball manufacturers all tell the same story – 'records destroyed, or almost all destroyed during the war – Second World War'.

Therefore up to the early 1920s, during which time squash was becoming organised and formalised, there had been no official attempt to standardise a ball and there were a number of manufacturers making squash balls of diverse properties, often just for specific groups of players to use on a particular court or courts.

Before delving into what the minutes of the various committees reveal about the development of the ball and the scanty snippets of information provided by the manufacturers it is helpful to understand in general terms the ball's evolution.

In the early days a ball of quite high resilience (bounciness) was used, but as players became more skilled it was found that lower resilience balls were more desirable – with a bouncy ball it is difficult to

make winning shots and rallies become long and boring. This reduces the advantage of the good player over the poorer player, but with a less resilient ball the skilled player can produce shots which his opponent cannot return.

This requirement for a hysteretic or non-resilient ball produces manufacturing complications since most rubber compounds and particularly those from which squash balls are made become more resilient at high temperatures. Also the internal pressure in the ball rises with temperature which also increases resilience. So as a ball is continually struck against a wall its temperature rises with the consequences already outlined. This is why squash balls have to be warmed up before play so that they reach the right temperature and produce the correct playing properties.

But as can be appreciated the different levels of temperatures in courts and the widely differing abilities of players able to strike the ball correctly means that there has to be a range of balls with different speed specifications to satisfy the needs of the sport.

The temperature which a ball will reach in play depends very much on the standards of the performers. With internationals a temperature of 55 °C (131 °F) has been recorded but for average players 45 °C (113 °F) is more typical. Therefore the top player prefers to use a ball which has suitable resilience at 55 °C (131 °F), and if the average player used it not enough heat would be generated and the ball would be too 'slow'. He would be better off using a ball made from a rubber compound which has inherently more resilience or bounciness and is satisfactory at 45 °C (113 °F).

There are two other reasons for different ball specifications and why the widely accepted colour coding of a yellow dot for extra super slow, white dot for slow, red dot for medium and blue dot for fast has been formulated. Firstly, poorer players are generally less mobile and need a ball which does not die in the back of the court, and secondly the ball temperature reached in play is simply an extra over the temperature of the court. So if the court temperature is only 5 °C (41 °F) rather than 15 °C (59 °F) the ball might only warm up to 45 °C (113 °F) instead of 55 °C (131 °F) and a 'faster' ball would be required.

This knowledge has only come about through the extensive research and development carried out by the sport's leading manufacturers over many years and has led to the current situation whereby the sport's followers can enjoy their games more fully by using products suited to their standard and which have been tried and tested. Moreover, these standards are constantly being monitored by governing bodies who do not issue their approval lightly.

An advert for Gradidge's standard 'Nigger' ball as approved by the Tennis and Rackets Association. The advertisement appeared in the 1929–30 SRA handbook

---

What then were the players of the 1920s and earlier using? The Avon India Rubber Company began manufacturing balls of various sizes and hardness in 1925, the sizes being $1\frac{7}{16}$ in diameter (small), $1\frac{9}{16}$ in (medium and the 'standard') and $1\frac{11}{16}$ (large). In some instances balls were dipped in varnish and others were buffed to give a matt finish. The large ball had a hole burned in it to slow it down and was known as the 'Bath Club holer' and from other records it is clear that this ball was being made before 1925, if not by Avon then by some other company.

The general rubber goods department of Dunlop in Manchester is known to have made squash balls around 1919/20, but this is believed to have been a resumption of work after the First World War, implying that it went on before. In 1928 they began to make the SRA standard ball and this responsibility was taken up in 1947 by the Dunlop Sports Company.

The Gradidge Company, now amalgamated with Slazenger, began making their 'nigger' ball for the

officers at the Woolwich barracks, close to their factory, between 1900 and 1905. And in spite of its name the ball was coloured either white, red or black.

The Royal Automobile Club licensed the Silvertown Company to manufacture a squash ball for their members' use and this is thought to have been on sale from 1914 onwards. This ball, subsequently known as the RAC number one ball, was made from a top grade quality red rubber with a high gloss, black enamelled surface carrying the RAC name painted in red monogram style. Its diameter was $1\cdot54$ in.

Due to a requirement for a change in pace the RAC number two ball was produced in 1924 and this ball remained a favourite with squash players up to about 1926.

At about this time the Tennis and Rackets Association issued a standard specification for an authorised ball which with its general adoption by clubs and players eliminated any further demand for such non-standard balls as the RAC ball. However, before the Tennis and Rackets Association reached their historic decision much work had gone on behind the scenes initiated by the Joint Clubs Squash Committee in 1923. Four different balls were put through a series of tests on courts at Lords and the RAC and notes taken to show the comparative weights, sizes and percentages of bounce. This led to the adoption in February 1923 of the RAC standard ball for amateur championship matches. No dates or details can be given concerning the manufacture of this ball – the Wisden 'Royal' – as that company's records were all destroyed. However, by September 1923 a minute had appeared which could well have come from any present-day squash committee. Members were complaining that the official ball was 'too fast' and that approaches should be made to another company with a view to producing two balls, one 3 per cent slower, the other 5 per cent.

The task fell to the India Rubber and Gutta Percha Company who duly supplied samples, one of them being accepted after tests by a number of well-known players of the day, including Britain's first professional Charles Arnold. There is no further mention of the ball until late October 1925 when the committee met again to instigate a new series of tests on balls – both existing ones and those made to new specifications. This latter requirement inferred that although the minutes had been silent on the subject there must have been plenty of unofficial discussion.

In the following year (July 1926) the Tennis and Rackets Association received a proposal that the two balls manufactured by the Silvertown Company and by Gradidge should be adopted as standard. These two balls had come up to the investigating committee's requirements: 'capable of being killed by a

THE BALL How a Dunlop championship black squash ball is made

Two pellets of rubber compound are used to make a squash ball – one for each half of the ball. Varying the ingredients in the compound can determine whether the ball will be fast, slow, extra super slow, etc. The pellets are placed in a press to be moulded into the shape of half a ball. They are subjected to a pressure of 1100 lb per sq in for 12 minutes.

After the half balls have been moulded they are 'spotted' using a syringe and special paint. The colour of the spot denotes the speed of the ball.

The half balls are knocked out from their sheet to become individual 'shells'.

The smooth edges of the shells are buffed – slightly roughened – in a way which helps them accept the solution which will eventually join the two halves together. After this process the shells are washed.

The shells are put into trays ready to accept the solution – adhesive – which is used to join the two halves.

The solution is applied by roller. Three coats are applied at half-hour intervals.

The two halves of the ball are brought together in an operation called 'flapping'.

When the two halves of the ball have been joined they are put into another press for the final moulding cycle – 178 balls at a time are subjected to a pressure of 1000 lb per sq in for 15 minutes.

After moulding the balls are placed in an automatic buffing machine. This smooths down the seam and gives the balls their essential matt surface.

The balls are again washed thoroughly.

Every ball is inspected to ensure that it is perfect and acceptable for play. In addition to this visual check each ball is also subjected to a bound test which guarantees that they conform to the playing characteristics specified by the Squash Rackets Association.

Only when the balls have been confirmed as being perfect are they printed with the logos.

well-played drive, responded to "gentler" treatment and gave more chance than the RAC number two ball of winning points by well played drops and angled shots'. The proposal was approved and Silvertown and Gradidge given permission to mark the ball 'T and RA – Standard', the Tennis and Rackets Association still being the recognised governing body of the sport.

Only two balls had been approved as standard, but it was not long before other firms were modifying their previously divergent products to bring them into line with this new specification. No step since the standardisation of the court dimensions did more to produce a uniform game in all clubs than the introduction of the standard mark for squash balls. Just as after 1923 it became less necessary for a player from one club visiting another to adapt himself to a court five or ten foot longer or shorter than to which he was accustomed, so he need no longer be faced with a ball bigger or smaller, heavier or lighter, harder or softer, with or without a hole.

By 1926 the ball with a hole was abandoned and the only hole which appeared was the one when it broke – the slower ball had an immediate advantage in that this occurred less frequently. The old 'nigger' ball and its contemporaries, especially when used on a stone floor, as many were, broke quickly.

With the formation of the Squash Rackets Association (SRA) in 1928, responsibility for the ball passed to the new body and in the first three years there are occasional references to firms submitting their makes of ball for approval for the standard mark – a procedure that helped to ensure consistency and quality in ball manufacture.

And so the standard had been set, although it is interesting to note that when the Women's Squash Rackets Association (formed 1934) got around to considering the ball best suited to them, they opted for the Gradidge ball. This was in contrast to the SRA who gave more importance to the Silvertown ball by adopting it as the official ball for the Amateur Championship.

The Second World War handicapped squash rackets heavily, particularly in relation to the ball since supplies of rubber stopped and virtually no balls were manufactured during this period. The result was that by the end of the war much of the manufacturing skill had been lost and on resumption of play the performances of all makes was so erratic that the SRA faced an extremely difficult task in re-establishing standards.

Dunlop took over as principal ball supplier, the SRA requirement being for a slower ball than the Silvertown due to the fact that the Amateur Championship had now transferred from the Bath Club (destroyed by fire) to the Lansdowne Club where the courts were appreciably warmer and faster. Other grades – medium and slow – were manufactured and these types eventually gave way to the butyl ball in 1960 which Slazenger (already amalgamated with Gradidge) had successfully launched on to the Australian market. Butyl is a synthetic substance mixed in various quantities and qualities with ordinary rubber to help overcome the problems of hot and cold court conditions.

In turn came the present 'dot' varieties and more recently the 'non-marking' ball, in response to complaints from club owners. Several non-marking balls have been made with different degrees of success but none have matched the resilience and temperature characteristics of the black ball which remains the only ball used in major championships. There is now a swing back to the black ball on the grounds that the marks which it makes, although more visible, are easier to clean off than those of the 'non-marking' variety!

Grays have now taken over as producers of the official SRA ball with their 'Grays Merco ball', while Dunlop's range is now endorsed by the International Squash Players Association.

Research is being done to produce a ball suitable for televising squash and linked with this are suggestions for a further reduction in the pace of the ball. This latter request has come about because of the high degree of fitness of the modern player who can maintain lengthy rallies and shift the emphasis to physique and stamina and away from skill. The television ball, if such a product can be manufactured, would be white, yellow or whatever colour enables the non-squash spectator to easily follow play. It may even be bigger. The squash ball it seems is destined to stay always uppermost in the minds of every player.

3 Champions of squash

To try and select the champions of squash is to invite criticism not only about the players that are chosen but for the ones that are omitted.

The following section therefore is not intended to be a comprehensive guide to all those great players who have graced the sport but to feature many of those who have made their names synonymous with the World and British Opens.

It would be impossible, certainly within the confines of this book, to do justice to every competitor who has won an international title of significance. Suffice therefore that all the names are recorded in the championship results section and the brief portraits that follow will give the reader a feel for the personalities and characters that have made their mark in squash.

Don Butcher (Eng)
British Open champion 1930, 1931

Don Butcher became the first winner of the British Open in 1930 when he challenged and defeated the designated champion Charles Read. Read was British professional champion of rackets and lawn tennis but was no match on a squash court for Butcher who, like many who followed him, was a great believer in rigorous training. His accuracy on court was unmatched by his contemporaries and he developed this facet of his game by attempting in practice to hit a penny which was placed edge-on on top of the tin. He also had a half-penny on the court floor a yard from the front and next to the sidewall on which he tried to drop the ball by playing drop shots into the nick.

Butcher retained the title in 1931 by beating Charles Arnold but the emergence of Amr Bey as a top-class player ensured that he enjoyed no further successes.

He was suspended by the SRA in 1938 for taking Benzedrine before a match but was reinstated after a doctor explained that the incident was part of an experiment to discover the effects of the drug on sports people. However, he never fully managed to shake off the nickname 'Benzedrine Kid'. After the war Butcher concentrated on coaching until 1957 when he emigrated to Australia with his wife and son and was sadly virtually lost to the sport.

Don Butcher who became the first British Open champion in 1930, pictured with Amr Bey who dispossessed him of the title. If Butcher set new standards in the sport for accuracy on court and physical fitness he was more than matched by the graceful, athletic Egyptian who had a wide range of strokes coupled with an extraordinary retrieval ability. *From* The Art of Squash Rackets

Although his name will always appear on squash's roll of honour as the first winner of the British Open, Butcher will be best remembered for the variety of shots which he introduced to the game when most other players were simply adapting those of rackets.

F. D. Amr Bey (Abdel Fattah Amr) (Egy)
British Open champion 1932–37
British Amateur champion 1931–33, 1935–37

When Abdel Fattah Amr arrived in England in 1928 nothing could have been further from his mind than the game of squash. He was a highly-respected Egyptian diplomat, renowned horseman and polo player and had come to represent his country in the Davis Cup tennis competition.

He was introduced to squash at Queen's Club, Hurlingham by Dan Maskell who, in later years, became world-famous for his commentaries from Wimbledon. Maskell was so impressed that he suggested the young Egyptian should concentrate on the game. Amr took his advice and went to train under professional Oke Johnson at the RAC Club in Pall Mall, London. He showed tremendous natural aptitude, already had fine eye–hand co-ordination developed through his tennis career and was exceptionally quick around the court. Johnson provided the one missing link – the ability to deal with the more physical demands of the newly-adopted sport – and the diminutive Egyptian quickly went from strength to strength.

He reached the semi-finals of the British Amateur Championship in 1930 and won it in the following season. In 1933 he became the first man – and the only one other than the great Jonah Barrington – to achieve the 'double' of winning the British Amateur and British Open titles in the same season.

His graceful style, wide range of strokes and his ability to retrieve almost anything brought him six British Amateur titles, 1931–38 and 1935–37 (he did not compete in 1934), and six British Open victories, 1932–37. He also won the inaugural Egyptian Amateur Championship in 1936. The extent of his popularity and influence on British squash was indicated in 1935 when he was invited to captain the British side against the USA at the Bath Club.

He would undoubtedly have added to his tally of major wins had he not decided in 1938, at the age of 28, to retire from serious competition to concentrate on his diplomatic career in which, by then, he had reached the exalted position of Egyptian Ambassador to the United Kingdom.

NB: Abdel Fattah Amr's name appears in many record books as F. D. Amr Bey. 'Bey' was an Egyptian title of rank resulting from his diplomatic work as was 'Pasha' in his full title as Ambassador to the UK – H.E. The Ambassador to the Court of St James, F. D. Amr Pasha. The 'D' was apparently inserted early in his life to avoid confusion with a nephew who possessed exactly the same name.

Jim Dear (Eng)
British Open champion 1938

The fact that Jim Dear's name appears only once on the British Open roll of honour is a far from true reflection of his quality as a squash player. He was one of the best exponents of the game ever produced in England but his attempts to win major prizes were

frustrated by two great Egyptian champions and the break-out of the Second World War.

Initially he was a rackets player who first became prominent in squash when he contested the 1933 British Professional Championship final with Don Butcher. The match was played on a two-leg basis and, although he lost the first quite easily, he kept the twice British Open champion on court for two hours in the second encounter before going down 8–10 in the fifth. He exacted revenge when he defeated the same opponent in the finals of the 1935 and 1936 competitions.

However, the British Open title remained tantalisingly out of reach as he finished runner-up to Abdel Fattah Amr in 1935, 1936 and 1937. Finally, with the retirement of the little Egyptian, he beat Bert Biddle to win the championship in 1938 – just in time to leave on active service with the RAF!

He returned, at the age of 36, to defend his title in 1946, the first competition after the war. Amr was

Jim Dear, seen playing an overhead shot against Don Butcher during the final of the Professional Championship of the British Isles in November 1935. Dear's victory earned him the right to challenge Amr Bey in the British Open. It was a bid that failed that year and for the following two years until in 1938 Dear won his only Open title – just before he had to leave squash for active service in the RAF. *Illustrated London News*

gone but now standing in the Englishman's way was another talented Egyptian, Mahmoud Karim. Dear lost both of the 1946 challenge matches to Karim although he led 2–0 in the second. The 1947 competition was the first played under the knock-out system but Dear battled through to face Karim once again in the final. It was one of the event's finest climaxes. The Egyptian opened up a two-game lead but Dear levelled the match and only just failed to complete a tremendous comeback when he was beaten 10–8 in the fifth. Dear did not compete again in the British Open but he did record one more major win when he beat Abdul Bari in the 1949 final of the British Professional Championship – 14 years after his first victory in the event.

Dear's collection of squash trophies may have been less than his talent deserved but he ensured that his name would be indelibly written into sporting history when he completed a remarkable treble. After winning the British Open in 1938 – then the equivalent of the world title, he became world rackets champion from 1947 to 1954 and world real tennis champion in 1955.

Mahmoud Karim, who established Egyptian domination of the Open title after Amr Bey's retirement and the solitary win by Dear. He defeated Dear in the first final after the Second World War and remained champion until the arrival of Hashim Khan who ushered in the era of the Khans

---

Mahmoud Karim (Egy)
British Open champion 1946–49

Like his great Egyptian predecessor Abdel Fattah Amr, Mahmoud Karim was introduced to squash by a fluke of fate. His main sporting interests had been golf, tennis and football until, at the age of 15, he was asked to play by an American officer who was in need of a partner. Karim took to the game immediately, began to play as often as possible and soon saw it as a way to improve the lifestyle to which, because of his poor family background, he had become accustomed. He regularly played Amr Bey in Egypt and was soon beating him more often than not.

Further progress was inhibited by the outbreak of the Second World War. He was ready to travel to England when hostilities heightened and had to postpone his trip until 1946. His challenge for the British Open title was further delayed when he badly injured a knee during a practice match with England's Brian Phillips and was out of action for several weeks.

He eventually faced Jim Dear in the rearranged final and won the opening match 9–4, 9–1, 9–3 at the Lansdowne Club. If that confrontation was somewhat one-sided, the return leg at the RAC Club was a decidedly different affair. Dear led by 2 games to love and 8–4 in the third before the Egyptian staged the greatest fightback in the history of the competition to win 5–9, 7–9, 9–8, 9–7, 9–4.

A new champion had arrived and he reigned supreme for the next three years with final victories over Dear, Phillips and Abdul Bari. He reached the

following two finals but, now in his late-30s, he proved no match for the legendary Hashim Khan who beat him for five and twelve points. Although Karim smoked cigarettes – even when in training – he was very quick around the court, had fine anticipation and was regarded by many of those privileged to see him play as the greatest stroke-player of all time. Hashim paid tribute to him thus: 'Never before do I see a man like this. . . . He moves about the court like a ballet dancer. You never hear his feet on the floor and how he turns, runs and strokes – you want to watch all day. His play has rhythm . . . he has many different strokes, some I see for the first time anywhere.'

Karim emigrated to Canada in 1953 where he became an immensely popular figure in coaching and tournament organisation. He adapted easily to the hardball game in which he became very successful but was responsible for spreading the popularity of the international code in his adopted country – particularly at junior level.

Hashim Khan (Pak)
British Open champion 1950–55, 1957

Anyone who has spotted a short, bald man with a pot-belly and baggy shorts taking to the court in the British Open Vintage Championship in recent years could be excused for dismissing him as another of squash's extrovert enthusiasts . . . until he starts to play. Then all the old flair, ability and impish humour come to the fore and he is at once recognisable as the great Hashim Khan.

Hashim started playing squash when he was around eight years old at the Peshawar Club where his father Abdullah was chief steward. Because he was so small,

31

Left: The legendary Hashim Khan in his younger days during the 1950s when he won 7 British Open titles.
Below: He returned to the same British Championship in 1978 and showed that his natural flair and artistry had not been diminished by the passing years, beating England's Jack Dengel in the final of the Vintage event

he had to hold the racket halfway up the shaft – a grip which he never discarded and which became his trademark. He was much faster than other boys of his age and so quickly developed a reputation for retrieving from what appeared impossible positions.

He was appointed professional at the RAF base in Peshawar in 1942 and in 1944 won the All-India Professional Championship beating Abdul Bari in the final. He continued to dominate squash in his own country until, in 1950, he was sent to London to try and wrest the British Open title from Egypt's Mahmoud Karim who had won the championship for the previous four years and was regarded as the world's best player at the time. Not only did Hashim win the Open but he demolished Karim in the final for the loss of just five points to notch the first of an incredible run of successes.

Although it has never been possible to ascertain his exact birth date, he was somewhere between 35 and 37 when he recorded this first victory – an age when the majority of players have ceased to be involved in serious competition!

For the next five years Hashim was virtually unbeatable and he held the British Open title throughout this period – twice beating his brother Azam in the final. The tournament of 1956 was a 'failure' by such high standards – he lost in the final to cousin Roshan but bounced back in 1957 to win the title, again beating Azam in the final. The following year he lost in the semi-finals to his brother and this proved to be his last Open Championship.

He moved to America where his name and legendary achievements provided him with rich pickings and he has lived there ever since. He adapted easily to the American game and recorded a string of US Open wins.

The little man has returned to Britain each year since 1977 to win the British Open Vintage Championship. In April 1981 he watched Geoff Hunt beat his record of seven Open victories but, by then, he had won four Vintage titles – a record in itself and even more remarkable when one considers that he was approximately 68 years of age at the time.

His great run in the fifties may finally have been eclipsed by Hunt and, perhaps, will be again by the precocious talent of Jahangir, but no one will ever again be called the father of squash or the founder of the modern game. Hashim Khan has earned the right to regard those titles as his own personal property.

Roshan Khan (Pak)
British Open champion 1956

Roshan Khan's victory against Hashim Khan in the final of the British Open in March 1956 was the culmination of a fight against poverty and intense clan rivalry. When Hashim, a relative by marriage from the same village, won the first of his British Open titles in 1951, Roshan was working as assistant squash professional to his father at the Rawalpindi Club. That year Roshan won the Pakistan Professional Championship and, somewhat impulsively, gave up his job at Rawalpindi to join elder brother Nasrullah in Karachi.

For the next two years he was frustrated that, despite retaining the national championship, he had to remain in Karachi while Hashim and his brother Azam were funded to travel to England for the world's premier event. As he explained to Rex Bellamy in *The Story of Squash*, this period in his life was immensely depressing. 'I was lying on the street, with no house, no job, no racket, no shoes. All day I helped Naz with tennis to get some money. They would not allow me to play squash. At night I used to go to open ground to run. I couldn't afford to buy a racket to practise and, even if I could, I couldn't play. There were much politics against me.'

He seriously considered giving up the game but, just as this seemed the only solution, the Pakistan Navy came to his rescue. He was offered a job and promised a trip to England if he won the Pakistan Professional Championship for the third time. He won the title and was dispatched to Britain, but that was not the end of his worries. He arrived with the minimum of clothing, no squash gear, just £5 in his pocket – most of which was spent on rent and a taxi to the Pakistan Embassy. But generously an official of the SRA kitted him out and, when cousin Abdul Bari invited him to play at the Junior Carlton Club, life was looking considerably brighter. He won his first tournament and 105 guineas by beating Azam and Mahmoud Karim.

Despite this victory and the subsequent upturn in his fortune, the brothers Azam and Hashim frustrated his attempts to win the British Open for three years. First he lost in the semi-final to Azam and then at the same stage and in the final to Hashim. But finally in 1957 he defeated another member of the clan, Mohibullah, in the semi-final before going on to beat Hashim 6-9, 9-5, 9-2, 9-1 to win the championship.

After that triumph first his right and then his left knee began to cause him pain and he was never again able to reproduce his very best form. He did not compete in the next two British Opens, took just one point from Azam in the final in 1960 and lost in the semi-finals of the next three competitions – to Azam, Mohibullah and Aboutaleb. He won his last overseas tournament when he lifted the Canadian Open title in 1961.

Although he was offered many lucrative posts overseas, Roshan has always remained in Pakistan where

Roshan Khan's British Open win in 1956/7 interrupted the run of victories by Hashim, related to him by marriage. His triumph was a tribute to his success over poverty and inter-clan rivalry which at one time threatened to deprive him of a chance to show what he could do on a squash court

he coached two of his sons to the top of his beloved game. His youngest, Jahangir, is current world champion and destined to become the greatest-ever player while Torsam, his eldest, had reached the world's top ten before he died tragically of a heart attack during a tournament in Australia in late 1979. It is therefore perhaps fitting to leave the last words to the late Torsam who once described his father's game as: 'classy and characterised by fantastic ball control but his strokes, particularly his backhand volley drop and the delayed short shots on the backhand were his unforgettable weapons. His game might have looked straightforward but he always moved his opponent around the court. He always had you chasing.'

Azam Khan (Pak)
British Open champion 1958–61

Azam Khan, younger brother of Hashim, lived in the shadow of the great man for six years before emerging to win four consecutive British Open titles between 1958 and 1961.

He was rescued from a relatively unimportant tennis coaching job and taught squash by his elder brother before travelling to England in December 1952. At first he showed little indication of the talent that would make him such an accomplished player in later years. 'I was hopeless to begin with. But Hashim kept pushing me and finally I could stay on court

Azam, younger brother of Hashim, won four consecutive Open titles and many an argument has raged as to how many he might have won if an Achilles tendon injury had not cut short his career

longer and longer without getting exhausted and my strokes improved also' he explained once.

Early in 1953 he played his first genuine competitive match against England's Roy Wilson and lost in five. Less than three months later he reached the semi-finals of the British Open where he was beaten in five by Hashim who went on to defeat Wilson in the final. For the next five years Hashim stopped his younger brother's progress in the Open beating him twice more in semi-finals and three times in the final.

Azam finally got his reward in 1958 when he beat nephew Mohibullah to win the title. He retained it in 1959 by demolishing Roshan Khan for the loss of one point and notched up two further final victories against Mohibullah in 1960 and 1961.

Azam's career was tragically cut short in 1962 when a badly damaged Achilles tendon forced him to abandon tournament play.

It is still a matter for heated debate as to how many

British Open titles Azam could or should have won were it not for the presence of Pakistani family politics. Many people believe that he was capable of beating Hashim towards the end of the great man's run of victories but either chose or was encouraged not to. On the other hand, there are those who would suggest that the young Mohibullah was capable of winning the title in 1960 and 1961 – he lost to Azam in five games on both occasions. Still more expert observers deny both these arguments but do feel that, had it not been for his tendon injury, he might well have gone on to beat Hashim's record of seven successive victories. The whole truth is unlikely ever to be revealed but there is no doubt that Azam is – and fully deserves to be – ranked among the very best to have played the game.

Mohibullah Khan (Pak)
British Open champion 1962

Having finished runner-up on three occasions to his uncle Azam, Mohibullah Khan finally won the British Open Championship in 1962 to complete a remark-

Mohibullah Khan after three unsuccessful British Open title bids when he was defeated by his uncle, Azam, eventually recorded the 13th consecutive win by a Khan when he beat a complacent Aboutaleb in the 1962 final. The Egyptian should have won comfortably and squandered an 8–1 lead in the fourth game when he led by 2 games to 1

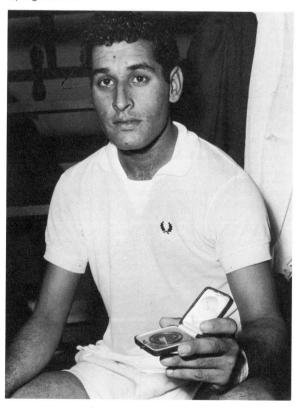

able run of 13 successive victories by the amazing Khan clan.

Many observers feel that he could have beaten Azam in 1960 and 1961 and his failure to do so nearly cost him his place on squash's roll of honour. In the 1962 final he looked destined to finish second-best yet again as he trailed Aboutaleb 1–2 and 1–8 in the fourth before the Egyptian, perhaps thinking it was all too easy, allowed him to get back in the match. Mohibullah gratefully seized his opportunity and staged a fine comeback to win 9–4, 5–9, 3–9, 10–8, 9–6.

Mohibullah started playing squash at the age of 10 under the supervision of his father Safirullah who was professional at the Sind Club. When he won the Pakistan junior title in 1956, without dropping a game, Hashim took charge of his training.

In 1958 he won the Pakistan Open – admittedly in the absence of Hashim, Roshan, and Azam – and in the same season reached the final of the British Open where he lost to Azam. In the previous two years he had reached the last four where he lost to Hashim and Roshan in straight games.

In 1959 he was defeated in the quarter-finals by Scotland's Mike Oddy who again beat him, in the semi-finals this time, the year after his only title win.

After his 1962 triumph Mohibullah emigrated to the USA where he became professional at the Harvard Club in Boston on the recommendation of John F. Kennedy. He was not seen again on the international circuit after 1963 but transferred his allegiance very successfully to the hardball game reaching three US Open finals in succession, losing to Hashim in 1963 and defeating the same opponent in the following two years.

A. A. Aboutaleb (Egy)
British Open champion 1963–65

Someone had to end the Khan rule of the British Open and, after 13 glorious years, the honour fell to the Egyptian Aboutaleb.

He should have won in 1962 when he led Mohibullah Khan 2 games to 1 and 8–1 in the fourth but complacency allowed it to slip from his grasp. The following year he was not to be denied and, in the first Open since 1949 not to feature a Pakistani in the semi-finals, he defeated Scotland's Mike Oddy to take the title.

He retained the title in 1964 when he defeated Ibrahim Amin in the first all-Egyptian final and completed his hat trick with a victory over Pakistan's Aftab Jawaid in 1965. Between 1961 and 1969 he reached the quarter-finals in every British Open – apart from his three wins, he was runner-up twice and losing semi-finalist once.

The decision to take up squash had little to do with Aboutaleb himself. When he was ten he was dispatched to the National Sporting Club in Cairo to act as a general helper to the professional. His elder brother, who was a tennis professional, had suggested that, as Aboutaleb was too small to be a tennis player, this was the next best step! He developed into a highly-talented player and a great entertainer although, like many of that mould, a fiery temperament was to prove a problem on more than one occasion.

In fairness it is difficult to compare him with the champions who immediately preceded him since the standard of opposition during his title-winning run was not as high as in previous years. This shortage of high-class opponents and the acclaim and rewards which he achieved as British Open champion led him to neglect his fitness and this was to prove his downfall when the great Jonah Barrington arrived on the scene. Barrington beat him in the British Open quarter-finals of 1966 and in the final of 1967 as the Irishman grasped firmly the mantle of the world's leading player. He never fully recovered from the blow of losing to Barrington and had to suffer many indignities, including being ignored by his own country's Press.

Aboutaleb had the distinction of ending the Khan domination. However, his own susceptibility to the victory acclaim of being champion and lack of attention to fitness eventually contributed much to his downfall

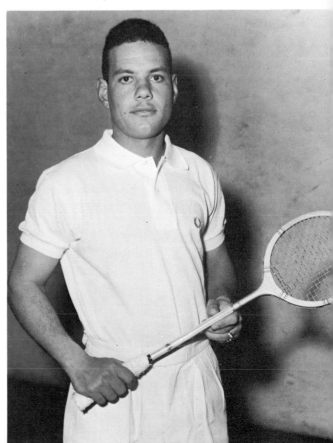

Aboutaleb returned to Egypt as he was still in the Egyptian Air Force and found that a complaint had been made by the English SRA about his behaviour on court. As a punishment he was confined to camp for three months but fortunately the Major in charge was keen on squash and in return for lessons allowed the fallen star to go home each day. Once over this very unhappy period of his life he contested five further Opens with limited success and eventually took up a position as resident professional at the North Kent Priory Club in Blackheath near London and then moved to Bexley. He worked as a coach but the lack of training and love of good food had by now added several inches to his waistline. Sadly he died from a heart attack at the age of 44 in the summer of 1983.

NB: Aboutaleb's real name was Abdelfattah Ahmed Aboutaleb. When he first came to England he was asked, via an interpreter, for his name, he replied Aboutaleb which was misunderstood as Abou Taleb. Officials were unwilling to juggle with the rest of his name and until 1976 the record books listed him as A. F. A. Taleb. The records were then corrected but the 'Abou' tag stuck.

Jonah Barrington (GB & Ire)

British Open champion 1966–67, 1969–72
British Amateur champion 1966–68

That so many people have discovered the pleasure – and pain – of playing squash, can be traced in part to an extraordinary contribution from one man, Jonah Barrington.

Barrington, a Cornishman born of an Irish father, won the British Open title six times (recognised as the unofficial world title until the 1975 British Open officially incorporated that status into that event).

His run of victories forever marks him as one of the world's greatest players and when Barrington claimed his first open title in 1966 he was the first Briton to do so for 28 years. That year he also became the first British player to win the Open and British Amateur titles in the same year. Barrington's string of open wins covered the years 1966–67 and 1969–72. The amateur title he claimed from 1966–68.

He turned professional in 1969 and by his dedication and enthusiasm both on and off the court he set an example that was to be eventually followed by all the world's leading players, since by 1976 it was rare to find an amateur who could survive to the last eight of the British Open. At international level he has

Jonah Barrington cherishes the memories of his six Open wins, yet one victory that gave him almost as much pleasure was that in the 1980/1 British national championship against Gawain Briars, pictured here. Barrington achieved that at the age of 39. *Robin Eley Jones*

represented both Great Britain and Ireland and as a coach had the satisfaction of training the Great Britain team which won the 1979 World Amateur Team Championship in Australia.

His playing success was founded upon fitness and a fanatical desire to win. How he did it is a tale that would seem better coming from the pages of a story book, since it describes how a dissipated, out-of-work 23-year-old, with poor eyesight and unimpressive physique drove himself to the top of one of the world's most physically demanding sports.

Barrington's devotion to the physical side of the game gave him advantage over his contemporaries and a head start on younger players such as Geoff Hunt from Australia who was to become one of his most formidable rivals. Hunt and others applied themselves diligently to Barrington's example, linking fitness to skill and eventually surpassing the former master who once knew that he could grind most opponents into the boards through sheer exhaustion.

This transformation took place in the early seventies and after his Open title success in 1972 Barrington was destined not to win another major Open championship. Age, a gathering horde of talented rivals, plus the reaction that Barrington's body now began to show for the punishing fitness disciplines, all took their toll; reducing his ability to compete on a regular basis, eroding the consistency of his performance at the highest level. But by then the Barrington name had become synonymous with squash. He had travelled the world popularising the sport by his deeds on court, by his vibrant personality off it. As far as British squash was concerned there was no other name; particularly on the occasion of an Open championship when the press coverage of the event would frequently centre upon the form of Barrington.

Here, including the years of his Open victories, he has set a formidable record of reaching the quarter-final stages of the British Open no less than 15 times during the period from 1966 to 1981. During that time he truly dominated the home scene, never having lost to a home player since 1966 when he was beaten by Jeremy Lyon.

That record promised to fall in 1980 when Jonah challenged for the British national title and pitted his wits and resources against young challengers such as Gawain Briars and Phil Kenyon. But Barrington on an evening of tremendous emotion triumphed over Briars and proved that even at the age of 39 he could still beat anyone in the country.

Injury prevented Barrington from defending his title in 1981 and he was unable to enter the 1982 British Open. Prudence now dictates that this most formidable sportsman will not compete at international level in squash, except in age group events and in those he could begin another period of domination.

Competition, however, is only one facet of the game and Barrington has made considerable contributions in two other important areas – juniors and the advancement of the playing professional through the International Squash Players Association (ISPA). Barrington has fired many a youngster's enthusiasm through his involvement with coaching – both national and on his own schemes – and admits that this area of involvement gives him great satisfaction.

His role with the ISPA was no less important since Barrington has always championed the professional's cause, being an integral part of the Association since it was founded in 1973, either as an officer or member. Barrington has been chairman and president, but never secretary because even the most fervent Barrington admirer would never be able to sing Jonah's praises as a king of paperwork! But people do listen to what Jonah has to say. He has a warm engaging personality and an enthusiasm which still reflects the flame of single-mindedness that drove him on in the early years. Rouse him and you will observe the abrasiveness which frequently brought him into head-on collision with authority, the Celtic spirit that even now occasionally pushes him to act and think later about the consequences.

Barrington feels that he still has a lot to contribute and commercially this fact has been quickly recognised by a leading sports goods manufacturer who has signed him to endorse a range of equipment despite Barrington's fade-out from playing.

Age group, veterans and vintage tournaments lie ahead and he has already taken a notable step on that path, winning the 1984 British Open Over-35 title.

Geoffrey Hunt (Aus)

British Open champion 1968, 1973, 1975–80
British Amateur champion 1969
World Open champion 1975, 1977, 1979, 1980
ISRF World Individual champion 1967, 1969, 1971

The retirement of Geoffrey Hunt from competitive squash at the age of 35 in April 1982 left a gap in the playing scene that will never be filled. The eight times British Open champion and four times World Open champion set standards of physical fitness, mental discipline and court behaviour that moulded him into the classic concept of a sporting ambassador. He bridged a gap from the days of the amateur player to the hard-nosed professionalism of the later seventies having himself had to come to terms with new levels of fitness required to succeed when he turned professional in 1971. The nonchalant air of the amateur,

expressing surprise that anyone should train so vigorously on and off court as Barrington did at that time, was transformed into a grim, inner determination to improve his stamina and widen his range of shots.

Yet, even at the heights of his success, he outwardly retained his diffident, casual manner; often it seemed shying away from publicity but never shirking the responsibility of a champion. His rivalry, first with Barrington and then later with a number of brilliant Pakistanis, built Hunt's reputation as the most resourceful player of modern times.

When Barrington faded, the Pakistanis led by Qamar Zaman, Mohibullah Khan, Hiddy Jahan and Gogi Alauddin all tried to knock the champion off his perch. They had limited success and what was more frustrating for his challengers was that Hunt developed a Houdini-like quality of surging to victory from the brink of defeat. He repeated his escape act on so many occasions that it had the effect of psyching his opponents into defeat before a match had begun. The Pakistanis faced the awful prospect of knowing they had to stay on court for two hours to have a chance of beating Hunt and then even if a winning position had been manoeuvred, the memory of Hunt's recoveries would eventually erode their confidence.

Although Hunt carried this air of invincibility, built it must be said by the Press and squash followers – he would never underestimate any opponent – his championship clashes were never foregone conclusions. The tightness of his play, the ball control, changes of paces and tactics, development of a greater range of strokes in later years, the strength of character to fight back, made Hunt a number 1 crowd puller. People would buy tickets for tournaments if they knew Hunt was competing, and the prospect of a Hunt v. Zaman final or later a Hunt v. Jahangir Khan would ensure a sell-out.

Jahangir Khan appeared as a threat to Hunt's many crowns when the Australian's physical abilities were beginning to fade. He kept the teenager at bay until November 1981 when he had to concede his world title to him, although the seeds of that defeat had been sown earlier that year when it was clear that Jahangir's outrageous ability would eventually swamp the gallant but ageing Hunt. In a five game match with Jahangir in the final of the Chichester tournament in March 1981 he was reduced to jelly-legged defeat. This sight shocked Hunt's followers and everyone knew then that it was only a matter of time.

The Australian came back to Britain in the spring of

The winning smile of a super champion. Geoff Hunt became accustomed to success but never assumed and always seemed pleasantly surprised when his skills and fitness brought him victory

1982 to defend his British Open crown and at that time looking to be the only player likely to be able to beat the awesome Jahangir. He went out early in his first three events and it was obvious that he was no longer the Hunt that everyone remembered. The pace, the sharpness, the movement had gone. The reason, a cracked vertebra, was revealed. Hunt withdrew from the Open and shortly after returning to Australia he announced his retirement. A lion of squash had gone. A last roar would have been appropriate but the doctor's warnings of the likely damage if he played on were wisely heeded.

His career in squash had started at the age of 12 after several years of tennis and at the age of 14 he gave up tennis completely. In 1965 at the age of 18 he became the youngest player to win the Australian Amateur and the youngest-ever finalist in the British Amateur, losing to Aftab Jawaid of Pakistan.

By 1967 he had won the first World Amateur Championship, a feat he repeated in 1969 and 1971 when he turned professional. He developed an intense rivalry with Barrington and the pair played many fierce matches with Hunt enjoying the best of their duels. His aggregate record against Barrington made him, his supporters argued, the better player although he was always in trouble against Barrington's attritional tactics. Their meetings frequently became a race to see whether Hunt's stamina could last before Barrington succumbed to Hunt's wider range of shots. When Hunt's level of fitness equalled and eventually surpassed that of Barrington he looked set to take over but by then Zaman and Mohibullah were on the scene.

Zaman won the 1975 British Open and Hunt once again had to re-think his approach in view of the artistry that Zaman had brought to the game. Hunt's character and resource saw him through and, in the process, squash was treated to a series of matches between himself and Zaman that will always be remembered by those privileged to watch them. These encounters left the audiences exhausted, marvelling at the respective skills. The 1978 British Open final, if not typical, highlighted their many encounters. The opening game lasted 50 minutes and was played at a furious pace. A well known press man was heard to comment 'If they go on at this pace they'll kill themselves'. Zaman won that cruel first game and Hunt's reply was to move up the court and take the ball earlier. The tactic crucified Zaman; the psychological lift of drawing first blood being totally nullified by Hunt's ability to adjust to a situation mentally and physically. Hunt went on to win the battle.

Hunt's departure has been missed, particularly by the Pakistanis who held him in the highest regard. Yet

Hunt's phlegmatic disposition will have allowed him to come quickly to terms with an enforced retirement. He always missed his family, increasingly so as his children reached school age. The public always saw him as the quietly-spoken champion going efficiently about his business. What they didn't see was the suitcase lifestyle and loneliness of hotel bedrooms.

Qamar Zaman (Pak)
British Open champion 1974

Qamar Zaman has often been dubbed the 'magician of the court', the undisciplined artist, the player who breathes humour and creativity into squash. All descriptions are accurate and well deserved and squash can be thankful that in an age prone to produce sportsmen whose forte is clinical precision there are exceptions such as Zaman.

Zaman's armoury is diverse. Opponents are astonished by the drop shot played from the back of the court with stunning accuracy; audiences are won over by the raising of an eyebrow, the soulful shrug of the shoulders or the casual droll, dry remark.

True comedians are rare in squash for the sport is too punishing, too exhausting for players to have the time, let alone the inclination, to view the proceedings with anything more than a desperate eye on the score and a mental check on stamina levels.

If one photograph ever captured the real Qamar Zaman it is this, depicting the deadpan humour which the Pakistani frequently uses to entertain a crowd, fluster a referee or unsettle an opponent. *Stephen Line*

Zaman's chunky physique, the ungainly walk, the deadpan face might seem more suited to a theatre setting, and certainly there have been many times when Zaman, the showman, has used the squash court as his own special stage. He has an impish sense of humour and a delicate understanding of timing, knowing just the moment to deliver a one-liner or raise his bushy eyebrows in such a way that an audience will dissolve into laughter.

His unpredictability makes him a nightmare opponent for all but his close Pakistani colleagues who can read his game better than most through the familiarity of practice sessions and many years of match play. Hunt learned to combat him by reducing his opportunities to play shots and occasionally, just occasionally, a player with fine racket ability, such as Britain's Gawain Briars, will be able to run him close, trading shot for shot. Zaman would enjoy such matches, even running the risk of losing if he were allowed to play in his own unfettered style, going for shots with a high percentage chance of error and succeeding more often than not.

He entered the international scene in 1972, having initially had a preference for tennis. His father Mohammed Ayub was a tennis and squash coach. The Zaman family came from Peshawar but Qamar was born in Quetta, the hill city of wild Baluchistan.

It was in Peshawar, however, that he began his squash preparation, joining his contemporary and future rival, Mohibullah Khan, under the watchful eye of Mohammed Yasin, now coach at Wembley Squash Centre.

The accent was always upon court training, practising shots and routines, a philosophy extolled by Zaman's father. Mohibullah Khan was the perfect foil for Zaman, possessing many of the qualities of skill, speed and stamina that Zaman was to meet later against Hunt.

He came to Britain in 1972 to contest the British Amateur Championship, reaching the semi-finals and failing only by one point to beat the Australian Billy Reedman. A month later he reached the last 16 of the Open, losing in five games to his uncle Aftab Jawaid, and in both appearances there was clear evidence that Zaman was destined for greater things.

The experience gained in Britain made him a better player, improved his method and stamina, so that when he returned the following year he progressed to the final of the Amateur, losing to Mohibullah, and to the semis of the Open, falling to Yasin. Mohibullah again beat him in 1974 in the Amateur although this disappointment for Zaman was soon to be allayed by a famous victory in the 1975 British Open. It was not an easy draw for Zaman. He had to beat Britain's Phil Ayton in the third round, holder Geoff Hunt in the quarters, Hiddy Jahan in the semis and finally Gogi Alauddin.

The match against Hunt predictably went to five games and was one of the few occasions that Hunt allowed Zaman to 'slip away' when apparently in a winning position. The Australian led 7–5 in the fifth and Zaman responded with an onslaught of devastating winners, a tremendous risk to take at such a stage but underlining the Zaman approach of 'go for your shots at all times'.

For a few heady weeks Zaman was on top of the world. He beat Hunt again and it forced the Australian to re-think his game. Many people made snap decisions that Zaman was destined for a long reign as Open champion. His game at times seemed unplayable and to the orthodox western eye it was inconceivable that such stroke play could be subdued. What happened is well known. Hunt did come back and Zaman was destined to stand for the most part in his shadow. Somehow Zaman has never seemed to quite make up his mind whether he is a competitor or entertainer. His natural instinct to play shots often gains him initiatives, even commanding leads. If this could be combined with a ruthless efficiency to resort to a more clinical game to exploit match advantages then Zaman would have undoubtedly added further British Open titles to his list of triumphs. After a while the Hunt dominance seemed to get him down. To Zaman, two hours of slugging up and down sidewalls was not squash, although to be fair to Hunt the Australian did learn from Zaman and introduce many more varied strokes to his repertoire.

Zaman often did get the better of Mohibullah, achieving, it seems, a psychological ascendancy through the development of his own extrovert character at the expenses of the shy, wistful Mohibullah. The exchanges were often rugged affairs, sometimes bad tempered; born of two players who knew each other's strengths and weaknesses.

Zaman won the World Masters in 1979 and the International Squash Players Championship in 1977 and 1979. He has four times been runner-up in the British Open and three times in the World Open. In the 1983 ISRF World Individual Championship he was again runner-up. However, now that Jahangir Khan has appeared, the future for Zaman once again takes on the shape of a supporting role, as was shown by his defeat by Jahangir in the 1984 British Open final.

Jahangir Khan (Pak)

British Open champion 1981, 1982, 1983
World Open champion 1981, 1982, 1983
ISRF World Individual champion 1979, 1983

As recently as 1980 any discussion about the 'greatest squash player of all time' would have been dominated by three names – Hashim Khan, Jonah Barrington and Geoff Hunt. Since then the remarkable success story of a young Pakistani player has added another dimension to that fascinating argument – the name of Jahangir Khan. That Jahangir should turn out to be a talented performer is hardly surprising. His pedigree is impeccable. The Khan family dominated world squash in the 1950s and early 1960s. Hashim, a cousin of Jahangir's father Roshan, contested seven British Open finals between 1950 and 1957 and won seven. His only 'failure' was in 1956 when he was beaten by none other than Roshan! Besides that win, Roshan was losing finalist in 1955 and 1959 and reached the semi-finals on five other occasions. Hashim's brother Azam took over the mantle of champion in 1958 – the first of four consecutive victories. He reached the semi-finals in each of the six previous years and was losing finalist three times. Cousin Mohibullah added

One player who is young enough and good enough to overhaul Geoff Hunt's record of eight British Open and four World Open wins is Jahangir Khan. His ability does not seem in doubt and his domination is such that his entry into any tournament prompts the question – 'who's going to be second?' *Robin Eley Jones*

his name to the list of winners in 1962 to complete 13 years of family rule in the world's premier event. What *is* stunning is that Jahangir should achieve so much in such a short time and at such a tender age in squash-playing terms. When he travelled to the World Amateur Championships in September 1979 he was not yet 16 and virtually unknown outside Pakistan. His own country's selectors did not even consider him good enough to play in the team event and he was asked to qualify for the individual competition. Within a few days he had astounded everyone by beating four seeded players to become the youngest-ever World Amateur champion.

That win prompted Jonah Barrington to comment: 'He really is a revelation. He has a very athletic heart which can only improve and he has a most un-Pakistani feeling for running and other general training. His length and width hitting are of a very high order already and he has an obvious talent for the short game which within five years will provide his unfortunate opponents with a great deal of misery. I have no doubt that by the time he is 21 he will have won the World Open.' A bold prediction and accurate in every respect apart from the length of time that Jahangir needed to win the Open.

Jahangir's first period of glory was marred by a tragedy just a few weeks later when his elder brother Torsam, an exceptionally talented player who was ranked in the world's top 10 and had undertaken to guide the youngster through the early stages of his career, collapsed and died during a tournament in Adelaide. At the time Jahangir's future looked in doubt, but his cousin Rahmat stepped in, virtually sacrificed his own playing career and took the new champion under his wing at his home in Wembley.

Jahangir's grief was compounded by frustration when he was robbed of the opportunity to add the British Amateur title to his world crown when an injury sustained in training forced him to withdraw from the championship. He made his professional debut in the ISPA Championship in February 1980 and immediately served notice that his victory in Australia was no fluke by leading world number 4 Hiddy Jahan two games to one before going down in five. That match prompted Jahan to add his name to the growing list of Jahangir's admirers by announcing that the youngster would be champion within two years.

That assessment still seemed somewhat extravagant when Jahangir finished the season ranked equal 26th in the world alongside Australian Frank Donnelly. However, his improvement in the next twelve months was the most dramatic in the history of the game and confounded even his most optimistic supporters.

He beat Maqsood Ahmed to reach the last eight of the 1980 World Open before losing 2–3 to Qamar Zaman. He won the New Zealand Open, beating Bruce Brownlee in the final, the Pakistan Open, with victories over Zaman and Mohibullah Khan, and had his first win over Geoff Hunt in the Canadian Club tournament in Germany. In England he added to his list of notable scalps by beating Gamal Awad in the Prodorite Invitation final, Ross Norman in the British Under-23 Open and Zaman in the Durham and Cleveland Open. Hunt avenged his earlier defeat in Germany by beating the youngster 3–0 in the 1981 ISPA final and so the scene was set for an enthralling climax to the British season. What transpired was even more than anyone could have hoped as Hunt and Jahangir fought out two of the most dramatic, competitive and brutal battles ever waged on a squash court. The ultra-fit Australian was reduced to immobility as Jahangir emerged victorious from the 1981 Chichester Festival final which lasted 2 hours 11 minutes. Many pundits felt that the Pakistani would end Hunt's run of British Open victories by repeating the win in Bromley two weeks later. It looked as if they would be proved correct as Jahangir recovered from 0–2 to take the third game and lead 6–2 in the fourth. Hunt was thoroughly exhausted but somehow he discovered a fresh reservoir of strength to recover and win 3–1 after 2 hours 14 minutes.

Although his season had finished on a relatively disappointing note, Jahangir was now ranked number 2 in the world – an incredible 27 places above Donnelly with whom he had been bracketed just a year before – and now all the earlier predictions about his future were, incredibly, being made to look understated.

Jahangir achieved his number 1 ranking by beating Hunt in the World Open final in December 1981 and he was still eleven days short of his eighteenth birthday! He has since gone from strength to strength recording a remarkable string of major victories. He took the coveted British Open title in April 1982 without dropping a game, even though five of his six opponents were ranked in the world's top 20 and he retained the world title later in the year when he beat Dean Williams of Australia in the final.

Both of these latter victories were achieved without having to do battle with Geoff Hunt who had been forced into premature retirement through injury. Anyone who witnessed either of their two meetings at the end of the 1980/1 season will forever regret that these two great athletes were not to share the same court more often. Jahangir has not tasted defeat since that British Open final with Hunt and currently none of the other top players seem capable of challenging his seeming invincibility.

During the 1983 Chichester Festival, the Egyptian Gamal Awad attempted to run Jahangir into submission. The result was a final lasting 2 hours 46 minutes, the longest match on record and another win for Jahangir by 3–1 who showed that his physical fitness can hold up to such tests.

Awad, psychologically dispirited after losing, could not raise the same enthusiasm two weeks later in the final of the British Open and subsided in straight games for the loss of eight points.

The 1983 ISRF world individual title fell to Jahangir and two months later he collected his third World Open crown in Munich, winning the championship without dropping a single game in all his matches.

Such is his dominance of the sport that when the 'greatest ever' argument is aired in years to come the discussion may be very short and amicable. It may well revolve around just one name – Jahangir Khan.

Janet Shardlow (née Morgan) (Eng)
British Women's Open champion 1950–58

Whenever women's squash is discussed, the name of Janet Shardlow will never be far from people's lips. As Janet Morgan she was indisputably the best in the game during the 1950s when she won 10 British Open titles in succession. Since her enforced retirement in 1960 she has worked tirelessly to promote and develop the sport in her role as President of the English Women's Squash Rackets Federation. Her retirement from the latter position in 1983 left a void that will be noticeable within the women's game for many years to come.

Like many of the great players, she came to squash through her first love – tennis. She competed at Wimbledon on 14 occasions, represented her home county of Surrey and was selected for the first post-war Wightman Cup squad.

In 1946, at the age of 24, she was invited by a friend to play a game of squash until the rain was blown from the courts of Surbiton Lawn Tennis Club. She began to concentrate on squash during the winter months and just four years later she won her first British title. 'I'd been in the final the two previous years but lost both times to another tennis player, Joan Curry,' she recalls. 'The first time went to five games and 10–8 or so in the fifth. The second time I lost more easily but after that I was home and dried.'

Ten years and another nine titles later she was compelled by persistent back and leg trouble to retire undefeated. Her competitive instincts were channelled instead into golf in which she achieved a seven handicap.

In most sports a run of ten successive victories in the world's premier event would remain permanently on the record books. But women's squash produced

Like many of the great players Janet Shardlow came to squash through her first love – tennis, but eventually achieved greater fame through her squash exploits, winning ten successive British Open titles. *Central Press*

Heather McKay, and Shardlow's record was eclipsed. Ironically McKay's development can be attributed in no small measure to Shardlow herself.

In 1954 Shardlow and Sheila Speight were invited to tour Australia and New Zealand where they played, coached and put on exhibition matches in front of enthralled audiences. Few women played there at the time, but the tour did much to popularise the game and helped produce the environment from which McKay developed. When the Australian travelled to England for the first time, she brought with her a letter of introduction to Shardlow who housed the youngster and encouraged her through those early, lonely months of what developed into the most successful career in the game to date.

The two have remained close friends over the years, but it is small wonder that Shardlow still recalls with immense satisfaction the personal significance of that trip in 1954: 'That was the year I won the three big ones, the Australian, British and American Open titles – the only thing Heather hasn't taken from me.'

44

Heather McKay (née Blundell) (Aus)
British Women's Open champion 1962–1977
Women's World Open champion 1976, 1979

If you won your sport's premier event for ten years in succession you would not expect a close friend and erstwhile lodger to repay your hospitality by making your achievement seem almost pedestrian. But that's exactly what happened to Janet Shardlow, president of the Women's Squash Rackets Association!

As Janet Morgan she caused the record books to be rewritten when, having twice finished runner-up, she was unbeaten in the British Open Championship throughout the 1950s before retiring from major competitions.

Then, early in 1962, a 20-year-old Australian girl arrived on her first visit to England. She was travelling on her own for the first time, was very shy and knew no one in Britain. Janet Shardlow welcomed her to the country and offered her accommodation in her home. And so was born the strong and lasting friendship between the 10-times champion and the girl who was destined to become the greatest-ever female squash player – Heather Blundell.

Heather was the eighth of eleven children born to a baker and his wife in the small town of Queanbeyan, New South Wales. Her mother played tennis, her father rugby league and she had concentrated on tennis and hockey until, at 17, she took up squash to improve her fitness. Just two years later she was Australian champion.

That had been a remarkable achievement but, when she travelled to England, no one could have forecast the impact she would make on the game during the next two decades.

In January 1962 she reached the final of the Scottish Open where she lost to British Open champion Fran Marshall. A month later she avenged that defeat with a 3–0 victory in the British Open final and was never again to lose a competitive match!

She won the next three British Opens as Miss Blundell and, after marrying professional coach Brian McKay in 1965, eclipsed Janet's record with a win over South African Kathy Malan in 1972 before going on to complete an astonishing run of 16 successive victories when she beat compatriot Barbara Wall in the first all-Australian final in 1977. Her domination of the event during those years was such that she dropped just two games during the 16 tournaments – to Anna Craven-Smith in 1964 and Sue Cogswell on her final appearance in 1977. She conceded only 99 points in the 16 finals (an average of just over 6 per match) and recorded the only 27–0 final scoreline in the history of the competition when she destroyed the unfortunate Bev Johnson in only 15 minutes in 1968 –

her opponent did not serve once during the second or third games. She also amassed 14 consecutive Australian titles before rendering herself ineligible for the championship by turning professional in January 1974.

She won the first-ever WISRF World Individual Championship in Brisbane in 1976, during which she conceded just 15 points, and, despite having ceased to compete in the British Open, returned to England in 1979 to retain her world title at Sheffield.

She moved with husband Brian to Toronto in 1975 and, after winning the second world title, retired there to concentrate on the relatively lucrative sport of racquetball. It was a move not without criticism, since there were those who felt that she was deserting the game that had made her famous. In a letter to an English squash magazine, she explained the thinking behind the decision: 'I have given squash much during the last 19 years. I tried where possible to advance interest in the game and help promote

Heather McKay holding aloft the British Women's Open Trophy, a gesture that became second nature since she took the title for 16 successive years. Her total domination of the sport has no modern-day parallel.
United Press International

women's role in active competition. In return I have gained great personal satisfaction and extremely modest financial reward. But I loved the game and that's what counted the most. I don't apologise for being a winner, I'm proud of my record. I have always said I would leave the game undefeated and have not changed my mind. Racquetball has been my moneymaker and I believe I deserve the winning purses because I learned to play with, and beat, the best.' If the controversy worried her, it didn't affect her performances. Within a year of taking up racquetball she had become Canada's best player.

It was not the first time she had displayed such determination and ability to adapt. When she first arrived in Britain she was not particularly fit and was so painfully shy that she was horrified at the thought of meeting strangers, attending parties or making speeches. She developed the athleticism that became one of the hallmarks of the game by regularly playing against men, and she fought bravely to combat her natural shyness. Indeed, on future tours, she readily made herself available for speeches, interviews and broadcasts.

This personal courage together with great powers of concentration, unbounded enthusiasm, exceptionally competitive spirit and an ability to learn quickly, combined to make Heather McKay the most successful female squash player and, arguably, the finest sportswoman of all time.

Vicki Cardwell (née Hoffman) (Aus)
British Women's Open champion 1980–83
Women's World Open champion 1983

November 1983 and Vicki Cardwell can retire contented. She announced her intention to do so after her fourth successive British Open victory earlier in the year, but one very significant gap in her impressive list of achievements led one to believe that it would be an uneasy rest. For over three years – first as Miss Hoffman and then Mrs Cardwell – the Australian had been the undisputed world number 1 but she had failed to win the world championship. The title is only contested every two years and in 1981 when firm favourite, she had been beaten in the final by good friend and compatriot Rhonda Thorne who thus settled on the throne left vacant by the retirement of the legendary Heather McKay.

That defeat was a blemish on a highly successful career and it rankled. Therefore, in 1983, at Perth, Western Australia, Cardwell reversed that result, was crowned world champion and reaffirmed her desire to quit the game and settle down to family life with husband Ian. On this occasion the statement could be totally accepted as that of a woman who had achieved everything in her chosen game.

Aggression is written all over Vicki Cardwell's face as she moves in to crack the ball away down the sidewall.
Robin Eley Jones

13', the tournament made a lasting impression. She saw for the first time some of the greats of squash – McKay, Hunt, Hiscoe, Mohibullah Khan – and determined to give up tennis and hockey to concentrate on squash. That event was in Perth and ten years later the squash enthusiasts of the same city witnessed the culmination of her efforts.

During the years in between her progress had been remarkable. In 1974 she was promoted from the State Juniors to number 5 in the senior side and was selected for the national under-23 team. The following year she played number 3 for the seniors; lined up at number 2 to Lyle Hubinger in 1976 and was number 1 in 1977. She was also the third ranked amateur in Australia that year having been number 6 in 1976. In 1978 she won the Australian Amateur title and in 1978 captured her first Australian Open (in Perth, naturally!) – both against Rhonda Thorne. She also reached the British Open final in 1978 where she lost to Sue Newman. In 1980 she won the Australian and British Open Championships, beating Sue Cogswell in both finals.

She reigned supreme in Britain from then, completing her run in the Open with victories over Margaret Zachariah and Lisa Opie twice.

It is a fine record and one that places her alongside the greats of the women's game, Heather McKay and England's Janet Shardlow. Comparisons with McKay are unavoidable but Cardwell refuses to add fuel to the debate. 'It would be unfair of me to make comparisons,' she says, 'I was just starting as she was nearing the end. But she was extraordinary, probably the greatest athlete that ever graced the earth.'

So the relative talents of the two women must remain a matter of conjecture but there is no disputing that Cardwell recorded her major victories at a time when the women's game could boast many players of greater skill and fitness than those with which McKay had to contend.

Cardwell was the fittest of all, hitting the ball with a ferocity unexpected from such a small frame and possessed an enormous 'will to win' which intimidated opponents even when they appeared to be in winning positions.

The little Australian is aggressive, fun-loving, outspoken and hates to lose – a combination that has seen her in trouble more than once with the games' authorities. All great sports people detest defeat. Cardwell is no exception. Some can conceal their emotions. Others need to vent them. Cardwell is decidedly in the latter category. Conflict is inevitable but in years to come, Vicki Cardwell should be remembered not for her off-court exploits but as one of the most talented, competitive and successful women ever to grace the game of squash.

Remarkably, but for encouragement from her tennis coach, Cardwell might have never taken squash seriously. She had first played when she was 12 but that was a one-off experiment and during most of her teens she concentrated on tennis and hockey.

Her tennis career blossomed. She became South Australian hardcourt champion and holder of the under-17 and under-19 state titles. Then, when she was 17, came the discussion that was to change her life. Her tennis coach, also secretary of the local Squash Rackets Association, suggested she had a natural flair for squash. She was not convinced but she entered the State Junior Championship and finished runner-up. She represented her State Junior team at the Australian Championships later in the same year and, although she recalls: 'I was absolutely hopeless and the only match I won was against a girl of

4 Spectator squash

Today's squash enthusiasts who enjoy the privilege of viewing major tournaments on an all-transparent court from the comfort of cushioned theatre seats could be excused for assuming that these innovations are a result of continuous development throughout the history of the game.

In reality nothing could be further from the truth. Little of significance happened to the squash court or its spectator facilities in the 100 years following the building of the first courts at Harrow in 1864. In terms of spectator numbers it was accepted that only a handful of people could watch. For instance when the Amateur Championship was held at the Old Bath Club in Dover Street, London from 1923–38, the audience could never be more than 50. The largest gallery at the time was the RAC Club which could accommodate 100 and it wasn't until improvements were made to the Lansdowne Club in the mid-thirties that spectator capacity was doubled. The Abbeydale Club, Sheffield and Edgbaston Priory, two of England's most famous clubs only had space for 100 spectators before bold redevelopment schemes in the 1970s made more room for the public. A glass back-wall did the trick for Abbeydale while at Edgbaston the idea of glass was given a new dimension by siting another court immediately opposite the championship court, on the back to back principle. When events are held, the 'portable' backwall of court No. 2 moves to make way for an audience seating system which racks back into the recess of the court enabling spectators to have an excellent view of play through the glass. This technique has since been utilised to good effect at many clubs.

Before the advent of glasswalls, watching squash could be a hazardous occupation for the few who could actually get a view of the play. Galleries were quite inadequate to cope with the numbers of people who wanted to watch, as typified in this scene at Queen's Club, London during the final of the 1939 British Women's Open between Margot Lumb and Susan Noel. Stools, tables and ladders were pressed into service, but even the British Amateur champion, K. C. Gandar Dower, at the top of the tallest ladder, cannot have seen much more than the front wall. *Illustrated London News*

Overseas the trend was to go higher and add additional galleries around the sides of a championship court. This approach extends capacity considerably, examples being The Wanderers Club, Johannesburg (400), Victoria SRA Centre, Melbourne (500), Harare, Zimbabwe (800), and Peshawar (800), although customers at the latter centre who are allocated seats in the 'gods' could well end up suffering from vertigo. Generally, however, those in the gallery in the early 1960s still risked permanent neck damage as they strained to see action in the back-corners while hanging precariously over the top of the solid-walled court.

The first tentative steps in the march towards the current dramatic settings were not taken until the latter part of the sixties although research into 'all glass assemblies', as they were then called, began at

the Pilkington Laboratories in 1961. The immediate aims were to improve spectator viewing and enjoyment of squash, linked with the fascination that eventually squash could be successfully filmed and televised. By the early 1970s the latter ambition of attracting television was at least sharing equal billing in the minds of the court constructors concerned. As television coverage of all sport increased in that decade it was clear that squash had to find a way to enhance its appeal as a television sport if it was to maintain the momentum of popularity and compete with emerging sports.

The fact that the game has to be played within four walls be they brick, glass or plastic, with two players moving swiftly, striking a small ball, poses tremendous difficulties for the television camera. Translating the action on court to the small screen has so far met with only qualified success.

The first recorded occasion of squash being televised for general broadcast was in Perth for the 1962 men's Australian championship. This was achieved by removing the middle located back door of the court and televising through the open doorway.

The story was continued in 1965 at Hobart, Australia when a court door was fitted with a glass window through which play could be filmed (see p. 61). This idea was expanded in December 1966 when Pilkington Glass installed a glass panel in the backwall of a court at the Birkenhead SRC in Merseyside. However, the panel, 5 ft (1·5 m) high by 16 ft (4·9 m) long and made of 1 in (25 mm) thick glass glazed along four edges, did little to improve spectator capacity as the wall backed on to a narrow passageway.

The 1967 inaugural ISRF World Championship at Albert Park, Melbourne received television coverage although the court did not have a glass backwall. The walls above the out of play lines opened into galleries and this allowed cameras at the rear and side.

Two years later in Brisbane a court was built with a glass panel across the full length of the backwall but the presence of metal supports seriously hindered spectating and filming. The development encountered a further problem as reflection on the inside of the glass caused difficulty in defining the surface.

The first major breakthrough came in October 1971 at the Abbeydale Club in Sheffield. Ellis Pearson installed the world's first all-glass backwall consisting of six plates including the door, supported by four glass fins which replaced the hitherto obstructive steel adjuncts. The designers also overcame the Brisbane reflection problem by etching into the glass vertical lines $\frac{1}{16}$ in (1·6 mm) wide and 1 in (25 mm) apart which permitted clearer sighting of the ball. To complete the package, seating was provided behind the glass wall and a white screen was placed before the first row to

improve competitors' vision. The British Open was held at the club in 1972 when the spectator capacity enabled the first prize to be increased five-fold from that of the previous year (1971 – £100, 1972 – £500).

Two years later BBC Television was at Abbeydale to record the final of the British Open for screening on *Grandstand*. Unfortunately, for the first time in the history of the event, the final failed to take place. Mo Yasin was unable to face Geoff Hunt due to injury – but the cameras focused instead on an exhibition match between Hunt and Jonah Barrington.

In November 1974 the first court designed specifically with television in mind was opened at the Wembley Squash Centre. It had a glass backwall, seating for 240, and standing room for up to 100. Blocks of seats on each side of the front rows and halfway back in the centre of the gallery were removable to make way for cameras. Most significantly, a glass-sided commentary box was placed to the side of the gallery behind the backwall. This set-up staged six consecutive British Opens including the event in February 1976 which incorporated the first World Open Championship.

In 1976 Pakistan International Airlines opened their magnificent five-court complex in Karachi which incorporates two championship courts. The No. 1 court has seating for 256 people and standing room for 100 more, plus a television position built into the seating five rows up from the backwall. In No. 2 court there is accommodation for 150 spectators. This centre must currently rate as the finest purpose-built championship play complex anywhere in the world and it is a pity that it is not utilised more often for international events. For comfort the championship court is unrivalled with wide walk-ways between the rows of seats which gives plenty of leg room – exactly the opposite of the Wembley facility.

Early in 1977 Ellis Pearson announced that it was ready to make final tests on the first all-glass court and a sample panel was featured on BBC Television's *Tomorrow's World*. Although the court failed to appear as planned, the developers had taken considerable strides towards solving viewing and ball-skid problems. Two-tone ceramic dots – white towards the inside, black towards the spectators – were baked on to the glass during the toughening process. One fifth of the glass area was covered by dots ensuring that 20 per cent of the light which would normally travel outwards was deflected back into the court, making the wall seem white to the players and

Recipe for a packed gallery anywhere in the world was the appearance together on court of Geoff Hunt (*right*) and Qamar Zaman, rivals in many international finals. *All Sport*

reducing the black mirror effect of normal glass. At
the same time the view of those in the audience was
virtually unaffected. Additionally, the inclusion of
the dots produced a rough surface on the glass which
eliminated the ball-skidding problem.

In September 1978 the Swedish company Perstorp
erected a prefabricated court in two days at the Kung-
liga Tennishallen in Stockholm in which 600 people
watched part of the Swedish leg of the PIA series.
This was the first instance of a demountable court
erected in a leisure complex to take advantage of
greater seating capacity although, on this occasion,
everyone was still seated behind the backwall.

Five months later the first event in England to use a
demountable glass backwall court was staged at the
Kings Hall, Belle Vue, Manchester. The Lookers
Masters was played on a court erected in the circus
ring and over 1000 people watched the final. Unfor-

The use of demountable courts *(see above)* hastened the
prospect of major events being played before audiences
of several thousand, and it was the Swedish company,
Perstorp, who showed the way. Perstorp's prefab-
ricated court was erected in the Kings Tennis Hall,
Stockholm for the final stages of the Pakistan
International Airlines World Series in September 1978.
Although everyone had to be seated behind the glass
backwall there was an audience of 600 for the final.
And five months later this figure was swelled to 1000 as
the court made its debut in England for the Lookers
Masters at Belle Vue, Manchester

The Twin-Vue portable four glass wall court made its debut in England at the Marina Centre, Great Yarmouth for a special television test event in November 1983.
Andrew Perkins

tunately there were holes in the roof and there was the unusual sight of snowflakes drifting down on a section of the audience. This did not dampen spectators' enjoyment of the play however.

At the same time the works canteen of a company called Fisher Karpark was the unlikely setting for another innovation. A court was built adjacent to the canteen and the furniture was removed to accommodate tiered seating for the final stages of the FKI International tournament.

The demountable Perstorp court was transported in 44 pieces to Canada in September 1979 where it was used for the first time at a major tournament – the World Open at the Etobicoke Olympium sports centre in Toronto. In February 1980 it was hoisted on to the stage of Southampton's Gaumont Theatre for the ISPA Championships and a month later it was used for the British Open at Wembley Conference Centre's Grand Hall where approximately four times as many spectators were able to watch as at the Wembley Squash Centre.

A similar demountable court, manufactured by the German company ASB, was then utilised for the 1981 and 1982 British Opens; the setting being the stage of the Bromley Theatre, South London. Again this gave an audience capacity of between 800 to 1000.

In July 1981 the world's first transparent sidewall was installed at the Walton Hall Hotel and Leisure Complex near Wakefield, Yorkshire. American company Twin-Vue was responsible for the development and the glass contained a series of tiny black and white dots superimposed on each other.

In October of the same year Swedish firm Andren and Sons produced a plexiglass all-transparent court called Transwall. The Stockholm company used the same dot principle as that already developed on glass but surmounted patent problems by not using glass. The court made its first appearance at the German Masters in an air-hall in Cologne.

A month later Twin-Vue took a mammoth step forward by producing a glass frontwall for the World Open at the Columbus Community Centre in Toronto. The court had a clear glass Ellis Pearson backwall and laminated demountable sides.

The Transwall all-transparent court made its British debut at the Chichester Festival in March 1982. Hurried repairs were needed following damage in transit and the supporting steel structure obstructed spectators' view but the event proved a major step forward for television coverage.

August 1982 and, in the Audi Warehouse in Milton Keynes, Twin-Vue demonstrated a court with one solid sidewall and glass back, front and other side. Generally, playing characteristics were heralded as good but some difficulty was encountered seeing a ball played low across court. This problem fortunately did not arise when Twin-Vue used the same combination – three glass walls and a solid right forehand wall – for the 1982 Audi World Open held in November of that year at the National Exhibition Centre, Birmingham. The event was a great success and attracted a record audience for squash of 1600 for one session – a figure that has now been beaten. Also in November 1982, Campbell Reith and Partners and ICI combined to produce the Safe-Screen court which was unveiled at the World Masters in Leicester. It was made from Perspex, ICI's acrylic sheet, and the Granby Hall venue allowed viewing from all four sides for the first time ever. Only one day is required to erect and dismantle the court which is claimed to be unique in several ways. No steelwork obstructs the view – the stability of the walls depends on in-built plastic fins. When the court is lit and the spectator area is in relative darkness the dot patterns enable the audience to see in but players cannot see out. The panel floor has been developed for quick erection and

the panels run the length of the court to avoid lateral joints. There is a uniformly non-glare illuminated ceiling which, combined with high-intensity lighting, enables television coverage through the walls. Between the top of the court walls and the illuminated ceiling is a perforated section of polyester which maintains the one-way effect but allows ventilation. A 2 ft (0·6 m) deep illuminated banner for advertising purposes surrounds the court above the level of the ceiling and additional illuminated signs cover the outside of the tin where they are visible to television and spectators but not to players. This style of presentation was used for the 1983 British Open at the Assembly Rooms, Derby and for the 1984 tournament when the event returned to the Wembley Conference Centre and attracted a world record audience of 2603 for the final.

Yet despite the high level of professionalism that is now evident in many promotions it is clear that although squash has established its spectator appeal, the television programme controllers do not share this enthusiasm. Nowhere is this scepticism for television

The Twin-Vue Court with three glass walls and one solid sidewall used at the National Exhibition Centre, Birmingham, for the 1982 World Open. At the time the event set a record audience of 1600 for one session.

squash more deep rooted than in the UK where network coverage for the sport is little more than one hour per year. This is not to denigrate the efforts of regional television companies – Anglia, TVS and Grampian – or the BBC. Nor should the many excellent hours of coverage given by television companies in Australia, New Zealand, Singapore, Pakistan and Canada be ignored. But the fact remains that to the non-squash viewer the sport generally remains a mystery with rules that are difficult to follow and a ball that is difficult to see. So far the 'opening-up' of squash via transparent courts has failed to produce the television breakthrough expected and this has motivated a group of leading promoters in England to try and tackle the problem head-on.

Under the banner of World Championship Squash Ltd (WCS), a new format has been introduced. This utilises 'American' scoring whereby a point is scored at the end of every rally as opposed to the traditional idea of scoring only when holding service. Matches are still the best of five games, but up to 13 points and a tie-break system operates if the score reaches 12–12. In parallel with this change, WCS has also adopted a dark blue floor, using yellow marking lines and a white squash ball.

The idea of a blue floor and a white ball was first successfully used during the 1983 French Open in Paris. The French also made history by becoming the first people to use a four wall Twin-Vue court made of glass. For their test event at Great Yarmouth, WCS also used the all-glass court, the first time it had been seen in the UK. Modifications were made, notably by painting the floor a much darker blue to produce a greater contrast with the white ball. This was found to improve visibility of the ball. Eight leading professional players then played to the new rules and the result was aggressive, entertaining squash and much shorter matches (the tendency of some matches to last more than two hours being another major television criticism). Anglia Television put in five cameras, experimenting with different angles and shooting a lot of the play through the front wall. Vision of the white ball against the blue floor was much improved and Anglia were of the opinion that real progress had been made with television coverage of the sport. Other possibilities being discussed are to make the ball an 'ultra white' and also to manufacture a slightly larger ball.

The 1984 British Open used the combination of a yellow ball and blue floor and for a Test match against Pakistan an experiment was made with a special light-reflective ball.

Whether all these changes, some of them radical and understandably hard for the traditionalist to accept, will result in regularly attracting television to squash, cannot be assessed at this stage. It is hard to believe that such developments have sprung from the insertion of a small glass window in a court door at Hobart. It is perhaps less difficult to accept that in another 20 years we will look back on these happenings as nothing more than the infancy of squash spectating . . . but for the moment at least the last two decades certainly remain the most exciting period in the history of the game.

5 Who runs squash?

Squash, unlike many other sports, has a simple, easy to understand administrative structure.

Each country where the sport is sufficiently developed has a national association – in most cases the interests of men and women are combined in one association but three countries, England, Ireland and South Africa, still have separate bodies for women.

The national associations are all represented by the International Squash Rackets Federation (ISRF) which is the game's single rule-making body. All official changes in the sport have to be implemented by the ISRF who also assume general responsibility for the welfare of the game and for the running of world individual and team championships every two years.

Within this structure, but without any real authority, are the federations such as the European and Asian group of countries organised on a geographical basis. The federations try to foster the sport in much the same way that the ISRF does, but within certain sectors of the world, and also run their own championships, usually every year.

The Women's International Squash Rackets Federation, established in 1978, is very much a newcomer and came about as a result of a desire to run women's world team and individual championships and to encourage international competition. It is possible however that it will eventually be amalgamated with the ISRF.

The professional male players have their own association, the International Squash Players Association (ISPA), set up in 1973 to look after the interests of the tournament player. The ISPA runs its own World Open Championship which tends to lead to some confusion with the events run by the ISRF and is a situation yet to be clarified. This dates from the time when there were amateurs and professionals and the official World Open did not exist and although the 1976 British Open was given 'world status' by the ISRF, the players took matters into their own hands and instituted their own championship. The ISPA also brought in their own system of grading events for computer ranking points and issue their own world ranking list.

A separate women's association, the Women's Squash Professionals Association, was constituted in April 1984.

The ISPA's accord with the ISRF and general relations with national associations is currently good but there have been skirmishes in the past and no doubt there will be in the future, although it is hoped that the disputes which plague tennis do not develop. Matters such as organisation of events, the calendar, prize money and discipline are sensitive areas.

International Squash Rackets Federation

Chairman: Ian Stewart, 259 Steelcase Road West, Markham, Ontario, L3R 2P6 Canada, Tel: (416) 485 0800
Vice Chairman: Ronnie Sinclair, 5 Barnton Gardens, Edinburgh EH4 6AF, Scotland, Tel: (031) 336 2309 (home); (031) 225 7515 (office)
Executive Dir: Roger Eady, National Sports Centre, Sophia Gardens, Cardiff, Wales CF1 9SW, Tel: Cardiff 374771 (STD code 0222)

No official body existed in the early days of squash with responsibility for establishing and standardising rules. The Canadian Squash Rackets Association was founded in 1915, the United States association in 1920 and the English association in 1928 but these developments were too late to prevent the growth of two differing codes – the 'hardball' version in North America and the 'international game' throughout the rest of the world.

After the Second World War overseas visits by national sides became popular and in 1962 representatives of Britain, Australia and South Africa met in London to agree on rule policies for such tours and inaugurated an international body, if only in embryonic form.

In January 1965, the Australian SRA asked Britain, Egypt, New Zealand, Pakistan, South Africa and the USA to consider the formation of an international federation with a view to setting up regular world championships.

A year later representatives of Australia, Britain, Canada, Egypt, India, New Zealand, Pakistan, South Africa and the USA met in London and decided to form the International Squash Rackets Federation (ISRF). A constitution was agreed to promote the welfare of the game, to uphold the rules of squash rackets, co-ordinate international matches and investigate the holding of annual international championships.

The ISRF's inaugural meeting was held in London on 5 January 1967 at which Australia, Egypt, GB,

The International Squash Rackets Federation was established in 1967 and one of the first tasks it undertook was to organise a world team championship. Seen here are the 1969 winning Australian team of Ken Hiscoe, Geoff Hunt, Frank Boyle (from the Australian Embassy in London), Dick Carter and Cam Nancarrow

India, New Zealand, Pakistan and South Africa became founder members. Britain's Peter Phillips and John Horry were elected chairman and secretary respectively, and Roy Wilson of Australia became vice-chairman. The Squash Rackets Association's rules, as formulated in 1929, were adopted with an agreement that future changes would only be made at a full meeting of the Federation. Canada and the USA became founder associate members and it was decided that the first ISRF championships would be held in Australia in August 1967.

The host country dominated the first championships – all seven founder members except Egypt took part – with Geoff Hunt beating Cam Nancarrow in the final of the individual event and the same two players together with Ken Hiscoe and Dick Carter winning the team title.

In 1968 Canada and the USA were upgraded to founder members and it was decided that the founder members would stage the world championships at approximately two-yearly intervals.

Politics infiltrated the Federation in 1970 when an 'Emergency General Meeting' was held in London to discuss a resolution to exclude South Africa from the ISRF because of its government's racial policies. The resolution was withdrawn when South Africa agreed not to send a team to the 1971 World Championships in New Zealand where, together with the host country, Australia, Britain, Canada, Egypt, India and Pakistan competed. Hunt and his fellow countrymen

again won both competitions. South Africa was the venue in 1973 but only Australia, Britain, New Zealand and the USA made the trip. Both trophies were retained by Australia. In that year, a new constitution was adopted which recognised the rules of the 'hard-ball' game on an equal footing with those of the international code.

Britain ended Australia's domination of the team event when 10 countries competed in England in 1976 but the individual trophy went 'down-under' for the fourth successive time when Kevin Shawcross won at Wembley. Britain retained the title in Australia in 1979 and squash received its first glimpse of a future world champion when the unseeded fifteen-year-old Jahangir Khan of Pakistan won the individual event. The same player led Pakistan to its first team triumph in Sweden in 1981 from a field of 20. Steve Bowditch restored Australian supremacy in the individual event by beating New Zealand's Craig Blackwood in the final of a competition which included none of the Pakistan stars. In 1980, the ISRF organised the first world junior championships in Sweden when Preter Nance won the individual event and led his side to victory in the team competition. Sohail Qaiser of Pakistan completed the same double when the tournaments were held in Singapore and Malaysia in 1982.

The 1983 championships were held in New Zealand with 19 countries competing and Jahangir Khan and Pakistan, respectively, winning the individual and team titles.

Women's International Squash Rackets Federation

Chairman: Mrs Prue Hamilton, 10 Thorndale Road, North Carryduff, Belfast BT8 8HY, Northern Ireland, Tel: Belfast 813343 (STD code 0232)
Liaison Committee: Mrs Suzie Simcock (NZ)
Vice-Chairmen: Mrs Jackie Robinson (England); Miss Marion Matchett (Ireland); Robyn Blackwood (WSPA)

The foundations of the Women's International Squash Rackets Federation (WISRF) were laid in Brisbane in August 1976 when a meeting took place between international players and administrators from Great Britain, South Africa, Canada, Ireland, New Zealand and Australia.

The Australian Women's SRA had invited players worldwide to take part in a World Open Squash Championship, the first non-national Open championship held for women.

It was felt, at this time, that a women's organisation at international level was needed, since for many years both individuals and the strongest women's squash playing countries had been promoting international squash for women but little interest had been expressed by the ISRF.

In February 1978 a further meeting was held in Birmingham to consider the results of a questionnaire sent out following the Brisbane meeting. The outcome of the responses received from the leading countries' associations in women's squash clearly indicated that:

(a) they would like to hold both a team and individual world championship;
(b) they did not wish these events to be held in conjunction with the ISRF events;
(c) they wished to form a women's international squash rackets federation.

Outline agreement was reached on the main points to be included in the constitution and rules for the championships. A committee under the chairmanship of Mrs Janet Shardlow was formed with the objective of preparing a draft constitution for the next meeting.

The purpose of the WISRF was to organise and control the championships and to act as an informal link between women in member countries, whether or not the countries had joint men and women national associations. There was no question of the WISRF being a governing body, and the meeting expressed a wish for close co-operation and communication with the ISRF. During the Women's World Championships, hosted by Great Britain in 1979, the constitution and rules were approved at a meeting held on 17 March in Birmingham, which was attended by representatives of eight countries.

The following countries were accepted as members, having fulfilled the criteria for membership: Great Britain, South Africa, Ireland, Australia, New Zealand, Canada and the USA. Mrs Janet Shardlow MBE (Eng), was elected chairman of the newly formed WISRF, Dr Sue Pexman (Can) vice-chairman, and Mrs Ina Osborn (SA) and Mrs Jackie Robinson (Eng) were elected to serve on the liaison committee until the next General Meeting.

In 1981 Canada hosted the Women's World Team and Individual Championships in Toronto, and an Invitation Junior World Championship was introduced with a view to formalising it if sufficient support was shown.

By this time the WISRF membership had increased to 16 countries, England, Scotland and Wales having become members separately, and 14 of these countries played in the team championship.

In 1981 Miss Jan Honeycombe (Aus) and Mrs Prue Hamilton (Ire) were elected to the liaison committee, the chairman and vice-chairman being re-elected.

Most recently the Women's World Championships were hosted in autumn 1983 by Australia, this time in Perth. Four world titles were contested – the Women's Open Individual, the Senior (Over-40) Women's Open Individual, the Women's Junior and the Women's Team Championships. Although the membership has remained constant during the past few years only seven countries played in the team event in Perth, while 78 players played in the individual championship. Mrs Shardlow retired after six years as chairman and it should be recorded that through her personal endeavours many countries were brought into the international scene.

The establishment of the WISRF and with it, the firm resolve to advance the game of squash for women, in particular through international com-

The WISRF introduced two new events for their 1983 world championship in Perth, Australia – for players aged 35 and over, and 40 and over. First winner of the Over-40 was Jenny Webster of New Zealand (*right*) and runner-up, Anne Smith of Australia. *Greg Wood*

petition on a regular basis, has created a climate whereby amalgamation of the WISRF with the ISRF is being considered.

Since 1979 a significant number of national associations which were separate for men's and women's squash have become one. Currently only three countries have separate associations, these are England, Ireland and South Africa. This situation may have accelerated talks regarding the joining of the two international federations, however it is recognised that this will not impinge on the autonomy of the SRA's within these countries.

European Squash Rackets Federation
Chairman: Lou Zandvliet, Stalperstraat 107, 2597RS, Den Haag, Netherlands Tel: 70 727895 (office); 70 240582 (home)
Vice-Chairmen: Bo Skough, Klavervagen 74, 32545 Vaxjo, Sweden Tel: 0470 45100 (office), 0470 21954 (home); Mrs Jean Reynolds, 8 Sir Harry's Road, Edgbaston, Birmingham B15 20Y, England Tel (021) 440 5243; Brian Fitzgerald, 9 Netherleigh Park, Belfast BT4 3GR, Northern Ireland Tel: Belfast 63686 (STD code 0232) (home); Belfast 238877 (STD code 0232) (office)
Secretary: Ian D. W. Wright, 50 Tredegar Road, Wilmington, Dartford, Kent DA2 7AZ, England Tel: Dartford 72200 (STD code 0322)

The European Squash Rackets Federation (ESRF) was formed in 1973 during the inaugural European Team Championships at which ten countries participated. Since then the Federation has grown quickly in stature and now has 21 members.

The objects of the body are to promote the welfare of the sport in Europe, uphold the rules of the game and ensure their observation in national and international competitions, organise annual European championships, co-ordinate matches between member countries and national team tours, and settle disputes between member countries.

The first officers were: Lennart Jepsen (Swe), chairman; Aris Vatimbella (Mon) and Lou Zandvliet (Net), vice-chairmen; Robert Dolman (Wal), treasurer; Peter Woods (Eng), secretary. A technical committee was set up in 1976 to supply members with technical details essential to setting up and maintaining standards.

Initially, the annual European Championships comprised only a men's team event, but in 1978 a women's tournament was introduced.

England has been far the most successful country. The men have won nine times from eleven starts – they were surprisingly beaten into second place by Sweden in Helsinki in 1980 and again in Munich in 1983 – while the women have yet to taste defeat in six years of competition. Each year a trophy is awarded to the man and woman who, in the view of a panel, 'has

shown the greatest spirit of fair play and has demonstrated great perseverence or has won unexpectedly during the championship'. The first men's winner was Ken Watson of Denmark in 1973 and when the women's award was introduced in 1980 it was won by Sweden's Agneta Samuelsson.

International Squash Players Association
President: Ahmed Safwat (Egypt)
Vice-President: Richard O'Connor (South Africa)
Chairman: Greg Pollard (Australia)
Correspondence to: Roger Eady, National Sports Centre, Sophia Gardens, Cardiff, Wales CF1 9SW Tel: Cardiff 374771 (STD code 0222)

The International Squash Players Association (ISPA) was founded in 1973 following a meeting in Birmingham of most of the world's leading full-time players. The move was, to some extent, promoted by dissatisfaction among many of the professionals at the seedings for certain British tournaments. At the time the stated aims of the Association were 'to co-ordinate as a men's professional players body and to protect that body's interest on an international basis; to liaise and work with all the sport's governing bodies, tournament organisers and sponsors to further safeguard the future development of competitive professional squash throughout the world'.

It was hoped that, by communication among its national delegates, up-to-date match results could be gathered throughout the world from which accurate advice could be given on seedings. The Association also offered advice on breakdown of prize money and expenses. Now, apart from the Executive Committee, the Association also has committees responsible for ranking/seeding, rules and refereeing and discipline.

To be eligible to join the Association, the professionals had to play at least three Open tournaments in 12 months. Since that somewhat disorganised beginning, the ISPA has gone from strength to strength and now represents over 100 of the world's top full-time players. A working ranking list is produced on 1 January every year reflecting the results of the previous year and a seeding list is issued based on a 'rolling' 12-month period. Seedings and rankings are worked out by allotting points to a player dependent on his progress in certain recognised tournaments. Over 20 events – in one of seven different grades depending on total prize money – are taken into account.

The Association first held its own official championship at Sheffield in March 1978 when Qamar Zaman defeated fellow-Pakistani Hiddy Jahan to become champion. The event has been staged annually since then. In 1982 in another all-Pakistani match Jahangir Khan completed a 9–0, 9–0, 9–0 victory

ISPA Seeding and World Ranking List

The International Squash Players Association (ISPA) establish their 'seeding list' on the performance of their players on a rolling twelve-month period and formulate a points table as a function of the grade of tournament and the progress in that tournament made by each player. The ISPA tournament circuit is graded in accordance with the total prize money available to the players as follows:

Grade A £30 000 plus
Grade 1 £20 000–£29 999
Grade 2 £15 000–£19 999
Grade 3 £10 000–£14 999
Grade 4 £ 7 500–£ 9 999
Grade 5 £ 5 000–£ 7 499
Grade 6 £ 2 000–£ 4 999

The merit points per grade of tournament range from 200 for the winner of a Grade A event to a single point for a first round loser in a draw of 64 in a Grade 5 event (see table).

Place	Grade						
	A	1	2	3	4	5	6
1	200	140	120	100	90	80	40
2	150	105	90	75	67	60	30
3	106	75	64	54	48	43	22
4	92	65	56	46	42	37	18
5/8	64	45	38	32	28	26	13
9/16	38	27	23	19	17	16	8
17/32	14	10	8	7	6	5	3
33/64	4	3	2	2	1	1	—

To encourage players to compete in as many tournaments as possible, each player's total points are divided by 6 until such time as he has played more than 6 tournaments, when the total points are divided by the actual number of tournaments played.

At the end of an ISPA calendar year – 31 December – the 'seeding' table becomes the world ranking list.

over world number 4 Maqsood Ahmed to record the first whitewash in a major final since the great Heather McKay demolished her Australian compatriot Bev Johnson in the 1967/8 British Women's Open Championship.

Women's Squash Players Association

Chairwoman: Robyn Blackwood, 188 Richmond Road, Ponsonby, Auckland, New Zealand. Tel: 789747
Secretary/Treasurer: Rae Anderson, 3 Kew Court, Donvale, Melbourne, Australia 3111. Tel: 8743729
Committee: Rhonda Thorne (Australia), Sue Cogswell (England), Heather Wallace (Scotland)

After several abortive attempts by a number of players an effective professional women's association was formed in March 1984 with the aim of co-ordinating tournaments, players and rankings. The membership includes most of the world's leading players and foundation members are the executive members as named above plus Renee Aucamp, Vicki Cardwell, Carin Clonda, Sue Devoy, Barbara Diggens, Lynne Ferry, Martine Le Moignan, Jan Miller, Lisa Opie, Angela Smith, Ruth Strauss, Alison Cumings and Jayne Ashton. The two patrons of the association are Mariann Greenberg (USA) and Jan Shuttleworth (Australia).

One of the first priorities of the Association is the implementation of international ranking lists adapted from the system used by the men. By forming themselves into an official body the women achieved the important function of creating a cohesive group of players accessible to promoters, organisers and national associations to assist the development of women's professional squash.

Arab Squash Rackets Federation

Secretary: Ibrahim Abu Jubara, PO Box 7872, Amman, Jordan

No further information supplied.

Asian Squash Rackets Federation

Executive Dir: Air Vice Marshall Sharbat A. Changazi, S. Bat Headquarters, Central Air Command, PAF, Sargodha, Pakistan.
Member countries: Bahrain, Bangladesh, Hong Kong, India, Japan, Jordan, Kuwait, Lebanon, Malaysia, Pakistan, Palestine, Philippines, Singapore, Sri Lanka, Thailand

No further information supplied.

Caribbean Area Squash Rackets Association

President: Reid T. Young (Bermuda)
Secretary: Nick Cochrane (Bermuda)
Member countries: Antigua, Bahamas, Barbados, Cayman Islands, Guyana, Jamaica, St. Lucia, St. Vincent, Trinidad & Tobago, Venezuela

The Caribbean Area Squash Rackets Association (CARASRA) was conceived at the first regional tournament held at the Village Club in Nassau, Bahamas during September 1977. The representatives of the original six countries – Bahamas, Bermuda, Jamaica, Guyana, Trinidad and Barbados – agreed that a regional controlling body was needed and the main objects of the new association were to promote and control squash in the region and to stage area team and individual championships.

The Northern Caribbean territories were more advanced than the southern countries since they had been organising inter-territorial matches for some time – indeed, both Trinidad and Barbados at that time had not formed national associations and were asked to do so immediately since it was imperative for CARASRA to deal with the national representative body.

The first officers of the Association were voted in, they being Peter Higgs (Bahamas) president, Ronnie Nasralla (Jamaica) vice-president, Ivern Davis (Bahamas) treasurer, Keith Parker (Bahamas) secretary, Godfrey Chin (Guyana) 5th Officer, and Ralph Johnson (Barbados) 6th Officer.

Through the hard work, wisdom and foresight of its first president, the fledgling Association was nurtured into a cohesive body and a draft constitution circulated, discussed and adopted.

By September 1979, when the second General Meeting was held in Jamaica, the president was also able to have adopted rules governing the running of the championships, criteria governing various categories of membership, and recommendations on how the officers of the Association should be elected. Using the latter guidelines, since Jamaica was now the hosting nation, Ronnie Nasralla was elected the 2nd president, Mr Clyde Cunningham (Jamaica) vice-president, Ivern Davies (Bahamas) was re-elected treasurer, Douglas Beckford (Jamaica) secretary, Ralph Johnson (Barbados) 5th Officer and Gordon Gatt (Trinidad & Tobago) 6th Officer. It was unanimously agreed that the past president would also continue to be a member of the committee.

At this meeting in Jamaica, full membership was granted to St. Vincent and associate membership was granted to the Caracas Sports Club. Since then, Cayman and Antigua have become members.

CARASRA has initiated a calendar of events which includes all national championships and other prestigious tournaments which are promoted by various territories, highlighted by the two area championships which are held in the north for the Rosebowl and in the south for the British Airways Trophy.

CARASRA is now affiliated to the International Squash Rackets Federation and is a seasoned body, having taken a firm grip on the organisational process of squash in the Caribbean.

South American Squash Rackets Federation
President: Dr Carlos Salem, Avda Paolista 1765, 4º andar, Conj 41, Sao Paulo, Brazil
Secretary: Peter Kingston, Asociacion Argentina de Squash Rackets, Carlos Pellgrini 763, 1009 Buenos Aires Tel: 392 7152
Member countries: Argentina, Brazil, Peru, Uruguay

The Confederacion Sud-Americana de Squash Rackets was formed on 8 November 1982 with four affiliated countries – Argentina, Brazil, Peru and Uruguay. Paraguay has officially applied for membership and Chile, who has sent delegates and players to meetings and tournaments, is expected to apply in the near future.

Squash in South America is still an underdeveloped sport despite the fact that the first squash club was formed in 1929 in Buenos Aires and is still functioning. Brazil took up the sport a little later, followed by Peru and Uruguay. The breakthrough which gives hope for the future, took place in Argentina and Brazil with commerical centres being built and each country now has an estimated 200 courts. Peru has 20 courts, with commerical centres under consideration, Uruguay and Chile each has eight clubs, while Paraguay has three courts with five under construction.

Each year the Confederation holds four Grand Prix events restricted to South American players and which count for South American ranking. The major event is the individual championship but team events are also held and in Montevideo in 1984 the first veterans (over-40) championship was held plus the first South American women's championship. A junior event is planned.

6 Squash nations of the world

Squash is now played by six million people worldwide, a truly phenomenal participant following for a sport that prior to the 1960s was considered a select pastime for those attending public schools, pursuing a military or government service career or living in a Commonwealth country.

In 20 years squash has become internationally known and accepted and membership of the International Squash Rackets Federation (ISRF), the game's rule-making body, has more than doubled to 51 countries.

Its appeal and success is based on the fact that it is played indoors and is not affected by the weather. It is easy to learn and provides an entertaining and invigorating way of taking a lot of exercise within a short space of time. It has become particularly popular among businessmen seeking escape from sedentary lifestyles, and squash has also fitted the bill for those wanting a change from the diluted challenge of team sports.

In an age when more time and money is available for leisure pursuits and when individuals are conscious of image and lifestyle, squash has become the vogue and shows no sign of going out of fashion. In this respect the sport has been successful in retaining the more positive aspects of its cloistered past; its up-market image attracting followers who tend to be aspirational by nature and wish to look after themselves, stay fit and be healthy.

Sports goods manufacturers and club owners have been quick to recognise the commercial appeal of the image-conscious squash player. The sport has prospered from the vigorous growth of private, commercial and local authority centres, and manufacturers, in addition to providing the basic hardware, are now turning their attention to creating styles of squash clothing that are fashionable as well as functional. Squash has therefore now firmly established itself in the sporting and social fabric of many countries, its future and growth assured by its own inherent appeal and the financial investment in buildings, courts and equipment. The growth pattern of the game can clearly be charted with the original Commonwealth countries of the United Kingdom – Australia and New Zealand – providing the foundation and then booms in the UK and Australia subsequently fuelling popularity in Europe and south-east Asia.

The timespan in which modern-day development has taken place is also easily identifiable since out of the 51 member associations of the ISRF, 32 of them (nearly two-thirds) came into being from the year 1970 onwards. This spectacular development did not happen solely because squash became a popular sport to play, but was due to the solid administrative base achieved through the English Squash Rackets Association founded in 1928 and effectively the game's controlling body until 1967, and other founder nations of the ISRF such as Australia (founded 1935) and New Zealand (1939).

Established countries are able to offer a ready source of expertise to aid newcomers and they also had, and still have, the strength and depth of competition necessary for emergent players to improve their standards. Other important areas such as the training of officials and the setting and maintenance of standards for courts and equipment were also reasons why the rest of the squash-playing world have tended to look to England and other countries for initial help.

England is still regarded as the best training ground for players since the structure of the seasonal tournament calendar is so wide and varied that it offers opportunities for all standards of competitors. This pattern is changing, however. The English SRA, once the focal point of squash, is just one member nation of the ISRF. The Federation itself is run from Canada who, although founded in 1913 and able therefore to claim to be the oldest association, did not become a full member of the Federation until 1969.

Other area federations have been formed to assist and channel views and opinions, the European Federation being formed in 1973 and with 21 members being the strongest group outside of the ISRF. But federations in Asia, the Caribbean and even South America, where the sport has barely a toe hold, again reflect the ability of squash to appeal to all nationalities. Only the USSR, the Eastern bloc countries and China have yet to fall under its spell.

Technical developments have kept pace with the sport's popularity – equipment is well designed, courts and clubs are built to high specifications and within the clubs the use of glass has been one of the features of the last decade. Glass walls opened up the sport to the playing public and now side and front walls have been used in permanent and portable situations. This has led to the exciting prospect of spectator squash and linked with this the possibility that one day television will be able to do justice to the sport. Sweden, the first 'European' country to embrace squash, could justifiably claim to be a pacemaker in this respect since they led the way with the use of the first demountable court. This court, manufactured by the Swedish company Perstorp, was conventional in the sense that it had three solid walls and a glass back but erected in the main arena of the Kings Tennis Hall, Stockholm in 1978 it enabled 600 people to watch.

Since then the Germans, who have some of the best appointed clubs in the world, hosted the 1983 World Open on a four glass-wall court in Munich and the French ran the first event to use a demountable four glass-wall court in Paris in the same year. A court with glass walls in Zurich means that the Swiss also have facilities for staging major championships.

Expansion of squash in mainland Europe during the 1980s is likely to be one of the major aspects of the sport's development. Germany now has half a million players, 350 complexes and 2700 courts, Switzerland 120 000 players, Finland 100 000, France 45 000 and Holland 40 000. Even in Austria where squash was not introduced until 1976 there are 10 000 followers. Other key areas for growth must inevitably be Canada and south-east Asia where Malaysia, Singapore and Hong Kong are all reporting a surge of court building.

Singapore, which has hosted several world class championships including the world junior event, now has 85 centres and 400 courts while in Hong Kong the pressure on its 38 centres and 158 courts is intense. The Hong Kong Government aims to provide one court for every 10 000 head of population and this has set a building target of 520 courts for the colony.

In Canada the international or 'softball' version of squash has enjoyed spectacular growth at the expense of the traditional American hardball version, yet if *rapprochement* could be made between the two codes who knows what the effect could be on the whole North American continent where a healthy sport such as squash could take off in a big way. Already there are signs of the two codes coming closer together with the United States Squash Rackets Association officially adopting 'softball' for its summer game.

Clearly squash travels well and appeals to many races and temperaments. The bricks and mortar base it has established worldwide has demonstrated that it is not a passing fad to be discarded after a few months. The sport woos people with its simplicity and once it has taken hold proceeds to infuriate, frustrate and continually challenge as the player realises that mastery of its art will never ever be realised, that a skill or shot can always be improved and with the certain knowledge that someone, somewhere is better than you.

Every effort has been made to make all the country details as complete as possible. However in some instances, not all information has been forthcoming.

ARGENTINA

Courts: 250 *Players:* 10 000
Association: Asociacion Argentina de Squash Rackets, Carlos Pellgrini 763, 1009 Buenos Aires. Founded: 1983. Secretary: Peter Kingston

Although squash has been played continuously in Argentina since 1929, the year 1983 was of paramount importance for the game. The first commercial centres were opened at the beginning of the year and immediately gained favour with the general public. This sudden but predictable flowering of interest in squash in turn led to other results – the previous association, an informal grouping of the leading clubs, was transformed into the actual association, designed to meet the new demands. Press coverage was greatly increased and a magazine, *Squash Rackets* dedicated entirely to the game, is being published monthly. Sponsors, previously spurned by the traditional clubs, have shown a welcome interest in supporting squash. The Association is receiving enquiries concerning construction and organisation of courts and centres at the rate of 40 per month. Clubs are spread from north to south of the country.

The major tournaments staged during 1983 included the South American Grand Prix (Buenos Aires leg) and the Argentine Open. Francisco Frizoni and Paulinho Troyano, both from Brazil, shared the Grand Prix title and Claudio Miguens won the Open. The team championship was won by Argentina but Uruguay reversed the result with a 3–2 win in the River Plate Cup in Montevideo.

The main problem areas are shortage of qualified coaches and referees but with the enthusiasm shown by the juniors, the future of squash in Argentina seems assured.

AUSTRALIA

Clubs/centres: 1200 *Courts:* 6000 *Players:* 500 000
Association: Squash Rackets Association of Australia, PO Box 356, Spring Hill, Queensland 4000. Founded: 1935. President: Victor C. Belsham; Secretary/Executive Dir: Simon L. Boegheim

Squash rackets in Australia saw its beginning in Melbourne in 1913 at the private and prestigious Melbourne club. The club at the top end of tree-lined Collins street was, as now, the social venue of the leaders of most of the professions. Two courts were built at the club by converting a rackets court which had in turn been converted from a wood shed around 1880.

During the 1920s and early 1930s a few squash courts were built at some of the private clubs around Melbourne and Sydney. Public courts were very few and their development did not commence until the 1950s.

The Squash Rackets Association of Australia (SRAA) was established in Melbourne in 1935 to service a few Melbourne based clubs which were then commencing rounds of what is now the established Pennant competition. During the 1930s the Association attracted membership from other clubs and organisations outside Victoria including the Royal Sydney Tennis Club, the New South Wales Squash Rackets Association, the South Australian Association and the Naval and Military Club of South Australia.

In 1938 because they felt that the SRAA was more interested in national rather than local affairs the State of Victoria formed their own association but since then the national body has become totally representative and has its headquarters in Brisbane.

The Australian Women's Squash Rackets Association existed from 1933 to 1980 when it amalgamated with the SRAA to become the Australian Squash Rackets Association.

There was considerable growth in squash court construction between 1947 to the late 1970s, a good example being the number of courts built in Victoria where the figure jumped from 30 to 738. Although the game of squash is still booming, the year of 1982 saw a slow down in the building of courts as a result of over development of the market, the high cost of building and the world economic recession.

While there were a number of Australian teams engaged in tours of New Zealand and South Africa in the 1950s the first major international team development took place in 1961. In that year an official Australian team composed of K. Hiscoe, O. Parmenter, R. Carter and D. Stevenson toured the UK and won all tests and matches. Further successful official visits took place in 1963 and 1965 with Geoff Hunt getting into the 1963 side and Cam Nancarrow, a contemporary of Hunt touring in 1965.

In 1967 the inaugural ISRF Championship was held in Melbourne beginning an era of Australian dominance in both the team and individual events that was to last until 1975. Since then Australia has not been so successful, finishing third in 1976, fifth in 1977, equal third in 1979, runners-up in 1981 and third in 1983.

In 1976 the Women's Association staged a world invitation event in Brisbane and, following the success of this, the Women's International Squash Rack-

The great Ken Hiscoe in full flight. A typical action shot captured during the 1976/7 British Open at Wembley while he was playing the Swede, Leif Leiner. Hiscoe formed a solid partnership with Geoff Hunt and together the pair helped to blaze the trail for professionals in the early 1970s. *Robin Eley Jones*

ets Federation was formed to run regular championships for individuals and teams. Heather McKay won the title in 1976 and again in 1979 in England when a team event was held for the first time and in which Australia finished runners-up to the host country. Australia got their revenge in 1981 in Toronto, beating England 2–1 and held on to the title by the same margin against England when the championships were held in Perth. Rhonda Thorne and Vicki Cardwell, respectively, ensured total Australian domination by winning the individual titles.

Squash was first televised for general broadcast in Perth in 1962, the occasion being the final of the 1962 men's Australian Championship. Prior to the development of see-through walls, squash was a difficult game to photograph or televise and the Perth telecast was done by removing the middle located back door of the court and televising through the open doorway!

The next major tournament to be covered was the world championship at the large galleried Albert Park Stadium in Melbourne in 1967. The court, while not having a glass backwall, had the walls open above the out of court lines and this enabled cameras to be located in the rear and side galleries.

During the formative years of the 1960s it can safely be said that the Australian Broadcasting Commission pioneered the televising of squash and did much to assist public awareness of the sport, although subsequently squash has not attracted large television audiences and there has been a reluctance by commercial stations to give coverage and promote sponsorship. However, many stations developed extensive news and magazine type television coverage during the latter years of Geoff Hunt's record breaking performances.

Sponsorship has also played a vital role with the game receiving solid support from the Government and companies such as Ansett, Consolidated Sporting Goods, Sun Alliance Insurance, AMF Head, Dunlop, Slazenger and Staminade.

There has always been interest in the youngest and oldest players to have won major titles, although there are few records of the exact ages of the participants.

The youngest player to have won the men's Australian Amateur Championship was Geoff Hunt at the age of 17 in 1965 while the two youngest to win the Australian Open were Mohibullah Khan (1975) and Jahangir Khan (1982), both 19.

The oldest player to win the Australian Open was almost certainly Hashim Khan who at the time of his victory in 1957 would have been approximately 42.

International Championship
(formerly Australian Amateur Championship)

MEN

1931 F. R. S. Strickland	1976 M. Donnelly
1932 R. A. Henderson	1977 D. Williams
1933–34 H. C. Hopman	1978 G. Briars (Eng)
1935 N. M. Heath	1979 F. Donnelly
1936 H. C. Hopman	1980–81 G. B. Hunt
1937 M. G. Weston	1982 Jahangir Khan (Pak)
1938 W. Vestey	1983 R. Thorne
1939 M. G. Weston	
1940–45 No competition	WOMEN
1946–47 I. R. Carson	1933 R. Grey-Smith
1948–49 R. L. Harris	1934 P. Walker
1950 I. R. Carson	1935 L. Long Innes
1951 E. Metcalf	1936 J. Long Innes
1952 W. E. Anstee	1937 R. Grey-Smith
1953–55 B. Boys	1938–45 No competition
1956 A. McCausland	1946 B. Meagher
1957 J. Cheadle	1947–48 V. Watts
1958 B. Stuart	1949–50 B. Meagher
1959 M. A. Oddy (Sco)	1951 V. Watts
1960–64 K. Hiscoe	1952 J. Tissot
1965 G. B. Hunt	1953 J. Watson
1966–67 K. Hiscoe	1954 J. Morgan (GB)
1968 J. Barrington	1955 M. Maher
(GB & Ire)	1956–57 J. Tissot
1969–71 G. B. Hunt	1958 J. Fitzgerald
1972 C. Nancarrow	1959 P. Parmenter
1973 Q. Zaman (Pak)	1960–65 H. Blundell
1974 S. Muneer (Pak)	1966–73 H. McKay (née
1975 K. Shawcross	Blundell)
	1974 M. Jackman

1975–76 S. Newman	1981 R. Thorne
1977 M. Zachariah	1982–83 V. Cardwell (née
1978–80 V. Hoffman	Hoffman)

Open Championship

MEN

1939 G. J. Watson	1958–69 No competition
1940–45 No competition	1970 J. Barrington
1946–48 G. J. Watson	(GB & Ire)
1949 M. Karim (Egy)	1971 G. Hunt
1950 A. Bari (Ind)	1972 No competition
1951 E. Metcalf	1973 G. Hunt
1952 J. H. Garrett	1974 No competition
1953–56 B. A. Boys	1975 Mohibullah Khan
1957 Hashim Khan (Pak)	(Pak)
	1976–80 G. Hunt

AUSTRIA

Courts: 120 *Players:* 10 000
Association: Oesterreichische Squash Racket Verbans, Landstrasse Haupstrasse 2A, 1030 Vienna. Founded: 1935. President: M. Kapeller

International Championship

MEN

1979 S. Bowditch (Aus)	1980 Karimullah Khan
	(Pak)
	1981 S. Bowditch (Aus)

National Championship

MEN	WOMEN
1978–79 H. W. Selden	1978–80 A. Trestler
1980 E. Stepanek	

BAHAMAS

Clubs/centres: 3
Association: Bahamas Squash Rackets Association, PO Box F765 Freeport. Founded: 1972. President: Neville Garcia; Secretary: Ann Wilson

The Bahamas is one of the latest additions to the list of squash-playing nations and recent developments show that the game is growing in stature.

In 1980/1 emphasis began to be placed on the progress of younger players. Shell Bahamas Ltd sponsored a junior development programme which at the time was organised by individuals outside the Bahamas SRA. Improvement in the standard of younger players has been significant since then and this has contributed to the increased popularity of the sport. Lester Cox and John Wilson are two of the most promising juniors to have emerged from the programme and have already made a tour of the UK.

In the same year a club in the Bahamas employed a professional for the first time when England's Angela Smith was appointed to the Racquets Club, Nassau.

Several leading players including Aziz Khan, Ian Robinson and John Le Lievre have visited the island's three clubs and played a series of exhibition matches before enthusiastic crowds. Despite these innovations, the Bahamas' teams were unable to compete seriously with local rivals Jamaica and Bermuda until 1982 when their forces, previously split into Nassau and Freeport, were joined to form a combined side. This decision further increased interest in the game and should help the Bahamas become a real competitive force in the region.

National Championship

MEN	
1965 M. Melotte	1979 K. Parker
1966 I. Davis	1980–82 P. Williams
1967 K. Parker	1983 L. Cox
1968 A. Lancaster	
1969 D. Trimble	WOMEN
1970–71 R. Montgomery	1980–81 S. Carey
1972–73 D. Trimble	1982 C. Higgs
1974–78 A. Newell	1983 G. Martin

BARBADOS

Clubs/centres: 5   *Courts:* 14   *Players:* 350
Association: Barbados Squash Rackets Association, c/o Harris Paints Barbados Ltd, Wildey Industrial Park, St. Michael. Founded: 1978. President: Geoffrey Atkinson; Secretary/Executive Dir: Susan Colby

The game was introduced by a group of expatriates who built the first court in the early 1970s. The first national championships were played in 1974/5 and Barbados Squash Club formed in 1976. The first official Barbadian team competed in the inaugural Caribbean Championships in 1977. Two further courts were built at the Rockley Resort Hotel in 1977, since when two other hotels have erected their own courts. In 1979 Barbados Squash Club built a championship court with a seating capacity of 150 and added a third court in 1980. Two more were erected in 1981 at a boys' college in an attempt to introduce the game to schools. There are also two private courts on the island. This spate of activity bore fruit when Barbados won the overall South Caribbean title in 1979, 1980 and 1981.

Squash sponsorship was introduced in 1979 when Barbados Fire and General Insurance backed the Junior Championships and the biggest sponsorship to date was supplied by the same company when they put up $5000 BD to host the North/South Caribbean Championships in 1980. British Airways and United Insurance have also sponsored major tournaments.

National Championship

MEN		WOMEN	
1974–75 B. Tudor		1974 T. Tipping	
1976 S. Mantell		1975 S. Edghill	
1977 B. Tudor		1976 J. Atkinson	
1978–79 M. Armstrong		1977 A. Webber	
1980 R. Goodridge		1978–79 S. Edghill	
1981 C. Franklin		1980 A. Webber	
1982 No competition		1981–83 C. Choy	
1983 S. Faulkner-Lee			

The Barbados national team which contested the 1981 Caribbean Championships. *Back row –* Robin Johnson (ladies' team manager), Chris Frankland, Leon Truss, Richard Browne, Lynn Johnson, Bruce Tudor, Brian Allan, Rudy Goodridge, Mickey Armstrong (men's captain), Ralph Johnson (men's manager); *front row –* Tessa Newsam (youngest ever national finalist), Angela Webber (ladies' captain), Liz Johnson, Kris Choy (national champion)

Most international appearances: men: R. Brown/B. Tudor 8; women: S. Edghill/A. Webber 5. **Youngest international:** D. Edghill represented Barbados at the Caribbean Junior Championships in St. Vincent in 1981, aged 8. **Youngest national finalist:** T. Newsam, aged 13 at Barbados Squash Club in 1982.

BELGIUM

Clubs/centres: 100 *Courts:* 300 *Players:* 15 000
Association: Federation de Squash Rackets de Belgique, Weidelaan 10, B-1900 Overijse. Founded: 1974.
President: Clarence Steininger; Secretary: Mrs Magda Jennes

Squash started in Belgium in the mid-thirties but there were still only two clubs by 1973. Since then new centres have opened regularly and the game in general has expanded very rapidly. By the end of 1983 15 000 players were registered and this figure is expected to rise quickly with many new clubs opening.

This trend was also noticeable in the heavy tournament calendar for the 1983/4 season with no fewer than 100 competitions in all categories. Moreover, the inter-club league has seen a considerable expansion with 144 teams participating. New on the tournament scene was the introduction of a Belgian Championship 'D' for non-ranked players, in which at least 350 players participated, another indication of the game's growing popularity at the grass-roots level. A regional junior inter-club league designed to raise the level of the game among the youngsters, was also started.

International Championship

MEN	
1945 A. Fyler (Eng)	1969 J. D. Ward (Eng)
1946 M. Blo	1970 R. Ratinac (Aus)
1947 J. P. Hye de Crom	1971 R. Lewis (Aus)
1948 B. C. Phillips (Eng)	1972 J. N. C. Easter (Eng)
1949 H. A. de Coninck	1973 P. G. Verow (Eng)
1950 No competition	1974 P. G. Kirton (Eng)
1951–52 A. A. T. Seymour-Haydon (Eng)	1975 S. H. Courtney (Eng)
1953 B. C. Phillips (Eng)	1976 J. L. Richardson (Eng)
1954 N. H. R. A. Broomfield (Eng)	1977 No competition
1955 J. Lyon (Eng)	1978 G. Brumby (Aus)
1956 M. van den Bemden	1979–80 I. Yeates (Aus)
1957 D. B. Daniels (Eng)	1981 P. Chaplin (Eng)
1958 D. I. Medway	1982 G. Williams (Eng)
1959–60 No competition	1983 E. Van der Pluym (Hol)
1961 P. Robinson (SA)	
1962 A. Frazer (Eng)	WOMEN
1963 M. van den Bemden	1978 B. Wall (Aus)
1964 D. B. Daniels (Eng)	1979 B. Anderson (Eng)
1965 C. G. Daniels (Eng)	1980 B. Wall (Aus)
1966 W. van Rooyen (Net)	1981 J. Shuttleworth
1967–68 B. H. Woodbridge (Eng)	1982 R. Best (Ire)
	1983 R. Strauss (Eng)

National Championship

MEN	
1942 F. E. Dens	1968 R. Goosens
1943 H. A. de Coninck	1969–71 J. Narinx
1944 F. E. Dens	1972 J. Roersch
1945 P. Washer	1973 J. Narinx
1946–47 M. Blomme	1974–79 A. Ceurvorst
1948 J. P. Hye de Crom	1980–81 P. Dieudonne
1949 M. Blomme	1982 A. Ceurvorst
1950–53 H. A. de Coninck	1983 P. Dieudonne
1954 P. Washer	
1955–63 M. van den Bemden	WOMEN
1964–65 R. Goosens	1978 I. Miller
1966 S. Abraham	1979–80 E. Lloyd-Michelli
1967 M. van den Bemden	1981 B. Vuylsteke
	1982–83 E. van Exter

Youngest winner of men's national title: A. Ceurvorst, aged 16, in 1974. **Oldest winner of men's national title:** S. Abraham, aged 40, in 1966.

BERMUDA

Clubs/centres: 5 *Courts:* 10 *Players:* 500
Association: Bermuda Squash Racquets Association, PO Box 176, Hamilton 5. Founded: 1962. President: Reginald A. F. Rawlins; Secretary: Susan Foster

The first two courts in Bermuda were built in 1930 by the British Government for the use of the Royal Navy and British garrison and they are still maintained and used. It was not until 1959 that 12 enthusiasts got together to promote the game and eventually formed the Bermuda SRA. In 1966 the first official team competed against Nassau Squash Club for the Caribbean trophy. Two further courts were built in 1968 and two more were completed in 1974. In 1975 a private club at Coral Beach erected two more. A glass-backed court with seating for 180 was opened in May 1983 during a visit by world champion Jahangir

Above left
Stuart Davenport who quickly took over as New Zealand's number 1 player when a serious injury threatened the career of Ross Norman. Norman has since made a comeback and an intriguing battle for supremacy seems likely. *Robin Eley Jones*

Above right
Jahangir Khan (*left*) and Qamar Zaman disputing the final of the ICI Perspex World Masters at Warrington. *Tim Pike*

Below
Vicki Cardwell (*right*) and Lisa Opie during the 1981/2 British Open final, won by Cardwell. *Robin Eley Jones*

Khan, and other famous names who have been to the island include Geoff Hunt, Heather McKay and Sharif Khan. Television coverage and sponsorship has been difficult to encourage although part of the 1983 Caribbean Championship has been screened and the event was supported by Ballantines Whisky.

International Championship

MEN		WOMEN	
1979	R. Beck (USA)	1977–79	B. Marshall
1980	G. Anderson (Can)	1979–82	J. Peake
1981	T. K. Boyce		
1982	R. D. Thompson		

National Championship

MEN		WOMEN	
1964	E. McLay	1973–74	S. Hartley
1965	E. Roberts	1974–75	B. Marshall
1966–68	C. Donald	1975–76	E. Driscoll
1969	G. Hunn	1976–79	B. Marshall
1970	C. Donald	1979–80	D. Kyme
1971–72	N. Kelly	1980–81	J. Peake
1973–76	E. Kyme	1981–82	E. Driscoll
1977	J. Bennett		
1978–80	E. Kyme		
1981	T. K. Boyce		
1982–83	R. Thompson		

BRAZIL

Courts: 200
Association: Federacao Carioca de Squash, R. Candido Mendes, 581 CEP 20241, Rio de Janeiro. Founded: 1982.
President: John L. Hughes

Squash continues to be a growing sport in Brazil. In 1983 more courts were inaugurated and plans and projects drawn up for further courts to be built in homes, clubs and commercial centres.

The main competition during 1983 was the International Championship held again at Itaparica Island at the Club Mediteranee, in the State of Bahia. The best players in South America plus Ross Norman of New Zealand and Martin Bodimeade of England competed. The latter, as expected, met in the final. They beat the top ranked players in Brazil and South America, Kiko Frisoni and Paulo Troyano in the quarter-finals and Ross Norman had no difficulty in beating Martin in the final 3–0.

The South American Grand Prix was played in

The 1982 ISPA final at Sheffield. Maqsood Ahmed (*left*) attempts to put the ball away as Jahangir Khan moves forward, but for Maqsood it was a night to forget. He lost 9–0, 9–0, 9–0 and Jahangir became the first player to win a men's international final without dropping a point. *Robin Eley Jones*

Uruguay, Peru and Argentina with the last round in Brazil in November. This year was a tie with Kiko Frisoni and Paulo Troyano in first place but Kiko had a slight advantage having won three out of the four championships. Kiko won the Brazilian Championship for the fourth time in succession beating Paulo 3–1 in the final.

The Rio de Janeiro Championship, held in March 1983, was won by a promising young player, Rodrigo Soares.

Work is going ahead to attract young players which is meeting with some success and efforts are also being made to improve marking and refereeing.

National Championship

MEN	
1982–83	K. Frisoni

CANADA

Clubs/centres: 350–375 *Courts:* 1400 *Players:* 200 000
Association: Canadian Squash Racquets Association, 333 River Road, Vanier, Ontario KIL 8B9. Founded: 1913.
President: David Hetherington; Secretary/Executive Dir: Alan Smith

Although squash has been played in England since the mid-1800s, the Canadian SRA was one of the first formal associations, being founded in 1913, 15 years before the English SRA. The country had its first national champion as far back as 1912 and the Lapham Cup was first competed for by Canada and the USA in 1922.

Until the early 1970s the game was played almost exclusively in private clubs, private schools and universities and was predominantly the North American 'hardball' version except for one or two pockets of the 'international' variety. There followed a dramatic development of commercial facilities and, with it, a major transition from the hardball to softball game. The number of players increased from 10 000 in the late sixties to a present-day figure of around 200 000, and now 95 per cent of the squash played in the country is the 'international' game.

During 1983 squash continued its steady growth across the country in spite of economic restraint. Particular enthusiasm and development was evident in the western provinces where programmes were very active. In addition the National Senior and Junior Softball Championships were held in the west and were also scheduled to take place there in 1984 along with the ISRF World Junior Championships.

It should be stated that hardball squash continues to be very much alive in the Toronto, Hamilton, and Montreal areas, as well as in other centres in southern

Ontario. Doubles and mixed doubles are showing significant growth in the above areas as well as in British Columbia. In fact the Canadian Doubles Championship was awarded to Vancouver, BC in March 1984, as a result of the renewed enthusiasm for the game on the West Coast.

The men's and women's national teams both improved their performances in the 1983 ISRF World Championships, the men's team being placed eighth after defeating both Scotland and Singapore 3–0 in preliminary play. Dale Styner showed that he is now competitive with many of the top international players by his narrow 3–2 losses to Ahmed Safwat and Lars Kvant.

The women's team finished seventh again behind Scotland but actually defeated Scotland 2–1 and only lost by a slim margin of 1–2 (2–3 in one of the losses) to Wales. Eighteen-year-old Diana Edge, playing number two, won all of her matches in the team championships except against Angela Smith.

International Championship

MEN	
1974 G. Anderson	1976 H. McKay (Aus)
1975–76 M. Desaulniers	1977 J. Cartmel
1977 B. Brownlee (NZ)	1978 N. Ballantyne
1978 J. Walia	1979 B. Paton
1979–80 M. Desaulniers	1980 A. Thompson
1981–82 D. Whittaker	1981 N. Ballantyne
1983 J. Barrington (GB & Ire)	1982–83 J. Maycock
1984 D. Styner	1984 J. A. Harris (Aus)

WOMEN	
1975 P. Faulkner (USA)	

CAYMAN ISLANDS

Clubs/centres: 1 *Courts:* 2 *Players:* 150
Association: Cayman Islands Squash Racquets Association, PO Box 1847, George Town, Grand Cayman, British West Indies. Founded: 1977. Chairman: John Hephill; Secretary: H. Annesley

Squash started in the Cayman Islands when the Cayman Racquet Club opened its first court in June 1977. Regular knockout tournaments were held over the next few months with Ken Dunlop taking the first men's title from an entry of 65 and Chris Benbow winning the women's event in which 24 participated. The second court was built in March 1978 complete with glass backwall and seating for 100 spectators. In April of the same year the first league, comprising 30 teams, was set up.

Matches are played regularly against visiting Royal Navy ships and touring clubs. Opportunities for coaching and exhibition matches are taken when players from Britain or Jamaica visit the islands.

DENMARK

Clubs/centres: 14 *Courts:* 50 *Players:* 3000
Association: Dansk Squash Forbund, Idraettens Hus, Brondby Stadion 20, 2620 Glostrop. Founded: 1971.
Chairman: Flemming Bulow; Secretary: Soren Skov

Squash has been played in Denmark since the late 1930s. However, for many years it was played in just one three-court club in Copenhagen and significant expansion did not start until the mid seventies. In 1978 the Association was accepted as a member of the National Sports Council thus becoming eligible for official financial support. Thirty of the 50 courts have been built since 1981. The game has still not developed sufficiently to interest major sponsors although Adidas and, latterly, Nassau have sponsored the national team. Television coverage is practically non-existent – just 10 minutes of national screening in the last 10 years!

International Championship

MEN	
1936 H. Grut	1976 D. Williams (Aus)
1937 O. Claussen	1977 L. Kvant (Swe)
1938 H. Wigg	1978 S. Wall (Aus)
1939 O. Claussen	1979 M. Awad (Egy)
1940 No competition	1980 D. Williams (Aus)
1941–43 O. Claussen	1981 M. Saad (Egy)
1944 No competition	
1945 O. Rasmussen	WOMEN
1946–47 J. Andersen	1957 I. Gerlardi
1948–54 O. Rasmussen	1958–59 E. Prior
1955 M. J. Perkins (Eng)	1960 D. Corbett (Eng)
1956–57 Per Rodikjaer	1961 No competition
1958–64 P. Gerlow	1962 E. Prior
1965 A. Lange (SA)	1963–70 No competition
1966 D. Woods (SA)	1971 M. Dymock (Eng)
1967 J. N. Smith (Eng)	1972 T. Lindfors (Swe)
1968 J. D. Ward (Eng)	1973 G. Agerbaek
1969 K. Watson (Aus)	1974 S. Boyd (Sco)
1970 No competition	1975 G. Baeck
1971 R. Zacks (Rho)	1976 D. Gilstrup (Eng)
1972 G. Alauddin (Pak)	1977–78 B. Wall (Aus)
1973 K. Watson (Aus)	1979 Y. Nygren (Swe)
1974 A. Aziz (Egy)	1980 E. Lundquist (Swe)
1975 R. Carter (Eng)	1981 K. Due-Boje (Swe)

National Championship

MEN	WOMEN
1978 P. Gerlow	1978 M. Olsen
1979–81 A. Jacobsen	1979 L. Troelsen
	1980 A. Osby
	1981 C. Thomas

EGYPT

Clubs/centres: 17 *Courts:* 72 *Players:* 1700
Association: The Egyptian Squash Rackets Association, c/o

Heliopolis Sporting Club, Heliopolis, Cairo. Founded: 1935. Chairman: Yousef Aloba; Secretary: Gen. Mohammed Sabet

Despite the country's remarkable list of world-class players – some of whom are listed below with their major achievements – squash is still not very popular in Egypt! The Egyptian SRA is attempting to rectify this by creating interest amongst youngsters. Every effort is made to send the most promising to England to take part in the Open, Junior and Under-23 events. Despite the cost, this is deemed necessary because of the poor standard of home-based coaches. World-class Egyptian players living abroad are also encouraged to return home on holidays or between tournaments to play and assist local players.

It is hoped that further interest will be generated in 1985 when Egypt, for the first time, will host the ISRF World Championships. A nine-court centre is being built in Cairo to house the event. News of the championships has also prompted several other new developments in the city including the erection of eight glass-backwalled courts at the Arab Contractors Club, two at the Nasr City Club and one at Cairo University.

EGYPTIAN GREATS

F. D. Amr Bey
6 consecutive British Open wins 1932–37
6 British Amateur titles between 1931 and 1937

Mahmoud Karim
4 consecutive British Open wins 1946–49
British Open runner-up 1950 and 1951

A. Aboutaleb
3 consecutive British Open wins 1963–65
British Open runner-up 1962 and 1967

Ibrahim Amin
Winner of British Amateur 1959
Runner-up British Amateur 1960 and 1961

Tewfik Shafik
British Amateur runner-up 1962 and 1963

Mo Asran
British Amateur runner-up 1971

A. Aziz
British Amateur runner-up 1975

Gamal Awad
Winner of British Amateur 1977 and 1978

Ahmed Safwat
7 consecutive British Professional Championship wins 1973–79

Nicknamed the 'rubber man' or the 'grasshopper', Gamal Awad has done much to restore Egypt's former squash glories. *Robin Eley Jones*

International Championship – Open

MEN

1958 M. Dardir	1968 T. Shafik
1959–66 A. Aboutaleb	1969–70 M. Khalifa
1967 J. Barrington (GB & Ire)	1971 M. Asran
	1972 A. Aziz
	1973 S. Ali
1974 Q. Zaman (Pak)	1954 S. Sidky
1975 G. Allam	1955–57 No competition
1976 A. Aboutaleb	1958 I. Amin
1977–78 A. Soliman	1959 T. Shafik
1979 N. Zahran	1960 No competition
	1961 K. Zaghhoul

Amateur

MEN	1962 T. Shafik
1936 F. D. Amr Bey	1963–64 I. Amin
1937 A. T. Casdagli (Eng)	1965 No competition
1938 C. P. Hamilton (Eng)	1966–68 T. Shafik
1939 H. A. Lascelles (Eng)	1969–71 M. Asran
1940–44 No competition	1972 G. Allam
1945 C. A'D. Consett (Eng)	1973 A. Aziz
1946 D. I. Burnett (Eng)	1974 A. Helal
1947 A. Zeitoun	1975 A. Aouba
1948 A. A. T. Seymour-Haydon (Eng)	1976–77 G. Awad
1949 M. Nour	1978 No competition
1950–53 M. Fakhry	1979 A. Soliman
	1980–82 N. Zahran

ENGLAND

Clubs/centres: 2803 *Courts:* 8419 *Players:* 2 463 000
Association: The Squash Rackets Association, Francis
House, Francis Street, London SW1P 1DE. Tel: 01–828
3064. Founded: 1928. President: Norman Borrett; Chief
Executive: Bob Morris

Squash had the reputation for many years of being
played only in public schools, London clubs and in
the Services. This was largely true until the mid 1950s
when the game started to become more popular
among the whole population. The turning point in the
history of the game in England and throughout the
UK was undoubtedly the sudden emergence and out-
standing successes of Jonah Barrington in national
and international competitions in the mid 1960s. His
many successes in the British Amateur and British
Open Championships produced for the first time
press coverage which brought the game to the attention of the whole country. At the same time the concept of getting fit and keeping fit was becoming more
popular and squash provided an ideal means of fulfil-
ling these objectives.

As the game became more popular, two major areas
of expansion appeared together. Firstly, many
commercially-minded people and companies saw an
opportunity to invest in a profitable business and the
number of commercial clubs quickly reached 200
with many having six or more courts. Secondly the
Government vigorously promoted the policy of establishing local authority sports' centres to the extent
that today nearly 20 per cent of all courts in England
are under public ownership.

The SRA continues to develop plans to ensure the
future growth and well-being of squash in England.
New courts continue to be built, and there are now
some 9000 in the country; a drive has been initiated to
increase full use of these facilities by encouraging
more and more of the population to take up squash as
their leisure time activity.

Links with squash enthusiasts in England and
abroad have been significantly strengthened by continuing improvements to the SRA's own publication,
Squash News. This magazine is now a major benefit of
SRA membership. Free copies are also circulated to
ISRF member countries to keep active the links which
prove so valuable at ISRF Annual General Meetings.
Work continues with a view to increasing television
exposure of the sport. Transparent courts providing
spectator capacities of 1500 and more are now standard
for the SRA's own two major tournaments, and the
British Open returned to Wembley in 1984 and was
played in front of audiences of up to 2700.

The SRA issued a special souvenir
cover to commemorate the
Association's Golden Jubilee and the
50th Amateur Championship. The
stamps depicted the championship
court at Wembley and the covers were
posted at Harrow School where the
game is believed to have started

Phil Kenyon – a fine example of the SRA's encouragement of talented junior players. Phil won several important national junior titles before establishing himself in the world's top ten. *Robin Eley Jones*

England continues to consolidate its playing strength at all age levels and has an encouraging array of younger players striving to achieve selection to represent their country in 1985 and beyond. The SRA is proud that its representative team was second only to Pakistan in the 1983 ISRF World Team Championships which were generally considered to have been the best yet.

(For full details of the British Open Veterans, Vintage, and British Amateur Championships see Chapter 8.)

National Championship (Closed)
FINALS

1974 J. Leslie beat S. Courtney 6–9, 8–10, 9–3, 9–3, 9–2
1975 P. Ayton beat S. Courtney 7–9, 9–7, 9–10, 9–7, 9–1
1976 J. Leslie beat J. Richardson 2–9, 9–4, 5–9, 9–6, 9–5
1977 P. Kenyon beat J. Leslie 2–9, 9–5, 9–3, 9–6
1978 P. Verow beat P. Kenyon 7–9, 9–6, 9–10, 9–4, 9–0
1979 G. Briars beat I. Robinson 9–5, 9–5, 9–0
1980 J. Barrington beat G. Briars 4–9, 9–3, 9–0, 9–2
1981 P. Kenyon beat G. Briars 9–5, 9–4, 9–6
1982 G. Briars beat P. Kenyon 9–7, 9–0, 9–2
1983 P. Kenyon beat G. Briars 5–9, 9–4, 1–9, 10–8, 9–1

Most caps: Phillip Ayton 76 from 1968–79 (includes representing GB in 1974). Peter Verow 62 from 1972 (includes seven appearances for GB). Andy Dwyer 44 from 1977 (includes representing GB in 1979). Philip Kenyon 36 from 1975 (includes representing GB in 1979). Gawain Briars 33 from 1977.

Women's Association: Women's Squash Rackets Association, 345 Upper Richmond Road West, Sheen, London SW14 8QN. Tel: 01-876 6219.
Founded: 1934. President: Mrs Janet Shardlow; Secretary: Miss Christina Myers

Recent years have seen the women's game in England grow in popularity to the extent that current estimates of those playing squash are well on the way to one million. An estimate of the established core of women players who play more than once a week is between 400 000 and 500 000, and this growth in the women's game is mirrored to a greater or lesser extent in other countries. This rapid increase in the number of women playing squash was welcome news for the WSRA whose specific brief is to develop the game at all levels in England.

At the highest level, the position of England as a world leader in the sport has been maintained. In 1979 England won the inaugural World Team Championship, putting up a convincing performance on home ground to defeat Australia 3–0. The positions were reversed in 1981, and in November 1983 Australia clung on to the title by the narrowest of margins with the advantage of home territory.

England has dominated the European Championship since its inception in 1978, but the emergence of players of talent in Europe is beginning to provide a stronger challenge rather closer to home than Australasia.

Players of international calibre develop through a healthy competitive structure which provides competitive match experience on most weekends of the squash season. The number of events run directly from the WSRA office has increased from 7 in 1975, to 12 in 1979 and 20 in 1984.

The growth in competitive opportunities has led to the development of a small but significant group of professionals who earn their living from the game. Women's competitions were declared 'Open' in 1974, and in 1979 all restrictions on coaching/playing for remuneration were lifted.

Great emphasis within the WSRA has always been placed upon the development of the junior game even though sponsorship is negligible. A full range of competitive and coaching opportunities are provided for juniors from beginners' coaching to national training and representative play. Of particular value in the junior programme is the beginners' coaching scheme funded by BP which began in 1981 and has since provided thousands of children aged between 8 and 12 with some basic training in the game. The inauguration of international competition between the home counties at Under-19 and Under-16 levels over the past two years completes the broadening of the spectrum so desirable for future progress.

So, progress over the recent past has been steadily based on the phenomenal increase in the number of women players in the late seventies. Not all the implications have yet been fully realised, but the WSRA aim to match the broadening of participation in squash with the realisation of as high a standard of performance and funding at all levels as is possible.

National Championship (Closed)
FINALS
1975 S. Cogswell beat T. Lawes 9–4, 9–7, 9–1
1976 A. Smith beat S. Cogswell 9–3, 9–5, 9–7
1977 S. Cogswell beat T. Lawes 9–2, 9–0, 9–1
1978 S. Cogswell beat A. Smith 10–8, 9–1, 9–4
1979 S. Cogswell beat A. Smith 5–9, 10–9, 10–8, 9–4
1980 S. Cogswell beat M. Le Moignan 9–7, 9–4, 9–1
1981 L. Opie beat A. Smith 10–8, 9–4, 9–7
1982 A. Cumings beat M. Le Moignan 7–9, 9–4, 7–9, 9–2, 9–4
1983 L. Opie beat M. Le Moignan 10–9, 9–1, 9–4

Lisa Opie, tipped as the English player with the skill to win world titles but who has yet to master an uncertain temperament. *Robin Eley Jones*

Most caps: (Great Britain): Fran Marshall 21 from 1959–72. Sue Cogswell 18 from 1973–80. Sheila Macintosh 18 from 1952–68. (England): Angela Smith 32 (plus 7 for GB). Barbara Diggens 29 (plus 8 for GB). Martine Le Moignan 25. Lisa Opie 25. **Youngest competitor in women's Open:** Susan Noel, aged 9 years 8 months, in 1922. **Youngest players to represent England:** Alice Isaacs and Jayne Ashton, both aged 16. Miss Isaacs played against Wales on 19 February 1950 and Miss Ashton against Scotland on 13 January 1974. **Youngest player to win British Closed title:** Lisa Opie, aged 18, in December 1981.

FINLAND
Clubs/centres: 78 *Courts:* 460 *Players:* 100 000
Association: Finnish Squash Rackets Association, c/o Finnish Central Sports Federation, Topeliuksenkatu 41a, 00250 Helsinki 25. Founded: 1971. President: Mauno Rintanen; Secretary/Executive Dir: Jorma Vertainen

Finland's first courts were built in 1968 by Thelma and Sakari Salo – the best known of the country's tennis players during the 1940s and 1950s. The main boom arrived during the second half of the seventies when the majority of the centres were built, and the highpoint came when Helsinki hosted the 1980 European Championships. The main squash areas are Helsinki, Turku and Tampere but the game is gathering momentum throughout the country.

More than 100 000 Finns now play squash rackets weekly, as there are good playing facilities in almost every town and the growth has continued to be strong in the countryside. Competition activities have expanded and in 1983 there were some 15 000 participants, with 60 teams in the national league.

The major squash rackets competition arranged in Finland is the Finnish Open, which is annually arranged at the end of February. There is a strong foreign participation in the Finnish Open, and in the 1983 final Gregg Pollard from Australia beat Jan-Ulf Soderberg from Sweden by 3–1. The most successful Finnish player was Markku Sainio, who played as a pro in Western Germany for the season 1982–83.

As for future prospects, the Nordic Championships won by the juniors was a very important achievement. In the European Championships in Western Germany Finland was placed fifth in men and sixth in women. The Finnish champions of 1983 were Kale Leskinen and Tuula Myllyniemi.

International Championship
MEN	WOMEN
1977 D. Williams (Aus)	**1981** K. Sauerwald
1978 M. Awad (Egy)	**1982** T. Myllyniemi
1979–80 B. Bostrom (Swe)	
1981 C. Erikson (Swe)	
1982 G. Pollard (Aus)	
1983 G. Williams (Eng)	

National Championship

MEN	
1970–72 H. Salo	**1983** K. Leskinen
1973 K. Leskinen	
1974–76 H. Bucht	WOMEN
1977 K. Leskinen	**1970** A. Swanljung
1978 H. Salo	**1971–75** E. Jones
1979 K. Leskinen	**1976** R. Oro
1980 H. Bucht	**1977–78** N. Mohell
1981 K. Leskinen	**1979** M. Saari
1982 M. Sainio	**1980–82** K. Sauerwald
	1983 T. Myllyniemi

Most international appearances: *Men:* H. Bucht 79, P. Salo 70. *Women:* K. Sauerwald 82.

FRANCE

Clubs/centres: 180   *Courts:* 500   *Players:* 45 000
Association: Fédération Française de Squash-Raquettes, 70 avenue Kléber, 75116 Paris. Founded: 1974. President: Guy Quennouelle; Secretary/Executive Dir: Pierre Gehanne

There were only 2500 registered players in France in 1979 but by the end of 1982 the figure had risen to 15 000 with another 25 000 playing regularly. There are expected to be over 100 000 players by the end of 1986.

The year of real expansion was 1983: countrywide leagues were established; there were over 100 club tournaments with prize money ranging from 2000–20 000 francs; the FFSR produced its first handbook and distributed 8500 copies; and a national training scheme involving over 100 coaches was run.

The 1982/3 season marked the introduction of a Grand Prix circuit with 25 regional tournaments, computer rankings and a Masters final. Non-ranked players have a circuit of 12 tournaments.

Sponsorship has only really developed since 1981. The national team is sponsored by Lacoste and Siporex back the French Open. Donnay, Unsquashable, Bred Bank, Martini, Pernod, Sacedi and ELS are involved with lesser tournaments. Television coverage is normally limited to the occasional 5–10 minute spot although Antenne 2 did show the final of the 1982 and 1983 Open Championships. The 1983 Open was significant in that it saw the first use of the four wall glass court with a blue floor and white ball. This event attracted major sponsorship from Guy La Roche in 1983 and 1984.

International Championship

MEN	
1974–75 Shah Jahan Khan (Pak)	**1979** Mohibullah Khan (Pak)
1976 Abbas Khan (Pak)	**1980** A. Safwat (Egy)
1977 F. Donnelly (Aus)	**1981–83** Jahangir Khan (Pak)
1978 G. Brumby (Aus)	

French champion – Sabine Amigorena

National Championship

MEN	WOMEN
1974 D. Grozdanovitch	**1977** F. Millet
1975 G. Quennoulle	**1978** H. Guilaud
1976–78 D. Grozdanovitch	**1979–80** C. Teulieres
1979–81 C. Clauss	**1981** C. Largeau
1982 P. Chautard	**1982** S. Amigorena

GERMANY, Federal Republic of

Clubs/centres: 350   *Courts:* 2700   *Players:* 500 000
Association: Deutscher Squash Rackets Verband e.V., Lange Worth 2, 2125 Garlstorf, West Germany. Founded: 1973. President: Hartmut Kautz; Secretary/Executive Dir: Thomas Ziegler

Germany is almost certainly the fastest growing squash nation in terms of the building of new clubs and increase in the number of players. Its facilities also encourage some of the world's leading players to have their base there – currently the group includes Steve Bowditch, Ali Aziz and Zahir Hussein Khan.

The German SRA celebrated their tenth year in existence by staging the European Team Championships in Munich in May 1983. Munich, and its immediate surroundings, is today the stronghold of German squash with over 30 centres and more than 200 courts. This was further emphasised by the staging of the 1983 World Open there, sponsored by Canadian Club. However, the best players still come from Hamburg where the boom started in the 1970s.

International Championship

MEN		WOMEN	
1976–77	G. Alauddin (Pak)	1979	T. Lawes (Eng)
1978	M. Hellstrom (Swe)	1980	K. Due-Boje (Swe)
1979–81	L. Kvant	1981–82	No competition
1982	G. Awad (Egy)	1983	S. Devoy (NZ)
1983	H. Jahan (Eng)		

National Championship

MEN		WOMEN	
1976–78	R. Rothenberger	1976–79	J. Lange (née Burrows)
1979	C. Hasselbach		
1980–83	C. Martini	1980–83	C. Thomalla

GREECE

Courts: 10
Association: Greek Squash Committee, c/o Greek Tennis Federation, 89 Patision Str, GR-104 34 Athens. Founded: 1974. President: Costis Th. Vranas

International Championship

MEN			
1945	Capt. Casdagli	1969	No competition
1946	Police Officer Cock	1970	A. Kaoud (Egy)
1947	Maj. Sedwick	1971	M. Asran (Egy)
1948	Wing Cdr. Lee	1972	G. Allam (Egy)
1949	Wing Cdr. Willis	1973–74	A. Safwat (Egy)
1950	Police Officer Cock	1975	Mohibullah Khan (Pak)
1951	Maj. Forte		
1952–53	A. Vatimbella	1976–77	A. Safwat (Egy)
1954–55	D. Codounis	1978	J. Barrington (GB & Ire)
1956–57	Lt. M. H. Packard RN		A. Kaoud (Egy)
1958	No competition	1979–82	M. Awad (Egy)
1959	D. Codounis	1983	H. Jahan (Pak)
1960–62	Lt. (later Lt. Cdr.) M. H. Packard RN	WOMEN	
1963	S. Demetriades	1982–83	M. Le Moignan (Eng)
1964	G. Barletti		
1965	Lt. Cdr. M. H. Packard RN		
1966	S. Demetriades		
1967	Lt. Cdr. M. H. Packard RN		
1968	S. Demetriades		

National Championship

MEN			
1947	P. Pappadopoulo	1958–61	D. Codounis
1948	N. Demetriades	1962–68	S. Demetriades
1949–50	G. Louzy	1969	G. Barletti
1951	A. Vatimbella	1970–78	L. Gavalas
1952–53	No competition	1979–82	P. Vassilou
1954–56	D. Codounis		
1957	S. Demetriades	WOMEN	
		1982	E. Melachrinou

HONG KONG

Clubs/centres: 38   *Courts:* 158   *Players:* 19 000
Association: Hong Kong Squash Rackets Association, c/o Jubilee Sports Centre, 18 Borrett Road. Founded: 1961. Chairman: W. J. Downey; Secretary/Executive Dir: Mrs B. MacAnaney

Interest in squash has been spreading significantly throughout Hong Kong since the late seventies. A number of new clubs are being built or are at the planning stage and the number of registered players has increased by 25 per cent over the last two years. Nearly 200 teams currently compete in the leagues. The Government would like to see an official provision of one court per 10 000 of the population and this gives a building target of 520 courts over the next few years. The Urban Council have outlined plans for an 18-court centre with an exhibition court seating 300 spectators.

The country's enthusiasm has been fired by visits from Jonah Barrington, Steve Bowditch, world champion Jahangir Khan and a series of exhibition matches organised by Pakistan International Airways involving Qamar Zaman, Maqsood Ahmed, Gogi Alauddin and Mohibullah Khan.

In 1981 Hong Kong hosted the East Asian Championships and the home teams produced very creditable performances to win the women's event and finish third behind Singapore and Malaysia in the men's tournament.

Although sponsorship is not yet very well established, the national championships are supported by British Caledonian and Dunlop.

National Championship

MEN			
1950–51	D. I. Bosanquet	1960	Capt. M. F. Perkins
1952	Lt. Col. A. R. Fyler	1961–62	Lt. (later Capt.) A. Marsden
1953	Lt. Cdr. L. L. Rigge	1963	P. D. Mather
1954	R. M. MacPherson	1964	M. Kamien
1955	D. G. Coffrey	1965	P. Bencharit
1956	Lt. Col. J. J. Sullivan	1966	T. D. Phillips
1957	D. G. Coffrey	1967	J. W. Haines
1958	Flt. Lt. D. L. F. Thornton	1968	M. R. V. Clinch
1959	Capt. J. M. Booth	1969	F. Khan
		1970–72	T. D. Phillips

1973 Y. C. Lai	1965 J. K. E. King
1974–76 J. R. Cooper	1966–68 G. Piercy
1977 K. K. Chan	1969 P. Roberts
1978 S. Swallow	1970 G. Piercy
1979–80 K. K. Chan	1971 L. Wilkinson
1981 Capt. D. Armstrong	1972–73 Capt. S. Taylor
1982–83 K. K. Chan	1974–75 H. Cooper
	1976 P. Ewing
WOMEN	1977–79 F. Sella
1962–63 A. Gladstone	1980–81 J. Hawkes
1964 G. Piercy	1982–83 T. Brooke

INDIA

Clubs/centres: 58   *Courts:* 450   *Players:* 25 000
Association: The Squash Rackets Federation of India, c/o
The Calcutta Racket Club, nr. St Paul's Cathedral,
Chowringhee, Calcutta 700 071. Founded: 1954.
President: Narenda N. Atal; Secretary/Executive Dir:
Pranam Wahi

There are signs that, after a number of years of
decline, there is a resurgence of interest in squash in
India. The national association was reconstituted in
1980 in an effort to accelerate the growth and promote
the game as a discipline in its own right. The standard
of play has, as yet, shown little improvement but it is
noticeable that more youngsters are playing and
taking part in tournaments. Incentives are being provided with the opportunity for overseas travel for the
more promising players. In 1981, a new championship was started which is played for by teams
representing the Indian States.

Although the standard of squash has remained sta-
tic there are signs of a new crop of young players
developing into future champions. Maj. R. K. Manchanda had dominated the men's game for seven years
until losing the 1983/4 title to a 20-year-old, M.
Daruwalla. The interest in women's squash is limited
to a few centres and Miss B. Kumari, although only
24, has won the title for seven consecutive years.

Growth, however, is still slow and facilities are less
than ideal. The country does not yet have a court with
suitable viewing capacity to stage a major tournament.

National Championship

MEN	
1953–55 R. N. Singh	1968 A. Ispahani
1956–57 Capt. K. K.	1969–70 S. Roy
Hazari	1971–73 A. Nayar
1958–63 Lt. (later Capt.)	1974–76 No competition
K. S. Jain	1977–82 Maj. R. K.
1964 A. Nayar	Manchanda
1965 S. Roy	1983 M. Daruwalla
1966 A. Nayar	
1967 A. Akhtar Ali	WOMEN
	1977–83 B. Kumari

INDONESIA

Clubs/centres: 11   *Courts:* 25   *Players:* 700
Association: represented by the Bandung Squash Club,
Jalan Cilaki 49, Bandung, Java. Founded: 1979. President:
Ray Wilson; Secretary/Executive Dir: Mrs Jill Atkins

The game was played in purely expatriate sports clubs
until the Bandung Squash Club was founded in 1979.
Since then the Centre has concentrated on introducing the sport to the Indonesian people and considerable progress has been made.

In 1980 the club was accepted as a provisional
member of the ISRF and the following year it opened
a glass backwalled squash court which was designed
and built by its first Indonesian member, Jeffrey
Kijono. The club now has more than 150 members
and it is planned to add a third court to expand the
membership still further.

Efforts to encourage Indonesians to play squash are
now paying dividends and in 1983, a home player Joni
Effendi won the club championship for the first time.
The club is also encouraging other squash centres in
Bandung and other cities in Indonesia.

A national association is in the embryonic stage and
it is eventually hoped to meet the requirements of the
Ministry of Sport and for squash to be recognised as a
national sport. For this squash must be represented in
eight of the country's 27 provinces and good progress
has been made towards this goal.

International Championship
MEN
1983 R. Yam (Phi)

National Championship

MEN	WOMEN
1982–83 G. S. Bambang	1983 No competition

IRELAND

Clubs/centres: 180   *Courts:* 650   *Players:* 115 000
Association: Irish Squash Rackets Association, 38
Woodlawn Park Grove, Firhouse, County Dublin. Tel:
Dublin 521689. Founded: 1934. President: Ivan Carter;
Secretary/Executive Dir: Tom Cantwell

As with many other countries, squash flourished in
Ireland in the middle and late 1970s. In 1972 there
were 94 courts and around 600 players. By 1979 the
figures had increased phenomenally to 468 courts and
74 000 players. Now there are 650 courts and
approximately 115 000 regular participants.

Although the rate of increase has understandably
slowed, the numbers are still climbing. The province
of Ulster has recorded the greatest upsurge of interest

with 35 courts in 1972, 220 in 1979 and over 350 today.

Sponsorship is proving difficult to secure, especially for the national teams in overseas events. However, things are brighter on the tournament front. Dunlop sponsored the Irish Open until 1979 and is now involved, together with Audi, in junior developments. The Open Championship has been sponsored for the last two years by the Star & Crescent Club in Drogheda to a level which has allowed 16 world class players to compete. Guinness sponsor the Women's Open Championship and Mahon Merchant Bankers the All-Ireland Club tournament.

The Irish television station RTE was one of the pioneers of televised squash when a specially devised tournament, sponsored by Dunlop, was first shown in 1979. The coverage, then and since, has prompted many experts and players to suggest that other countries' television companies are overplaying the difficulties of screening the sport.

International Championship

1931 A. Hamilton	**1956** H. E. O'Donoghue
1932 R. W. Beadle (Eng)	**1957–59** D. M. Pratt
1933 R. W. S. Greene	**1960** B. Kilcoyne
1934–36 T. G. McVeagh	**1961–65** D. M. Pratt
1937 R. A. McNeile	**1966–67** J. Barrington
1938 S. G. S. Pawle (Eng)	**1968** D. M. Pratt
1939 Sir W. B. Golding Bt.	**1969** J. Barrington
1940–41 P. D. MacWeeney	**1970** W. Barr
1942 T. J. O'Driscoll	**1971** D. M. Pratt
1943 C. A. Kemp	**1972–73** G. B. Hunt (Aus)
1944–45 J. O'Keefe	**1974** G. Alauddin (Pak)
1946–47 W. S. M. Jameson	**1975–76** G. B. Hunt (Aus)
1948 D. N. Sell	**1977** Q. Zaman (Pak)
1949 A. G. Aitchison (Sco)	**1978** P. S. Kenyon (Eng)
1950–51 J. P. MacHale	**1979** J. Barrington
1952 W. R. Howson (Eng)	**1980–81** H. Jahan (Pak)
1953–54 H. E. O'Donoghue	**1982–83** Jahangir Khan
1955 P. Knox-Peebles	(Pak)

National Championship

1972 J. R. Young	**1981** J. Fleury
1973–75 J. H. D. Magrath	**1982** D. Gotto
1976–78 D. Gotto	**1983** W. Hosey
1979–80 R. Power	

Most international caps: Ben Cranwell 77.

Women's Association: Irish Women's Squash Rackets Association. President: Miss Pamela Paxton, 29 Gray's Park, Belvoir Park, Belfast BT8 4EG. Tel: Belfast 645754; Secretary: Mrs Prue Hamilton, 10 Thorndale Road North, Carryduff, Belfast BT8 8HY. Tel: 0232 813343

Founded in 1951 to promote squash for women in Ireland when the players numbered about 200, the IWSRA is now engaged in representing over 20 000 women players.

In the early fifties very few clubs in Ireland permitted women the use of their courts, and this directly led to the formation of the Women's Squash Rackets Association of Ireland, as the Association was then known. The primary aim at that time was to encourage more women to play squash by providing some form of regular competition in the few clubs which permitted such 'irregular' activity for women.

It is worthy of note that one of Ireland's foremost clubs, the Fitzwilliam Lawn Tennis Club, Dublin which had squash courts and was the base of the ISRA, gladly permitted women the use of the squash

Geraldine Barniville – Ireland's and the world's most capped woman player

courts at off-peak times, although the women could not become members of the club. This help and encouragement to the newly-formed IWSRA has continued over the past 30 years and the Association continues to enjoy the facilities of Fitzwilliam for its meetings and many of its major championships.

It was recorded in *The Sunday Times*, 11 November 1951 that 'the first president of the IWSRA is Mrs Vera McWeeney, the all-round games player who has represented her country at tennis and hockey'. Sadly, her death four years ago deprived Irish women's squash of a great friend.

Clubs throughout Ireland were invited to join the Association at an annual subscription of one guinea, the individual fee was 2s 6d. The most replies came from the Northern Province, Ulster, and competition between Leinster and Ulster soon followed. These matches served as selection matches for fixtures arranged against the Edinburgh Sports Club, in the first instance.

The first 'International' was played against the USA in Dublin in April 1953 which the visitors won 6–0. Wales provided the first 'European' competition in March 1954. One of the most hotly contested championships is the annual meeting of the teams from each of the four provinces. This championship started first between Ulster and Leinster back in the 1950s and has continued to flourish with Munster and Connacht now taking part.

Until 1958 the organisation of the Association was based in Dublin. It is believed that at this time it was centred in Trinity College but, perhaps due to students moving, the records disappeared. The lost threads were picked up again in the early sixties by Mrs Dorothy Boyd, then honorary secretary of the Women's Association in Ulster. Through her interest during the real growth period of squash in Ireland, the IWSRA returned from oblivion. Again it functioned primarily in the competitive fields at inter-provincial, national and international levels.

A demand for a more active administration came in the mid seventies from the leading players who felt their labours could best be rewarded at home by an association which could supply funds for travel, the organisation needed to run training squads and the support for juniors. While most of the coaching courses for coaches and juniors was carried out by the provincial associations a large area of development, mainly financial and organisational, was required at Irish level.

At this time there was much talk of amalgamating with the ISRA but unanimous opinion was not forthcoming. Through determination and the leadership of the new president, Mrs Prue Hamilton, from 1977 the confidence of the women in administration was restored. Since then the Association has continued to support not only its leading players, but it has slowly been able to develop other areas of the game particularly the setting up of coaching courses for coaches, under the guidance of Mrs Dorothy Boyd, Ireland's only woman squash tutor.

The dominant Irish players of the past decade are well known throughout the world: Geraldine Barniville – 71 caps, Dorothy Armstrong – 64 caps; Barbara Sanderson – 54 caps; and Irene Hewitt – 35 caps. The new generation of young players have taken their places on the international side – four of the squad of six are under 23.

In 1976, G. Barniville, D. Armstrong and I. Hewitt represented Ireland in the first Women's World Championship (Individual); in 1978 the team was placed third in the team championship behind England and Australia; in 1981 the team was fifth in Canada in the team championship; and in 1983 in Perth they were placed fourth behind Australia, England and New Zealand. Since the inception of the European Championship in 1979 the Irish team has finished second behind England.

On the home front the Irish Women's Open has, since 1974, had a very strong overseas entry. The draw is limited to 32 so the top 16 Irish players have the opportunity to meet the cream of women's squash on their home ground.

The commitment to the administration by a small number of women from all over Ireland, working in concert with the ISRA and the provincial associations has culminated in Ireland being the next venue for the Women's World Squash Championships in 1985. In addition, the Association has been greatly honoured by the election of the honorary secretary, Prue Hamilton to the highest office in international women's squash – chairman of the WISRF.

International Championship

1948–49	A. Mann	1968	B. Sanderson
1950	H. Cole	1969–70	J. Menzies
1951	R. J. Hackett	1971	S. Lynas
1952	H. Cole	1972	D. Armstrong
1953	D. Kilbride	1973	G. Barniville
1954	M. Gowthorpe	1974	F. Marshall (Eng)
1955	H. Flinn	1975	S. Newman (Aus)
1956–57	G. Horsley	1976	M. Zachariah (Aus)
1958–62	No records	1977	B. Wall (Aus)
1963	D. Boyd	1978	J. Ashton (Eng)
1964	T. Hopkins	1979	S. Cogswell (Eng)
1965	D. Boyd	1980	R. Anderson (Aus)
1966	J. Wallace	1981	S. Cogswell (Aus)
1967	D. Boyd	1982	L. Opie (Eng)

National Championship

1973	I. Hewitt	1975–76	I. Hewitt
1974	D. Armstrong	1977	G. Barniville

1978	D. Armstrong	1981	G. Barniville
1979–80	I. Hewitt	1982	M. Burke

ISRAEL

Clubs/centres: 9   *Courts:* 31   *Players:* 3000
Association: Israel Squash Rackets Association, PO Box 919, R. Gan 52109. Founded: 1982. Secretary: Mervin Muravitz

As recently as 1976, squash was barely known in the country, but now Israel has two major commercial centres and there are plans to erect a new complex at Haifa. The kibbutz is a popular place for facilities.

In 1976, the Israeli Squash Centre at Ra'anana was constructed with two collapsible courts and the demand for additional courts increased. More modern complexes were built at the Maccabi Village in Ramat-Gan and Herzlia.

The first Israeli Open Championships were held at Herzlia in 1983 with television coverage. Peter Verow (Eng) beat Moussa Helal (Egy) in the men's event and Angela Smith (Eng) beat Jayne Ashton (Eng) in the women's event. John Easter (Eng) won the Masters (Over-35) Championships.

Peter Brown (Eng) is leading a band of some 25 coaches to help improve the standard of play and many tournaments are being added to the calendar including the Israeli Closed and a national league.

International Championship

MEN		WOMEN	
1983	P. Verow (Eng)	1983–84	A. Smith (Eng)
1984	R. Hill (Aus)		

National Championship

MEN			
1980	M. Rabinowitz	1982	N. Berman
1981	M. Lurie	1983	B. Zimmerman

ITALY

Clubs/centres: 10   *Courts:* 30   *Players:* 350
Association: Associazione Italiana Badminton Squash, Via Valsolda 157, 00141 Rome. Founded: 1976.
Secretary/Executive Dir: Aurelio Chiappero

Squash, which started to boom in 1976, is still growing. Organisation and playing levels are improving all the time and the numbers of clubs and players are increasing steadily. A new centre at Rimini was completed in 1982 and others are expected to be built in Rome, Florence, Cuneo, Genoa, Lecce, San Remo and Trieste.

International Championship

MEN			
		1979	J. Goernerup (Swe)
1977	P. Carmell (Eng)	1980–81	M. Awad (Egy)
1978	P. East (Eng)		

WOMEN		1980	J. Arleklo (Swe)
1979	J. Burrows (Aus)	1981	B. Hartmann (Swz)

National Championship

MEN		WOMEN	
1978–81	M. Nerozzi	1979–81	R. Rota
		1982	M. Sisti

JAMAICA

Clubs/centres: 6   *Courts:* 14   *Players:* 1000
Association: Jamaica Squash Rackets Association, c/o NCM Ltd, NCM Buildings, 7 Oxford Terrace, Kingston 5. Founded: 1973. Chairman: Dougie Beckford; Secretary/Executive Dir: Ronald Nasralla

International Championship

MEN		1980–81	No competition
1973	J. Simmonds	1982	M. Lilley (NZ)
1974–75	No competition	1983	G. Williams (Eng)
1976–79	O. Haslam		

National Championship

MEN		WOMEN	
1982–83	W. Burrowes	1982–83	S. Lawrence

Susan Lawrence and Wayne Burrowes, 1983/4 Jamaica and Caribbean champions

JAPAN

Clubs/centres: 22   *Courts:* 80   *Players:* 10 000
Association: Japan Squash Rackets Association, c/o Roi
Building, 9F 5-5-1 Rappongi, Minato-ku, Tokyo 106.
Founded: 1971. Chairman: Shintaro Ishihari;
Secretary/Executive Dir: Mike Y. Hara

Japan's first commercial court was built in 1971.
Since then the sport has developed quickly and there
are now more than 80 courts in 22 clubs. The sport is
one of the fastest growing in Japanese history and
seems set to continue in this fashion particularly as
squash courts take up relatively little space – an
important factor in a country where there is a shortage
of land.

International Championship

MEN		
1975–76 S. Sakamoto	1978–81 S. Sakamoto
1977 No competition	1982 I. Robinson (Eng)

National Championship

MEN	WOMEN
1973–80 S. Sakamoto	1976 M. Kamata
1981–83 H. Ushiogi	1977 M. Miyagishima
	1978–83 E. Watanabe

JORDAN

Association: Jordanian Squash Rackets Association, c/o
A. L. Hussen Sports City, Amman. Founded: 1980.
President: Capt. Jawdat Munim; Secretary: Istlag Jarallah

Squash in Jordan was given a boost by the hosting of
the second Asian Championships in January 1984
when seven nations competed. The success of this
event is expected to lead to Jordan staging the Asian
Junior Championship in 1985.

KUWAIT

Clubs/centres: 14   *Courts:* 80   *Players:* 1000
Association: Kuwait Tennis, Table Tennis & Squash
Federation, PO Box 20496, Safat. Founded: 1968.
President: Ali Najaf Abdullah; Secretary/Executive Dir:
Ya 'qoub Al-Husseini

Since the Federation was founded in 1968 the number
of players and facilities has steadily increased. There
are several centres currently under construction. To
the relief of overseas visitors, all courts have recently
been modified to include air-conditioning systems to
help combat the previously unbearable heat and
humidity.

In 1976 a training centre for under-14s was set up
and the country now has a full-time junior coach. The
national team has competed in many international
events, including the ISRF World Team Championships and the Asian Championships. The training of
officials has also not been neglected – the Federation
organised a referee/marker course in 1978 which was
conducted by the European Squash Rackets Federation secretary Ian Wright, who also held a follow-up
course in 1980. Television coverage of the sport has
been limited but both referee/marker courses were
screened, as were a series of exhibitions between
Qamar Zaman and Maqsood Ahmed during the
Kuwait Open in 1982.

National Championship

MEN	
1981–82 T. Owayesh

LUXEMBOURG

Courts: 13   *Players:* 600
Association: Federation Luxembourgoise de Squash
Rackets, 33 Boulevard Prince Henri, L-1724. Founded:
1973. President: Chris Clarke; Secretary: Philip Aspden

The standard of squash in the Grand Duchy remains
astonishingly high for a country where there are only
300 players. The number of courts has remained at
seven (two of which are restricted to the EEC institu-
tions and one of which has a concrete floor). However,
there are encouraging signs that more courts will be
built in the country's second city, Esch-sur-Alzette.

Leagues for both men and women have been introduced and it is hoped that this will stimulate the
growth of squash and, more importantly, attract the
support of the young people of Luxembourg.

International Championship

MEN	
1982–83 R. Maasen (Net)

National Championship

MEN	
1973–78 C. McIntosh
1979–83 C. Irrthum

MALAYSIA

Clubs/centres: 55   *Courts:* 173   *Players:* 3000
Association: Squash Rackets Association of Malaysia, PO
Box 10164, Kuala Lumpur. Founded: 1972. President:
Yam Tunku Imran Ibni Tuanku Ja'afar;
Secretary/Executive Dir: N. Prasad Pillai

Squash was originally introduced to Malaysia by the
British and played almost exclusively in private clubs.
The boom started in 1978 when the first public courts
were built in Kuala Lumpur. Now the largest complex just outside the city has 20 courts, including a
championship court with a gallery for 550 spectators.
A new 26-court complex opened in 1983 and further
courts are being erected in Penang, Perak and Treng-

ganu. The game is now the fastest growing sport in Malaysia, and the country hosted the second World Junior Championships (individual event) in 1982 and the Asian Junior Championships in 1983. The national team was runner-up in the 1981, 1982 and 1983 East Asian Championships in Hong Kong, Thailand and Papua New Guinea, and finished fourth in the first Asian Championships in Karachi in 1981.

Television coverage in the past has been limited to international events held in Malaysia but interest is now being shown in national tournaments and hopes are high of live coverage in the near future. Sponsorship of major events is encouraging. Anchor Beer began sponsoring the national championships for five years starting in 1982; the Malaysian Open is supported by Magnolia who also sponsored the Asian Championships; and the World Junior event was backed by Dunlop, Milo and Kentucky Fried Chicken.

International Championship

MEN	WOMEN
1975 G. Alauddin (Pak)	1975 H. Chinchen (Sin)
1976 M. Ahmed (Pak)	1976–78 A. Andrews (Sin)
1977 F. Gul (Pak)	1979 M. Miyagishima (Jap)
1978–79 Atlas Khan (Pak)	1980–82 S. Paton (Sin)
1980 F. Gul (Pak)	1983 C. C. Lan (Sin)
1981 Atlas Khan (Pak)	
1982 A. Aziz (Egy)	
1983 Jahangir Khan (Pak)	

National Championship

MEN	WOMEN
1973 T. Imran	1974 A. Kronenberg
1974 N. M. Din	1975 S. Liew
1975 H. M. Salleh	1976 A. Kronenberg
1976–77 N. M. Din	1977–78 S. Liew
1978–79 T. Tiah	1979 A. Kronenberg
1980–82 J. Loo	1980 S. Liew
1983 S. Manlam	1981–82 A. Kronenberg
	1983 O. S. Mee

MEXICO

Association: Federation Mexicana de Squash AC, Avenida Chapultepec 18, 3er piso 06720. Founded: 1968. President: Francisco Suinaga Andrade; Secretary/Executive Dir: T. C. Ehrenberg

Although the game is popular in Mexico, few of the estimated thousands of players are registered or organised in leagues. No statistics are available regarding the number of players. The general standard of play appears to be improving and Mario Sanchez has won the USA Amateur Hardball Championship twice and there are several other very competent players including Juan and Raul de Villafranca, Raul Sanchez and Jose Musi. Courts are now being built in hotels, large

industrial complexes and private homes in the more fashionable city suburbs.

International Championship

MEN	
	1973 G. Anderson (Can)
1970 R. Sanchez	1974 V. Niederhoffer (USA)
1971 T. Poor (USA)	1975–76 J. de Villafranca
1972 A. Nayar (Ind)	1977–82 Sharif Khan (Pak)

National Championship
MEN

1982 J. Martinez

MONACO

Clubs/centres: 2 *Courts:* 6 *Players:* 150
Association: Federation Monegasque de Squash-Rackets, c/o Single Buoy Moorings, 24 Avenue de Fontvielle, MC. Founded: 1969. President: Michael Chiappori; Secretary/Executive Dir: Graham Gray

Squash was introduced to Monaco in 1925 when two courts were built for the use of the large British community. The courts fell into decay after the war but were renovated when the Monte Carlo Squash Rackets Club was founded in 1969 thanks to Prince Rainier III who is a keen player. Four additional courts have been built in a new multi-sport complex scheduled to be completed in 1984. The national team has finished runner-up in the French Championships each year since 1977. Teams have been entered in the European Championships in 1973 when they finished 10th, 1976 (15th), 1979 (15th), 1980 (15th), 1981 (12th), 1982 (15th) and 1983 (14th). A women's team entered for the first time in 1982 and were 15th, achieving the same position in 1983.

Sponsorship was introduced in 1980 when Yellow Dot and British Caledonian sponsored the Monaco Open which is now supported by Goudie. Fila provide equipment for the national team.

The attitude of the local television companies has been very positive considering the low number of players and Tele-Monte-Carlo and French regional station Attitude have screened events.

International Championship

MEN	
	1975 P. White (Eng)
1970 A. Swift (Eng)	1976 Shah J. Khan (Pak)
1971 M. Abaza (Egy)	1977 Atlas Khan (Pak)
1972 S. H. Courtney (Eng)	1978–79 Abbas Khan (Pak)
1973 No competition	1980 H. Jahan (Pak)
1974 I. R. G. Dowdeswell	1981 D. Williams (Aus)
(Zim)	1982 R. Thorne (Aus)

National Championship
MEN

1969 A. Vatimbella	1973 I. Henderson
1970 J. Crovetto	1974–76 J. Crovetto
1971–72 P. Rubino	1977–79 B. Fissore

1980	M. Ballerio	WOMEN	
1981–82	E. Janvier	1978–79	P. Elder
		1980	C. Mace
		1981	J. Ventorino
		1982	C. Mace

NETHERLANDS

Clubs/centres: 120   *Courts:* 400   *Players:* 35 000
Association: Netherlands SR Bond, Catsheuvel 6, 5e Etage
Torenflat, Netherlands Congresgebouw, 2517 JZ Den
Haag. Founded: 1938. President: F. Nijkerk;
Secretary/Executive Dir: Henk Smies

Squash was introduced in Utrecht in 1932 but progress was slow and there were no more than seven courts at the outbreak of the war. In 1973 the first new courts were erected in the Hague and by the end of the year there were four clubs. Since then the spread of the game has been rapid. The 500th court is expected to be erected in 1984 by which time it is hoped that 50 000 people will be playing regularly.

During 1983 the Hague club was extended to seven courts, including a championship court, and the occasion was honoured by HRH Prince Claus who performed the opening ceremony. HRH Prince Bernard opened centres at Warmond (six courts) and Gonda (two courts).

Since the late seventies Midalgan, de Kuper and Ambiro Sports have sponsored a tournament circuit

Ric Zandvliet, nearer the camera, and Louk Klippel, two of the leading players in the Netherlands

and in 1981 Equity and Law started a national club competition. The current sponsorship is running at approximately 75 000 Dutch fl. per annum.

Television coverage is practically non existent although an exhibition match between Qamar Zaman and Mohibullah Khan was shown as long ago as 1975.

International Championship

MEN			
1963	M. W. Corby (Eng)	1979	P. Chaplin (Eng)
1964	J. G. A. Lyon (Eng)	1980	M. Saad (Egy)
1965	G. D. Massey (Eng)	1981	No competition
1966	J. Barrington (GB & Ire)	1982	A. Safwat (Egy)
1967	P. D. Stokes (Wal)	1983	R. Hill (Aus)
1968	M. W. Corby (Eng)		
1969–71	P. N. Ayton (Eng)	WOMEN	
1972	No competition	1974	J. Courtney (Eng)
1973	P. N. Ayton (Eng)	1975	J. Ashton (Eng)
1974	P. G. Verow (Eng)	1976–77	T. Lawes (Eng)
1975	P. N. Ayton (Eng)	1978–79	C. Rees (Wal)
1976	D. Scott (SA)	1980	A. Samuelsson (Swe)
1977	P. S. Kenyon (Eng)	1981	No competition
1978	G. Awad (Egy)	1982	R. Best (Ire)
		1983	J. Freeman

National Championship

MEN		WOMEN	
1940	H. Timmer	1948–68	J. Jamin
1946–60	A. G. Maris	1969	A. Bakker
1961–62	H. van der Straaten	1970	J. Jamin
1963–64	H. Herok	1971–74	A. Bakker
1965–68	W. van Rooyen	1975	I. Zeevenhoven-Koster
1969	H. Herok	1976	A. de Laive-Bakker
1970–78	R. Anjema	1977–79	I. Zeevenhoven-Koster
1979	R. Zandvliet		
1980–82	R. Anjema	1980	A. de Laive-Bakker
1983	E. van der Pluijm	1981	I. Zeevenhoven-Koster
		1982–83	M. Remijnse

NEW ZEALAND

Clubs/centres: 238   *Courts:* 645   *Players:* 51 000
Association: New Zealand Squash Rackets Association, PO Box 1040, Tauranga. Founded: 1939. President: Andrew Doig; Secretary/Executive Dir: Bill Murphy

The Association, although founded in 1939, formally got under way in 1946 but it has only been since 1966 that the present administration system of a management committee meeting on a regular basis has been operating. In recent years squash has become one of the country's leading participant sports, and continues to grow in popularity as does the ability and status of the country's top players. The Association now runs its own centre in Wellington where the present eight courts are soon to be increased to twelve. In 1979 the Association appointed a full-time execu-

Bruce Brownlee, former New Zealand number 1, who in 1981 had to retire through injury when at the peak of his career. *Robin Eley Jones*

tive officer and director of coaching and development which has provided further impetus to the sport.

Since the advent of the 'Open' game more sponsorship and tournaments have been introduced and the New Zealand calendar of events now covers practically the whole year. In 1981/2 a tournament players' championship was started which is contested on a points system throughout the various district championships.

New Zealand squash received a cruel blow in 1982 when their number 1 and world-ranked number 6 Bruce Brownlee was forced to retire through injury. However with Stuart Davenport, Ross Norman, Craig Blackwood and Neven Barbour, the country still boasts a very strong squad and finished fifth in the 1981 ISRF World Team Championships in Sweden and fifth in the 1983 event in New Zealand. Blackwood was runner-up in the 1981 individual event although the competition lost most of its prestige when the field was severely depleted by a series of

withdrawals including all the top Pakistani players. But this was not the case in 1983 when Davenport got to the semi-finals and was put out by Jahangir Khan. The women have played consistently well and in the 1981 world team event in Canada and the 1983 event in Australia finished third on both occasions. Sue Devoy became the first New Zealander to win the British Women's Open with her victory in April 1984.

International Championship (Open)

MEN	WOMEN
1976 B. Brownlee	**1976** P. Buckingham
1977 C. Nancarrow (Aus)	**1977** No competition
1978–79 G. B. Hunt (Aus)	**1978** B. Wall (Aus)
1980 Jahangir Khan (Pak)	**1979** J. Ashton (Eng)
1981 K. Shawcross (Aus)	**1980** J. Webster
1982–83 Jahangir Khan (Pak)	**1981–82** V. Cardwell (née Hoffman)
	1983 R. Blackwood

National Championship

Since 1981 this event has been open only to New Zealand citizens or players who have resided in the country for a period of not less than 12 months.

MEN	
1932 G. E. F. Kingscote	**1981** B. Brownlee
1933–35 P. D. Hall	**1982** R. Norman
1936–37 W. R. Fea	**1983** S. Davenport
1938–39 W. E. Renton	
1940–45 No competition	WOMEN
1946 A. H. Malcolm	**1951–55** N. New
1947 A. M. Johns	**1956** B. Patterson
1948 M. J. Souter	**1957–58** A. McKenzies
1949 A. M. Johns	**1959** B. Patterson
1950–52 J. A. Gillies	**1960** A. McKenzies
1953 D. D. Mochan	**1961** A. Stephens
1954 P. R. Vesty	**1962** P. McGlenaughan (Aus)
1955 D. D. Mochan	**1963** A. Stephens
1956 D. G. Green	**1964** D. Deacon
1957 D. D. Mochan	**1965** H. Blundell (Aus)
1958 J. Cheadle (Aus)	**1966** P. Mills
1959 M. A. Oddy (Sco)	**1967** M. Waugh
1960–64 C. R. Waugh	**1968** V. Biss
1965 R. Carter (Aus)	**1969** P. Buckingham
1966 T. Johnston	**1970** T. Lawes
1967 D. Burmeister	**1971** P. Buckingham
1968 T. Johnston	**1972** C. Fleming
1969–70 D. Burmeister	**1973** P. Buckingham
1971 M. Asran (Egy)	**1974** J. Webster
1972 L. M. Greene	**1975** P. Buckingham
1973–74 N. S. Barbour	**1976–77** J. Webster
1975 T. Johnston	**1978** P. Guy
1976 H. Broun	**1979–80** J. Ashton (Eng)
1977 B. Brownlee	**1981** A. Owen
1978 P. Kenyon (Eng)	**1982** R. Blackwood
1979–80 F. X. Donnelly (Aus)	**1983** S. Devoy

NIGERIA

Clubs/centres: 100   *Courts:* 350   *Players:* 8000
Association: Nigeria Squash Rackets Association, National
Sports Commission, PO Box 145, Lagos. Founded: 1972.
Chairman: Cmdr. Edwin Kentebbe; Secretary/Executive
Dir: Frances S. Gbiri

The game was first played in Nigeria during the pre-
independence days of the 1940s and 1950s. At that
time it was based mainly in Lagos but after independence it spread to other areas. As with most countries,
the 1970s heralded a boom, the National Sports
Commission took an active interest in the sport and
Nigeria was accepted into the ISRF in 1975. The
national men's team entered the World Team Championships in Australia in 1979 when they finished
11th out of 14 and again in 1981 in Sweden when they
came 14th out of 23. The country's women were the
only black nation to compete in the World Championships in Canada in 1981.

Sponsorship is remarkably well developed with the
Elephant Cement Company having supported the
Open Championships for the last eight years to the
tune of ₦30 000; Milo sponsor the Lagos Open
(₦6000); Five Star Textiles have invested ₦25 000 in
the Ikoyi Tournament over five years; Voxmobile
sponsor an annual event for ₦45 000; and NEM
Insurance put up ₦30 000 for the Nigerian Closed.

Television coverage has so far been limited to opening and closing ceremonies and discussion programmes, but the stations appear to be coming alive to
the potential of screening matches.

International Championship

MEN	WOMEN
1975 P. Ani	1975–78 S. Bowner
1976 S. Oladunjoye	1979 C. Hood (Ken)
1977 O. Martins	1980 J. Maycock (Can)
1978 G. Awad (Egy)	1981 T. Tikili
1979 P. Chaplin (Eng)	1982 T. Owoyemi
1980 L. Kvant (Swe)	
1981 M. Mfuk	
1982 O. Martins	

National Championship

MEN	
1970 M. Sofoluwe	1980 O. Martins
1971 E. Enebeli	1981 F. Omoben
1972 S. Oladunjoye	1982 O. Martins
1973 B. Solomon	1983–84 M. Olubo
1974 P. Ani	**WOMEN**
1975 S. Oladunjoye	1980 T. Tikili
1976–78 O. Martins	1981–82 T. Owoyemi
1979 F. Omoben	1983 T. Tikili
	1984 T. Owoyemi

Longest recorded match: 1982 Nigerian Open quarter-
final. M. Mfuk beat M. Olubo in 5 games lasting 2 hours 30
minutes.

NORWAY

Clubs/centres: 23   *Courts:* 60   *Players:* 6000
Association: Norges Squashforbund, PO Box 1652, Vika,
Oslo 1. Founded: 1978. Chairman: B. Nilssen;
Secretary/Executive Dir: Knut Amundsen

Since the late seventies the overall standard of play has
improved but the country is still the weakest of the
Nordic nations. There is considerable concern over
the shortage of younger players who are taking up the
game. Most of the new recruits are from the senior
and middle age groups. The main reason for this is
that all centres are operated on a profit-making basis
making it very expensive to play – usually around £9
per hour.

International Championship

MEN	WOMEN
1979 P. Bostrom (Swe)	1979 K. Due-Boje (Swe)
1980 L. Kvant (Swe)	1980 P. Anderson
1981 J. Stockenberg (Swe)	1981 C. Bjornstom (Fin)
1982–83 C. Ericsson (Swe)	1982–83 T. Johnson (Eng)

National Championship

MEN	WOMEN
1978–79 G. Bretteville-Jensen	1978 H. Skog
	1979 K. Robsham
1980–83 J. Aabyholm	1980–82 A. Aabyholm
	1983 G. Lenth

PAKISTAN

Clubs/centres: 400   *Courts:* 120   *Players:* 1500

The championship court at the PIA Squash Complex,
Karachi, with seating for 256 and standing room for 100
more. The complex is probably the best purpose-built
traditional championship venue in the world

Association: Pakistan Squash Rackets Federation, Air Headquarters, Peshawar. Founded: 1947. President: Air Chief Marshall Muhammed Anwar Shamin; Joint Secretaries: Wing Cdr. Manzur-ul-haq Awan, Air Vice Marshall Sharbat A. Changazi

International Championship

MEN

1953–54	A. J. Quraishi	1970	M. Saleem
1955	Capt. A. Hamid	1971	No competition
1956	No competition	1972	M. Yasin
1957–59	A. J. Quraishi	1973	Mohibullah Khan
1960–62	No competition	1974	No competition
1963	A. A. Jawaid	1975	Mohibullah Khan
1964–66	No competition	1976–77	M. Ahmed
1967	M. Saleem	1978	Daulat Khan
1968	A. A. Jawaid	1979–82	Jahangir Khan
1969	J. Barrington (GB & Ire)		

PAPUA NEW GUINEA

Association: Papua New Guinea Squash Rackets Federation, PO Box 1818 Boroko. President: Michael Wilson; Secretary/Executive Dir: Mrs P. Bastion

The highlight of the 1983 season was the hosting, for the first time, of an international squash tournament – the 8th East Asian Squash Championships being played at Port Moresby. Teams came from Indonesia, Singapore, Hong Kong, Japan, Malaysia, Philippines and, of course, Papua New Guinea. It was the first occasion on which team and individual events were played at the same time in the eight-year history of the championships.

St. Vincent team which contested the fifth Southern Caribbean Championships in Guyana in 1982. From the left, Jim Lockhart, Paul Cyrus, Dr Cecil Cyrus, Clive Cyrus, Garfield Cyrus, Mark Cyrus and Leroy Edwards

Competing in the South Pacific region, Papua New Guinea won gold medals at the 1977 South Pacific Games and the 1980 and 1982 South Pacific Cup. At the 1980 East Asian Championships, held in Kuala Lumpur, the Papua New Guinea men's team finished last and the women's team was fifth. In 1981 the team improved its performance and in 1982 the men came fourth and the women third.

The team also participated in the 1983 ISRF World Championship in New Zealand and gained valuable experience, meeting players from the northern hemisphere. Papua New Guinea finished 16th out of 19 teams pushing Japan, Kuwait and Hong Kong below them.

National Championship

MEN		WOMEN	
1979–81	P. Gertzel	1979–80	K. Daisley
1982	B. Foster	1981	D. Sims
		1982	P. Bastion

PHILIPPINES

Association: Squash Rackets Association of the Philippines, 3rd floor, Diadem Building, Herrera Str Corner de la Rosa Str, Legaspi Village, Makati, Metro Manila. Dir: Bob de la Rosa

Squash in the Philippines is getting under way and a national inter-club competition has been formed to improve the standard of play.

A team was entered in the 8th East Asian Championships in Papua New Guinea and the Association hope to host the 10th Championship in 1985. Junior teams have also contested the Asian Junior and Malaysian Junior Championships.

ST. VINCENT

Clubs/centres: 3   *Courts:* 8   *Players:* 200
Association: St. Vincent and the Grenadines Squash Rackets Association, PO 359 Montrose, St. Vincent, West Indies. Founded: 1979. President: Dr Arthur Cecil Cyrus; Secretary/Executive Dir: Kathryn Cyrus

Squash was introduced to St. Vincent in 1963 by Dr Cecil Cyrus on his return from Belfast where he played for the University. He erected a court in a small converted garage and three years later built a medical clinic beneath which a full-sized court was housed. It took him ten years to encourage local players during which time his court was used by expatriates and visiting Navy personnel.

Although two further private courts were erected in subsequent years the most significant development came in January 1983 when a portion of land was leased to the Association by the Archbishop of the

West Indies for the building of 3 national championship courts. Construction work was begun in the autumn of 1983. The addition of the courts mean that the Association will host the 1984 Southern Caribbean Championships.

Representative matches began in 1976 with a visit to Barbados, quickly followed by a match with Guyana when the teams competed for the Cecil Cyrus Challenge Cup, a trophy still contested annually.

All four Cyrus children, Paul aged 15, Garfield 16, Mark 17 and Clive 19, play for St. Vincent and during the 1983 Southern Caribbean Senior Championship, young Paul beat the number 1 seed Tom Fortson of Venezuela. Paul is also the Caribbean Boys Under-16 champion as well as being the St. Vincent national champion, a title he first took in 1982 at the age of 14.

Although squash is becoming popular with the local people a coaching programme and more interest is needed to prevent the game stagnating. Sponsorship is non-existent and television coverage has been limited to interviews with Dr Cyrus and visiting international Angela Smith.

National Championship

MEN		WOMEN	
1980	T. Sardine	1980	M. Ferrari
1981	J. Barnard	1981–83	R. Cyrus
1982–83	P. Cyrus		

SCOTLAND

Clubs/centres: 170   *Courts:* 500   *Players:* 221 000
Association: Scottish Squash Rackets Association, 18 Ainslie Place, Edinburgh EH3 6AN. Tel: 031-226 4401. Founded: 1936. President: Dr D. Geoffrey Smith; Secretary/Executive Dir: Brenda Carmichael

The first known courts were built at Fettes College in Edinburgh in 1928. By 1939 there were approximately 30 courts, mostly attached to military establishments and schools. When the SSRA was formed it had six or seven affiliated clubs and six individual members. Post-war progress was slow with only around another 15 courts being built by 1964. In 1968 the 'boom' started and in the following 10 years approximately 210 courts were erected. Although numbers are not continuing to grow at the same rate, no season passes without the appearance of several new clubs. Present estimates put the number of clubs in Scotland at over 200 although only 121 are around Edinburgh and Glasgow, but there are clubs as far apart as Shetland and Stranraer.

International matches started prior to 1939 with games against Wales and England. Matches continued to be played against the other home countries and occasional touring sides until the European Championships started for men in 1972 and women in

One of Scotland's most famous players – Mike Oddy, runner-up in the 1963 British Open, and winner of the British Amateur in 1960 and 1961

1978. Scotland is now struggling to maintain playing standards against the rising levels of newer squash nations.

Sponsorship has varied from year to year with few companies continuing over extended periods. Television coverage is minimal – Grampian Television has shown the most interest and have screened several events since 1978. In 1982 one hour of the men's open final was shown and similar coverage from Grampian was given to the 1983 Open.

A women's association was founded in 1937 but it became amalgamated with the SSRA in 1972.

International Championship

MEN			
1935	I. A. W. Crabbie	1951–53	D. W. D. Shaw
1936–38	W. B. Scott	1954	I. C. de Sales la Terriere (Eng)
1939–45	No competition	1955	M. A. Oddy
1946–47	P. Harding-Edgar	1956	D. J. Callaghan (SA)
1948	T. I. Johnson-Gilbert	1957	M. A. Oddy
1949–50	W. R. Howson (Eng)	1958	I. Amin (Egy)
		1959	O. L. Balfour

83

1960–61 M. A. Oddy	**1951** L. McInroy
1962 K. Hiscoe (Aus)	**1952** S. Speight
1963 M. A. Oddy	**1953** L. R. Bryne
1964 G. B. Hunt (Aus)	**1954** E. E. Knox
1965 Sharif Khan (Pak)	**1955** J. Gidwell
1966–67 O. L. Balfour	**1956** S. Speight
1968–69 P. N. Ayton (Eng)	**1957** F. Marshall (Eng)
1970 C. Nancarrow (Aus)	**1958–59** J. R. Sands
1971 A. Swift (Eng)	**1960** B. J. Whitehead
1972–73 A. Jawaid (Pak)	**1961** F. Marshall (Eng)
1974 A. Colburn (SA)	**1962** A. Picton (Eng)
1975 M. Donnelly (Aus)	**1963** S. C. F. McClure
1976 D. Williams (Aus)	**1964–65** H. McKay (née
1977 F. X. Donnelly (Aus)	Blundell) (Aus)
1978 G. Brumby (Aus)	**1966** F. Marshall (Eng)
1979 Z. Hussein Khan (Pak)	**1967** S. Macintosh (Eng)
1980 Karimullah Khan	**1968** S. C. F. McClure
(Pak)	**1969** M. Roche (SA)
1981 C. Blackwood (NZ)	**1970** B. Carmichael
1982 T. Wilkinson (SA)	**1971** F. Marshall (Eng)
1983 N. Harvey (Eng)	**1972** L. Meuleman (Aus)
	1973 T. W. Cowie
WOMEN	**1974** T. Lawes (Eng)
1938 E. E. Knox	**1975** S. Newman (Aus)
1939–45 No competition	**1976** S. Cogswell (Eng)
1946 C. Russouw (SA)	**1977** I. Hewitt (Ire)
1947 J. R. M. Morgan (Eng)	**1978** R. Thorne (Aus)
1948 D. O. Liddell	**1979–80** V. Hoffman (Aus)
1949 J. R. M. Morgan (Eng)	**1981** M. Zachariah (Aus)
1950 H. J. R. Townsend	**1982** R. Blackwood (NZ)
(Eng)	**1983** S. Devoy (NZ)

National Championship

MEN	
1972 D. Smith	**1983** C. McManus
1973 A. K. Bruce Lockhart	
1974–75 N. D. T. Martin	**WOMEN**
1976 C. M. N. Wilson	**1974** D. H. McNeill
1977 R. R. Chalmers	**1975–77** D. Sharp
1978 C. M. N. Wilson	**1978–79** A. Bostock
1979 N. H. Stewart	**1980** R. Gregg
1980–81 G. Dupre	**1981** R. Lynch
1982 M. MacLean	**1982–83** H. Wallace

Most international appearances: *Men:* C. M. N. Wilson 106, A. K. Bruce Lockhart 61, N. H. Stewart 59. *Women:* D. Sharp 65, B. Carmichael 53, A. Smith 37. **Longest period at international level:** *Men:* P. Harding-Edgar 1938–59. *Women:* B. Carmichael 1957–78.

SINGAPORE

Clubs/centres: 58 *Courts:* 400 *Players:* 27 000
Association: Singapore Squash Rackets Association, Room 32, Sports House, Rutland Road, Farrer Park, Singapore 0821. Founded: 1970. President: Dr Eddie Jacob; Secretary/Executive Dir: Maj. Haridas Nair

The game had its origins in the police force but there was a significant move forward when the Singapore

Armed Forces began building courts in military camps and armed forces personnel started playing the game in considerable numbers in the early 1970s. The Singapore Sports Council built the nine-court Kallang Squash Club in the late seventies and this was followed by the erection of several public complexes. In 1982 The East Coast Recreation Centre was completed with 20 courts, of which three were glass-backed. This was the venue for the ISRF World Junior Team Championship in the same year.

While social squash has boomed with no sign of a slackening in demand for courts, the competitive game has also shown spectacular growth over the last five years. Besides the SSRA organised tournaments there are events held at club, community centre and business house level. The game is also steadily finding its way into secondary schools.

Just as the game has caught the imagination of the public, the potential of squash has been recognised by many commercial concerns. The main sponsors are Malayan Breweries (Anchor Beer), Nestles (Milo), Pakistan International Airlines and Wander (Singapore) Pty Limited. Many sports goods manufacturers have also provided strong financial backing, the foremost of which is Sunrise & Co. the sole agents for Ascot in Singapore. Milo and Sunrise teamed up in 1982 to jointly sponsor the ISRF World Junior Team Championships by contributing $50 000 each. Milo has sponsored the national championships for the last 10 years while Malayan Breweries have backed the Singapore Open for 13 consecutive seasons. An age-group training scheme is also sponsored by Pepsi Cola to the tune of $30 000 every year.

Television coverage started in 1977 and since then the Singapore leg of the PIA World Series, the national and open championships have been screened regularly. The final of the World Junior Team Championships between Pakistan and Australia was covered live in 1982.

International Championship

MEN	WOMEN
1970–71 M. Simons	**1972–73** M. Hocking
1972 B. Thoma	**1974** B. King
1973–74 Q. Zaman (Pak)	**1975** H. Cooper (HK)
1975 G. Alauddin (Pak)	**1976–78** R. Tablante (Phi)
1976 M. Ahmed (Pak)	**1979–81** S. Paton
1977 R. Gul (Pak)	**1982** J. Harris (Aus)
1978–81 Atlas Khan (Pak)	**1983** L. S. Hui
1982 A. Aziz (Egy)	
1983 Q. Zaman (Pak)	

National Championship

MEN	
1973–74 H. Ibrahim	**1978** V. Gopal
1975 T. C. Guan	**1979–82** Z. Abidin
1976–77 H. Ibrahim	**1983** P. Hill

WOMEN	
	1975 O. S. Ngoh
1973 O. S. Ngoh	**1976–80** T. Oh
1974 O. S. Lin	**1981–83** L. S. Hui

SOUTHERN AFRICA

Clubs/centres: 435 *Courts:* 1250 *Players:* 240 000
Association: Squash Rackets Association of South Africa,
PO Box 81235 Parkhurst, Johannesburg 2120. Founded:
1947. Chairman: David L. Quail; Secretary/Executive
Dir: Joy Williams

Squash was introduced to South Africa by the British at the beginning of the century. The first national championship was played in 1910/11. Until the mid seventies the game was played only in the club environment and at that time 500 courts had been constructed. In 1976 the first public centre was opened and since then the game has exploded. There is still a demand for courts and there remains a vast untapped potential in the country's black communities. There seems no reason why the growth over the last ten years should not be repeated over the next ten.

The first squash sponsorship was obtained in 1968 when Coca Cola backed the Champion of Champion tournament in Johannesburg for US $300. Today the men's Open Championship has sponsorship of US $40 000 while the women's circuit of five events has US $30 000. There are few tournaments where sponsorship does not play some part. At present there is a known US $34 000 tied up but an estimate of the total amount, taking into consideration the 'hidden' sponsorship and the local backing, would be approx. US $400 000. In addition there are various sponsored coaching schemes.

Television was introduced to South Africa in 1975 and squash has been screened every year since. Five or six events are shown each year with approximately 45 minutes of live coverage for each. South African television has not yet overcome the problem of creating an exciting squash telecast and is therefore reluctant to 'overdo' the coverage.

International Championship
1974–81 G. B. Hunt (Aus)
1982 D. Williams (Aus)
1983 R. Thorne (Aus)

National Championship
Until 1982 known as South African Amateur Championship.

1910–11 H. K. Reed	**1928–29** H. D. Clinch
1912 B. MacNaughten	**1930–32** H. W. P. Whiteley
1913 C. Reunert	**1933** D. O. Beckingham
1914–24 No competition	**1934** T. W. T. Baines
1925 C. Reunert	**1935–38** H. W. P. Whiteley
1926–27 M. McMaster	**1939–45** No competition

1946 B. H. Callaghan	**1964–65** F. P. A. Robinson
1947 D. C. Beckingham	**1966** C. Nancarrow (Aus)
1948 H. W. P. Whiteley	**1967** D. H. Botha
1949 G. Hildick-Smith	**1968–69** J. Barrington
1950–52 B. H. Callaghan	(GB & Ire)
1953 D. L. Hodgson	**1970** P. N. Ayton (Eng)
1954 B. H. Callaghan	**1971–72** D. Barrow
1955 D. J. Callaghan	**1973** C. Nancarrow (Aus)
1956 R. K. Jarvis	**1974** P. N. Ayton (Eng)
1957 C. B. Kaplan	**1975** I. Holding
1958 N. H. R. A. Broom-	**1976** J. C. Leslie (Eng)
field (Eng)	**1977** S. Machet
1959 M. L. Melvill	**1978** D. Scott
1960 D. J. Callaghan	**1979–80** L. Kvant (Swe)
1961 M. L. Melvill	**1981** T. Wilkinson (Zim)
1962 M. A. Oddy (Sco)	**1982** R. Watson
1963 K. Hiscoe (Aus)	**1983** I. Holding

Most international appearances: D. Barrow, D. H. Botha 8. **Youngest:** Only two teenagers have won the South African Amateur title – Bill Whiteley in 1930 aged 18 and Ian Holding in 1957. Whiteley is also the **oldest** player to win the event, aged 36 in 1948, and holds the record for the **most championship wins** – 8. **Longest:** The longest recorded match in the country was in the South African

Roland Watson, ex Johannesburg policeman, who has been South Africa's top player on the professional circuit

Open in 1957 between Cam Nancarrow of Australia and Ireland's Jonah Barrington – 2 hours 17 minutes. **Shortest:** The shortest match was in Harare, Zimbabwe (then Salisbury, Rhodesia) when Geoff Hunt beat fellow Australian Kevin Shawcross in just 12 minutes. **Most Open wins –** Geoff Hunt has won the South African Open Championship on eight occasions, 1974–81 inclusively. **Longest reign –** Roland Watson was first ranked number 1 in South Africa in 1973 and was still at number 1 in 1983. **Marathon effort –** Geoff Hunt played various matches against teams during his many visits. He played against South Africa twice, winning both matches 3–0, but it was against a five-man provincial team from Natal that he remained on court for 2 hours 45 minutes to win 5–0.

Women's Association: Women's Squash Rackets Association, PO Box 2202, Clareinch 7740, South Africa. Tel: (021) 617825. Founded: 1964. Chairwoman: Ina Osburn; Vice-Chairwoman: Elaine Smaller; Secretary: Val Carris; Treasurer: Janet McClarty

A separate association to promote and run women's squash in South Africa came into being on 8 September 1964 after a meeting at the Wanderers Club in Johannesburg. Since then the women's game has grown in strength and the Association now has 17 affiliated provincial associations under its control.

An interesting feature of recent years is that several top players have held important administrative posts within the Association at the height of their careers – Jill Eckstein was chairwoman from 1975–78 (and South African women's champion in 1975 and 1976) while Kathy Hardy, chairwoman from 1978–80, won the title in 1979. These appointments are an encouraging sign of players contributing to a sport that has served them well.

A number of South African players have distinguished themselves over the years in major championships. In 1969 Marcia Roche (now Cormie) reached the finals of the British Open before losing in straight games to Heather McKay and three years later in the same event, Kathy Malan lost to Heather, also in the final. In 1976 Jill Eckstein reached the finals of the Australian Amateur losing 0–3 to Sue Newman.

A national circuit has now been set up by the Association and is run by various provincial associations, taking in Johannesburg, Pretoria, Durban and Cape Town before culminating in the national championship. The circuit provides for up to almost six weeks of continuous play and is a main event on the international calendar with prize money increasing all the time.

International Championship

1947–48	P. Pentelow	1954	D. Lange
1949	C. Rossouw	1955	S. van Coller
1950–51	No competition	1956–57	D. Lange
1952	V. Lowe	1958	No competition
1953	S. van Coller	1959	E. A. Rous

1960–62	B. Murgatroyd	1975–76	J. Eckstein
1963	F. Marshall (Eng)	1977–78	S. Cogswell (Eng)
1964	C. van Veen	1979	K. Hardy
1965–68	G. Erskine	1980	V. Hoffman (Aus)
1969	M. Roche	1981	S. Cogswell (Eng)
1970–71	J. Eckstein	1982	V. Cardwell (née
1972–73	K. Malan		Hoffman) (Aus)
1974	K. Hardy	1983	S. Cogswell (Eng)

National Championship

1978	V. Bridgens
1979–83	R. Aucamp

SPAIN

Clubs/centres: 12 *Courts:* 50 *Players:* 4000
Association: Real Asociacion Nacional de Squash, Comite Adherido a La Real Federation Espanola de Tenis, C Cuarto No 24, Madrid 16. Founded: 1978. President: Eduardo Gongora; Secretary/Executive Dir: Victor Ruiz

Squash has expanded rapidly in the last two years with a significant increase in court construction especially in Catalonya where two new clubs with five courts each were opened in 1982. There are now clubs in almost all cities but Madrid and Barcelona are the main centres. Although accurate figures are difficult to obtain, it is estimated that the number of players is doubling each year. Competitive activity is also growing rapidly and 1981 saw the introduction of an all-year round events calendar. Although the playing level is still low compared to most of Europe, several promising juniors are coming through.

Representing Spain are (*left to right*): back row – M. Inchausti (national champion), S. Nisto, J. Dominguez (captain), A. Sainz, J. Pellon; front row – J. Pombo, C. Sainz, J. L. de la Guardia

In 1982 in Cardiff the team obtained its best result to date finishing 13 out of 19. Their first major success was in 1981 when they won a six nations tournament in Innsbruck against Austria, Italy, Monaco, Luxembourg and Switzerland.

Sponsorship of tournaments is not developed to any extent but the national team is supported by Indesa, Goudie and Inter footwear.

International Championship

MEN	
1979 F. X. Donnelly (Aus)	**1983** G. Awad (Egy)
1980 R. Norman (NZ)	WOMEN
1981 D. Williams (Aus)	**1983** R. Strauss (Eng)
1982 No competition	

National Championship

MEN	WOMEN
1979 C. Sainz	**1979** R. Ros
1980–82 S. N. Lopez	**1980–82** A. Zamora
1983 M. Inchausti	**1983** P. Armet
1984 J. L. de la Guardia	**1984** M. Bachs

Youngest national finalist: Agustin Adarraga, aged 12, lost 1979 final to Carlo Sainz who was only 16.

SRI LANKA

Courts: 17
Association: Squash Federation of Sri Lanka, c/o Heath and Company (Ceylon) Ltd, PO Box 71, Colombo 2.
Founded: 1980. Secretary: Milroy de Silva

In March 1981 the Federation was accepted and registered by the Ministry of Sports as the controlling body for squash in Sri Lanka. The founder affiliates were the Gymkhana Club (the leading squash playing club in Sri Lanka with a playing membership of 125–150), Sri Lanka Air Force (25–35), Sri Lanka Army (10–15), Sri Lanka Navy (15–20), plus one school (15–25). There are a total of 17 courts on the island, not including hotels (six courts) which cater for their own guests. National championships for men and women and in many categories have been introduced with the number of entries rising each year.

Teams were entered in the 1981 and 1984 Asian Championships, finishing 10th out of 14 on the first occasion which was very creditable considering that prior to the event none of the team had been able to play on a court with a wooden floor or glass back as all courts in Sri Lanka at that time had cement floors. On the second occasion in 1984 they were sixth out of seven competing nations.

SWEDEN

Clubs/centres: 85   *Courts:* 450   *Players:* 75 000
Association: Svenska Squashforbundet, Idrottens Hus, 123 87 Farsta. Founded: 1965. President: Henrik Malm; Secretary/Executive Dir: Otto Zethelius

Sweden's first court was built in 1929 in a private house in Stockholm. In the same city in 1937 two

Sweden, in a short space of time, has produced a number of world class players and one of the best is the flamboyant Lars Kvant. *Robin Eley Jones*

three-court centres were opened to the public. One centre was closed within two years although one of the courts is still in existence and used as a dancehall. The other centre is still operating successfully. In 1942 the Swedish Air Force built two courts and the Swedish Navy one for their members. Nothing further happened until 1959 when a new court was opened in Linkoping, which was the first court outside Stockholm. In 1967 the boom really started and in the following eight years a vast number of clubs and courts were erected. Since then the sport has continued to grow but at a much slower pace.

Internationally Sweden continues to improve and has now won the European team championship title on two occasions. With several young players regularly competing on the professional circuit, national standards are expected to rise.

Squash was first mentioned on Swedish television in 1969 when the Swedish SRA joined the Sports Federation. Since then coverage has been limited to a couple of minutes on two or three occasions per year.

International Championship

MEN	
1968–69 J. D. Ward (Eng)	**1980–81** L. Kvant
1970 P. G. Kirton (Eng)	**1982** M. Saad (Egy)
1971 P. E. Millman (Eng)	**1983** J. Soderberg
1972–73 H. Jahan (Pak)	
1974 Mohibullah Khan (Pak)	WOMEN
1975 No competition	**1976** T. Johnson (Eng)
1976 D. Scott (SA)	**1977** R. Blackwood (NZ)
1977 M. Hellstrom	**1978** No competition
1978–79 M. Awad (Egy)	**1979–81** A. Samuelsson
	1982 T. Myllymiemi (Fin)
	1983 V. Cardwell (Aus)

National Championship

MEN		
1937 C. Dickerson	**1967** B. Ahlstrom	
1938 T. Wissnell	**1968** R. Jonasson	
1939–42 L. Johncke	**1969** B. Ahlstrom	
1943 G. Lundgren	**1970** B. Almkvist	
1944–45 A. Froander	**1971–72** P. Stiller	
1946 T. Johacke	**1973** T. Tovar	
1947 G. Westerlund	**1974** M. Nathanson	
1948 E. Froander	**1975** M. Hellstrom	
1949 A. Froander	**1976** T. Tovar	
1950–51 E. Froander	**1977–80** L. Kvant	
1952–54 B. Jacobsson	**1981** M. Awad (Egy)	
1955 U. Jacobsson	**1982** L. Kvant	
1956 B. Salen	**1983** J. Soderberg	
1957 U. Jacobsson		
1958 B. Jacobsson	WOMEN	
1959 R. Jonasson	**1973** P. Skoog	
1960 B. Jacobsson	**1974** C. Ehinger	
1961 U. Jacobsson	**1975** M. Wicklen	
1962 R. Jonasson	**1976–77** K. Due Boje	
1963 B. Jacobsson	**1978** T. Dahl	
1964 R. Jonasson	**1979–80** K. Due Boje	
1965 B. Ahlstrom	**1981** A. Samuelsson	
1966 R. Jonasson	**1982** E. Lundquist	
	1983 L. Friden	

SWITZERLAND

Clubs/centres: 115 *Courts:* 400 *Players:* 120 000
Association: Swiss Squash Rackets Association, Obere Zollgasse 75, Postfach 3, CH–3072 Ostermundigen, Bern. Founded: 1973. President: David Burton; Secretary/Executive Dir: Cristina Camporovo

In 1970 only one court existed in Switzerland on which an estimated 150 people played! Despite the foundation of the Swiss SRA in 1973, by 1977 there were still only seven clubs with 19 courts and around 2000 participants. Since then the growth has been dramatic – by the beginning of the 1980s there were 58 clubs, 160 courts and 3500 players and in the last three years the number of clubs has doubled and the players have more than trebled. In 1983 the first three-glass-wall court was opened at the Vitis Centre near Zurich.

Television coverage and sponsorship are still in their infancy but Dunlop, Grays and Patrick have all invested money.

International Championship

MEN	
1973–74 J. N. C. Easter (Eng)	**1980** M. Saad (Egy)
	1981 D. Williams (Aus)
1975 P. S. Kenyon (Eng)	**1982** P. Verow (Eng)
1976–77 J. C. A. Leslie (Eng)	**1983** D. Williams (Aus)
1978 F. X. Donnelly (Aus)	WOMEN
1979 D. Williams (Aus)	**1982** M. Le Moignan (Eng)
	1983 V. Cardwell (Aus)

National Championship

MEN	WOMEN
1975 P. Kubil	**1975–77** N. Henderson
1976 X. Notari	**1978** S. Sandmeier
1977–78 K. Fleishmann	**1979** N. Henderson
1979–81 W. Zollinger	**1980** H. Fletcher
1982 I. Schnider	**1981** N. Henderson
	1982 H. Fletcher
	1983 B. Hartman

THAILAND

Courts: 29
Association: Thailand Squash Rackets Association, 108 Soi Attavimol, Rajaprarop Road, Bangkok 4. Founded: 1979. President: Dr Kalaya Isarasaena; Secretary: Mrs Auranuch Issarangkul

The year 1983 was a period of unspectacular but steady progress for squash in Thailand, during which, at last, clear signs began to emerge that squash is expanding from the traditional private club environment into a more public status. This transition is exemplified by the growth of squash courts and the wider participation in the Thailand SRA national team leagues.

During the year, eleven squash courts were constructed, two each at the Oriental and Hilton Hotels, one at the Dusit Thani Hotel, four at the Polo Club, and two at the new Shell Building. Further courts are planned or under construction at several other locations, including the Peninsula Hotel. As far as can be estimated, this brings the total number of squash courts available in Bangkok at the present time to 29, which is a significant increase on just a few short years ago when only 8 courts could be mustered throughout the entire city.

Unfortunately, in several cases, the design and measurements of the courts do not meet accepted international and competition standards. The TSRA, through its committee and membership, is always ready and willing to provide advice and guidance in such matters, and it is a pity that in the instances mentioned (mainly those courts constructed in hotels) the assistance of the TSRA was not sought earlier.

Such problems do not exist, however, with the two superb new air-conditioned courts at the Shell Building which were officially opened in September 1983 by Dr P. J. Merki of Shell, in the presence of the then TSRA president, Dr Chirayu Issarangkun na Ayudhya and a large gathering of squash enthusiasts. Although built essentially for the Shell Staff Sports Club, Dr Merki has offered the use of these courts to the TSRA for competitions, matches and coaching purposes. This is an important development for the TSRA which, hitherto, has had no courts at its disposal in this way.

National Championship

USA

Clubs/centres: 187 *Courts:* 3000 *Players:* 400 000
Association: United States Squash Rackets Association, 211 Ford Road, Bala-Cynwyd, Pennsylvania 19004. Founded: 1920. President: John F. Herrick; Secretary/Executive Dir: Hamilton F. Biggar III

In 1975 the USSRA had only 650 members, but the total is now close to 7000 with the number of players increasing by about 5 per cent per annum. The 'hardball' variation is the predominant game in the USA and there are still only nine 'international' courts of which only six are used regularly. However, in a development which could eventually have far reaching implications, the USSRA has adopted the international 'softball' code officially for their summer game. This means the use of 'softballs', USSRA rackets and the ISRF 'softball' rules.

The first National Soft Ball Championships were held in Baltimore in September 1983 and squash is now officially an all-year round sport in the United States.

The 70+ hardball game continues to grow steadily and the estimated number of regular league players is put at around 250 000. The professional side, administered through the World Professional Squash Association, has developed a very successful tournament tour. Sharif Khan's dominance in the North American Open has been broken by Mike Desaulniers and Mark Talbot and Talbot himself has had to make way for world Open 'softball' champion Jahangir Khan who has the distinction of holding the two main titles in two codes of squash at the same time. The USA were especially pleased with its 'softball' team which finished seventh in the ISRF World Team Championships in Stockholm in 1981 and in New Zealand in 1983.

Sponsorship is flourishing throughout the country with Coca Cola, Insilco, and many drinks and sportswear manufacturers (Slazenger, Dunlop, etc.) supporting the game. Television coverage is virtually nil as the television companies feel that the viewing market is too small.

North American Open Championship

Amateur Championship

National Championship

Kenton Jernigan (*right*), aged 18, in a match against Joseph Swain on his way to becoming the youngest-ever finalist in the USSRA men's singles championship in 1982. Jernigan lost 3–1 to John Nimick in the finals

1956–59 B. Constable (née Howe)	**1971** C. Thesieres
	1972 N. Moyer
1960–63 M. Varner	**1973–74** G. Spruance
1964 A. Wetzel	**1975** G. Akabane
1965 J. Davenport	**1976–78** G. Spruance
1966–68 B. Meade	**1979** H. McKay (Aus)
1969 J. Davenport	**1980–81** B. Maltby
1970 N. Moyer	**1982–83** A. McConnell

VENEZUELA

Association: Venezuela Squash Rackets Association, Apartado De Altamira 68158, Caracas 1062–A. Founded: 1982. Secretary: Robert L. Jones

WALES

Clubs/centres: 112   *Courts:* 298   *Players:* 155 000
Association: Welsh Squash Rackets Federation, Trienna, Quarella, Bridgend, Mid Glamorgan. Tel: 0656 56752. Founded: 1947. President: Stan Williams; Secretary/Executive Dir: Christine Barton

Sponsorship is very difficult to obtain at present but the Federation have a three-year agreement with Dunlop to supply kits and financial assistance to the national teams. Individual events have a history of being backed by local companies or national concerns on a one-off basis. The Sports Council for Wales assists with funds for training of international squads, coaches and officials.

Television coverage is virtually non-existent despite facilities at the National Sports Centre in Cardiff which lend themselves admirably to the small screen. There was some encouragement when part of the action was shown from the European Championships in Cardiff in 1982.

International Championship

MEN	
1948 P. E. Hare	**1962** J. L. Ramsden
1949 A. A. T. Seymour-Haydon	**1963** D. Barrow (SA)
1950 D. J. Townsend	**1964** J. L. Ramsden
1951–53 A. A. T. Seymour-Haydon	**1965** J. Barrington (GB & Ire)
1954 P. M. H. Robinson	**1966** M. W. Corby (Eng)
1955 S. J. S. Lam (Ind)	**1967** A. M. H. Hill (Eng)
1956 Capt. M. J. Perkins	**1968** M. W. Corby (Eng)
1957 D. B. Hughes	**1969** P. N. Ayton (Eng)
1958 R. S. Bourne	**1970** M. Yasin (Pak)
1959 L. I. Verney	**1971–73** H. Jahan (Pak)
1960 R. S. Bourne	**1974** Torsam Khan (Pak)
1961 T. Pickering	**1975** S. H. Courtney (Eng)
	1976 B. Brownlee (NZ)
	1977 S. H. Courtney (Eng)

1978–79 J. C. A. Leslie (Eng)	1963–64 A. Craven-Smith
1980 P. Verow (Eng)	1965 S. Macintosh
1981 M. Helal (Egy)	1966 A. Craven-Smith
1982 G. Williams (Eng)	1967 B. Johnson (Aus)
1983 A. Allouba (Eng)	1968 P. Goodall
	1969 A. M. Price
	1970 J. Wilson
WOMEN	1971 J. Barham
1948 S. Speight	1972 S. Newman (Aus)
1949 A. Bates	1973 J. Wilson
1950–51 A. Isaac	1974–75 T. Lawes
1952–53 S. Speight	1976 A. Smith
1954 R. Walsh	1977 J. Ashton
1955–56 S. Speight	1978 A. Smith
1957 H. Bond	1979 F. Hargreaves
1958–59 R. Campion	1980 A. Smith
1960 J. Gidwell	1981 D. Murray
1961 B. Whitehead	1982 S. Washer
1962 H. Blundell (Aus)	1983 L. Opie

National Championship

MEN	WOMEN
1974 I. Carlisle	1974 B. Davies
1975 D. Jude	1975–76 J. Ganz
1976 I. Carlisle	1977 B. Davies
1977–79 D. Jude	1978 S. Washer
1980 P. J. Wilson	1979–82 D. Murray
1981–82 T. Salisbury	1983 D. Turnbull
1983 C. Jones	

Most international appearances: *Men:* R. A. Dolman 68, *Women:* D. Murray 54. **Longest international career:** *Men:* R. A. Dolman 1966–80. *Women:* P. Connies-Laing 1954–76. R. Campion 1947–69. **Youngest and Oldest:** Glyn Evans, aged 30 and Adrian Davies, 15, both won their first caps for Wales at the 1982 European Championships.

ZAMBIA

Clubs/centres: 15   *Courts:* 32   *Players:* 2500
Association: Zambia Squash Rackets Association, PO Box 20919, Kitwe. Founded: 1964. Chairman: Crawford Masson; Secretary: Mrs Heather Belshaw

ZIMBABWE

Courts: 160   *Players:* 3000
Association: Squash Rackets Association of Zimbabwe, PO Box 8383, Causeway, Harare. Founded: 1956. President: Johannes Andersen; Secretary/Executive Dir: Mrs Anne Smith

The first squash court in South Africa was built in Bulawayo in 1898 and Salisbury's first was erected in 1924. The first inter-town tournament was played in 1930 between Salisbury and Bulawayo and the first national men's championships were held in 1932 at Bulawayo.

Further courts were erected at RAF stations during the Second World War but the growth of the game was slow until the late 1960s. At that time world-class players such as Jonah Barrington and Geoff Hunt visited the country and enthusiasm for the sport started to spread.

During the years of the Federation of Rhodesia and Nyasaland, 1953 to 1962, Southern Rhodesia, as it was then, established squash ties with other African countries. The first national team played in the Transvaal in 1952. The first South African Inter-Provincial Tournament, now known as the Jarvis Cup, was held in 1960 and Salisbury hosted the event in 1964, 1968 and 1972. A court with capacity for 150 spectators was built in Salisbury in 1966 and, soon after, the first Test Match between South Africa and Australia was played there.

Interest grew so much in the late sixties that a court was erected in Salisbury in 1974 and 850 people watched a match between Hunt and Barrington played there. This is still believed to be the largest spectator capacity of any permanent court in the world. The court is sunk so that the top of the front wall is at ground level. It has a glass backwall with seats up to and above ground level behind it. The sidewalls are winged back above the court lines and seats may be placed at the sides and behind the front wall at ground level.

Squash is continuing to grow in popularity with over 160 courts throughout the country. The largest centre is the Harare Sports Club which has eight courts and 450 members.

National Championship

MEN		WOMEN	
1932 A. Howard	1975–76 T. Tarr	1952–54 K. Thomas	
1933 T. H. Cooke	1977 R. Plumstead	1955 No competition	
1934 B. R. W. Johnson	1978–79 D. Scott	1956 K. Thomas	
1935–36 G. R. Johnson	1980 T. Wilkinson	1957 No competition	
1937–38 B. R. W. Johnson	1981–82 N. Ingledew	1958 K. Thomas	
1939–46 No competition		1959 D. Warburton	
1947 C. V. Irvine	WOMEN	1960–62 No competition	
1948 H. Downey		1963–64 G. Warburton	
1949 C. V. Irvine		1965–66 G. Erskine	
1950 D. L. Hodgson		1967 J. Warburton	
1951 G. Mennie		1968 G. Erskine	
1952–54 J. W. Field		1969 J. Donaldson	
1955 C. J. English		1970–71 G. Erskine	
1956 B. D. M. Sutter		1972 A. Papenfus	
1957–58 A. W. Mallett		1973–77 G. Erskine	
1959–60 E. Cary		1978 S. Paton	
1961 D. G. Warburton		1979 S. Pichanick	
1962 J. B. H. Castle		1980 P. Haig	
1963 D. G. Warburton		1981–82 S. Bromhead	
1964 I. Dowdeswell			
1965 T. N. Erskine			
1966 R. D. Haddad			
1967–69 I. Dowdeswell			
1970–73 S. Sherren			
1974 D. G. Warburton			

7 Tournament players

Maqsood Ahmed (Pak)

Born Peshawar 30 August 1957. Lives in Pakistan. Maqsood started playing in 1968 and turned professional in 1978. A very consistent player, Maqsood has been in the world's top ten for a number of years, although he is often under-rated because of the success of fellow-countrymen such as Zaman, Alauddin, Mohibullah and Jahangir. In 1977 Maqsood became the first player to win the Pakistani Amateur and Open titles in the same year. His most memorable victory came when he beat Geoff Hunt of Australia in the final of the 1981 Swiss Masters although his win in the individual event of the ISRF World Championship in 1977 ranks almost as high. He reached the last four in the 1979 World Open in Canada and just failed to make the final when he lost in five to Zaman. Maqsood also knows the agonies of defeat since he suffered the indignity of being beaten, when ranked number 4 in the world, 9–0, 9–0, 9–0 by Jahangir Khan in the 1982 ISPA Championship final in Sheffield.

Major achievements (winner unless stated otherwise): 1972 Pakistan Junior Championship (r/u); 1973 Pakistan Junior Championship; 1976 Pakistan Amateur, Malaysian Open, Singapore Open; 1977 Pakistan Amateur and Open, ISRF World Individual Championship, British Amateur (r/u); 1979 British Open (s/f), ISPA Championship (s/f), World Open (s/f); 1980 British Open (q/f), German Masters (s/f), Pakistan Open (s/f), ISPA Championship (s/f); 1981 British Open (q/f), ISPA Championship (s/f), Swiss Masters; 1982 World Open (q/f), ISPA Championship (r/u); 1983 World Open (q/f); 1984 Asian Individual Championship (r/u), British Open (q/f). Represented Pakistan in the 1976, 1977 and 1983 ISRF World Team Championships, 1981 and 1984 Asian Team Championships.

Gogi Alauddin (Pak)

Born 1950. Lives in Lahore. Son of Ahmed Din and uncle of bright new prospect Sohail Qaiser who is another in the long line of exceptionally talented players produced by Pakistan in recent years. Gogi has always had tremendous ability to move an opponent around the court, teasing with delicate drop

Gogi Alauddin of Pakistan – one of the founding fathers of modern tournament squash. *Robin Eley Jones*

shots and precision lobs. His control of the ball is legendary and his appearance as a touring player in this country in the early seventies makes him one of the founding fathers of tournament squash as it is known today. His thin spidery frame earned him the nickname of the 'pipe cleaner' but anyone who thought Gogi would snap easily was usually in for a shock. Gogi's ability never quite brought him the rewards that he deserved – perhaps it was a slight lack of confidence on his part at the vital time that robbed him of many successes. Why Gogi should have this weakness is difficult to assess since he was and is still rated a most difficult player to beat. Even now in the latter part of his career when he is not training or competing on a regular basis he is capable of beating most players in the top ten.

Major achievements (winner unless stated otherwise): 1967 Pakistan Junior Championship; 1970 British Amateur; 1971 British Open (s/f), British Amateur, South of England Open, Essex Open, Midland Open, Middlesex Open, Surrey Open, North-West Open; 1972 British Open (r/u), Danish Open, North-West Open; 1974 British Open (r/u), Irish Open, British Caledonian–Yellow Dot Grand Prix (3rd); 1975 British and World Opens (combined event) (s/f), Malaysian Open, Singapore Open; 1976 PIA World Series, German Open, Victorian Open (r/u); 1977

World Open (s/f), British Open (q/f), German Open; 1978 British Open (q/f); 1979 World Open (q/f), British Open (q/f); 1980 World Open (q/f).

Gamal Awad (Egy)

Born Alexandria 9 August 1955. Lives in Dartford, Kent. Gamal is Egyptian number one and the younger brother of fellow squash professional, the world-ranked Mohammed Awad. He has well earned his nickname of the 'grasshopper' or 'rubber man' due to his amazing powers of reflex shots and retrieval which often involves diving full-length to return the ball. He twice won the British Amateur Championship (1977 and 1978), and the year he beat Maqsood Ahmed of Pakistan at Wembley (1977) is still remembered as one of the most spectacular finals of all time. However he is probably best known for his exploits in a relatively new event, the World Masters. In 1980 he beat Geoff Hunt in the first round at Wembley and reached the final where he lost to Mohibullah Khan. In 1982 he defeated Hiddy Jahan in the semi-final but again finished runner-up, this time to Jahangir Khan. He has given Jahangir many problems and has striven hard to match the brilliant Pakistani. His almost fanatical attempts to beat Jahangir came to a head in the 1983 Patrick Chichester Festival final when the pair played for 2 hours 46 minutes, a world record for any professional match. Gamal played probably the best squash of his career and was close to beating Jahangir. The first game took 71 minutes, also a record, and the Pakistani eventually won 9–10, 9–5, 9–7, 9–2.

Major achievements (winner unless stated otherwise): 1966 Egyptian Under-13 Championship (r/u); 1968 Egyptian Under-13 Championship; 1973 Egyptian Under-19 Championship; 1976 Egyptian Championship; 1977 British Amateur, World Amateur (s/f), Egyptian Championship; 1978 British Amateur, Netherlands Open, Nigerian Open; 1979 Guernsey Open; 1980 British Open (s/f), World Open (q/f), World Masters (r/u), Irish Open (r/u), Prodorite Invitation (r/u), Welsh Open (r/u); 1981 ISPA Championship (s/f), World Open (q/f); 1982 World Open (q/f), World Masters (r/u), German Open; 1983 ISPA Championship (s/f), Chichester Festival (r/u), British Open (r/u), World Open (s/f). Represented Egypt in the 1976 and 1977 ISRF World Team Championships.

Mohammed Awad (Egy)

Born Alexandria 5 February 1949. A player who is somewhat overshadowed by his younger brother Gamal but has had considerable success in Europe. Mohammed finished 1982 just outside the world's top 20 and in the 1982/3 British Open reached the last 16, only to have to retire from his match against Dean Williams due to a thigh injury. His interest outside squash is football.

Major achievements (winner unless stated otherwise): 1972 Egyptian Championship (r/u); 1975 Egyptian Championship (r/u); 1977 Swedish Open; 1978 Swedish Open, Finnish Open; 1979 Danish Open; 1980 Italian Open. Represented Egypt in the 1976 and 1977 ISRF World Team Championships.

Ali Aziz (Egy)

Born Alexandria 1 October 1947. Lives in West Germany. Ali started playing in Cairo aged 13 and turned professional in 1957. He is now one of the most experienced and consistent players on the circuit, although still seeking his first major title win. He considers his best achievement was finishing runner-up to Kevin Shawcross of Australia in the 1975 British Amateur Championship. Ali rates his most difficult opponent as Qamar Zaman of Pakistan 'because of his deception'. Once ranked as high as number 10 in the world, Ali does not do the training that is now required to keep at the top but is a brave and resilient opponent for all that. His dislikes about squash: 'unorganised tournaments'. His interests outside squash are fishing and cooking.

Major achievements (winner unless stated otherwise): 1973 Egyptian Amateur and Open; 1974 Danish Open; 1975 British Amateur (r/u); 1982 Malaysian Open. Represented Egypt in the 1981 ISRF World Team Championship.

Craig Blackwood (NZ)

Born Whanagarei 28 May 1956. Lives in Auckland. Craig started playing at the age of 11 in the Auckland North Shore Club but only broke into world rankings in the 1981/2 season. His sister Robyn is ranked among the world's top 10 women. Craig is a former New Zealand Under-23 champion and was a quarter-finalist in the British Amateur Championship in 1977. He first represented his country in the Hashim Khan Team Trophy event in Pakistan in 1976. His interests outside squash include music and reading.

Major achievements (winner unless stated otherwise): 1974 New Zealand Junior Championship (r/u); 1975 New Zealand Under-23 Championship; 1976 British Amateur (q/f); 1978 New Zealand Under-23 Championship; 1980 East of England Championship; 1981 ISRF World Individual Championship (r/u), Scottish Open. Represented New Zealand in 1974 as a junior and then at senior level in the 1976 Hashim Khan Team Trophy, 1978 tour of Australia, 1979 and 1981 ISRF World Team Championships.

Steven Bowditch (Aus)

Born Darwin 9 August 1955. Lives in West Germany. Steve started playing in 1966 and turned professional in 1977. His early progress in the professional ranks was hampered by a back injury. But he is now one of the most exciting, adventurous and unpredictable players in the world with a remarkable range of shots. He does not train regularly, but when he does a normal day might consist of two hours on court plus long-distance running. He rates Jahangir Khan as his most difficult opponent because 'he nullifies my percentage of winning shots'. His favourite shot is the cross-court drop to the nick from the back of the court. He has strong views on how squash should be changed and would like to see the tin lowered by up to 6 inches (15 cm) and a new time-out system introduced. He thinks television coverage could be improved by showing highlights in slow-motion replay and employing better commentators. His interests outside squash are music, cross-country, skiing and golf.

Major achievements (winner unless stated otherwise): 1971 Darwin Open; 1973 New South Wales Junior Championship, Australian Junior Championship (r/u); 1976 Victorian Amateur; 1977 South Australian Open (r/u), Northern Territory Open (r/u); 1978 Guernsey Open; 1979 Merseyside Open; 1980 ISPA Championship (q/f), German Open (r/u), Prodorite Invitation (s/f); 1981 ISRF World Individual Championship. Represented Northern Territory as a junior from 1970–73, Australia in the 1974 junior tour of New Zealand, Northern Territory (as captain) in the 1976 Australian Team Championship, 1978 Hashim Khan Team Trophy, 1981 ISRF World Team Championship.

Gawain Briars (Eng)

Born Witney, Oxfordshire 4 April 1958. Lives in Nottingham. First played at Greshams School in 1970 and turned professional in 1979. A 6 ft 4 in (1·93 m) attacking player, he is now established as one of England's leading players and in the world's top 10. Among the top players he has beaten are Qamar Zaman, Hiddy Jahan and Maqsood Ahmed. The major influences on his career have been his parents and coach Malcolm Willstrop. Gawain trains four hours every day, including running, weight training and court practice. He considers that Geoff Hunt was his most difficult opponent because Hunt's 'complete preparation' enabled him to 'close down' the game and seek out his opponent's smallest weakness. He doesn't have a favourite shot and gets as much satisfaction from hitting a good length as pulling off a delicate drop. His longest match was when he lost 7–9 in the fifth to Jonny Leslie in the 1979 British Amateur after 1 hour 40 minutes. His most memorable match he rates as being when he lost 2–3 to Geoff Hunt in the final of the 1981 South African Open. Gawain would not like to see the game changed but if

forced he would advocate lowering the tin slightly. Television coverage he feels could be improved by experiments with camera angles, colour of walls and balls. His main dislikes about squash are what he calls the elements of 'back-biting' in the game which occurs because of the small number of players and the intimate nature of the professional circuit. His interests outside squash are socialising with close friends, light tennis, golf and swimming.

Major achievements (winner unless stated otherwise): 1975 British Under-19 Closed Championship, British Under-19 Open (Drysdale Cup) Championship; 1976 East of England Championship, British Under-19 Closed Championship, British Under-19 Open (Drysdale Cup) Championship, British Under-23 Closed Championship; 1977 East of England Championship, Dutch Open (r/u), North of England Open (r/u), British Amateur (q/f), British Under-23 Closed Championship; 1978 Australian Amateur, North of England Open, Midland Championship; 1979 British Closed, Mercia Open; 1980 British Closed (r/u), British Under-23 Closed Championship; 1981 British Closed (r/u); 1982 British Closed, ISPA Championship (s/f); 1983 Pakistan Open (s/f), Chichester Festival (s/f); 1984 French Open (q/f), British Open (q/f). Represented England and Great Britain 34 times since 1977 in the ISRF World Team and European Team Championships and home internationals.

Glen Thomas Brumby (Aus)

Born Maylands, South Australia 11 May 1960. Lives in West Germany. During the 1982/3 season injury forced Glen to reduce his commitment to the circuit, a setback that could not have come at a worse time as he had consolidated his place among the world's top 10 players. Although still very young he seems to have been around a long time, an impression partly due to his distinguished career as a junior when he twice won the Australian junior title. As a junior he had one of his most famous victories beating a certain Jahangir Khan in the semi-final of the 1977 Drysdale Cup (British Under-19 Open). Glen always adhered to a very strict training schedule and this coupled with the enormous amount of competition squash he has played in a comparatively short time has taken its toll on his body. His longest match was 1 hour 45 minutes against Roland Watson of South Africa in the quarter-final of the 1981 Irish Open and he regards his most memorable victory as one over Hiddy Jahan, then ranked number 2 in the world in the 1982 Lookers Masters. He would like to see balls and courts standardised throughout the game and believes that television coverage would be enhanced by better match commentary and the use of a specially-designed venue that conveyed the true atmosphere of the sport. His interests outside squash are chess, world events and music.

Major achievements (winner unless stated otherwise): 1975 Australian Under-16 Championship; 1976 Australian Junior Championship, South Australian Under-21 Championship; 1977 Australian Junior Championship, South Australian Under-21 Championship, British Under-19 Open (Drysdale Cup) Championship, South Australian Championship (r/u); 1978 British Under-19 Open (Drysdale Cup) Championship, Scottish Open, Belgian Open, French Open; 1979 New South Wales Open; 1980 South Australian Open, Western Cape Open; 1981 British Open (s/f), Australian Open (s/f), South African Open (s/f), British Under-23 Open Championship (r/u); 1982 World Open (s/f). Represented Australia in the 1978 Under-23 tour, 1978 World Junior Team Championship, 1979 and 1981 ISRF World Team Championships.

Stuart Davenport (NZ)

Born Auckland 21 September 1962. Lives in Beaconsfield, England. Stuart is a very bright prospect and at the height of 6 ft 4 in (1·93 m) he rivals Gawain Briars as one of the tallest players on the circuit. He is a very crisp striker of the ball, a fine volleyer and has a range of front court deceptive shots. He really came to the fore as a professional during the latter part of 1982 when he reached the last 16 of the World Open. This promise was fulfilled in 1983 with a string of high quality and consistent performances, the highlights of which were in reaching the semi-finals of the ISRF World Individual Championship in New Zealand and the World Open in Germany. In the ISRF event he won the third place play-off, defeating England number 1 Hiddy Jahan and in Munich he produced an even better display to knock out the number 2 seed Qamar Zaman of Pakistan at the quarter-final stage.

Major achievements (winner unless stated otherwise): 1979 British Under-19 Open (Drysdale Cup) Championship; 1981 British Under-23 Open Championship; 1982 reached last 16 of World Open; 1983 ISPA Championship (s/f), Irish Open (s/f), British Open (q/f), ISRF World Individual Championship (s/f), World Open (s/f); 1984 British Under-23 Open Championship (r/u); French Open (q/f), British Open (s/f). Represented New Zealand in the 1983 ISRF World Team Championship.

Christopher Simon Dittmar (Aus)

Born Alberton, South Australia 16 January 1964. Lives in Nottingham. Chris first experienced squash at the age of three and has subsequently developed into a hard-hitting, high promising youngster who many see as Geoff Hunt's ultimate successor as the Australian number 1. This view has gained strength after Dittmar's outstanding achievement of finishing runner-up in the 1983 World Open. He had a distinguished junior career winning the Australian junior title in 1981 and finishing as runner-up in the 1980 and 1982 World Junior Championships. He also performed usefully in rugby and Australian rules football before deciding to concentrate on squash. Chris has no particular schedule but he does train every day. He finds all the top players difficult to play but singles out his compatriot Dean Williams as being most difficult

Chris Dittmar of Australia – representing the 'post-Hunt' era of Australian squash and at 19 already runner-up in the World Open. *Robin Eley Jones*

because 'I play him more than most and you have to cover every millimetre of the court in every rally'. His longest matches he recalls were in the 1980 ISRF World Junior Championships when his quarter-final against Christy Willstrop of England and his semi-final with Stuart Davenport of New Zealand both lasted two hours. His favourite shot is the volleyed drop on either side of the court. If any changes were to be made he would like to see 'turning' banned completely to 'do away with the obvious dangerous situations'. His interests outside squash are Australian football, cricket and music.

Major achievements (winner unless stated otherwise): 1980 ISRF World Junior Individual Championship (r/u); 1981 Australian Junior Championship, British Under-19 Open (Drysdale Cup) Championship, Midland Open, ISRF World Junior Individual Championship (r/u); 1982 reached last 16 in the World Open; 1983 British Open (q/f), World Open (r/u). Represented Australia as a junior in 1980, as junior captain at the 1981 and senior level at the 1983 ISRF World Team Championships.

Andrew Dwyer (Eng)

Born 2 November 1956. Lives in Hove, Sussex. Andrew's squash career began at Withdean, Brighton and his career was strongly influenced by Peter Sice and British international Phillip Ayton. He won recognition with England as a junior, and in 1977 graduated to the senior team since when he has represented his country on 43 occasions in the European and Home International Championships. His best achievement undoubtedly was being a member of the Great Britain team which won the 1979 ISRF World Team Championship, the last world amateur championship before the game went open.

Rod George (Aus)

Born Perth 1954. Now based as club professional in West Germany. He has been around the world circuit for some time without claiming any major titles, and was ranked 25 in the world at the end of the 1982/3 season after victories over Magdi Saad and Mohammed Ali Somjee in France. His interests outside squash are reading and swimming.

Fahim Gul (Pak)

Born Rawalpindi 12 August 1956. He is the brother of Rahim and Jamshed, both world-ranked professional players. He had a fine season in 1982/3 when he won the Lifting Gear Tournament in Leigh, England by beating Roland Watson, Steve Bateman and Daulat Khan, reached the last 16 at the Chichester Festival when he beat Zahir Hussein Khan and John Easter before losing to world ranked number 6 Maqsood Ahmed in five games.

Moussa Helal (Egy)

Born Cairo 30 November 1949. Lives in Warley, West Midlands. Moussa won the Egyptian Amateur title in 1975 but, despite being in or around the world's top 30 ever since, he has never figured in the latter stages of any of the major tournaments. However, he has a lively and likeable personality which has won him many friends on the circuit. Since he now spends six or seven hours per day coaching this leaves him little time for training so he does not expect to make further progress up the ranking. He dislikes swearing and arguing on court and feels that there should be stricter rulings and penalties for misbehaviour and dangerous play. He regards his most memorable match as losing 9–10 in the fifth to Jonny Leslie of England in the British Open in 1977 (Leslie went on to the quarter-finals). His most amusing memory is of his longest match against Mohammed Mustafa in Egypt: 'The match lasted well over two hours and the audience all went home. It finished when Mustafa went down with cramp for the umpteenth time and the referee counted 1, 2, 3, out and awarded me the match on a knock-out.' He considers television coverage could be improved by more often using a camera in the tin to see the game from the front of the court.

Major achievements (winner unless stated otherwise): 1975 Egyptian Amateur; 1976 British Open Plate; 1977 British Open Plate (r/u), Exeter Invitation; 1978 Exeter Invitation; 1980 British Open Plate, Exeter Invitation, Welsh Open, North of England Open, Mercia Open.

Ricki Hill (Aus)

Born Melbourne, Australia 7 September 1960. Ricki lives in London and is another in the seemingly never-ending list of talented youngsters produced by Australia in recent years. He moved to England to improve his game by more regular competition. He also places great emphasis on physical fitness and trains six days every week. Ricki regards Hiddy Jahan as his most difficult opponent 'because of his ability to change the pace and direction of the ball'. His most memorable matches were those against Jahangir Khan in the 1981 French and Irish Opens, both of which he lost 3–1. He would like scoring in squash to be changed to the 'American system' or, if left as it is, a player should only have one service. He believes that more 'close-ups' and player interviews would improve the standard of television coverage. He remembers his most amusing and embarrassing incident as removing his tracksuit pants on court during the French Open

Gamal Awad on court at Stockton-on-Tees for the Stockton Open, one of the oldest professional events on the British circuit. *Robin Eley Jones*

to find he was not wearing shorts! His interests outside squash are classical music and opera.

Major achievements (winner unless stated otherwise): 1980 World Open Plate, Wimbledon Cup; 1981 Mercia Open. Represented Australia in the 1978 ISRF World Junior Team Championship in Sweden when he won all five matches, 1983 ISRF World Team Championship.

Hiddy Jahan (Eng)

Born Quetta, Pakistan 15 March 1950. Lives in Wallington, Surrey. Became a British citizen in 1983 having lived in the UK for ten years, and is now eligible to represent England. He made his first appearance for England in the 1983 ISRF World Team Championship when England were runners-up to Pakistan. Hiddy is one of the most consistent and spectacular players of modern times striking the ball with ferocious power and earning himself the reputation of being the hardest hitter in the game.

His style of play has won worldwide acclaim and it is a pity that he has not been able to win either the World Open or British Open, a distinction which his performances and dedication would have earned him had he been playing in an era without the presence of a Geoff Hunt or Qamar Zaman. However, he has maintained his place in the world's top 5 for a decade, an achievement in itself, which is a tribute to his supreme talent.

Since the 1971/2 season he has only twice failed to reach the quarter-finals of the British Open and one was in 1976/7 when, like all other Pakistanis, because of the boycott he did not take part. He has figured in the semi-finals four times and in 1982 was runner-up to Jahangir Khan.

The World Open was inaugurated in 1975/6 and in that he has reached the quarter-finals each time, apart from 1983, and on three of those occasions moved on to the semis. Hiddy's explosive skills with the racket have frequently been matched with a fiery temperament, an aspect of his character that has undoubtedly lost him some matches he should have won. An extreme example of this was his disqualification from the 1983 Chichester Festival after a clash with the referee. This made him only one of two players of recent years (the other was Ali Aziz) who have paid the ultimate penalty for losing control of feelings. However, in contrast to this momentary lapse from grace, Hiddy is also known and respected for his work in furthering the progress of the professional game. For several years he was chairman of the International Squash Players Association. He still trains three hours

a day, six days a week and on current form looks capable of being a world force for a long time to come. He regards Gogi Alauddin as his most difficult opponent because 'he is one of the most clever players and is a great reader of the game'.

Not surprisingly he rates the forehand cross-court drive as his favourite shot and those who wonder how he does this with an apparent flick of the wrist should know that Hiddy developed his wrist skills and strength by playing badminton in his younger days.

He dislikes all the travelling involved with the game and feels that squash should be organised more by professional promoters than it is at present. He regards his most memorable matches as beating Qamar Zaman in 24 minutes in the 1976 Pakistan Masters and a victory over Geoff Hunt in the 1977 ISPA Championship. His interests outside squash are television and golf.

Major achievements (winner unless stated otherwise): 1971 British Amateur (s/f), British Open (q/f); 1972 Swedish Open, Welsh Open, North of England Open, British Open (q/f); 1973 Welsh Open, Mercia Open; 1974 British Open (s/f); 1975 British and World Opens (combined event) (q/f), New South Wales Open (r/u), Irish Open (r/u), Chichester Festival, British Caledonian–Yellow Dot Grand Prix (r/u), South African Open (r/u); 1977 World Open (q/f), British Open (s/f); 1978 British Open (s/f), ISPA Championship (r/u); 1979 World Open (q/f), British Open (q/f), Chichester Festival (r/u); 1980 World Open (s/f), British Open (q/f), Irish Open, Monaco Open, Pakistan Masters (r/u); 1981 World Open (s/f), British Open (r/u), Irish Open; 1982 World Open (s/f), Pakistan Open (r/u), World Masters (s/f); 1983 ISPA Championship (s/f), ISRF World Individual Championship (s/f), World Masters (s/f); 1984 French Open (q/f). Represented Pakistan in the 1978 Hashim Khan Team Trophy but did not play for that country in any team events recognised by the International Squash Rackets Federation. He was selected to play for England in the 1983 ISRF World Team Championship.

Abbas Kaoud (Egy)

Born Cairo 2 January 1948. Lives in Chatham, Kent. Abbas turned professional in 1973 and has been in the top 30 for many years without being able to make further progress or win any major tournaments. He trains every day but has to change routine very regularly in order to enjoy it. He regarded Geoff Hunt as his most difficult opponent because 'he kept you on court for a long time'. He feels that any game lasting 30 minutes should be decided by some form of tiebreaker and that the future of televised squash lies in the time limit format where players have to get as

Lisa Opie, youngest ever winner of the British Closed Championship. *Robin Eley Jones* many points as possible in a given period of time using 'American' scoring. His interests outside squash are tennis and football.

Major achievements (winner unless stated otherwise): 1968 Egyptian Junior Championship; 1969 Egyptian Championship; 1970 Egyptian Championship; 1970 Greek Open; 1972 Alexandria Open; 1973 Greek Open (r/u); 1975 Welsh Open (r/u); 1976 Mercia Open; 1978 Greek Open (shared with Jonah Barrington); 1980 Maidstone Open; 1981 Maidstone Open, Medway Open. Represented Egypt twice in the ISRF World Team Championships.

Philip Kenyon (Eng)

Born Blackpool, Lancashire 7 May 1956. Lives in Buckinghamshire. Philip is generally regarded as one of the fittest players on the circuit. He has held the England number 2 spot since 1980, was briefly at number 1 at the beginning of 1982 and surged back in 1983 by regaining the British Closed title from Gawain Briars. He had a very successful junior career, twice holding the British Under-19 Open and Closed titles and winning the Under-23 Closed Championship when only 19. Philip crowned his amateur days by playing a major role in the England side which won the World Team Championship and finished as runner-up to Jahangir Khan in the World Individual event in Australia in 1979. He reached the quarter-finals of the 1980/1 and 1981/2 British Open Championships and the 1982 and 1983 World Opens, making him the most successful British player in those particular major tournaments since the days of Jonah Barrington. He rates as his most difficult opponents all those 'up and coming hungry young pros'.

Philip has definite views about how the game might be changed and feels that 'American' scoring should be adopted for television coverage on transparent courts as well as the use of a different coloured ball. His longest match was 2 hours 15 minutes in beating Gamal Awad in the third round of the 1981 British Open, a match incidentally that saw Awad collapse from exhaustion. He regards his most memorable match as his first victory in 1973 in the British Under-19 Open (Drysdale Cup) (unofficial world junior title). His interests outside squash are motoring, surfing, waterskiing and do-it-yourself tasks.

Major achievements (winner unless stated otherwise): 1973 British Under-19 Open (Drysdale Cup) Championship, British Under-19 Closed Championship; 1974 British Under-19 Open (Drysdale Cup) Championship, British Under-19 Closed Championship; 1975 British Under-23 Closed Championship, Swiss Open; 1976 South of England Open, British Under-23 Closed Championship (r/u), Midland Open (r/u), Swiss Open (r/u); 1977 British Closed, Midland

Open, Netherlands Open, British Under-23 Closed Championship (r/u); 1978 British Under-23 Closed Championship, New Zealand Championship, Irish Open, British Closed (r/u), Midland Open (r/u); 1979 ISRF World Amateur Individual Championship (r/u), British Closed (s/f); 1980 British Open (q/f), British Closed (s/f); 1981 British Closed, British Open (q/f); 1982 World Open (q/f), British Closed (r/u); 1983 ISRF World Individual Championship, World Open (q/f), British Closed; 1984 French Open (q/f). Represented England and Great Britain 37 times since 1975.

Daulat Khan (Pak)

Born Peshawar 19 May 1957. Daulat began playing in 1968 and has been both junior and national champion, but has yet to stamp the same impression on the rest of the circuit.

Major achievements (winner unless stated otherwise): 1973 Pakistan Under-18 Championship (r/u); 1976 Pakistan Junior Championship; 1978 Pakistan National Championship; 1981 East of England Championship, Pakistan National Championship (r/u). Represented Pakistan in the 1977 and 1979 ISRF World Team Championships, 1981 Asian Championship.

Jahangir Khan (Pak)

Born Peshawar 10 December 1963. Lives in London with cousin and coach Rahmat Khan. He first played in Karachi at the age of 10 and is the son of British Open champion Roshan Khan and brother of the late Torsam Khan. Jahangir who seems destined to become the greatest player of all time, first came to prominence when, having had to qualify for the tournament, he won the ISRF World Amateur Individual title in Australia in 1979. He was just 15 and was not rated highly enough to be included in the Pakistan side for the team event! He became the youngest winner of the World Open at the age of 17 years 354 days in Canada, November 1981, and the British Open at 18 years 119 days the following April. He has not lost a tournament match since being beaten by Geoff Hunt in the British Open final in April 1981. His dominance over his fellow professionals was underlined when he beat Maqsood Ahmed, then ranked world number 4, 9–0, 9–0, 9–0 in the final of the ISPA Championship in March 1982. He is exceptionally fit and trains up to seven hours a day, five days a week. Like many other players he rated Geoff Hunt as his most difficult opponent because 'he was very fit and a good fighter'. He regards his most memorable matches as being against Hunt in the Patrick Chichester Festival final in March 1981 (he won 3–2 in 2 hr 10 min), British Open final in April 1981 (he lost 1–3 in 2 hr 13 min) and the World Open final

Right
Phil Kenyon of England – has consistently produced the best British performances in major events such as the British Open since the days of Barrington. *Robin Eley Jones*

Below
Jahangir Khan of Pakistan and Gamal Awad of Egypt – the world champion (*left*) catches his challenger off balance but Awad has not earned his nickname of the 'grasshopper' for nothing. *Tim Pike*

in November 1981 (he won 3–1 in 1 hr 50 min). He would like to see televised matches played over a set time period. Jahangir considers prize money in squash is too low in comparison to other sports. His interests outside squash are music, tennis, cinema, and reading sports magazines.

Major achievements (winner unless stated otherwise): 1978 Pakistan Junior Championship, Swedish Junior Championship, British Under-19 Open (Drysdale Cup) Championship (3rd); 1979 ISRF World Amateur Individual Championship; 1980 British Open (r/u), World Open (q/f), ISPA Championship (r/u), Pakistan Open, German Open, Belgian Open, New Zealand Open, Durham and Cleveland Open, British Under-23 Open Championship, Chichester Festival, Irish Open (r/u); 1981 World Open, British Open, French Open, German Masters, Durham and Cleveland Open, Patrick Chichester Festival, ISPA Championship, Lookers Masters, World Masters, Asian Individual Championship; 1982 World Open, World Masters, Pakistan Open, ISPA Championship, Patrick Chichester Festival, British Open, French Open; 1983 French Open, British Open, Patrick Chichester Festival, World Masters, World Open, ISRF World Individual Championship; 1984 French Open, British Open. Represented Pakistan in the 1978 and 1979 World Junior Championships, 1981 and 1983 ISRF World Team Championships, 1981 Asian Team Championship, 1981 Hashim Khan Team Trophy.

Zahir Hussein Khan (Pak)

Born 4 October 1960. Zahir now lives in West Germany and is one of the lesser-known Pakistani players who is just making his presence felt in the world's top 30. He trains two hours a day, five days a week. He rates Jahangir Khan as his most difficult opponent because 'he is much fitter than I am'. His most memorable match he regards as the final of the Augsburg Open in Germany when he lost 9–10 in the fifth to Karim. He would like squash scoring changed to the 'American' system and feels altering the colour of the ball would improve television coverage. His interests outside squash are tennis, the cinema, and music.

Major achievements (winner unless stated otherwise): 1978 British Under-19 Open (Drysdale Cup) Championship (r/u), German Masters; 1979 Scottish Open. Represented Pakistan in the 1978 and 1979 ISRF World Junior Team Championship, 1979 ISRF World Amateur Team Championship.

Lars Kvant (Swe)

Born Malmo 27 March 1955. Lars first started squash in 1973 which makes him a latecomer by modern standards so it says much for his ability that he is the first world-class player to emerge from continental Europe or Scandinavia. His flamboyant personality and occasionally volatile temperament have sometimes got him into trouble with squash administrators, but generally his good humour and zestful style have made him a popular figure on the circuit. He has performed solidly for Sweden over a long period and has had some notable individual successes, including reaching the last four of the 1980 World Masters, beating Geoff Hunt 3–2 in the 1982 ISPA Championship, and leading Sweden to successes in the 1980 and 1983 European Team Championships.

True to character Lars dislikes training and doesn't have a rigid fitness schedule, but despite that he has maintained a place in the world's top 20 on a regular basis. Lars rates as his most difficult opponent Qamar Zaman because 'he has you under pressure all the time'. His interests outside squash are fishing and music. •

Major achievements (winner unless stated otherwise): 1976 British Amateur (s/f), Swedish Closed; 1977 Swedish Closed, ISRF World Individual Championship (q/f), Danish Open; 1978 Swedish Closed; 1979 Swedish Open and Closed, South African Open, German Open; 1980 Swedish Open and Closed, South African National, German Open, World Masters (s/f), Nigerian Open, Norwegian Open; 1981 ISPA Championship (q/f), ISRF World Individual Championship (s/f), German Open, Swedish Open; 1982 Swedish Closed; 1983 Swedish Closed. Represented Sweden 80 times including the 1977, 1979, 1981 and 1983 ISRF World Team Championships, 1976–83 European Championships (in 1980 and 1983 he led Sweden to victory – the only occasions on which England have not won the title), 1976–79 Scandinavian Championships.

John Robert Le Lievre (Eng)

Born St. Peter Port, Guernsey 9 June 1956. John is one of the group of stylish and outstanding squash players to come from Guernsey, achieving international status with the England team. Although he has consistently achieved a high English ranking and has been on the fringe of the world's top 20 he has not really fulfilled the potential that his skilful play would seem to warrant. Partly this may be due to injury problems at critical times and partly to his own easy going relaxed nature which he finds difficult to translate into a 'killer instinct on court'. During 1983 he devoted more time to the development of the game, occupying the chair of ISPA for a year. He trains most days however and his schedule includes ball practice, running circuits, stretching, weights, and swimming. John, like a lot of players, rates Qamar Zaman as his most difficult opponent 'because you are never sure

where to go next!' His most memorable match was a
3–2 win over Glen Brumby in the 1979 England v.
Australia Test series, a win which helped to push the
series England's way. His interests outside squash are
golf, growing plants, chess and windsurfing.

Major achievements (winner unless stated otherwise):
1972 Guernsey Open; 1975 British Junior Championship (r/u); 1977 British Closed (s/f), South of
England Open (r/u), Guernsey Open (r/u); 1980 Midland Open, North of England Open (r/u); Mercia Open
(r/u). Represented England in 1978 and 1982 European Championships, 1978–79 Home Internationals
and the 1981 ISRF World Team Championship.

Ashley Naylor (Eng)

Born 23 August 1960. Lives in Batley, West Yorkshire. Ashley, who took up squash in 1973, has made
steady progress in English squash but has yet to make
his mark on the international scene. He rates his best
achievements as winning the Yorkshire title in 1983
and 1984, the North of England in 1983 and the
British Under-23 Closed title in 1982. He first represented England in the European Championships in
1980 and has made 15 appearances for his country
since then. His interests outside squash are current
affairs and the piano.

Ross Norman (NZ)

Born Whitiangi 7 January 1959. Lives in Middlesex,
England. First played squash in 1968. Ross was a
talented junior player and won his country's national
title at that level in 1977. He took over as the New
Zealand number 1 in 1981 when Bruce Brownlee was
forced to retire and quickly fought his way into the
world's top 10. In many ways his style is similar to
Brownlee in that he shows great determination and
resolution on court. During the summer of 1983 he
sustained a serious knee injury while parachuting and
this put his squash career in jeopardy. After many
months of medical treatment, Ross was able to make a
comeback during the early part of 1984, but in the
meantime his position as New Zealand's top player
has been taken over by Stuart Davenport. Normally
Ross would spend six days a week training but he has
no particular schedule. He regards Jahangir Khan as
his most difficult opponent because 'he is fit, strong,
fast and accurate'.

His longest match was 2 hours 2 minutes against
Ahmed Safwat in the quarter-finals of the 1981
French Open. He would like to see the rules of squash
changed to allow American scoring and possibly
introduce a time limit for matches. He thinks television coverage could be improved by using four
transparent walls and a brightly coloured ball. His
interests outside squash are snow-skiing, water
sports, hang gliding and photography.

Ross Norman of New Zealand – made a miraculous
recovery from a parachuting accident which all but
ended his career. *Robin Eley Jones*

Major achievements (winner unless stated otherwise):
1977 New South Wales Junior Championship, New
South Wales Under-23 Championship, Queensland
Junior Championship, Queensland Under-23 Cham-
pionship, New Zealand Junior Championship,
Australian Junior Championship (s/f), German
Amateur (r/u); 1979 British Amateur (r/u); 1980
British Open (q/f), South of England Open; 1984
French Open (s/f), British Open (q/f). Represented
New Zealand 1976/7 as a junior and 1978–81 12 times
as a senior.

Greg Pollard (Aus)

Born 5 November 1960. Lives in Nottingham. Greg
began playing squash at the age of 11 in Albury,
Australia and owes a lot initially to Maurice Horne
who owned the Albury Squash Centre and subsequently Neville Johnson who trained the New
South Wales junior team. Since then fellow professionals Glen Brumby and Hiddy Jahan have given
him valuable guidance.

He made a number of appearances for Australia as a

junior and won his country's junior title in 1979. Finishing as runner-up in the 1983 British Under-23 Open Championship he has begun to make steady progress on the professional scene.

Greg is a regular trainer six days a week, varies his schedule and unlike many players, enjoys training. He rates Jahangir Khan as his most difficult opponent because 'he is so good'. If the rules of squash were changed he would lower the tin a few inches, and to help television coverage he thinks that limited time period matches would help. His most memorable match was playing for New South Wales against Ross Thorne in the 1982 Interstate Teams Championship in the deciding rubber. Ross led 7–0 in the final game only for Greg to come back and win 9–7. His interest outside squash is reading.

Major achievements (winner unless stated otherwise): 1979 Australian Junior Championship; 1983 British Under-23 Open Championship (r/u). Represented Australia in 1978 on junior team tour of Australia and Sweden, 1979 junior tour to Papua New Guinea, 1981 ISRF World Team Championship.

Sohail Qaiser (Pak)
Born 1955. Lives in Lahore. The latest sensation to emerge from Pakistan showing tremendous class and potential. Sohail can change pace effortlessly and has all the shots from a ferocious drive to the most delicate of drops. He won the World Junior Championship in Kuala Lumpur in 1982 and emulated Jahangir Khan by winning the 1982 British Under-23 Open at Wembley. He beat Roland Watson in the 1981 British Open and defeated Phil Kenyon and Glen Brumby in the 1981 French Open before going down 1–3 to Jahangir in the semi-final. He is one of only a handful of players to take a game off the world champion since his unbeaten run began in April 1981 and will certainly trouble the top names in years to come.

Major achievements (winner unless stated otherwise): 1981 British Under-19 Open (Drysdale Cup) Championship (s/f), French Open (s/f); 1982 British Under-23 Open Championship, ISRF World Junior Individual Championship; 1983 Chichester Festival (q/f), French Open (q/f); 1984 British Under-23 Open Championship. Represented Pakistan in 1981 World Junior Team Championship.

Ian Robinson (Eng)
Born York 12 September 1952. Lives in Denby Dale, Yorkshire. First played squash in 1961 at St. Peters School, York. A tenacious performer on court, outspoken and articulate off it, Ian was vice-president of the Executive of the International Squash Players Association. He trains six days a week, mainly pressure and skill routines on court. He feels that some tournaments should play best of three games to

make the game more action-packed and thinks that co-operation is needed between players, promoters, sponsors and television companies to iron out the technical difficulties that exist with television coverage. When he finishes playing he would like to be involved with the promotion, management or television aspect of the game. He rates Gogi Alauddin as his most difficult opponent because 'he weaves a web of slow pace shots always to the extremities of the court calling for large reserves of power of retrieval and equal accuracy of shot to counter'. His most memorable matches were losing 9–10 in the fifth to Kevin Shawcross in the 1979 British Open after holding match balls, and beating John Le Lievre 3–2 in the quarter-finals of the 1980/1 British Closed. It took 14 minutes to score first point and the match finished at midnight. His interests outside squash are guitar, piano, golf, cricket, travel, snorkel and scuba diving.

Major achievements (winner unless stated otherwise): 1969 British Under-16 Open Championship (r/u); 1971 Yorkshire Junior Championship, British Under-19 Open (Drysdale Cup) Championship (r/u); 1974–81 Yorkshire champion 8 times; 1975 Zambian Open; 1978 Canadian Open; 1979 British Closed (r/u), World Open Plate; 1980 North of England Open, Mercia Open, British Closed (s/f); 1981 British Closed (s/f), Japan Open. He has more than 50 caps for England and Great Britain since 1975 including the 1977 ISRF World Amateur Championship when he won all his six matches.

Magdi Saad (Egy)
Born 1954. Magdi lives in West Germany where he is a club professional in Hamburg. He has reached a high level in world squash in a very short space of time having switched seriously to the sport in 1978, having been his country's junior tennis champion. In January 1980 he reached the semi-final of the British Amateur and since then his appearances on the circuit have been spasmodic. However, he has a number of good performances to his credit. In the summer of 1982 he reached the final of the South African Open beating Brumby, Briars and Kenyon before losing to Dean Williams. In the 1983 British Open he reached the third round, before losing to his countryman Gamal Awad. His interest outside squash is his old love – tennis.

Ahmed Safwat (Egy)
Born Cairo 6 June 1947. Lives in England. Ahmed, son of a diplomat, turned professional in 1971. He soon became known as a player with supreme style and grace, playing with a fluency that few of his contemporaries have emulated. His touch has never really deserted him and had he been physically stronger he would have undoubtedly challenged for

the very top honours in the game. He has won the British Professional Championship seven times and two of his best performances were in reaching the semi-finals of the 1976 British Open when he was beaten by Cam Nancarrow and the last eight of the 1981 World Open where he lost to Zaman.

After a spell as professional at one of England's most famous clubs, Abbeydale, he moved his family to Hamburg, but in the Spring of 1984 brought his family back to England again. Ahmed's squash has an enduring quality about it and even though he is now approaching the close of his competitive career his talent keeps him in the world's top 20. He may well continue with further success in age group competitions, an area where he has already won major titles – the 1982 World Grand Masters (Over-35) when he beat Jonah Barrington, and the 1983 British Open (Over-35) Championship.

Major achievements (winner unless stated otherwise): 1964–67 Egyptian Junior Championship; 1972 British Open (q/f), Mercia Open; 1973 North of England Open, 1973–79 British Professional Championship; 1975 Chichester Festival (r/u); 1976 British Open (s/f); 1980 French Open; 1981 World Open (q/f); 1982 World Grand Masters (Over-35); 1983 British Open (Over-35) Championship.

Ross Thorne (Aus)

Born 7 November 1957. Lives Aspley, Queensland. Since Ross's better half, Rhonda, is the former World Open champion it is not surprising that she is the person who has had most influence on his squash career. This has been very much to Ross' benefit as seen during 1983 when he made spectacular progress into the world's top 20, having previously languished well down the list. In that year he had notable successes in winning both the Australian and South African titles. He is a regular and hard working trainer, getting through three or four sessions a day, six days a week. These usually consist of a six-mile run or a series of 440s, followed by a light court practice and then a swim of up to one mile followed by practice games. His most difficult opponent he rates as fellow Australian Cam Nancarrow the former world amateur champion, an interesting choice as Nancarrow is now retired from the international circuit. 'I still don't know where Cam is going to hit the ball', he says. He dislikes the long, boring rallies that have crept into squash and would like to see a slower ball to encourage more attacking play. His interests outside squash are golf, cricket and most other sports.

Major achievements (winner unless stated otherwise): 1980 Queensland Open; 1982 Queensland Open; 1983 Queensland Open, South African Open, Australian Open; 1984 British Open (q/f). Rep-

resented Australia in the 1979, 1981 and 1983 ISRF World Team Championships.

Trevor Wilkinson (Zim)

Born 10 October 1960. Lives in Cape Town, South Africa. Trevor first began squash at the age of 13 in Harare (formerly Salisbury) and owes much to the guidance of his father. He won the South African Amateur Championship in 1981 and played for South Africa in matches against teams from the USA in 1979, from Egypt in 1982 and from Australia in 1983. His training schedule, which he enjoys, comprises daily sessions both on court and off court where he runs 400-metre sprints. His most difficult opponent, apart from Jahangir Khan, he rates as Zaman, because of the way he disrupts patterns of play and quickly saps an opponent's stamina. If he has a dislike about squash it is that the sport offers so little money for so much work. His interests outside squash are surfing and golf.

Major achievements (winner unless stated otherwise): 1979 ISRF World Junior Individual Championship (q/f); 1981 South African Amateur, British Under-23 Open Championship (q/f); 1982 British Under-23 Open Championship (q/f); 1983 British Under-23 Open Championship (q/f).

Dean Harley Williams (Aus)

Born Perth 22 April 1956. Lives in Perth. He first played in 1969 and did not turn professional until 1978. He is an extremely extrovert character both on and off court with an exciting range of shots. Dean has moved rapidly through the ranking list since becoming a professional and achieved his greatest success when he was runner-up to Jahangir Khan in the 1982 World Open after defeating world numbers 2 and 3 Hiddy Jahan and Qamar Zaman. He has clearly established himself as the Australian number 1 since Geoff Hunt's retirement in 1982 and is currently the highest ranked white player in the world. He trains every day but has no particular schedule. His favourite shots are overheads and drops. His longest match was 2 hours against Murray Lilley in Sweden in 1977, and he remembers his most amusing incident as: 'my pro debut in Sheffield in March 1978 in the ISPA Championship. Mo Asran withdrew so I replaced him in the draw to play Qamar Zaman. Asran then changed his mind and the three of us entered the court to much amusement and bewilderment. Zaman broke the tension by saying "no problem, I play both". Asran then left the court. I was thrashed.' Dean would like to see 3-minute rest periods between games and only one service per player. He feels television coverage would be improved by using three-quarter speed, and shooting from the tin and directly above the court. His interests outside squash are following all sports, reading, cinema, theatre, travelling and sightseeing, fishing, running, swimming, tennis, wine appreciation and cars.

Major achievements (winner unless stated otherwise): 1972 West Australian Junior Championship; 1973 West Australian Junior Championship; 1974 Australian Junior Championship; 1975 West Australian Championship; 1976 Danish Open, Scottish Amateur, West Australian Championship; 1977 Australian Amateur, Finnish Open, Prodorite Invitation, British Amateur (s/f), West Australian Championship; 1978 New South Wales Open, West Australian Championship; 1979 World Masters (s/f), Swiss Open, West Australian Championship; 1980 Spanish Open, Danish Open, Australian Open (r/u), New South Wales Open (r/u); 1981 Swiss Open, Monaco Open, Prodorite Invitation, Australian Open (r/u); 1982 World Open (r/u), 1983 ISPA Championship (q/f), British Open (s/f), World Masters (s/f), World Open (q/f); 1984 French Open (r/u). Represented Australia in the 1974 junior tour of New Zealand, 1977 and 1983 ISRF World Team Championship, 1979 Hashim Khan Team Trophy.

Geoff Williams (Eng)

Born 21 November 1957 India. Lives in Stockport. Geoff took up squash at Downside School and owes a lot of his 'squash education' to Australians Len Steward and Geoff Hunt and to Hiddy Jahan and Gogi Alauddin. He made a comparatively late entrance to the professional arena at the age of 24 in 1981 but in two years has made considerable progress becoming one of England's best players and moving into the world's top 20. He was selected for the England team that went to the 1983 ISRF World Championships and reached the last 16 of the individual competition. He finished off the year by winning through to the same stage of the World Open. In 1984 he reached the semis of the British Open, the first English player to do so since Jeremy Lyon in the 1967/8 event.

Most of his hard training is done between July and September when he puts in five hours a day for five days a week. During the season he does two hours a day, mainly court practice.

The ability of Jahangir Khan 'to keep getting the ball back' means that he rates him as his toughest opponent. On the subject of change in the game Geoff has revolutionary views and would make the court as 'big as a tennis court', with a faster, bigger ball. So that people can see, he says.

Interests outside squash are golf, snooker, windsurfing and disco music.

Major achievements (winner unless stated otherwise): 1982 Welsh Open; 1983 Jamaican Open, Belgium Open, reached last 16 of ISRF World Individual Championship, last 16 of World Open, British Closed (s/f); 1984 British Open (s/f). Represented England in the 1983 European Team Championship, 1983 ISRF World Team Championship, 1984 home internationals.

Qamar Zaman (Pak)

Born Quetta 11 April 1951. Lives in Peshawar. Son of squash and tennis professional Mohammed Ayub and nephew of former British Amateur champion Aftab Jawaid. He gave up tennis at 15 to concentrate on squash and is now regarded as one of the greatest players of all time with a range of shots second to none. He was first seen in Britain in 1972 and since then has had a remarkably consistent record in major tournaments. He has competed in 11 British Open Championships, winning one, finishing runner-up four times, losing semi-finalist five times and reached the last 16 at his first attempt. In seven World Opens (including the event combined with the 1975 British Open) he has been runner-up three times and lost in the semi-finals three times. His interest outside squash is tennis.

Major achievements (winner unless stated otherwise): 1967 Pakistan Under-16 Championship; 1968 Pakistan Under-18 Championship; 1969 Pakistan Under-18 Championship; 1972 British Amateur (s/f); 1973 British Amateur (r/u), British Open (s/f), Pakistan Amateur, Australian Amateur, Singapore Open; 1974 British Open, British Amateur (r/u), Australian Championship, Singapore Championship, Egyptian Championship, Durham and Cleveland Open; 1975 British and World Opens (combined event) (s/f), Chichester Festival; 1976 Pakistan Masters; 1977 World Open (r/u), British Open (r/u), ISPA Championship, Pakistan Masters, PIA World Series, Lookers Masters, Irish Open; 1978 British Open (r/u), ISPA Championship (r/u), Pakistan Masters; 1979 World Open (r/u), British Open (r/u), ISPA Championship (r/u), World Masters, Durham and Cleveland Open, Chichester Festival; 1980 World Open (r/u), British Open (s/f), ISPA Championship (q/f), Lookers Masters, Pakistan Masters, German Masters (r/u), Pakistan Open (r/u); 1981 World Open (s/f), British Open (s/f), World Masters (r/u), German Masters (s/f); 1982 World Open (s/f), World Masters (s/f), Pakistan Open (s/f), Chichester Festival (s/f), British Open (s/f), French Open (r/u); 1983 ISPA Championship (r/u), British Open (s/f), ISRF World Individual Championship (r/u), World Masters (r/u); 1984 Asian Individual Championship, French Open (r/u), British Open (r/u)). Represented Pakistan in the 1983 ISRF World Team Championship.

WOMEN

Rae Anderson (Aus)

Born Melbourne 8 April 1953. Rae first played squash at Ringwood, Melbourne in 1974. Like many squash players she was good at tennis before turning to squash at a relatively late stage in her life. She has had a very successful career in Australia, has had notable successes on the Continent but has not achieved a major title victory in England. Rae rates her favourite shots as the forehand short volley and backhand drop and regards her most difficult opponent as Vicki Cardwell who 'no matter how well you are playing, never gives up'. She remembers her most memorable match as defeating Vicki Cardwell in the semi-final of the 1981 Irish Open, and her longest match was 1 hour 45 minutes against Renee Aucamp in Cape Town in 1982. Rae trains twice a day and her schedule includes cycling or running 8 to 10 kilometres, sprints and gym work.

She would like to see an international testing system introduced for referees and markers which would include questions on video recorded action. Her ideas to improve televised coverage are for better camera positioning, more practise for cameramen and directors on tactics, use of action replay, coloured clothing and the American scoring system. She dislikes players who block the path to the ball and play the player instead of the ball. Interests outside squash include travelling, body-surfing, tennis, films, reading and horse riding.

Major achievements (winner unless stated otherwise): 1977 Western Victorian Open; 1979 Port Adelaide Open; 1980 Belgian Open, British Open (s/f), Prodorite Invitation (s/f), East of England Open (s/f); 1981 Irish Open, New South Wales Open (r/u); 1982 Swiss Open (r/u). Represented Australia in the 1981 ISRF World Team Championship.

Jayne Ashton (Eng)

Born Birmingham, England 31 August 1957. Jayne, who lives in Kenilworth, first played for England in 1973, the year she became British Junior champion, the title she was to hold for four consecutive seasons. Her distinguished junior career naturally led to selection by England at senior level and she has gained 28 caps. She assists training the England B squad, junior and senior in her capacity as a WSRA area coach, and her other interests are skiing and travelling.

Robyn Blackwood (NZ)

Born 22 April 1958 in Hamilton. New Zealand number 1 and sister of world ranked Craig Blackwood. An exceptionally stylish player, she is always smiling despite her fortunes on court. She has a very impressive list of New Zealand Junior, Under-23 and

Sue Cogswell of England – her class and consistency have kept her at the top for a decade. *Robin Eley Jones*

district titles to her credit and was unbeaten in her own country from 1981–83. In that year she won the Plate event at the ISRF World Individual Championship in Canada and led New Zealand to third place in the team event. She has yet to record her first major European tournament victory, but had the best win of her career when she beat Lisa Opie of England at the Chichester Festival in March 1983.

She ranks Vicki Cardwell as her most difficult opponent 'due to her physical and mental tenacity' and remembers her tussle with Angela Smith in the 1981 World Team event, which she lost 9–10 in the fifth, as her most memorable match. She would like to see more men's and women's tournaments run simultaneously as is common in New Zealand. Interests outside squash include travelling and pottery.

Major achievements (winner unless stated otherwise): 1977 Swedish Open; 1981 New Zealand Championship, New Zealand Open (r/u), British Open (q/f), Irish Open (s/f), Prodorite Invitation (s/f); 1982 New Zealand Championship, Chichester Festival (s/f), Scottish Open; 1983 New Zealand Championship; 1984 British Open (q/f). Represented New Zealand in the 1974 and 1975 junior team, 1983 WISRF World Team Championship.

Carin Clonda (Aus)

Born Sydney 1 March 1961. Lives in Dee Wye, New South Wales. Originally she took up squash at the age of 13 in an attempt to combat asthma and two years later in 1976 won the Australian Under-16 title. She arrived in England in 1979 as holder of the Australian Under-19 Championship and won the British Under-19 Open by beating Martine Le Moignan in the final. Carin lost four stone in weight during 1981 before returning to play the British circuit despite a doctor's advice that competing in England's climate could be fatal. She brought with her a respiratory machine which she had to use twice a day. With this handicap she put together a great run at the British Open beating seeded players Renee Aucamp and Sue Cogswell before losing in the quarter-finals to Angela Smith. In the 1982/3 season she reached the last 16 of the British Open before losing to the same opponent. In 1983 she was a member of Australia's team that won the WISRF world title in Perth and in the individual event she lost in the semi-finals to her compatriot Rhonda Thorne. She is now ranked number 4 in Australia after a period away from competitive squash during which she was unplaced in the list.

Major achievements (winner unless stated otherwise): 1976 New South Wales Under-16 Championship, Australian Under-16 Championship; 1978 British Under-19 Open Championship, Australian Under-19 Championship, captained Australian junior team v. New Zealand; 1979 New South Wales Under-23 Championship; 1981 British Open (q/f); 1982 British Open (q/f); 1983 WISRF World Individual Championship (s/f). Represented Australia in the 1983 WISRF World Team Championship.

Sue Cogswell (Eng)

Born Birmingham 7 September 1951. Sue started playing at school in Birmingham in 1961 and went on to become England's most successful player during the seventies and early eighties. At one stage she was ranked only second in the world to Heather McKay of Australia, whose performances she admits had a great influence on her career. Sue has won the British Closed title five times, been runner-up in the British Open on three occasions and finished second to McKay in the WISRF World Individual Championship in 1979. She was a member of the Great Britain team which won the WISRF World Team Championship in the same year. Since 1972 Sue has represented Great Britain and England more than 40 times. She took a game off McKay in the semi-final of the British Open in 1977 – the first game the Australian had dropped in 13 years.

A former county hockey and tennis player she rates her favourite shots as the backhand drop and the volley. She is disappointed that squash is not a bigger spectator sport and feels television could help by making personalities of the players. Interests outside squash include birdwatching and all sports, especially golf, tennis and surfing.

Major achievements (winner unless stated otherwise): 1972 Challengers Cup; 1973 British Open (r/u); 1974 Belgian Open, Midland Open, Wessex Open, Mercia Open, Middlesex Open, British Open (q/f); 1975 British Closed, British Open (s/f), Wessex Open, Essex Open; 1976 British Closed (r/u), British Open (s/f), WISRF World Individual Championship (q/f), Scottish Open; 1977 British Closed, British Open (s/f), South African Open, Scottish Open, Essex Open, South of England Open; 1978 British Closed, British Open (r/u), Midland Open, South of England Open; 1979 WISRF World Individual Championship (r/u), British Open (r/u), British Closed, Midland Open, Essex Open; 1980 British Closed, British Open (q/f); 1981 WISRF World Individual Championship (q/f), South African Open; 1982 Chichester Festival (r/u); 1983 British Open (q/f); 1984 British Open (q/f). Represented England in the 1979, 1981 and 1983 WISRF World Team Championships.

Alison Cumings (Eng)

Born Kent 18 November 1961. Lives in Reigate, Surrey. A very determined competitor, her anticipation and speed around court make up for a certain lack of flair. Alison came to the fore in the 1979/80 season when she won the British Under-19 Open title, finished runner-up in the Under-23 Open Championship and toured with the English team in Australia. She was then in the country's top 5 and seemed destined for the top but in the next two years her form suffered a surprising lapse and she slipped to number 9 in the ranking list.

In 1982/3 she fought back to number 3 when she won the British Closed Championship during which she defeated Barbara Diggens, Lisa Opie and Martine Le Moignan. In 1983 there was another major setback when an injury prevented her from taking her place in the England party contesting the WISRF World Team Championships in Perth. Interests outside squash include cooking.

Major achievements (winner unless stated otherwise):
1979 British Under-19 Open Championship, British
Under-23 Open Championship (r/u), Surrey Open;
1981 Surrey Open; 1982 British Closed, Surrey Open,
Wessex Open, Swiss Open (r/u).

Sue Devoy (NZ)

Born 4 January 1964. Sue is ranked number 1 in New
Zealand and won the British Women's Open title in
April 1984, the first New Zealand player to do so. She
came to England for the first time in 1982 after play-
ing number 3 for New Zealand in the 1981 WISRF
World Team Championships and reaching the semi-
finals of the world junior event. However Sue really
came good in the 1982/3 season when she beat Jayne
Ashton in the Irish Open, Felicity Hargreaves in the
Middlesex Open and Alison Cumings, from 0–2

Alison Cumings of England missed the 1983 world team
and individual championships through injury but has
proved before that she can make a comeback. *Robin
Eley Jones*

Sue Devoy of New Zealand who stunned the women's
squash world by winning the 1984 British Open. *Tim
Pike*

down, in the British Open where she reached the last
16. She also took games off three of the world's top
players Rhonda Thorne, Martine Le Moignan and
Robyn Blackwood. This promise was maintained in
1983 as she reached the semi-finals of the WISRF
World Individual Championship, losing to the eventual winner, Vicki Cardwell. Interests outside squash
include running and music.

Barbara Diggens (Eng)

Born 8 October 1949. Lives in Brighton, Sussex. First
played when aged 19 at Hove SC in Brighton. A
professional squash and tennis coach who has also
played county netball and lacrosse, Barbara was manager of the England team. She runs, with her husband
Paul, two sports shops in Sussex. She enjoys training
tremendously and trains almost every day in and out
of season. Her favourite shot she rates as the forehand
drive and regards her most difficult opponent as
Angela Smith, 'whom I never seem to perform at my
best against'. Barbara regards her most memorable
match and best squash achievement as beating Sue
King 3–0 in the final test of the England v. Australia
series in August 1980. She also recalls with affection
her defeat, in straight games, of Angela Smith in the
1977 British Closed Championship. She would like to
see the rules of the game altered by removing the tin,
and believes the scoring system should be changed to

improve televised squash. Interests outside squash include gardening, tennis and learning Russian.

Major achievements (winner unless stated otherwise): 1975 British Open (q/f); 1979 British Open (q/f); 1980 Kent Open; 1981 WISRF World Individual Championship (q/f), Kent Open; 1982 Kent Open; 1983 managed England team at WISRF World Championships. Represented England (as captain) in the 1983 WISRF World Team Championship.

Martine Le Moignan (Eng)

Born Guernsey 28 October 1962. Lives in Portsmouth. She started playing in 1975 and, like Lisa Opie, first developed her squash under the coaching of Reg Harbour before moving to the mainland to join Nottingham SRC. Since then she has moved her base to Portsmouth.

At her best she is a tremendously exciting, adventurous stroke player who is a match for anyone in the world. However, she can be frustratingly inconsistent and this flaw possibly cost her the 1982 British Closed Championship when she lost in the final to Alison Cumings. In 1983 she was again runner-up in the Closed, this time to Lisa Opie but could not complain about a straight games defeat. She went with the England party to the WISRF World Championships, losing in the quarter-finals of the individual and her

Martine Le Moignan of England – an exciting, adventurous stroke player whose bids for the major honours are hampered by inconsistency. *Robin Eley Jones*

match in the team final when she was hampered by injury. She recalls her most memorable match as the final of the 1980 British Closed: 'Although I lost to Sue Cogswell, reaching the final was a great thrill and it was the first time I felt I could reach the top'. Her favourite shots are volley nicks and boasts and she trains 1½ to 2 hours, 6 days a week – but admits she does not enjoy it. At Portsmouth she is under the guidance of professional Bryan Patterson who places great emphasis on physical fitness.

She would like to see a change to a slower ball to put emphasis on shot-making and attacking play and believes that more coverage of women's squash – with its shorter rallies and slower ball movement – would improve television presentation of the game. Her major complaint about squash is the lack of practice courts at most tournaments. After retiring from competitive play she would like to coach in Europe. Interests outside squash are all other sports, reading, cooking, music, discos, travel and looking after young children.

Major achievements (winner unless stated otherwise): 1979 Midland Open, Teesside Open; 1980 British Closed (r/u), British Open (q/f), British Under-23 Open Championship, North of England Open, Teesside Open; 1981 WISRF World Individual Championship (q/f), British Open (q/f), WISRF World Junior Individual Championship (r/u), East of England Championship, Isle of Man Open, World Cup Pairs (with Gamal Awad) (r/u); 1982 British Closed (r/u), Chichester Festival (s/f); 1983 British Closed (r/u), WISRF World Individual Championship (q/f); 1984 British Open (s/f). Represented England in the 1983 WISRF World Team Championship.

Jan Marie Miller (Aus)

Born 1 September 1957. Lives in Adelaide. For someone who did not take up the game until 1977, Jan has done remarkably well in a short space of time, culminating in gaining selection for the 1983 Australian team which won the world team championship. Some of this success she says, is due to the encouragement given in the early stages of her career by members of her home squash clubs, Campbelltown and Burnside. She is an enthusiastic trainer and likes to train every day, her schedule varying and depending on the timing of events with more emphasis on match practice during the season. Her most memorable match she recalls as being against her compatriot Barbara Oldfield in the 1981 Australian Women's Championship. Jan was unseeded and she beat Barbara, seeded number 4 in the last 16 and went on to reach the semi-finals. For that performance she received her first Australian ranking, that of number 8. She has much admiration for Vicki Cardwell, the retired world champion and rates her as the most difficult opponent because of her 'exceptional determination and retrieving ability'. Jan's interests outside squash are 'her husband, crosswords, music and reading'.

Barbara Oldfield (Aus)

Born 1 August 1950. Lives in Perth. West Australian number 1 and national number 3, she is married with one son. Barbara did not play the game until she was 21 but is now rated as one of the sport's most exciting exponents. She ranks Vicki Cardwell as her most difficult opponent because 'she never gives up' and recalls her most memorable match as that against Sue Cogswell in the 1981 WISRF World Team Championship which she lost 10–9 in the fifth. Despite that defeat, Australia beat England to win the event. Her favourite shot is the drop and, unlike many other leading players, she would be against any changes of rules or playing conditions within the game. However, she does dislike 'the cut-throat bitchiness of women wanting your position' in the sport. She feels that more careful selection of players who show flair and play exciting shots would improve the television coverage of squash. Although she enjoys training, she does not work to a set schedule and adapts according to mood and time of year.

Major achievements (winner unless stated otherwise): 1980 West Australian Championship; 1981 British Open (s/f), West Australian Championship; 1982 West Australian Championship. Represented Australia in 1980 Australia v. England, 1981 WISRF World Team Championship.

Lisa Opie (Eng)

Born Guernsey 15 September 1963. First played in 1976. Lisa was coached in Guernsey by Reg Harbour and Gavin Dupre before becoming part of the strongest club squad in England at Nottingham SRC. She rose steadily through the rankings until she broke into the country's top 10 in March 1980 and then soared to equal third with fellow Guernsey player Martine Le Moignan a year later after her first-ever win over the then England number 1 Sue Cogswell in the British Open. Lisa really came to world prominence between November 1981 and March 1982 when she won the World Junior title, reached the last four in the World Individual event, became the youngest-ever winner of the British Closed Championship, took over the top spot in the national rankings and defeated Vicki Cardwell in the final of the Patrick International Festival at Chichester. She was regarded as the girl most likely to end Australia's dominance of the women's game but lost this opportunity at the 1984 British Open when she went down to the brilliant

New Zealander Sue Devoy. Her behaviour in the final cost her a £1000 fine, imposed for bringing the game into disrepute. Lisa names the forehand volley as her favourite shot, Vicki Cardwell as her most difficult opponent because 'she is very determined, always attacks and takes the ball early', and her most memorable match as that final in Chichester which lasted 90 minutes. She would like to see more mixed tournaments (i.e. men's and women's events run together) on the circuit and believes that a luminous ball and more player interviews would improve television coverage of the game. Interests outside squash include fashion, parties and discos, music and art.

Major achievements (winner unless stated otherwise): 1979 Wessex Open; 1980 British Open (s/f), Midland Open, South of England Open, Middlesex Open, Ulster Open, British Under-19 Closed Championship (s/f); 1981 British Closed, WISRF World Junior Individual Championship, British Open (r/u), WISRF World Individual Championship (s/f), Chichester Festival, South of England Open; 1982 East of England Open, South of England Open; 1983 British Closed, British Open (r/u), WISRF World Individual Championship (q/f); 1984 British Open (r/u). Represented England in the 1981 and 1983 WISRF World Team Championships.

Angela Smith (Eng)

Born Stoke 3 July 1953. Formerly a physical education teacher, she was the first British girl to turn professional and was greatly responsible for increasing the popularity of the women's game in England. Angela's aggressive and competitive attitude has, at times, got her into trouble with the authorities and she was omitted from the English team that played a Test series in Australia in 1980 despite being British number 2 at the time. She has appeared in four British Closed finals – winning once – and finished third in the WISRF World Individual Championships in 1979 and 1981. She has reached the last eight of the British Open every year since 1975 – on four occasions making the semi-finals. She ranks Heather McKay and Vicki Cardwell as the most difficult opponents during her career and regards her win over Mrs Cardwell in the final of the WISRF World Team event in 1979 as her most memorable match. She rates the backhand drive as her favourite shot. She would like to see turning outlawed totally from the game and the American system of appeals introduced – i.e. extra referees. Angela considers prize money is too low considering the huge effort and dedication required on the part of players and feels that more camera positions, more slow motion replays and better commentary, explaining strategy and skill in detail, would improve the game on television. Interests outside squash include travel, music, soccer and sport in general.

Major achievements (winner unless stated otherwise):
1975 British Under-23 Open Championship, British Open (q/f), Midland Open, Mercia Open; 1976 British Closed, British Open (s/f), Midland Open, Welsh Open, North of England Open, West of England Open, Mercia Open, Wessex Open; 1977 British Open (q/f), Wessex Open, Mercia Open, Teesside Open; 1978 British Closed (r/u), British Open (s/f), Welsh Open, North of England Open, Warrington Invitation, Prodorite Invitation; 1979 WISRF World Individual Championship (s/f), British Closed (r/u), British Open (s/f), North of England Open; 1980 British Open (q/f), Welsh Open; 1981 WISRF World Individual Championship (s/f), British Closed (r/u), British Open (s/f); 1982 British Open (s/f); 1983 WISRF World Individual Championship (q/f); 1984 British Open (q/f). Represented England in the 1979, 1981 and 1983 WISRF World Championships.

Ruth Strauss (Eng)

Born 14 March 1963. Lives in Barling, near Southend. Ruth began squash at the age of 12, playing at her local club, Courtlands Park. She received considerable encouragement from her parents and subsequently from such professionals as Neil Harvey, Gogi Alauddin and the late Aboutaleb.

Like many good players she enjoyed a highly successful junior career and in 1978 in her first major championship appearance at the age of 14 took the British Under-19 junior title. She won it again in 1981, has also claimed two British Under-23 Open titles and won selection for England to the 1983 World Championships – an honour that she rates as one of her best achievements.

Training is an important part of her life and she enjoys going through a carefully prepared schedule on most days. Not many players would care to recall a 9–0, 9–0, 9–0 drubbing as their most memorable match but Ruth does so. It was against Heather McKay in the 2nd round of the 1979 British Women's Open and Ruth remembers also that she gained service only twice and served out on both occasions. Her interests outside squash are golf and all sports.

Major achievements (winner unless stated otherwise):
1978 British Under-19 Closed Championship; 1980 British Under-23 Open Championship; 1981 British Under-19 Closed Championship; 1982 British Under-23 Open Championship. Represented England in the 1982 and 1983 European Championships, 1983 WISRF World Team Championships, 1984 Home Internationals.

Rhonda Thorne (née Shapland) (Aus)

Born Queensland 6 February 1958. First played in 1969. Rhonda is married to world-ranked professional Ross Thorne. Winner of the Australian Junior Championship on four occasions, Rhonda has rarely reproduced her best form outside her own country but reached the pinnacle of her career when she beat Vicki Cardwell in the final of the WISRF World Individual Championship in Toronto in 1981. That was the longest match in which she has played – 1 hour 55 minutes. Despite that victory, she regards her most memorable match as a 3–0 win over Mrs Cardwell in the final of the 1981 Australian Open. Her favourite shot is an attacking boast from the back of the court and her most difficult opponent is named as Mrs Cardwell who 'has an enormous heart and doesn't know the meaning of giving up'. She would like to see the scoring system made easier for the general public to follow and the tin lowered to give the game more angle. Dislikes petty trivia among players and living in hotels. Interests outside squash – reading, all sports and enjoying time with friends.

Major achievements (winner unless stated otherwise):
1972 Brisbane Junior Championship, North Queensland Junior Championship, Queensland Junior Championship, Australian Junior Championship; 1973 Brisbane Junior Championship, Queensland Junior Championship; 1974 Brisbane Junior Championship, North Queensland Junior Championship, Australian Junior Championship; 1975 Brisbane Junior Championship, North Queensland Junior Championship, Australian Junior Championship; 1976 British Open (q/f), West of England Open, Australian Junior Championship, Queensland Championship (r/u); 1977 British Open (s/f); 1978 Scottish Open; 1980 British Open (q/f); 1981 WISRF World Individual Championship, Australian Open, British Open (q/f); 1982 British Open (q/f); 1983 WISRF World Individual Championship (r/u); 1984 British Open (s/f). Represented Australia in 1981 and 1983 WISRF World Team Championships.

Heather Wallace (Sco)

Born Kitwe, Zambia 4 December 1961. Heather was the first Scottish player to reach the quarter-finals of the women's World Open in Perth in 1983 and her performance reflected the improving standard of women's squash in her country. Scotland, under her leadership, finished in fifth place in the team event. In the 1983/4 Scottish Open she reached the semi-finals, losing to Angela Smith. Her interests outside squash are photography, outdoor pursuits, music and the theatre.

8 Championships of the world

World Open Championship

The first World Open event was incorporated in the Lucas-sponsored British Open Championship at Wembley in February 1976. It was won by Australian Geoff Hunt to add to his already impressive list of firsts – in 1976 he had become the first World Amateur champion and led Australia to the first world team title; then in 1969, while still an amateur, he won the British Open at his first attempt.

The Wembley final – against 20-year-old Mohibullah Khan – took five games and 2 hours 10 minutes to resolve which, at the time, was only three minutes short of the then longest recorded match – Hunt v. Barrington in the World Amateur team final in 1969. Sixty-four players had lined up for the first round proper of this first World Open – 14 of whom had fought through from a qualifying field of 56. Three of the semi-finalists were from Pakistan with Qamar Zaman losing to Mohibullah and Gogi Alauddin bowing out to Hunt. Jonah Barrington by then nearly 35, had been defeated by Zaman in their quarter-final match.

Adelaide was the venue for the second World Open in October 1977 when the same four players again contested the semi-finals. On this occasion Zaman exacted revenge over Mohibullah in five games but went down over the same distance to Hunt in the final which lasted 94 minutes and was televised live to a nationwide audience. Barrington's progress was again halted by Zaman in the quarter-finals.

Hunt demonstrated his superb fitness by flying to Sydney after winning his first round match to compete in a two-day Australian Superstars' contest. Despite the presence of athletics great Ron Clarke, cricketers Greg Chappell and David Hookes and double Olympic gold medallist from swimming, Michael Wenden, Hunt won the cycling and 800 metres and tied on points for first place with Graham Eddie from rugby league. On a 'countback' of events in which they took part, Eddie just got the verdict but Hunt returned to Adelaide $7000 richer and promptly beat fellow-countryman Steve Bowditch for the loss of eight points.

In a third round match Egypt's Ali Aziz was disqualified for failing to observe the rule which requires

The official World Open Championship came into being in 1976 when the winner of the British Open was also designated World Open champion. Subsequently the championship was taken over by the players' association – ISPA. Pictured is the first World Open trophy and winner's commemorative goblet, presented by the sponsors, Lucas Industries

play to be continuous, after having had several arguments with the referee. Unseeded New Zealander Bruce Brownlee was the revelation of the tournament, beating Cam Nancarrow and Ahmed Safwat to reach the last eight where he took a game off Hunt.

The Australian completed his hat-trick of wins when he beat Zaman for eight points in the 1979 final in Toronto and was even more ruthless in Australia a year later when he surrendered just six points to the same opponent. In Canada Hunt was joined yet again by three Pakistanis in the semi-finals – Mohibullah Khan and Maqsood Ahmed were losers – while Britain's most successful representative was Gawain Briars, reaching the last 16 before losing to Zaman.

In 1980 16-year-old Jahangir Khan, by then World Amateur champion, defeated sixth seed Maqsood Ahmed and took Zaman to five in their quarter-final clash.

In the 1981 event the young Pakistani proved himself to be the best player in the world by defeating Hunt in the final in Toronto – he was just 17 years 354 days old when he achieved his momentous victory over the four-times champion.

In 1982 the World Open returned to England for the first time since the inaugural competition. Audi sponsored the most ambitious event yet with the early rounds being played at 13 venues throughout the country and the quarter-finals onwards staged on a Twin-Vue portable glass court before 1595 spectators

Jahangir Khan moves in to crack the ball away during his semi-final match with Gamal Awad in the 1983 World Open in Munich

at the National Exhibition Centre in Birmingham. Phil Kenyon gave home supporters plenty to cheer about by reaching the last eight but the main head-lines belonged to Australian Dean Williams and – inevitably by now – Jahangir Khan. In the absence of Hunt – forced to retire from competition through injury – Williams thrilled Australian followers by defeating Qamar Zaman and Hiddy Jahan, seeded 3 and 2 respectively, to reach the final. There he took a game off Jahangir – the first the champion had dropped in the competition – before the young Pakistani powered his way to his second title. Another Australian, Glen Brumby, defeated fourth seed Maqsood Ahmed in the quarter-finals to ensure that, for the first time since the competition began, Pakistan had only two representatives in the last four. A World Grand Masters event was instituted for players over 35 and was won by Egyptian Ahmed Safwat who defeated Jonah Barrington in the final.

The scene for the 1983 World Open moved to Munich and the event was remarkable for some out-standing performances by young competitors.

Stuart Davenport, aged 21, the New Zealand

number 1 and Chris Dittmar of Australia, aged 19, had both had considerable experience at professional level and chose the occasion to put together a string of impressive results which brought them face to face in the semi-finals. Dittmar at the time ranked number 13 in the world, had struck the first blow by elimina-ting the number 3 seed Hiddy Jahan of England and quickly followed this with a quarter-final win over former World Amateur champion Maqsood Ahmed of Pakistan.

Davenport's path to the semis was barred by the number 2 seed Qamar Zaman, yet the New Zealan-der, in supremely confident form, put out the Pakis-tani in straight games. But against Dittmar it was a different story and the left-handed Australian coolly accepted the opportunity to move to his first World Open final without dropping a game.

In the other half of the draw Jahangir had made his inevitable progress, the only player to give him any-thing like a run being England's Phil Kenyon who kept the champion on court for 57 minutes and gleaned 12 points. Kenyon did not claim a game and the speculation concerning the final was whether Jahangir could become the first player to win the title without losing a game. Dittmar did his best, but managed only nine points in his 37 minutes on court.

It was 19-year-old Jahangir's third successive victory in the event and the first time that two teen-agers had battled for the title – an indication that squash players are maturing much more quickly and destroying the theory that the late twenties is the age when competitors can expect to reach the height of their physical strength.

1975 (Wembley, London)
Quarter-finals: Q. Zaman (Pak) beat J. Barrington (GB & Ire) 9–0, 9–1, 9–6; Mohibullah Khan (Pak) beat H. Jahan (Pak) 6–9, 9–1, 4–9, 9–7, 9–1; G. Alauddin (Pak) beat K. J. Hiscoe (Aus) 5–9, 9–0, 9–2, 9–1; G. B. Hunt (Aus) beat C. J. Nancarrow (Aus) 9–5, 9–6, 9–4.
Semi-finals: Mohibullah Khan beat Zaman 6–9, 9–5, 3–9, 9–2, 9–7; Hunt beat Alauddin 9–2, 9–5, 1–9, 9–5.
Final: Hunt beat Mohibullah Khan 7–9, 9–4, 8–10, 9–2, 9–2. (This event was incorporated in the 1975/6 British Open Championship.)
1977 (Adelaide, Australia)
Quarter-finals: G. B. Hunt (Aus) beat B. Brownlee (NZ) 9–2, 9–7, 9–3; G. Alauddin (Pak) beat H. Jahan (Pak) 7–9, 9–3, 5–9, 10–9, 10–8; Q. Zaman (Pak) beat J. Barrington (GB & Ire) 9–1, 9–5, 9–5; Mohibullah Khan (Pak) beat R. Watson (SA) 9–4, 9–6, 9–5.

The gallery at Wembley's championship court allows a less orthodox view of two of Britain's best young players – Martine Le Moignan, poised to strike the ball, and Ruth Strauss. *Tim Pike*

Semi-finals: Hunt beat Alauddin 9–6, 5–9, 9–2, 9–6; Zaman beat Mohibullah Khan 5–9, 9–4, 9–6, 8–10, 9–1.

Final: Hunt beat Zaman 9–5, 10–9, 0–9, 1–9, 9–4.

1979 (Toronto, Canada)

Quarter-finals: G. B. Hunt (Aus) beat R. Watson (SA) 9–6, 9–0, 5–9, 9–7; Mohibullah Khan (Pak) beat G. Alauddin (Pak) 5–9, 9–3, 9–2, 9–4; M. Ahmed (Pak) beat H. Jahan (Pak) 4–9, 9–4, 9–6, 7–9, 9–4; Q. Zaman (Pak) beat B. Brownlee (NZ) 9–1, 9–4, 9–6.

Semi-finals: Hunt beat Mohibullah Khan 9–3, 9–0, 9–2; Zaman beat Ahmed 9–7, 9–10, 9–4, 6–9, 9–4.

Final: Hunt beat Zaman 9–2, 9–3, 9–2.

1980 (Adelaide, Australia)

Quarter-finals: G. B. Hunt (Aus) beat G. Alauddin (Pak) 9–5, 10–8, 9–0; H. Jahan (Pak) beat G. Awad (Egy) 10–9, 9–1, 9–1; Mohibullah Khan (Pak) beat D. Williams (Aus) 9–5, 9–5, 9–1; Q. Zaman (Pak) beat Jahangir Khan (Pak) 5–9, 9–4, 9–0, 7–9, 9–2.

Semi-finals: Hunt beat Jahan 7–9, 10–9, 9–3, 9–5; Zaman beat Mohibullah Khan 10–8, 9–3, 9–3.

Final: Hunt beat Zaman 9–0, 9–3, 9–3.

1981 (Toronto, Canada)

Quarter-finals: G. B. Hunt (Aus) beat M. Ahmed (Pak) 9–0, 9–4, 9–1; Q. Zaman (Pak) beat A. Safwat (Egy) 9–5, 9–2, 9–4; H. Jahan (Pak) beat A. Aziz (Egy) 7–9, 9–4, 9–0, 9–2; Jahangir Khan (Pak) beat G. Awad (Egy) 9–6, 8–10, 9–5, 9–1.

Semi-finals: Hunt beat Zaman 9–5, 7–9, 9–2, 9–3; Jahangir Khan beat Jahan 9–3, 9–3, 9–3.

Final: Jahangir Khan beat Hunt 7–9, 9–1, 9–2, 9–1.

1982 (Birmingham, England)

Quarter-finals: Jahangir Khan (Pak) beat P. Kenyon (Eng) 9–2, 9–7, 9–6; G. Brumby (Aus) beat M. Ahmed (Pak) 9–7, 9–7, 9–6; D. Williams (Aus) beat Q. Zaman (Pak) 6–9, 5–9, 9–1, 9–3, 9–2; H. Jahan (Pak) beat G. Awad (Egy) 9–7, 9–3, 9–4.

Semi-finals: Jahangir Khan beat Brumby 9–1, 9–2, 9–0; Williams beat Jahan 9–6, 9–2, 0–9, 9–1.

Final: Jahangir Khan beat Williams 9–2, 6–9, 9–1, 9–1.

1983 (Munich, West Germany)

Quarter-finals: Jahangir Khan (Pak) beat P. Kenyon (Eng) 9–6, 9–0, 9–6; G. Awad (Egy) beat D. Williams (Aus) 10–8, 9–5, 9–4; C. Dittmar (Aus) beat M. Ahmed (Pak) 9–1, 9–7, 9–5; S. Davenport (NZ) beat Q. Zaman (Pak) 9–6, 10–8, 9–1.

Semi-finals: Jahangir Khan beat Awad 9–0, 9–1, 9–0; Dittmar beat Davenport 9–3, 9–3, 9–6.

Final: Jahangir Khan beat Dittmar 9–3, 9–6, 9–0.

ISRF World Championship

This biennial event was originally dubbed the International Squash Rackets Federation (ISRF) World Amateur Championship but, with the advent of

'Open' competition throughout the world, is now open to countries who are members of the Federation and all individuals who are members of an affiliated national association.

The team event – contested by three-man sides selected from a maximum of five nominated players – was played on an 'all-play-all' basis for the first four championships. In 1975, countries were divided into two groups with the top two in each playing off in a final pool. In 1977 the event reverted to its original format but, since then, thanks to the ever-growing list of entries, the competition has been structured on the pool system. The individual tournament is played on the traditional knock-out basis.

The first championships were held in Melbourne in 1967 when the host country dominated the team event by defeating Britain, New Zealand, South Africa, Pakistan and India without conceding a rubber. Britain finished second despite losing to New Zealand and, amazingly, Pakistan came last with only a victory over the Kiwis and one rubber against India to show for their journey. Australians also dominated the individual event providing three semi-finalists. In the final Geoff Hunt defeated fellow-countryman Cam Nancarrow who had beaten Jonah Barrington in the previous round.

Australia retained the team title in England in 1969 when they again defeated the other five competing nations although, on this occasion, they dropped rubbers to Britain, South Africa and Pakistan. Britain again finished second but Pakistan improved to fourth with wins over New Zealand and Egypt. Hunt beat Barrington in the final of the individual tournament – two other Australians Nancarrow and Ken Hiscoe reached the semi-finals.

Canada joined the fray in New Zealand in 1971 but only succeeded in winning one rubber – against India. Australia and Hunt completed their hat tricks. Britain finished second yet again and Pakistan moved up to third in the team event while Nancarrow was runner-up for the second time in the individual competition.

India, Egypt, Pakistan and Canada all decided against travelling to South Africa in 1973 but the USA brought the total of competing teams to five. Australia and Britain again took first places while, in the absence of Hunt, Nancarrow finally secured the individual title by beating England's Bryan Patterson in the final.

Australia's stranglehold on the team title was finally loosened in England in 1975. They could only finish third behind Pakistan and winners Great Britain – represented by Philip Ayton, Stuart Courtney, Jonny Leslie and Ian Robinson. Ten countries took part including, for the first time, Sweden and Kuwait.

The last ISRF world team trophy to be contested solely by amateurs went to the 1979 Great Britain side led by Jonny Leslie, pictured holding the award. On the left is team manager, Chris Stahl and on the right the coach, Jonah Barrington

There was no representative side from South Africa but in the individual event two of her players, Ian Holding and David Scott, contested a semi-final with Scott going on to lose in five to Australia's Kevin Shawcross in the final.

Two years later in Canada, Pakistan staked their claim as the world's leading squash nation by winning the team title and providing both finalists in the individual tournament. The team competition was the closest to date with Pakistan, New Zealand and Egypt all winning six of their seven matches and eventually being placed in that order by virtue of count-back on rubbers won. Pakistan beat Egypt 3–0 but lost 1–2 to New Zealand thanks to a fine win by Bruce Brownlee over Maqsood Ahmed who later defeated Mohammed Saleem in the individual final. Egypt then threw the competition wide open by beating New Zealand 2–1 with brothers Gamal and Mohammed Awad scoring wins over Bruce Brownlee and Murray Lillee. In the end it was Pakistan's performance against lesser teams that paved their way to the title. They beat Sweden and Australia 3–0 while both other leading contenders could only manage 2–1 victories against each of the nations. Great Britain finished a disappointing fourth after their victory two years earlier but Ian Robinson, playing second string, could be well pleased with his performance, winning in all six ties. Australia's demise was highlighted by the fact that only Dean Williams reached the last eight of the individual event where he lost to British Capt.

Jonny Leslie. Leslie put up a stirring performance in the semi-finals before losing 2–3 to eventual champion Maqsood Ahmed. The individual event in Melbourne in 1979 will forever be remembered as the occasion on which Jahangir Khan burst on to the world squash scene. The unseeded 15-year-old Pakistani, who was asked to qualify, recovered from two games to love down to defeat seventh seed Lars Kvant in the opening round. Later he defeated Australia's Ian Yeates to reach the quarter-finals where he trounced number 2 seed Jonny Leslie in straight games and then registered the same scoreline against Australian number 1 and sixth seed Frank Donnelly to reach the final. There he met England's Phil Kenyon who was seeded at 4 and had beaten top seed Atlas Khan in their semi-final. Kenyon took the opening game easily but the Pakistani was not to be denied and he captured the next three to become the youngest winner of the title.

Amazingly Jahangir was not considered good enough for the Pakistani side that defended the team title in Brisbane and his omission may well have cost them the championship. Atlas Khan, Daulat Khan and Fahim Gul safely negotiated their pool matches and a semi-final against Egypt to face Great Britain in the tournament's finale. The outcome rested on the result of the last rubber after Peter Verow had defeated Gul, and Leslie had gone down to Atlas Khan – both over five games. Phil Kenyon sealed Britain's second victory in the competition with a straight games victory over Daulat Khan but who knows what might have happened if Jahangir Khan had been included in the Pakistani line-up. Fourteen countries had competed with Ireland, Hong Kong, Malaysia and Nigeria making their first appearances.

Sweden played host to the championships in 1981 and the team event was littered with new entries: Singapore, West Germany, Finland, Holland, France, Norway, Zimbabwe and Monaco all sent sides while England and Scotland sent separate teams to replace Great Britain. India, Hong Kong and Malaysia did not enter. Pakistan with Jahangir Khan, Qamar Zaman and Maqsood Ahmed in the line-up cruised through the tournament without conceding a rubber to retain the team title.

Organisational mix-ups, off-court disputes and injuries deprived the individual competition of many leading players including all the Pakistanis. For the record, Steve Bowditch registered the sixth Australian victory by defeating New Zealand's Craig Blackwood in the final.

The ninth ISRF championships were held in New Zealand and they saw Pakistan maintain their dominance with that country winning the team title and the individual title through Jahangir Khan. Nineteen nations competed – it should have been 20 but Nigeria withdrew and their place was taken by an unofficial entry, New Zealand Youth.

The team event produced predictable results among the more established nations and the most improved team performances came from Ireland and Singapore who both moved up three places from positions attained in 1981.

In the individual championship Jahangir Khan dropped only one game in retaining his title but fortunately for the host country, Stuart Davenport, the New Zealand number 1, chose the occasion to produce some of his best form and finished in third spot. He had a notable win in his play-off against Hiddy Jahan who was representing England for the first time.

1967 (Australia)
TEAM
Australia beat Great Britain 3–0, New Zealand 3–0, South Africa 3–0, Pakistan 3–0, India 3–0. Great Britain beat South Africa 2–1, India 3–0, Pakistan 3–0. New Zealand beat Great Britain 2–1, South Africa 2–1, India 2–1. South Africa beat India 3–0, Pakistan 3–0. India beat Pakistan 2–1. Pakistan beat New Zealand 2–1.
Final positions: 1 Australia, 2 Great Britain, 3 New Zealand, 4 South Africa, 5 India, 6 Pakistan.

INDIVIDUAL
Quarter-finals: J. Barrington (GB & Ire) beat D. Botha (SA) 9–7, 10–9, 9–1; C. Nancarrow (Aus) beat R. Carter (Aus) 9–5, 7–9, 9–6, 3–9, 9–4; G. Hunt (Aus) beat M. Corby (GB) 9–3, 9–3, 10–8; K. Hiscoe (Aus) beat T. Burgess (Aus) 9–5, 9–3, 9–3.
Semi-finals: Nancarrow beat Barrington 9–7, 9–6, 9–7; Hunt beat Hiscoe 9–3, 9–7, 0–9, 10–8.
Final: Hunt beat Nancarrow 9–3, 9–2, 9–1.

1969 (England)
TEAM
Australia beat Great Britain 2–1, South Africa 2–1, Pakistan 2–1, New Zealand 3–0, Egypt 3–0. Great Britain beat South Africa 3–0, Pakistan 2–1, New Zealand 2–1, Egypt 2–1. Pakistan beat South Africa 2–1, New Zealand 2–1, Egypt 3–0. South Africa beat New Zealand 2–1, Egypt 2–1. New Zealand beat Egypt 2–1.
Final positions: 1 Australia, 2 Great Britain, 3 Pakistan, 4 South Africa, 5 New Zealand, 6 Egypt.

INDIVIDUAL
Quarter-finals: J. Barrington (GB & Ire) beat T. Johnson (NZ) 9–7, 9–1, 9–2; C. Nancarrow (Aus) beat R. Carter (Aus) 10–8, 9–7, 9–7; K. Hiscoe (Aus) beat M. Corby (GB) 9–7, 9–5, 9–6; G. Hunt (Aus) beat A. Jawaid (Pak) 9–5, 9–2, 9–2.
Semi-finals: Barrington beat Nancarrow 9–0, 9–2, 10–8; Hunt beat Hiscoe (Aus) 9–6, 9–5, 2–9, 9–7.
Final: Hunt beat Barrington 9–7, 2–9, 9–4, 9–0.

Results of matches played between top 6 seeds in past Championships

	Played	Won	Lost
AUSTRALIA			
v. Egypt	6	5	1
v. England	8	5	3
v. New Zealand	7	6	1
v. Pakistan	8	3	5
v. Sweden	5	5	0
Total	34	24	10
EGYPT			
v. Australia	6	1	5
v. England	8	4	4
v. New Zealand	4	3	1
v. Pakistan	6	0	6
v. Sweden	4	4	0
Total	28	12	16
ENGLAND			
v. Australia	8	3	5
v. Egypt	8	4	4
v. New Zealand	9	7	2
v. Pakistan	8	5	3
v. Sweden	2	2	0
Total	35	21	14
NEW ZEALAND			
v. Australia	7	1	6
v. Egypt	4	1	3
v. England	9	2	7
v. Pakistan	6	1	5
v. Sweden	6	6	0
Total	32	11	21
PAKISTAN			
v. Australia	8	5	3
v. Egypt	6	6	0
v. England	8	3	5
v. New Zealand	6	5	1
v. Sweden	3	3	0
Total	31	22	9
SWEDEN			
v. Australia	5	0	5
v. Egypt	4	0	4
v. England	6	0	6
v. New Zealand	6	0	6
v. Pakistan	3	0	3
Total	24	0	24
SUMMARY			
Australia	34	24	10
Pakistan	31	22	9
England	35	21	14
Egypt	28	12	16
New Zealand	32	11	21
Sweden	24	0	24

1971 (New Zealand)

TEAM

Australia beat Pakistan 2–1, Egypt 3–0, Great Britain 3–0, New Zealand 3–0, India 3–0, Canada 3–0. Pakistan beat Egypt 2–1, New Zealand 3–0, India 3–0, Canada 3–0. Egypt beat Great Britain 2–1, New Zealand 2–1, India 3–0, Canada 3–0. Great Britain beat Pakistan 3–0, New Zealand 3–0, India 3–0, Canada 3–0. New Zealand beat India 2–1, Canada 3–0. India beat Canada 2–1.

Final positions: 1 Australia, 2 Pakistan, 3 Egypt, 4 Great Britain, 5 New Zealand, 6 India, 7 Canada.

INDIVIDUAL

Quarter-finals: G. Hunt (Aus) beat A. Jawaid (Pak) 5–9, 9–6, 9–6, 9–7; K. Hiscoe (Aus) beat J. Easter (GB) 9–4, 9–7, 9–5; M. Asran (Egy) beat R. Lewis (Aus) 9–3, 9–7, 9–7; C. Nancarrow (Aus) beat P. Ayton (GB) 2–9, 10–9, 9–2, 9–7.

Semi-finals: Hunt beat Hiscoe 9–1, 9–3, 3–9, 9–1; Nancarrow beat Asran 9–3, 6–9, 9–7, 9–5.

Final: Hunt beat Nancarrow 9–0, 9–7, 8–10, 9–5.

1973 (South Africa)

TEAM

Australia beat Great Britain 2–1, South Africa 2–1, New Zealand 3–0, USA 3–0. Great Britain beat South Africa 2–1, New Zealand 3–0, USA 3–0. South Africa beat New Zealand 3–0, USA 3–0. New Zealand beat USA 3–0.

Final positions: 1 Australia, 2 Great Britain, 3 South Africa, 4 New Zealand, 5 USA.

INDIVIDUAL

Quarter-finals: C. Nancarrow (Aus) beat W. Reedman (Aus) 5–9, 9–3, 9–5, 10–8; M. Donnelly (Aus) beat P. Ayton (GB) 3–9, 10–8, 9–2, 10–8; B. Patterson (GB) beat J. Easter (GB) 9–4, 10–8, 9–1; D. Wright (Aus) beat L. Robberds (Aus) 9–4, 9–10, 9–4, 9–5.

Semi-finals: Nancarrow beat Donnelly 10–9, 9–2, 7–9, 9–6; Patterson beat Wright 5–9, 9–5, 9–7, 10–8.

Final: Nancarrow beat Patterson 9–2, 9–5, 9–3.

1975 (England)

TEAM

Pool A: Australia beat Egypt 2–1, Sweden 3–0, India 3–0, USA 3–0. Egypt beat Sweden 2–1, India 3–0, USA 3–0. Sweden beat India 3–0, USA 3–0. India beat USA 2–1.

Pool B: Great Britain beat Pakistan 3–0, New Zealand 3–0, Canada 3–0, Kuwait 3–0. Pakistan beat New Zealand 2–1, Canada 3–0, Kuwait 3–0. New Zealand beat Canada 3–0, Kuwait 3–0. Canada beat Kuwait 3–0.

Playoff series: Great Britain beat Australia 2–1, Egypt 2–1. Pakistan beat Australia 3–0, Egypt 2–1. New Zealand beat Sweden 2–1, India 3–0, USA 3–0. Sweden beat Canada 2–1, Kuwait 3–0. India beat Canada 2–1, Kuwait 3–0. Canada beat USA 2–1. USA beat Kuwait 3–0.

Final positions: 1 Great Britain, 2 Pakistan, 3 Australia, 4 Egypt, 5 New Zealand, 6 Sweden, 7 India, 8 Canada, 9 USA, 10 Kuwait.

INDIVIDUAL

Quarter-finals: K. Shawcross (Aus) beat N. Barbour (NZ) 9–5, 9–1, 9–4; M. Donnelly (Aus) beat B. Brownlee (NZ) 5–9, 9–7, 9–0, 9–0; D. Scott (SA) beat L. Keppell (Aus) 9–7, 9–4, 9–4; I. Holding (SA) beat P. Ayton (GB) 9–1, 9–3, 5–9, 9–6.

Semi-finals: Shawcross beat Donnelly 9–3, 9–4, 9–2; Scott beat Holding 2–9, 9–3, 9–10, 9–6, 9–2.

Final: Shawcross beat Scott 9–1, 0–9, 9–6, 6–9, 9–2.

1977 (Canada)

TEAM

Pakistan beat Canada 3–0, Egypt 3–0, USA 3–0, Great Britain 2–1, Sweden 3–0, Australia 3–0. New Zealand beat USA 3–0, Sweden 2–1, Pakistan 2–1, Great Britain 2–1, Canada 3–0, Australia 2–1. Egypt beat Great Britain 2–1, Sweden 2–1, Australia 2–1, New Zealand 2–1, Canada 3–0, USA 3–0. Great Britain beat Canada 3–0, USA 3–0, Australia 3–0, Sweden 2–1. Australia beat Sweden 2–1, USA 3–0, Canada 2–1. Sweden beat Canada 2–1, USA 2–1. Canada beat USA 3–0.

Final positions: 1 Pakistan, 2 New Zealand, 3 Egypt, 4 Great Britain, 5 Australia, 6 Sweden, 7 Canada, 8 USA.

INDIVIDUAL

Quarter-finals: M. Saleem (Pak) beat B. Brownlee (NZ) 10–8, 4–9, 9–5, 3–9, 9–1; G. Awad (Egy) beat Atlas Khan (Pak) 9–6, 9–0, 9–5; Maqsood Ahmed (Pak) beat L. Kvant (Swe) 9–0, 9–1, 9–4; J. Leslie (GB) beat D. Williams (Aus) 9–2, 6–9, 9–1, 9–0.

Semi-finals: Saleem beat Awad 9–7, 9–4, 1–9, 9–7; Ahmed beat Leslie 6–9, 9–2, 7–9, 9–5, 9–2.

Final: Ahmed beat Saleem 9–4, 9–7, 9–3.

1979 (Australia)

TEAM

Pool A: Pakistan beat Hong Kong 3–0, Ireland 3–0, Australia 2–1, Sweden 3–0, USA 3–0, India 3–0. Australia beat Sweden 3–0, India 2–1, USA 3–0, Hong Kong 3–0, Ireland 3–0. Sweden beat USA 2–1, Hong Kong 3–0, Ireland 3–0, India 2–1. India beat Ireland 3–0, Hong Kong 3–0, USA 3–0. USA beat Ireland 2–1, Hong Kong 3–0. Ireland beat Hong Kong 3–0.

Pool B: Great Britain beat Malaysia 3–0, Egypt 2–1, Nigeria 3–0, Kuwait 3–0, New Zealand 2–1, Canada 3–0. Egypt beat Canada 2–1, Nigeria 3–0, New Zealand 2–1, Malaysia 3–0, Kuwait 3–0. New Zealand beat Malaysia 3–0, Canada 3–0, Kuwait 3–0, Nigeria 3–0. Canada beat Nigeria 2–1, Malaysia 3–0, Kuwait 3–0. Nigeria beat Kuwait 3–0, Malaysia 3–0. Malaysia beat Kuwait 3–0.

Semi-finals: Great Britain beat Australia 2–1; Pakistan beat Egypt 2–1.

Final: Great Britain beat Pakistan 2–1.

Final positions: 1 Great Britain, 2 Pakistan, 3 Australia, 4 Egypt, 5 New Zealand, 6 Sweden, 7 India, 8 Canada, 9 USA, 10 Ireland, 11 Nigeria, 12 Malaysia, 13 Hong Kong, 14 Kuwait.

INDIVIDUAL

Quarter-finals: Atlas Khan (Pak) beat R. Norman (NZ) 9–6, 9–4, 2–9, 2–9, 9–3; P. Kenyon (GB) beat M.

Awad (Egy) 10–8, 9–0, 9–2; F. Donnelly (Aus) beat M. Hellstrom (Swe) 9–4, 2–9, 9–4, 9–2; Jahangir Khan (Pak) beat J. Leslie (GB) 9–7, 9–3, 9–4.

Semi-finals: Kenyon beat Atlas Khan 8–10, 9–1, 9–0, 9–4; Jahangir Khan beat Donnelly 9–4, 9–4, 9–3.

Final: Jahangir Khan beat Kenyon 2–9, 9–3, 9–3, 9–5.

1981 (Sweden)
TEAM
Pool A: Pakistan beat USA 3–0, Canada 3–0, Singapore 3–0. USA beat Singapore 2–1, Canada 2–1. Canada beat Singapore 3–0.

Pool B: Egypt beat England 2–1, Kuwait 3–0, Nigeria 3–0, West Germany 3–0. England beat Nigeria 3–0, West Germany 3–0, Kuwait 3–0. Nigeria beat Kuwait 2–1, West Germany 2–1. West Germany beat Kuwait 2–1.

Pool C: New Zealand beat Holland 2–1, France 3–0, Norway 3–0, Sweden 2–1, Finland 3–0. Sweden beat Norway 3–0, Holland 3–0, Finland 3–0, France 3–0. Finland beat France 3–0, Norway 3–0, Holland 2–1. Holland beat France 3–0, Norway 3–0. France beat Norway 3–0.

Pool D: Australia beat Scotland 3–0, Ireland 3–0, Zimbabwe 3–0, Monaco 3–0. Scotland beat Ireland 2–1, Zimbabwe 2–1, Monaco 3–0. Ireland beat Monaco 3–0, Zimbabwe 2–1. Zimbabwe beat Monaco 3–0.

Playoff series: Positions 1/8: Pakistan beat Australia 3–0, Egypt beat England 2–1, New Zealand beat Sweden 2–1, USA beat Scotland 3–0. Positions 9/16: Canada beat Finland 2–1, Zimbabwe beat Singapore 2–1, Ireland beat Nigeria 3–0, Holland beat West Germany 2–1. Positions 17/20: France beat Kuwait 3–0, Norway beat Monaco 3–0.

Final positions: 1 Pakistan, 2 Australia, 3 Egypt, 4 England, 5 New Zealand, 6 Sweden, 7 USA, 8 Scotland, 9 Canada, 10 Finland, 11 Zimbabwe, 12 Singapore, 13 Ireland, 14 Nigeria, 15 Holland, 16 West Germany, 17 France, 18 Kuwait, 19 Norway, 20 Monaco.

INDIVIDUAL
Quarter-finals: L. Kvant (Swe) beat M. Hellstrom (Swe) 10–8, 9–4, 9–7; C. Blackwood (NZ) beat P. Bostrum (Swe) 6–9, 6–9, 9–3, 9–6, 9–3; J. Soderberg (Swe) beat R. Henning (Swe) 7–9, 9–6, 9–3, 2–9, 9–4; S. Bowditch (Aus) beat M. Saad (Egy) 9–7, 9–7, 9–5.

Semi-finals: Blackwood beat Kvant 8–10, 8–10, 9–2, 9–1, 10–8; Bowditch beat Soderberg 9–7, 9–2, 9–3.

Final: Bowditch beat Blackwood 3–9, 7–9, 9–4, 9–3, 9–3.

1983 (New Zealand)
TEAM
Pool 1: Pakistan beat New Zealand Youth 3–0, Canada 3–0, Singapore 3–0, Scotland 3–0. Canada beat Singapore 3–0, Scotland 3–0. New Zealand Youth beat Scotland 3–0, Singapore 3–0, Canada 2–1. Singapore beat Scotland 2–1. Positions: 1 Pakistan, 2 Canada, 3 Singapore, 4 Scotland (New Zealand Youth had three wins but as an unofficial entry their results did not count in the final placings).

Pool 2: England beat Zimbabwe 3–0, Papua New Guinea 3–0, USA 3–0, Kuwait 3–0. USA beat Kuwait 3–0,

Zimbabwe 3–0, Papua New Guinea 3–0. Zimbabwe beat Papua New Guinea 3–0, Kuwait 3–0. Papua New Guinea beat Kuwait 3–0. Positions: 1 England, 2 USA, 3 Zimbabwe, 4 Papua New Guinea, 5 Kuwait.

Pool 3: Australia beat Hong Kong 3–0, Wales 3–0, Malaysia 3–0, Sweden 3–0. Sweden beat Malaysia 3–0, Hong Kong 3–0, Wales 3–0. Wales beat Malaysia 3–0, Hong Kong 3–0. Malaysia beat Hong Kong 3–0. Positions: 1 Australia, 2 Sweden, 3 Wales, 4 Malaysia, 5 Hong Kong.

Pool 4: Egypt beat Finland 3–0, Ireland 3–0, Japan 3–0, New Zealand 2–1. New Zealand beat Japan 3–0, Finland 3–0, Ireland 3–0. Ireland beat Japan 3–0, Finland 2–1. Finland beat Japan 3–0. Positions: 1 Egypt, 2 New Zealand, 3 Ireland, 4 Finland, 5 Japan.

Intermediate Pools

Pool A: Pakistan beat USA 3–0, New Zealand 3–0, Australia 3–0. Australia beat New Zealand 3–0, USA 3–0. New Zealand beat USA 2–1. Positions: 1 Pakistan, 2 Australia, 3 New Zealand, 4 USA.

Pool B: England beat Sweden 3–0, Canada 3–0, Egypt 2–1. Egypt beat Canada 3–0, Sweden 2–1. Sweden beat Canada 3–0. Positions: 1 England, 2 Egypt, 3 Sweden, 4 Canada.

Pool C: Singapore beat Papua New Guinea 3–0, Wales 2–1. Wales beat Finland 2–1, Papua New Guinea 3–0. Finland beat Singapore 2–1, Papua New Guinea 2–1. Positions: 1 Singapore, 2 Wales, 3 Finland, 4 Papua New Guinea.

Pool D: Ireland beat Malaysia 3–0, Scotland 2–1, Zimbabwe 3–0. Scotland beat Zimbabwe 3–0, Malaysia 3–0. Zimbabwe beat Malaysia 2–1. Positions: 1 Ireland, 2 Scotland, 3 Zimbabwe, 4 Malaysia.

Pool E: Japan beat Hong Kong 3–0, Kuwait 3–0. Kuwait beat Hong Kong 2–1. Positions: 1 Japan, 2 Kuwait, 3 Hong Kong.

Semi-finals: Pakistan beat Egypt 3–0, England beat Australia 3–0.

Final: Pakistan beat England 3–0.

Play-offs: 3/4 Australia beat Egypt 2–1, 5/6 New Zealand beat Sweden 2–1, 7/8 USA beat Canada 2–1, 9/10 Singapore beat Ireland 2–1, 11/12 Wales beat Scotland 3–0, 13/14 Finland beat Zimbabwe 2–1, 15/16 Malaysia w.o. Papua New Guinea. Japan, Kuwait and Hong Kong filled 17, 18 and 19 positions, respectively.

INDIVIDUAL
Quarter-finals: Jahangir Khan (Pak) beat P. Kenyon (Eng) 6–9, 9–1, 9–2, 9–3; S. Davenport (NZ) beat R. Thorne (Aus) 9–4, 1–9, 9–5, 9–2; H. Jahan (Eng) beat G. Briars (Eng) 9–6, 9–2, 9–5; Q. Zaman (Pak) beat Maqsood Ahmed (Pak) 9–7, 5–9, 9–5, 9–4.

Semi-finals: Jahangir Khan beat Davenport 9–4, 9–0, 9–2. Zaman beat Jahan 9–3, 9–5, 2–9, 9–3.

Final: Jahangir Khan beat Zaman 9–0, 9–4, 9–3. 3/4 play-off Davenport beat Jahan 9–7, 9–1, 4–9, 2–9, 9–6.

Final teams placings in past ISRF Championships

1967 (Australia)	2 Great Britain
1 Australia	3 New Zealand

4 South Africa
5 India
6 Pakistan

1969 (England)
1 Australia
2 Great Britain
3 Pakistan
4 South Africa
5 New Zealand
6 Egypt

1971 (New Zealand)
1 Australia
2 Pakistan
3 Egypt
4 Great Britain
5 New Zealand
6 India
7 Canada

1973 (South Africa)
1 Australia
2 Great Britain
3 South Africa
4 New Zealand
5 USA

1975–76 (England)
1 Great Britain
2 Pakistan
3 Australia
4 Egypt
5 New Zealand
6 Sweden
7 India
8 Canada
9 USA
10 Kuwait

1977 (Canada)
1 Pakistan
2 New Zealand
3 Egypt
4 Great Britain
5 Australia
6 Sweden
7 Canada
8 USA

1979 (Australia)
1 Great Britain
2 Pakistan
3 Australia
4 Egypt
5 New Zealand

6 Sweden
7 India
8 Canada
9 USA
10 Ireland
11 Nigeria
12 Malaysia
13 Hong Kong
14 Kuwait

1981 (Sweden)
1 Pakistan
2 Australia
3 Egypt
4 England
5 New Zealand
6 Sweden
7 USA
8 Scotland
9 Canada
10 Finland
11 Zimbabwe
12 Singapore
13 Ireland
14 Nigeria
15 Holland
16 West Germany
17 France
18 Kuwait
19 Norway
20 Monaco

1983 (New Zealand)
1 Pakistan
2 England
3 Australia
4 Egypt
5 New Zealand
6 Sweden
7 USA
8 Canada
9 Singapore
10 Ireland
11 Wales
12 Scotland
13 Finland
14 Zimbabwe
15 Malaysia
16 Papua New Guinea
17 Japan
18 Kuwait
19 Hong Kong

World Individual Over-45 Championship

Final: K. Hiscoe (Aus) beat F. Howell (Aus) 9–6, 9–0, 9–5.

World Junior Championship

(1973–79 known as Junior International Festival)

1973–75 England (England)   **1979** Pakistan (England)
1976 England (Wales)   **1980** (Sweden)
1978 Australia (Sweden)

TEAM
Pool I: New Zealand beat West Germany 3–0, Bahamas 3–0, Canada 3–0. Canada beat West Germany 2–1, Bahamas 3–0. West Germany beat Bahamas 3–0.
Pool II: Sweden beat Ireland 3–0, Wales 2–1, Denmark 3–0. Wales beat Ireland 3–0, Denmark 3–0. Ireland beat Denmark 3–0.
Pool III: Pakistan beat Australia 3–0, Switzerland 3–0, Norway 3–0. Australia beat Switzerland 3–0, Norway 3–0. Switzerland beat Norway 3–0.
Pool IV: England beat Scotland 3–0, Netherlands 3–0, Finland 3–0. Scotland beat Netherlands 2–1, Finland 3–0. Netherlands beat Finland 3–0.
Intermediate groups: (A) England beat Sweden 3–0, Canada 2–1. Australia beat England 2–1, Sweden 3–0, Canada 3–0. Canada beat Sweden 3–0. (B) Pakistan beat New Zealand 3–0, Scotland 3–0, Wales 2–1. New Zealand beat Scotland 3–0, Wales 3–0. Scotland beat Wales 2–1. (C) Finland beat West Germany 3–0, Switzerland 3–0, Denmark 3–0. West Germany beat Switzerland 2–1, Denmark 3–0. Switzerland beat Denmark 3–0. (D) Netherlands beat Ireland 2–1, Bahamas 3–0, Norway 3–0. Ireland beat Bahamas 3–0, Norway 3–0. Bahamas beat Norway 3–0.
Final: Australia beat Pakistan 2–1: S. Qaiser (Pak) beat P. Nance (Aus) 10–9, 9–2, 9–6; C. Dittmar (Aus) beat J. Gul (Pak) 9–6, 9–7, 9–3; C. Carter (Aus) beat Omar Hyat (Pak) 9–6, 9–5, 9–7. 3/4 New Zealand beat England 2–1. 5/6 Canada beat Scotland 3–0. 7/8 Sweden w.o. Wales. 9/10 Netherlands beat Finland 3–0. 11/12 Ireland beat West Germany 2–1. 13/14 Switzerland beat Bahamas 2–1. 15/16 Denmark beat Norway 3–0.

INDIVIDUAL
Semi-finals: C. Dittmar (Aus) beat S. Davenport (NZ) 9–1, 9–5, 3–9, 9–6; P. Nance (Aus) beat C. Carter (Aus) 9–4, 9–1, 9–4.
Final: Nance beat Dittmar 6–9, 9–7, 9–2, 9–6.

1982 (Singapore)
TEAM
Group A: Australia beat Hong Kong 3–0, Scotland 3–0. Scotland beat Hong Kong 3–0.
Group B: New Zealand beat Wales 2–1, Singapore 2–1, Thailand 3–0. Wales beat Singapore 2–1, Thailand 3–0. Singapore beat Thailand 3–0.
Group C: Pakistan beat Canada 3–0, Sweden 3–0. Sweden beat Canada 3–0.
Group D: England beat West Germany 3–0, Malaysia 3–0, Ireland 3–0. Ireland beat Malaysia 2–1, West Germany 2–1. West Germany beat Malaysia 2–1.
Round-robin play-offs (positions 9–13): West Germany beat Malaysia 3–0, Hong Kong 3–0, Singapore 2–1. Singapore beat Malaysia 3–0, Hong Kong 3–0, Canada 2–1. Canada beat West Germany 2–1, Malaysia 2–1, Hong Kong 3–0. Malaysia beat Hong Kong 2–1.
Positions: 9 West Germany, 10 Singapore, 11 Canada, 12 Malaysia, 13 Hong Kong.
Round-robin play-offs (positions 1–8): Pakistan beat Ireland 3–0, Scotland 3–0, New Zealand 3–0. Australia beat Wales 3–0, Sweden 3–0, England 3–0. England

Sohail Qaiser, the brilliant young Pakistani who is a nephew of the great Gogi Alauddin. In addition to two world junior titles he has quickly played his way into the world's top twenty. *Robin Eley Jones*

beat Sweden 3–0, Wales 3–0. New Zealand beat Scotland 2–1, Ireland 3–0. Ireland beat Scotland 2–1. Sweden beat Wales 3–0.
Final: Pakistan beat Australia 2–1: S. Qaiser (Pak) beat C. Dittmar (Aus) 5–9, 9–5, 9–5, 9–5; U. Hyat (Pak) beat T. Nancarrow (Aus) 8–10, 9–4, 9–3, 9–6; T. Pinnington (Aus) beat A. Gul (Pak) 9–0, 9–1, 9–3. 3/4 England beat New Zealand 2–1. 5/6 Ireland beat Sweden 2–1. 7/8 Wales beat Scotland 2–1.

INDIVIDUAL
Semi-finals: S. Qaiser (Pak) beat T. Nancarrow (Aus) 9–1, 9–6, 9–2; C. Dittmar (Aus) beat C. Willstrop (Eng) 9–4, 9–4, 9–3.
Final: Qaiser beat Dittmar 3–9, 10–8, 9–4, 9–3.

WISRF World Championships

In August 1976 the Australian Women's Association staged a Women's World Invitation Championship in Brisbane. The field was limited to 32 and the competition was designated 'Open' mainly in order to accommodate Heather McKay who had turned professional three years earlier. Mrs McKay duly repaid the honour by winning the title without dropping a game. Following the success of the event, the Women's International Squash Rackets Federation was formed to run regular world competitions for individuals and teams.

In 1979 England was chosen as the first venue for the combined team and individual world championship which was sponsored by hosiery company Pretty Polly. McKay retained her title from a field of 68 by beating England's Sue Cogswell in the final at Abbeydale Park, Sheffield after defeating Teresa Lawes and Angela Smith in earlier rounds. McKay did not compete in the team event at Edgbaston Priory, Birmingham and Cogswell, Smith and Lawes took full advantage of her absence by combining to win the title for Great Britain as they defeated Australia (Barbara Wall, Vicki Hoffman and Sue King) 3–0 in the final. Ireland, Sweden, Canada and the USA also took part with the Irish taking third place.

McKay did not defend her title in Toronto in 1981 but the trophy returned to Australia when Rhonda Thorne surprisingly beat compatriot and top seed Vicky Hoffman in a tense final which lasted just five minutes under two hours. The same two players were successful as Australia beat England 2–1 in the team final. In the first World Junior Championship final, English girl Lisa Opie beat Nottingham clubmate Martine Le Moignan.

For the next two years Vicki Cardwell (née Hoffman) was haunted by the memory of that defeat and she prepared for the 1983 Perth event knowing that it would be her last opportunity to win the title as she had announced earlier in the year her decision to retire after the next world championship. Her determination was clear for all to see as she stormed through to the final without losing a game and then crushed her colleague Rhonda Thorne in the final for the loss of only eight points.

The manner of her victory was fitting revenge for the defeat by Thorne in Canada. It was widely expected that England's Lisa Opie, seeded number 2 would have provided the opposition in the final but she lost a desperately close match with Thorne in the quarter-finals. Opie had match ball at 9–8 in the fifth only to waste the opportunity by serving out and seeing Thorne recover to win 10–9.

This result climaxed a disappointing championship for the English contingent, none of them progressing beyond the quarter-finals and their failures providing an opportunity for Australia's Carin Clonda and New Zealand's Sue Devoy to make unexpected appearances in the semis. England hoped to recoup lost glory in the team event and indeed reached the final against Australia but lost in disappointing and controversial fashion.

A gamble was taken to restore Martine Le Moignan, injured in the quarter-finals, to the England team and to drop Angela Smith down the order to number 3. This was good news for Clonda who was due to face Smith knowing she had lost twice to the English girl in the last two British Opens. Also Clonda had beaten Le Moignan earlier in the week in the individual event. Indeed the new playing order meant all the English team had to face opponents to whom they had lost in Australia. When Smith avenged her defeat by Jan Miller it seemed a good omen but this good start was quickly offset by Clonda beating Le Moignan for the loss of 10 points. This left Opie v. Thorne in the decider and Opie after leading one game to love and 5–0 was pulled back to two games all. In the fifth Opie led 5–0, had match ball at 8–7,

lost the verdict in a controversial refereeing decision at 8–8 and then the game and match at 8–10.

Although it was a close win for Australia, the victory was achieved without their number 1 Vicki Cardwell who was suspended from representing her country after incidents at the 1981 championship.

1976 (Brisbane, Australia)
Quarter-finals: Mrs H. McKay (Aus) beat Mrs J. Webster (NZ) 9–1, 9–1, 9–1; Miss M. Zachariah (Aus) beat Mrs J. Eckstein (SA) 9–3, 9–6, 9–0; Miss S. Newman (Aus) beat Miss S. Cogswell (Eng) 9–5, 9–5, 9–4; Mrs M. Jackman (Aus) beat Miss C. van Nierop (Aus) 9–5, 9–5, 10–8.
Semi-finals: McKay beat Zachariah 9–1, 9–4, 9–1; Jackman beat Newman 9–1, 9–5, 9–3.
Final: McKay beat Jackman 9–2, 9–2, 9–0.

Right
Robyn Friday (Aus) winner of the 1983 WISRF World Junior Championship, the first event of its kind to be run on an Open basis. *Greg Wood*

Below
Vicki Cardwell (Aus) dives full-length to retrieve a shot during her semi-final match with Sue Devoy of New Zealand in the 1983 WISRF World Championship. Cardwell got up to win the rally and eventually the match. *Greg Wood*

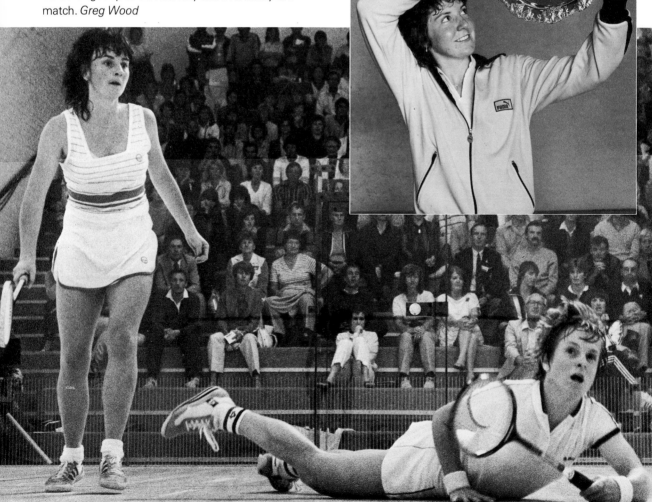

1979 (England)
INDIVIDUAL (Abbeydale Park, Sheffield)
Quarter-finals: Mrs H. McKay (Aus) beat Mrs Anne Smith (Aus) 9–2, 9–5, 9–4; Miss Angela Smith (Eng) beat Miss B. Wall (Aus) 9–5, 9–3, 9–3; Miss S. Cogswell (Eng) beat Mrs S. King (née Newman) (Aus) 9–1, 9–1, 9–0; Miss V. Hoffman (Aus) beat Mrs R. Thorne (Aus) 9–2, 9–1, 9–1.
Semi-finals: McKay beat Smith 9–10, 9–4, 9–3, 9–1; Cogswell beat Hoffman 9–6, 9–5, 7–9, 9–7.
Final: McKay beat Cogswell 6–9, 9–3, 9–1, 9–4.

TEAM (Edgbaston Priory, Birmingham)
Final: Great Britain beat Australia 3–0.
Miss S. Cogswell beat Miss B. Wall 9–6, 9–3, 9–1; Miss Angela Smith beat Miss V. Hoffman 9–7, 7–9, 9–3, 9–5; Miss T. Lawes beat Mrs S. King 5–9, 9–5, 7–9, 9–4, 9–5.
Final positions: 1 Great Britain, 2 Australia, 3 Ireland, 4 Canada, 5 Sweden, 6 USA.

1981 (Toronto, Canada)
INDIVIDUAL
Quarter-finals: Miss V. Hoffman (Aus) beat Miss M. Le Moignan (Eng) 9–1, 9–5, 9–3; Miss A. Smith (Eng) beat Miss M. Zachariah (Aus) 9–2, 9–2, 10–9; Miss L. Opie (Eng) beat Miss S. Cogswell (Eng) 8–10, 9–4, 7–9, 9–3, 9–2; Mrs R. Thorne (Aus) beat Mrs B. Diggens (Eng) 9–2, 9–1, 9–1.
Semi-finals: Hoffman beat Smith 9–2, 9–2, 10–9; Thorne beat Opie 9–2, 9–0, 9–4.
Final: Thorne beat Hoffman 8–10, 9–4, 9–5, 7–9, 9–7.

TEAM
Final: Australia beat England 2–1.
Mrs R. Thorne beat Miss A. Smith 9–1, 9–6, 9–0; Miss V. Hoffman beat Miss L. Opie 9–5, 9–7, 9–6; Miss B. Oldfield lost to Miss S. Cogswell 8–10, 9–3, 9–4, 7–9, 9–10.
Final positions: 1 Australia, 2 England, 3 New Zealand, 4 Scotland, 5 Ireland, 6 Wales, 7 Canada, 8 Zimbabwe, 9 Sweden, 10 Kenya, 11 USA, 12 Holland, 13 Germany, 14 Nigeria.

1983 (Perth, Australia)
INDIVIDUAL
Quarter-finals: Mrs V. Cardwell (née Hoffman) (Aus) beat Miss A. Smith (Eng) 9–6, 9–5, 9–4; Mrs R. Thorne (Aus) beat Miss L. Opie (Eng) 9–7, 9–6, 9–10, 3–9, 10–9; Miss S. Devoy (NZ) beat Miss H. Wallace (Sco) 7–9, 9–3, 9–4, 9–7; Miss C. Clonda (Aus) beat Miss M. Le Moignan (Eng) 9–3, 9–7, 5–9, 9–4.
Semi-finals: Cardwell beat Devoy 9–2, 9–5, 9–4; Thorne beat Clonda 6–9, 9–1, 9–1, 9–2.
Final: Cardwell beat Thorne 9–1, 9–3, 9–4.

TEAM
Final: Australia beat England 2–1.
Mrs R. Thorne beat Miss L. Opie 2–9, 9–6, 5–9, 10–8, 10–8; Miss C. Clonda beat Miss M. Le Moignan 9–4, 9–5, 9–1; Miss J. Miller lost to Miss A. Smith 6–9, 4–9, 6–9.

Final positions: 1 Australia, 2 England, 3 New Zealand, 4 Ireland, 5 Scotland, 6 USA, 7 Wales, 8 Canada, 9 Sweden.

World Individual Over-35 Championship

Final: M. Zachariah (Aus) beat M. Greenberg (USA) 9–7, 9–6, 9–8.

World Individual Over-40 Championship

Final: J. Webster (NZ) beat A. Smith (Aus) 9–7, 9–2, 9–4.

World Junior Championships

1981 (Ottawa, Canada) (Invitation event only)
Semi-finals: Miss L. Opie (Eng) beat Miss R. Strauss (Eng) 9–3, 7–9, 10–8, 9–1; Miss M. Le Moignan (Eng) beat Miss S. Devoy (NZ) 9–1, 3–9, 7–9, 9–5, 9–1.
Final: Opie beat Le Moignan 9–4, 9–6, 10–8.

1983 (Perth, Australia)
Semi-finals: Miss H. Paradeiser (Aus) beat Miss E. Irving (Aus) 5–9, 8–10, 9–7, 7–4, 10–8; Miss R. Friday (Aus) beat Miss L. Soutter (Eng) 7–9, 8–10, 9–6, 9–6, 9–7.
Final: Friday beat Paradeiser 10–8, 9–3, 9–2.

1984 (Calgary)
TEAM
Qualifying
Pool 1: Pakistan beat West Germany 3–0, Scotland 2–1. Scotland beat West Germany 3–0.
Pool 2: Australia beat Finland 3–0, Wales 2–1. Finland beat Wales 2–1.
Pool 3: England beat USA 3–0, Canada 2–1, Ireland 3–0. Canada beat Ireland 3–0, USA 3–0. Ireland beat USA 2–1.
Pool 4: Sweden beat Malaysia 3–0, Netherlands 2–1, New Zealand 2–1. New Zealand beat Netherlands 3–0, Malaysia 2–1. Malaysia beat Netherlands 2–1.

Intermediate Pools
Pool 1: England beat Finland 2–1, New Zealand 3–0, Pakistan 2–1. Pakistan beat New Zealand 3–0, Finland 3–0. New Zealand beat Finland 2–1.
Pool 2: Australia beat Scotland 3–0, Canada 2–1, Sweden 3–0. Canada beat Sweden 2–1, Scotland 2–1. Sweden beat Scotland 2–1.
Pool 3: West Germany beat Netherlands 2–1, Ireland 2–1. Ireland beat Netherlands 2–1.
Pool 4: Wales beat USA 2–1, Malaysia 2–1. USA beat Malaysia 2–1.
Semi-finals: Australia beat Pakistan 3–0, England beat Canada 2–1, Scotland beat New Zealand 2–1, Sweden beat Finland 3–0, USA beat West Germany 2–1, Wales beat Ireland 3–0, Malaysia beat Netherlands 3–0.
Finals: 1st place: Australia beat England 2–1. D. Lloyd (Eng) beat C. Robertson (Aus) 9–3, 9–0, 10–8; R. Martin (Aus) beat R. Owen (Eng) 9–4, 10–8, 9–4; S. O'Connor (Aus) beat G. Robinson (Eng) 9–2, 9–0, 9–3. 3/4 Pakistan beat Canada 3–0. 5/6 Sweden beat Scotland 3–0. 7/8 New Zealand beat Finland 2–1. 9/10 Wales

beat USA 2–1. 11/12 West Germany beat Ireland 2–1. 13/14 Malaysia beat Netherlands 3–0.

INDIVIDUAL
Semi-finals: D. Lloyd (Eng) beat Jansher Khan (Pak) 3–9, 7–9, 9–3, 9–6, 9–6; C. Robertson (Aus) beat R. Martin (Aus) 5–9, 9–3, 9–4, 9–6.
Final: Robertson beat Lloyd 9–0, 9–5, 9–0.

The British Open Championship

MEN

The birth of the world's most famous tournament was announced by a simple statement in the 1930/1 Squash Rackets Association handbook – 'An open championship has been instituted and, for purposes of challenge, C. R. Read has been designated open champion'. Don Butcher challenged and beat 'champion' Charles Read in a best-of-three match series to become the first winner of the event. In this system, which was discarded in favour of a knock-out format in 1947, the holder had to accept one challenge each season or surrender his title. The first match was played on the holder's home court, the second on the challenger's and if a deciding match had been necessary – it never was – it would have been at a neutral venue chosen by the SRA. Two thirds of the £100 purse went to the winner while the loser took one-third. If the gate receipts and player 'sponsorships' did not total £100, the challenger had to supply the difference. If either player was an amateur, the entire purse was given to the professional – win or lose.

The printed markers scoresheets with sponsor's names had not been thought about at the time of the first British Open in 1930. The back of an envelope was frequently pressed into service as Dugald Macpherson did when he marked the Open final that year, recording that Butcher beat Read by 9–3, 9–5, 9–3. *Courtesy of Ian Wright*

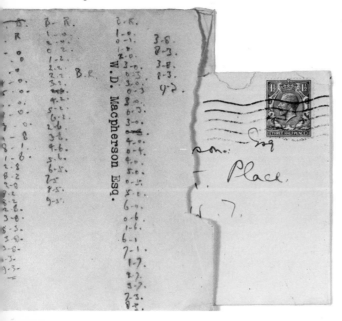

Egypt's Amr Bey was the most successful player while this format was in operation winning six times including 1933 when he did not receive a challenge. Jim Dear, who won the event in 1938, was an unsuccessful challenger on four occasions and was runner-up in the first tournament played as a knock-out when he was beaten by Mahmoud Karim in March 1948.

Since 1947 the event has been open to any player who, depending on his recent results, will either be placed directly in the main draw of 64 or asked to play through qualifying rounds.

Until 1974 the competition was regarded as the unofficial world championship and the roll of honour is in effect a list of players who are legends in the sport. Then in 1975 for one year it incorporated the World Open and since then a world championship has existed in its own right. Despite this innovation many players still regard the British Open as the 'one to win'.

The record number of victories is held by Australia's Geoff Hunt who won his eighth title at Bromley in 1980/1 beating by one the run of wins by Hashim Khan in the 1950s and by two the series by Barrington in the mid-sixties and early seventies.

The exploits of Hashim, Azam and Roshan Khan dominated squash, let alone the British Open, from 1950 until 1961 when the extraordinarily gifted and late lamented Aboutaleb briefly established Egyptian control of the title. By 1966 Jonah Barrington, the galvaniser, the forerunner of the modern professional game, had burst through to fire the enthusiasm of Britain's own squash players and begun a series of Open victories that threatened to overhaul Hashim.

Barrington's style of total commitment to physical fitness kept him ahead of the field while his opponents relied on a less professional approach although this is not to demean Barrington's Open successes since he defeated players with greater racket skills than his own.

The Barrington reign ended at the 1973/4 Championship, the great man beaten in the semi-finals by the wily Pakistani Mohammed Yasin. It was a sad championship for many reasons, not the least being Barrington's defeat. Yasin had to pull out of the final through injury and so lost his one and only chance of winning the title and BBC's cameras, present for the first time, had to film a meaningless exhibition match between Geoff Hunt and Barrington. To compound matters the match only went ahead after hours of bickering over terms and conditions for the appearance of both players – a situation that did not impress BBC or the sponsors, Benson and Hedges.

If this was a low point for the Open, the championship quickly reasserted itself as Hunt and the Pakistani Qamar Zaman began in 1974 a rivalry that captured the imagination of all squash followers. It was to extend through six championships until 1980, missing only the 1976/7 event when the Pakistanis boycotted the Open in a protest over South African participants. Zaman only won the title once (in 1974/5) and finished runner-up to Hunt on three occasions, the 1977/8 final being memorable for an incredible 50-minute opening game in which both players appeared intent on driving the other to exhaustion. Zaman was the one to crack. He had used all his stamina and had to capitulate weakly in the next three games.

Hunt just managed to sustain his own fitness long enough to set a new record of eight wins at the 1980/1 Championship before the awesome and youthful power of Jahangir Khan brought about the real prospect of a Pakistani domination of the title in much the same way the Khans did in the fifties.

The championship has also incorporated a Veteran's event since 1964 which India's Jamal Din has

Generations apart but linked by supreme sporting achievements – Hashim Khan, seven times British Open champion and the man who was to beat his record, Geoff Hunt, shown here at the start of the 1977/8 British Open Championship. Hashim had returned to this country to play in the Vintage Championship and at the time Hunt had recorded four Open victories

won five times and a Vintage Championship since 1975 in which the great Hashim Khan reigned supreme from 1977–82.

The rewards for the championship bear little resemblance to the £100 purse of early tournaments. The first £1000 winners' prize was offered in the 1973/4 season and the rewards have steadily risen – 74/5 (£1250), 75/6 (£1650), 76/7 (£1800), 77/8 (£2000), 78/9 (£2500), 79/80 (£2750), 80/1 (£3700), 81/2 (£4000). In 1982/3, due to reduced sponsorship the total prize money dipped from £25 000 to £13 500 with £2500 going to the winner, but an Over-35

Championship was inaugurated with £400 as first prize. However, in 1983/4 the level was raised again to £25 000 with a £4000 first prize.

Since 1981/2 the women's open, still under the control of the Women's Squash Rackets Association, has been run in conjunction with the men's event and while this has proved to be a very successful format, it does mean an increased requirement for sponsorship.

The Open has always been in the forefront in utilising the latest technical developments in squash and in 1980 the closing stages of the championship were held at the Wembley Conference Centre. A Perstorp demountable court with three solid walls and a glass back was used on the stage enabling an audience of up to 1000 to watch the play. For the next two years a similar style of presentation was employed at the Churchill Theatre, Bromley until in 1983 a four-wall transparent court (the ICI Perspex Court) was set up in the Assembly Rooms, Derby. This raised the audience capacity to around 1500, and further progress was made in 1984 when the event returned to the Conference Centre at Wembley. By siting the ICI court on the floor of the auditorium the Open final was played to its largest audience of 2603. Although the setting had changed the result of the men's final did not with Jahangir easily beating Zaman. Notable performances came from Gawain Briars and Geoff Williams of England in appearing in the quarter-finals with Williams going on to become the first English player in 17 years to reach the semi-final.

1930
D. G. Butcher beat C. R. Read 9–6, 9–5, 9–5 (Queen's Club, London) and 9–3, 9–5, 9–3 (Conservative Club, London).

1931
D. G. Butcher beat C. Arnold 9–0, 9–0, 9–0 (Conservative Club, London) and 9–3, 9–0, 9–5 (Bath Club, London).

1932
F. D. Amr Bey (Egy) beat D. G. Butcher 9–0, 9–7, 9–1 (Conservative Club, London) and 5–9, 5–9, 9–2, 9–1, 9–0 (Bath Club, London).

1933
F. D. Amr Bey (Egy) was not challenged.

1934
F. D. Amr Bey (Egy) beat D. G. Butcher 9–4, 9–10, 10–8, 9–0 (Conservative Club, London) and 9–6, 6–9, 9–2, 0–9, 9–5 (Bath Club, London).

1935
F. D. Amr Bey (Egy) beat J. P. Dear 9–3, 6–9, 8–10, 9–2, 9–4 (Bath Club, London) and 9–4, 9–7, 3–9, 9–7 (Royal Automobile Club, London).

1936
F. D. Amr Bey (Egy) beat J. P. Dear 9–7, 7–9, 9–7, 5–9, 9–6 (Royal Automobile Club, London) and 9–6, 8–10, 9–1, 9–6 (Bath Club, London).

1937
F. D. Amr Bey (Egy) beat J. P. Dear 10–8, 10–8, 4–9,

1–9, 9–4 (Royal Automobile Club, London) and 9–7, 8–10, 9–6, 9–5 (Bath Club, London).

1938
J. P. Dear beat A. E. Biddle 5–9, 9–6, 6–9, 9–6, 9–5 (Junior Carlton Club, London) and 6–9, 9–1, 9–2, 9–6 (Royal Automobile Club, London).

1939–45 No competition.

1946
M. Karim (Egy) beat J. P. Dear 9–4, 9–1, 9–3 (Lansdowne and Royal Aero Clubs, London) and 5–9, 7–9, 9–8, 9–7, 9–4 (Royal Automobile Club, London). (These matches were played in December 1947 having been postponed the previous season.)

1947
Quarter-finals: M. Karim (Egy) beat J. F. Stokes 5–9, 9–0, 9–1, 10–8; B. C. Phillips beat L. R. Hamer 6–9, 9–1, 9–4, 10–8; A. E. Biddle beat L. W. R. Keeble 10–8, 9–7, 9–2; J. P. Dear beat P. J. Phillips 9–7, 3–9, 9–3, 9–1.
Semi-finals: Karim beat Phillips 9–1, 2–9, 10–8, 9–3; Dear beat Biddle 9–4, 9–4, 9–2.
Final: Karim beat Dear 9–5, 9–3, 5–9, 1–9, 10–8.

1948
Quarter-finals: M. Karim (Egy) beat E. S. Hawes 9–0, 9–3, 9–2; N. F. Borrett beat N. E. Hooper 9–1, 9–3, 9–2; B. C. Phillips beat R. M. Boustead 6–9, 9–4, 10–8, 8–10, 9–4; L. W. R. Keeble beat W. E. Clements 9–7, 9–3, 9–0.
Semi-finals: Karim beat Borrett 9–2, 9–4, 9–0; Phillips beat Keeble 9–0, 4–9, 9–3, 9–7.
Final: Karim beat Phillips 9–4, 9–2, 9–10, 9–4.

1949
Quarter-finals: M. Karim (Egy) beat A. A. T. Seymour-Haydon 8–10, 9–5, 9–2, 9–6; J. P. Dear beat B. C. Phillips 9–0, 9–0, 9–3; G. J. Watson beat W. E. J. Gordon 9–1, 9–7, 7–9, 10–9; A. Bari (Ind) beat W. D. McLaggan 9–2, 9–1, 9–1.
Semi-finals: Karim beat Dear 9–0, 9–6, 10–8; Bari beat Watson 9–2, 9–2, 10–8.
Final: Karim beat Bari 9–4, 9–2, 9–7.

1950
Quarter-finals: M. Karim (Egy) beat L. W. R. Keeble 9–4, 9–0, 9–1; R. B. R. Wilson beat A. Bari (Ind) 9–6, 7–9, 4–9, 9–1, 9–4; G. Hildick-Smith beat R. M. Boustead 9–4, 9–5, 9–2; Hashim Khan (Pak) beat W. E. J. Gordon 9–3, 9–3, 9–0.
Semi-finals: Karim beat Wilson 9–2, 8–10, 10–9, 9–5; Hashim Khan beat Hildick-Smith 9–6, 9–2, 9–4.
Final: Hashim Khan beat Karim 9–5, 9–0, 9–0.

1951
Quarter-finals: Hashim Khan (Pak) beat A. Fairbairn 9–4, 9–0, 9–0; G. Hildick-Smith w.o. N. E. Hooper; B. C. Phillips beat Sir C. McLeod 6–9, 9–1, 9–2, 9–5; M. Karim (Egy) beat R. B. R. Wilson 9–3, 9–1, 9–6.
Semi-finals: Hashim Khan beat Hildick-Smith 9–2, 9–0, 9–2; Karim beat Phillips 9–2, 9–4, 9–3.
Final: Hashim Khan beat Karim 9–5, 9–7, 9–0.

1952
Quarter-finals: Hashim Khan (Pak) beat J. H. Giles 9–4, 9–5, 9–3; Azam Khan (Pak) w.o. A. A. T. Seymour-Haydon; R. B. R. Wilson beat A. Bari (Ind) 2–9, 9–1, 9–2, 2–9, 9–2; Safirullah Khan (Pak) w.o. M. Karim (Egy).
Semi-finals: Hashim Khan beat Azam Khan 9–6, 4–9, 9–7, 8–10, 9–4; Wilson beat Safirullah Khan 1–9, 9–7, 9–3, 9–4.
Final: Hashim Khan beat Wilson 9–2, 8–10, 9–1, 9–0.

1953
Quarter-finals: Hashim Khan (Pak) beat J. H. Giles 9–1, 9–2, 9–4; A. Bari (Ind) beat A. Fairbairn 6–9, 9–3, 9–2, 9–10, 9–7; Azam Khan (Pak) beat I. C. de Sales la Terriere 9–1, 7–9, 9–2, 9–2; Roshan Khan (Pak) beat Sir C. McLeod 9–3, 9–3, 9–6.
Semi-finals: Hashim Khan w.o. Bari; Azam Khan beat Roshan Khan 9–2, 6–9, 10–8, 9–3.
Final: Hashim Khan beat Azam Khan 6–9, 9–6, 9–6, 7–9, 9–5.

1954
Quarter-finals: Hashim Khan (Pak) beat J. H. Giles 9–4, 9–5, 9–4; Roshan Khan (Pak) beat A. A. T. Seymour-Haydon 9–1, 9–0, 9–4; R. B. R. Wilson beat A. P. Doggart 9–7, 9–5, 9–2; Azam Khan (Pak) beat D. B. Hughes 9–4, 9–0, 9–3.
Semi-finals: Hashim Khan beat Roshan Khan 9–2, 7–9, 2–9, 9–2, 9–5; Azam Khan beat Wilson 9–0, 9–1, 9–3.
Final: Hashim Khan beat Azam Khan 9–7, 7–9, 9–7, 5–9, 9–7.

1955
Quarter-finals: Hashim Khan (Pak) beat J. Din (Pak) 9–4, 10–9, 7–9, 9–5; Azam Khan (Pak) beat S. J. S. Lam 9–0, 9–1, 9–0; R. B. Hawkey beat J. H. Giles 9–1, 2–9, 8–10, 9–7, 9–0; Roshan Khan (Pak) beat M. Dardir (Egy) 9–2, 9–6, 9–2.
Semi-finals: Hashim Khan beat Azam Khan 10–9, 10–9, 4–9, 9–3; Roshan Khan beat Hawkey 9–1, 9–2, 9–0.
Final: Hashim Khan beat Roshan Khan 9–4, 9–2, 5–9, 9–5.

1956
Quarter-finals: Hashim Khan (Pak) beat J. H. Giles 9–5, 9–2, 10–8; Azam Khan (Pak) beat R. B. Hawkey 9–0, 9–3, 9–2; Mohibullah Khan (Pak) beat D. B. Hughes 9–5, 9–0, 9–2; Roshan Khan (Pak) beat M. J. Perkins 1–9, 9–4, 9–1, 9–4.
Semi-finals: Hashim Khan beat Azam Khan 9–4, 4–9, 9–6, 9–5; Roshan Khan beat Mohibullah Khan 10–8, 9–0, 9–5.
Final: Roshan Khan beat Hashim Khan 6–9, 9–5, 9–2, 9–1.

1957
Quarter-finals: Hashim Khan (Pak) beat Nasrullah Khan (Pak) 9–3, 9–2, 9–0; Mohibullah Khan (Pak) beat J. H. Giles 9–4, 9–3, 6–9, 9–3; D. B. Hughes beat Yusuf Khan (Pak) 10–8, 3–9, 3–9, 9–6, 9–4; Azam Khan (Pak) beat R. B. Hawkey 9–0, 9–3, 9–3.
Semi-finals: Hashim Khan beat Mohibullah Khan 6–9, 9–7, 9–3, 9–3; Azam Khan beat Hughes 9–2, 9–0, 9–0.
Final: Hashim Khan beat Azam Khan 9–7, 6–9, 9–6, 9–7.

1958
Quarter-finals: Nasrullah Khan (Pak) beat J. Din (Pak) 9–7, 9–4, 9–2; Mohibullah Khan (Pak) beat D. B.

Hughes 9–2, 9–6, 9–3; Ali Akbar Khan (Pak) beat R. B. Hawkey 9–5, 9–3, 9–1; Azam Khan (Pak) beat W. J. Ashford 9–3, 9–6, 9–2.

Semi-finals: Mohibullah Khan beat Nasrullah Khan 9–1, 9–0, 9–5; Azam Khan beat Ali Akbar Khan 9–1, 9–1, 9–1.

Final: Azam Khan beat Mohibullah Khan 9–5, 9–0, 9–1.

1959

Quarter-finals: Azam Khan (Pak) beat M. Dardir (Egy) 9–2, 9–5, 9–2; Hashim Khan (Pak) beat Nasrullah Khan (Pak) 9–6, 9–5, 9–6; M. A. Oddy beat Mohibullah Khan (Pak) 9–3, 6–9, 9–3, 9–0; Roshan Khan (Pak) beat J. Din (Pak) 9–7, 9–4, 2–9, 9–7.

Semi-finals: Azam Khan beat Hashim Khan 9–6, 5–9, 9–6, 9–6; Roshan Khan beat Oddy 6–9, 9–6, 9–3, 9–3.

Final: Azam Khan beat Roshan Khan 9–1, 9–0, 9–0.

1960

Quarter-finals: Azam Khan (Pak) beat J. Din (Pak) 9–1, 9–4, 9–4; D. Hughes beat I. Amin (Egy) 9–5, 9–6, 2–9, 9–4; Mohibullah Khan (Pak) beat M. A. Oddy 9–4, 9–5, 9–7; Roshan Khan (Pak) beat M. Dardir (Egy) 9–2, 0–9, 9–6, 4–9, 9–2.

Semi-finals: Azam Khan beat Hughes 9–0, 9–3, 9–2; Mohibullah Khan beat Roshan Khan 9–7, 9–0, 9–0.

Final: Azam Khan beat Mohibullah Khan 6–9, 9–1, 9–4, 0–9, 9–2.

1961

Quarter-finals: Azam Khan (Pak) beat M. A. Oddy 9–3, 9–5, 9–4; Roshan Khan (Pak) beat K. Zaghloul (Egy) 9–1, 9–0, 9–2; M. Dardir (Egy) beat I. Amin (Egy) 9–5, 9–1, 3–9, 10–8; Mohibullah Khan (Pak) beat A. Aboutaleb (Egy) 9–1, 9–2, 9–3.

Semi-finals: Azam Khan beat Roshan Khan 9–5, 9–3, 4–9, 1–9, 9–0; Mohibullah Khan beat Dardir 9–6, 9–6, 9–4.

Final: Azam Khan beat Mohibullah Khan 9–6, 7–9, 10–8, 2–9, 9–4.

1962

Quarter-finals: Mohibullah Khan (Pak) beat A. Aziz (Egy) 9–0, 9–0, 9–5; A. Jawaid (Pak) beat K. Zaghloul (Egy) 9–1, 6–9, 9–1, 6–9, 9–2; A. Aboutaleb (Egy) beat T. Shafik (Egy) 9–4, 9–0, 2–9, 9–3; Roshan Khan (Pak) beat G. R. Chisholm 9–4, 9–5, 9–3.

Semi-finals: Mohibullah Khan beat Jawaid 10–8, 9–3, 9–3; Aboutaleb beat Roshan Khan 2–9, 9–7, 9–0, 9–6.

Final: Mohibullah Khan beat Aboutaleb 9–4, 5–9, 3–9, 10–8, 9–6.

1963

Quarter-finals: Mohibullah Khan (Pak) beat T. Shafik (Egy) 9–1, 4–9, 9–5, 9–5; M. A. Oddy beat K. Zaghloul (Egy) 9–5, 9–5, 9–3; A. Jawaid (Pak) beat M. Yasin (Pak) 10–9, 9–6, 7–9, 10–8; A. Aboutaleb (Egy) beat I. Amin (Egy) 9–3, 9–2, 9–0.

Semi-finals: Oddy beat Mohibullah Khan 9–1, 9–6, 9–2; Aboutaleb beat Jawaid 9–3, 9–7, 9–1.

Final: Aboutaleb beat Oddy 9–3, 9–7, 9–0.

1964

Quarter-finals: A. Aboutaleb (Egy) beat D. R. Woods 9–2, 9–1, 9–3; T. Shafik (Egy) beat K. Zaghloul (Egy) 9–2, 9–4, 9–0; I. Amin (Egy) beat A. Aziz (Egy) 9–6, 2–9, 9–6, 9–7; A. Jawaid (Pak) beat J. G. A. Lyon 9–0, 9–6, 9–4.

Semi-finals: Aboutaleb beat Shafik 9–2, 9–3, 9–3; Amin beat Jawaid 1–9, 9–4, 6–9, 9–6, 9–6.

Final: Aboutaleb beat Amin 9–0, 0–9, 9–1, 9–6.

1965

Quarter-finals: A. Aboutaleb (Egy) beat J. N. H. Smith 9–7, 9–6, 9–7; T. Shafik (Egy) beat J. Barrington (GB & Ire) 9–6, 9–6, 9–6; K. Zaghloul (Egy) beat A. Aziz (Egy) 9–2, 9–4, 9–3; A. Jawaid (Pak) beat J. G. A. Lyon 6–9, 9–0, 9–1, 9–6.

Semi-finals: Aboutaleb beat Shafik 6–9, 9–7, 7–9, 9–2, 9–3; Jawaid beat Zaghloul 9–7, 9–4, 9–6.

Final: Aboutaleb beat Jawaid 9–5, 5–9, 9–3, 9–1.

1966

Quarter-finals: J. Barrington (GB & Ire) beat A. Aboutaleb (Egy) 9–4, 9–1, 8–10, 9–5; I. Amin (Egy) beat P. D. Stokes 9–6, 7–9, 9–5, 9–4; M. Yasin (Pak) beat K. Zaghloul (Egy) 9–2, 9–1, 9–2; A. Jawaid (Pak) beat A. Nadi (Egy) 9–10, 9–4, 9–6, 9–2.

Semi-finals: Barrington beat Amin 9–4, 4–9, 9–5, 9–3; Jawaid beat Yasin 4–9, 9–6, 9–2, 2–9, 10–8.

Final: Barrington beat Jawaid 9–2, 6–9, 9–2, 9–2.

1967

Quarter-finals: J. Barrington (GB & Ire) beat D. R. Brazier 9–2, 9–7, 9–5; K. Zaghloul (Egy) beat R. M. H. Boddington 9–7, 2–9, 9–5, 4–9, 9–3; J. G. A. Lyon beat A. Nadi (Egy) 9–0, 10–8, 9–7; A. Aboutaleb (Egy) beat D. B. Hughes 8–10, 9–2, 9–5, 5–9, 9–3.

Semi-finals: Barrington beat Zaghloul 9–2, 9–2, 9–0; A. Aboutaleb beat Lyon 5–9, 9–4, 7–9, 9–4, 9–2.

Final: Barrington beat Aboutaleb 9–6, 9–0, 9–3.

1968

Quarter-finals: J. Barrington (GB & Ire) beat A. M. H. Hill 9–3, 9–4, 9–2; C. J. Nancarrow (Aus) beat K. J. Hiscoe (Aus) 9–4, 9–1, 2–9, 9–7; A. Aboutaleb (Egy) beat R. Carter 1–9, 10–9, 9–6, 9–4; G. B. Hunt (Aus) beat M. W. Corby 9–4, 9–7, 3–9, 9–7.

Semi-finals: Nancarrow beat Barrington 9–4, 9–5, 10–8; Hunt beat Aboutaleb 9–5, 9–2, 9–5.

Final: Hunt beat Nancarrow 9–5, 9–4, 9–0.

1969

Quarter-finals: G. B. Hunt (Aus) beat P. E. Millman 9–3, 10–8, 10–9; A. Jawaid (Pak) beat M. W. Corby 7–9, 10–8, 9–1, 9–4; M. Yasin (Pak) beat A. Aboutaleb (Egy) 9–6, 9–0, 5–9, 9–2; J. Barrington (GB & Ire) beat J. N. C. Easter 9–6, 9–1, 9–4.

Semi-finals: Hunt beat Jawaid 9–7, 2–9, 9–1, 9–6; Barrington beat Yasin 9–5, 6–9, 9–5, 9–3.

Final: Barrington beat Hunt 9–7, 3–9, 3–9, 9–4, 9–4.

1970

Quarter-finals: J. Barrington (GB & Ire) beat M. Z. Hepker (Zim) 9–2, 9–1, 9–0; Sharif Khan (Pak) beat P. N. Ayton 9–0, 5–9, 9–2, 3–9, 9–5; M. Yasin (Pak) beat R. Ratinac (Aus) 2–9, 9–5, 9–3, 3–9, 9–5; A. Jawaid (Pak) beat J. N. C. Easter 9–4, 10–9, 9–6.

Semi-finals: Barrington beat Sharif Khan 9–0, 9–7, 3–9, 9–3; Jawaid beat Yasin 9–1, 9–2, 9–0.

Final: Barrington beat Jawaid 9–1, 9–2, 9–6.

1971

Quarter-finals: J. Barrington (GB & Ire) beat G. Allam (Egy) 9–6, 9–3, 9–7; G. Alauddin (Pak) beat A. Jawaid (Pak) 9–5, 9–4, 9–4; K. J. Hiscoe (Aus) beat M. Asran (Egy) 9–6, 3–9, 9–6, 9–3; G. B. Hunt (Aus) beat H. Jahan (Pak) 9–7, 10–9, 9–10, 9–1.

Semi-finals: Barrington beat Alauddin 10–8, 9–7, 9–2; Hunt beat Hiscoe 9–7, 10–9, 9–4.

Final: Barrington beat Hunt 0–9, 9–7, 10–8, 6–9, 9–7.

1972

Quarter-finals: J. Barrington (GB & Ire) beat A. Safwat (Egy) 9–3, 9–4, 9–10, 9–0; K. J. Hiscoe (Aus) beat H. Jahan (Pak) 2–9, 9–5, 9–0, 9–7; G. Alauddin (Pak) beat M. Yasin (Pak) 6–9, 9–2, 9–3, 9–3; G. B. Hunt (Aus) beat A. Jawaid (Pak) 9–6, 9–6, 9–3.

Semi-finals: Barrington beat Hiscoe 3–9, 9–1, 7–9, 9–1, 9–2; Alauddin beat Hunt 1–9, 9–7, 9–1, 10–8.

Final: Barrington beat Alauddin 9–4, 9–3, 9–2.

1973

Quarter-finals: M. Yasin (Pak) beat J. Barrington (GB & Ire) 1–9, 9–4, 10–8, 9–2; Q. Zaman (Pak) beat S. Muneer (Pak) 9–6, 9–2, 9–2; G. Alauddin (Pak) beat C. J. Nancarrow (Aus) 9–7, 9–7, 9–2; G. B. Hunt (Aus) beat H. Jahan (Pak) 9–4, 9–3, 9–6.

Semi-finals: Yasin beat Zaman 5–9, 9–7, 10–9, 9–7; Hunt beat Alauddin 9–4, 9–7, 9–3.

Final: Hunt w.o. Yasin.

1974

Quarter-finals: Q. Zaman (Pak) beat G. B. Hunt (Aus) 4–9, 8–10, 9–3, 9–2, 9–7; H. Jahan (Pak) beat Mohibullah Khan Jnr (Pak) 10–8, 9–3, 7–9, 10–8; G. Alauddin (Pak) beat J. Barrington (GB & Ire) 9–3, 9–6, 9–0; K. J. Hiscoe (Aus) beat C. J. Nancarrow (Aus) 9–4, 3–9, 6–9, 9–2, 9–6.

Semi-finals: Zaman beat Jahan 9–4, 9–2, 6–9, 9–4; Alauddin beat Hiscoe 9–3, 9–5, 9–5.

Final: Zaman beat Alauddin 9–7, 9–6, 9–1.

1975

Quarter-finals: Q. Zaman (Pak) beat J. Barrington (GB & Ire) 9–0, 9–1, 9–6; Mohibullah Khan Jnr (Pak) beat H. Jahan (Pak) 6–9, 9–1, 4–9, 9–7, 9–1; G. Alauddin (Pak) beat K. J. Hiscoe (Aus) 5–9, 9–0, 9–2, 9–1; G. B. Hunt (Aus) beat C. J. Nancarrow (Aus) 9–5, 9–6, 9–4.

Semi-finals: Mohibullah Khan Jnr beat Zaman 6–9, 9–5, 3–9, 9–2, 9–7; Hunt beat Alauddin 9–2, 9–5, 1–9, 9–5.

Final: Hunt beat Mohibullah Khan Jnr 7–9, 9–4, 8–10, 9–2, 9–2.

1976

Quarter-finals: G. B. Hunt (Aus) beat B. Brownlee (NZ) 9–4, 9–1, 9–4; J. Barrington (GB & Ire) beat R. Watson (SA) 10–8, 9–1, 5–9, 9–6; C. J. Nancarrow (Aus) beat J. C. A. Leslie 9–4, 7–9, 9–3, 9–5; A. Safwat (Egy) beat M. Asran (Egy) 9–6, 9–0, 9–7.

Semi-finals: Hunt beat Barrington 9–5, 9–2, 9–0; Nancarrow beat Safwat 9–1, 9–6, 6–9, 9–1.

Final: Hunt beat Nancarrow 9–4, 9–4, 8–10, 9–4.

1977

Quarter-finals: G. B. Hunt (Aus) beat J. Barrington (GB &

In 1977 at Wembley two Australians lined up for the final of the British Open – Geoff Hunt and Cam Nancarrow, a repeat of the 1968/9 final and only the second time in the history of the championship that two Australians have been finalists. The second occasion was mainly brought about by a Pakistani boycott of the championship in protest against South African participation. Hunt won by three games to one

Ire) 9–3, 9–2, 9–5; H. Jahan (Pak) beat G. Alauddin (Pak) 9–4, 9–7, 9–4; Mohibullah Khan Jnr (Pak) beat B. Brownlee (NZ) 9–1, 9–5, 2–9, 9–7; Q. Zaman (Pak) beat Torsam Khan (Pak) 9–10, 9–4, 9–1, 9–4.

Semi-finals: Hunt beat Jahan 9–4, 9–1, 9–3; Zaman beat Mohibullah Khan Jnr 9–5, 1–9, 9–7, 9–7.

Final: Hunt beat Zaman 7–9, 9–1, 9–1, 9–2.

1978
Quarter-finals: G. B. Hunt (Aus) beat G. Alauddin (Pak) 9–6, 9–1, 9–7; H. Jahan (Pak) beat J. Barrington (GB & Ire) 9–0, 9–4, 9–3; Mohibullah Khan Jnr (Pak) beat B. Brownlee (NZ) 9–4, 9–1, 9–1; Q. Zaman (Pak) beat M. Ahmed (Pak) 9–7, 5–9, 9–4, 7–9, 9–3.

Semi-finals: Hunt beat Jahan 9–3, 9–6, 9–10, 9–2; Zaman beat Mohibullah Khan Jnr 9–2, 9–1, 9–5.

Final: Hunt beat Zaman 2–9, 9–7, 9–0, 6–9, 9–3.

1979
Quarter-finals: G. B. Hunt (Aus) beat J. Barrington (GB & Ire) 9–3, 9–2, 7–9, 9–6; Mohibullah Khan Jnr (Pak) beat B. Brownlee (NZ) 9–1, 9–2, 9–0; M. Ahmed (Pak) beat H. Jahan (Pak) 10–9, 9–1, 9–6; Q. Zaman (Pak) beat G. Alauddin (Pak) 9–1, 7–9, 3–9, 9–1, 9–3.

Semi-finals: Hunt beat Mohibullah Khan Jnr 9–5, 9–1, 9–1; Zaman beat Ahmed 4–9, 9–1, 9–4, 9–1.

Final: Hunt beat Zaman 9–3, 9–2, 1–9, 9–1.

1980
Quarter-finals: G. B. Hunt (Aus) beat P. Kenyon 9–4, 9–3, 9–2; G. Awad (Egy) beat R. Norman (NZ) 9–4, 7–9, 9–2, 9–1; Jahangir Khan (Pak) beat H. Jahan (Pak) 9–4, 9–2, 9–6; Q. Zaman (Pak) beat M. Ahmed (Pak) 9–6, 4–9, 10–9, 9–6.

Semi-finals: Hunt beat Awad 9–10, 9–1, 9–0, 9–0; Jahangir Khan beat Zaman 9–5, 9–5, 9–7.

Final: Hunt beat Jahangir Khan 9–2, 9–7, 5–9, 9–7.

1981
Quarter-finals: Jahangir Khan (Pak) beat R. Norman (NZ) 9–5, 9–3, 9–3; Q. Zaman (Pak) beat D. Williams (Aus) 4–9, 9–5, 9–0, 9–2; H. Jahan (Pak) beat M. Ahmed (Pak) 7–9, 9–6, 9–0, 9–3; G. Brumby (Aus) beat P. Kenyon 9–4, 9–1, 9–5.

Semi-finals: Jahangir Khan beat Zaman 9–5, 9–5, 9–1; Jahan beat Brumby 3–9, 9–4, 9–3, 9–3.

Final: Jahangir Khan beat Jahan 9–2, 10–9, 9–3.

1982
Quarter-finals: Jahangir Khan (Pak) beat C. Dittmar (Aus) 9–0, 9–3, 9–4; Q. Zaman (Pak) beat R. Norman (NZ) 9–4, 9–1, 9–6; D. Williams (Aus) beat S. Davenport (NZ) 9–6, 9–3, 10–9; G. Awad (Egy) beat H. Jahan (Pak) 4–9, 9–2, 5–9, 9–2, 9–1.

Semi-finals: Jahangir Khan beat Zaman 9–6, 9–6, 9–2; Awad beat Williams 10–8, 9–0, 9–0.

Final: Jahangir Khan beat Awad 9–2, 9–5, 9–1.

1983
Quarter-finals: Jahangir Khan (Pak) beat R. Norman (NZ) 9–3, 9–0, 9–0; S. Davenport (NZ) beat M. Ahmed (Pak) 9–5, 9–7, 1–9, 9–1; G. Williams (Eng) beat R. Thorne (Aus) 9–4, 9–3, 9–6; Q. Zaman (Pak) beat G. Briars (Eng) 6–9, 9–1, 9–6, 9–2.

Semi-finals: Jahangir Khan beat Davenport 9–7, 9–6, 9–2; Zaman beat Williams 10–8, 9–5, 4–9, 9–3.

Final: Jahangir Khan beat Zaman 9–0, 9–3, 9–5.

Over-35 Championship
1982 A. Safwat (Egy) beat J. Barrington (GB & Ire) 9–6, 6–9, 9–3, 9–3

1983 J. Barrington (GB & Ire) beat A. Safwat (Egy) 9–10, 2–9, 9–6, 10–8, 9–2

Veterans Championship
(Players 45 and over)

1964 A. A. T. Seymour-Haydon beat F. R. D. Corbett 9–3, 5–9, 10–8, 10–8

1965 Nazrullah Khan (Pak) beat R. E. Mulliken 9–2, 9–1, 3–9, 9–7

1966 Nazrullah Khan (Pak) beat R. S. Bourne 9–1, 9–2, 9–0

1967 Nazrullah Khan (Pak) beat A. A. T. Seymour-Haydon 9–0, 9–0, 9–0

1968 J. Din (Ind) beat Nazrullah Khan (Pak) 9–5, 9–3, 7–9, 9–4

1969 Nazrullah Khan (Pak) beat J. Din (Ind) 3–9, 9–5, 9–5, 9–3

1970 J. Din (Ind) beat R. B. Hawkey 9–6, 9–0, 9–2

1971 J. Din (Ind) beat Nazrullah Khan (Pak) 6–9, 9–1, 9–5, 5–9, 9–6

1972 J. Din (Ind) beat W. D. N. Vaughan 9–3, 9–1, 9–5

1973 J. Din (Ind) beat R. B. Hawkey 9–7, 6–9, 9–7, 0–9, 9–3

1974 M. Buck (Aus) beat J. Din (Ind) 1–9, 9–2, 9–1, 9–3

1975 M. Buck (Aus) beat J. Din (Ind) 9–6, 9–10, 9–6, 0–9, 9–7

1976 K. E. Parker (Can) beat J. Platts (Wal) 9–5, 9–4, 9–4

1977 K. E. Parker (Can) beat J. Platts (Wal) 9–1, 9–0, 9–1

1978 K. E. Parker (Can) beat J. Platts (Wal) 9–2, 9–4, 9–6

1979 L. Atkins (Aus) beat J. F. Skinner 9–1, 9–3, 9–2

1980 J. G. A. Lyon beat L. Atkins (Aus) 9–6, 9–1, 9–5

1981 J. G. A. Lyon beat P. G. Kirton 3–9, 9–7, 9–0, 0–9, 9–2

1982 K. Hiscoe (Aus) beat P. G. Kirton 9–7, 9–6, 9–6

1983 K. Hiscoe (Aus) beat M. Grundy 9–4, 9–5, 9–6

Vintage Championship
(Players 55 and over)

1975 J. Din (Ind) beat R. S. Bourne 6–9, 9–5, 7–9, 9–7, 9–4

1976 J. Din (Ind) beat A. Amos (Aus) 9–6, 9–2, 9–10, 0–9, 9–1

1977 Hashim Khan (Pak) beat J. W. Dengel 9–5, 9–1, 9–0

1978 Hashim Khan (Pak) beat J. H. Giles 9–7, 9–1, 9–3

1979 Hashim Khan (Pak) beat A. E. Catherine 1–9, 9–10, 10–8, 10–8, 9–1

1980 Hashim Khan (Pak) beat A. E. Catherine 10–9, 6–9, 9–2, 9–6

1981 Hashim Khan (Pak) beat A. E. Catherine 9–5, 9–1, 5–9, 9–6

1982 Hashim Khan (Pak) beat T. Millican (Aus) 1–9, 9–4, 10–8, 0–9, 9–6

1983 K. Parker (Can) beat R. Griffin 9–0, 7–9, 9–7, 9–6

Notes

1 In all the above championship results the 1930/1 season is indicated by the date 1930, and similarly throughout for all years.
2 The 1975 events incorporated the World Championship.
3 Venues (from 1947): Lansdowne and Royal Aero Clubs, London 1947–57, 1962–67; Royal Automobile Club, London 1958–61; Abbeydale Park, Sheffield 1968, 1971–73; Edgbaston Priory, Birmingham 1969–70; Wembley, London 1974–79; Bromley, Kent 1980–81; Derby 1982; Brighton and Wembley 1983.

British Open Under-23 Championship

The concept behind the introduction of this championship was that it would provide a stepping stone for the up and coming player who had his sights set on the world's premier titles.

Ironically no British player has yet made the final and only Gawain Briars in the inaugural tournament in 1981 and Christy Willstrop and Jamie Hickox in 1984 have reached the semi-finals, so it might be said that other countries, other than the host nation have mostly benefited from the event. Jahangir Khan of Pakistan won the opening championship, graduated to higher things and since then two players Stuart Davenport of New Zealand and Sohail Qaiser of Pakistan have dominated proceedings. Davenport won in 1982 and was runner-up to Qaiser in 1984, Qaiser having won in 1983.

1981 (Wembley, England)
Quarter-finals: Jahangir Khan (Pak) beat R. Holmes (SA) 9–1, 9–0, 9–4; Zahir Hussein Khan (Pak) beat S. Bateman (Eng) 10–8, 6–9, 9–7, 9–5; R. Norman (NZ) beat A. Naylor (Eng) 9–7, 10–8, 9–3; G. Briars (Eng) beat T. Wilkinson (Zim) 9–5, 10–8, 9–2.
Semi-finals: Jahangir Khan beat Zahir Hussein Khan 9–7, 9–1, 9–5; Norman beat Briars 9–4, 3–9, 9–3, 9–3.
Final: Jahangir Khan beat Norman 9–5, 9–7, 9–3.

1982 (Wembley, England)
Quarter-finals: G. Brumby (Aus) beat T. Wilkinson (Zim) 9–7, 9–2, 9–1; R. Hill (Aus) beat Jamshed Gul (Pak) 3–9, 9–5, 9–4, 9–1; G. Pollard (Aus) beat R. Holmes (SA) 8–10, 9–4, 9–4, 7–9, 9–2; S. Davenport (NZ) beat A. Naylor (Eng) 9–3, 6–9, 9–3, 9–7.
Semi-finals: Brumby beat Hill 8–10, 9–6, 9–2, 9–6; Davenport beat Pollard 9–1, 9–5, 9–5.
Final: Davenport beat Brumby 9–2, 3–3 (retired).

1983 (Wembley, England)
Quarter-finals: C. Dittmar (Aus) beat A. Naylor (Eng) 9–6, 9–2, 9–6; G. Pollard (Aus) beat T. Wilkinson (Zim) 9–7, 9–6, 9–1; Zahir Hussein Khan (Pak) beat S. Davenport (NZ) 9–2, 5–9, 9–3, 10–8; S. Qaiser (Pak) beat Nasser Zahran (Egy) 9–6, 9–6, 9–0.
Semi-finals: Pollard beat Dittmar 9–5, 9–4, 9–6; Qaiser beat Zahir Hussein Khan 10–8, 9–1, 9–3.
Final: Qaiser beat Pollard 9–6, 3–9, 9–7, 9–1.

1984 (Wembley, England)
Quarter-finals: S. Davenport (NZ) beat Omar Hyat (Pak) 9–2, 9–2, 9–1; C. Willstrop (Eng) beat F. Johnsson (Swe) 9–4, 9–1, 10–8; S. Qaiser (Pak) beat M. Bodimeade (Eng) 9–3, 9–6, 9–5; J. Hickox (Eng) beat S. Hailstone (Zim) 9–2, 9–6, 9–4.
Semi-finals: Davenport beat Willstrop 9–5, 9–3, 9–2; Qaiser beat Hickox 9–5, 9–3, 9–2.
Final: Qaiser beat Davenport 9–1, 9–4, 7–9, 9–6.

The British Open Championship

WOMEN

This was the first women's major event to be inaugurated in Britain. The first championship was decided at Queen's Club, London in February 1922 – just over a year before the men's British Amateur Championship came into being and eight years in advance of the men's British Open. 'Open' competition for women (to include amateurs and professionals)' was introduced in the 1973/4 season.

The first six championships were played on an all-play-all group system with the top players progressing to semi-final and final knock-out rounds. (In the second round the leading player in each group went straight through to the final.) It was not until the sixth event in December 1926 that the modern-day scoring system of best five games to 9 points was introduced.

Sisters Nancy and Joyce Cave were the first players to dominate the competition. Nineteen-year-old Joyce was the first champion and the two contested three of the opening four finals. Altogether Nancy appeared in nine finals, winning three and Joyce won three from six appearances. One girl who must have been sick of the name Cave was Sylvia Huntsman who, having defeated Nancy to win the second championship, lost in the semi-finals of the next nine tournaments – four times to Nancy and twice to Joyce. Her other three defeats were inflicted by Cicely Fenwick who beat Nancy in three finals and lost once each to the two sisters.

Susan Noel was the first player to win three consecutive titles (1931–33), taking the first at the age of 20 – she had first competed in 1922 at the age of 9. She was succeeded by fellow tennis international Margot Lumb who won the five championships immediately prior to the outbreak of the Second World War. When the competition was resumed after the war, another tennis international, Joan Curry, completed a 'hat trick' of wins. The loser in the last two of these finals was Janet Morgan who was destined to become Britain's most successful woman player.

Janet Morgan (now Janet Shardlow MBE), president of the Women's Squash Rackets Association, followed these two narrow misses by beating Curry in the next three finals and went on to win 10 consecutive titles before retiring from major competition.

Sheila Macintosh (née Speight), who had been runner-up to Morgan five times, finally received her just deserts by winning the title in 1959/60 and Fran Marshall had her only victory – she also finished second on five occasions – in the following season.

That was Britain's last success in the tournament as Australian Heather Blundell (later Mrs McKay) arrived on the scene in February 1962 when she beat Marshall in the final. McKay proved herself to be the greatest woman player of all time as she played in 16 consecutive British Opens, won all of them and

As more women took up squash the subject of fashion on court became the subject of serious debate, particularly the issue of skirts v. shorts. Pictured are Joan Curry, the first Open champion after the war, and Miss M. Carlisle demonstrating the opposing styles

dropped just two games in the process! She also wrote her name in the competition's history books in several other categories. She was the first Australian to win the title, recorded the only 27–0 final scoreline when she beat Bev Johnson in the first all-Australian final in February 1968 and participated in the first all-professional final when she beat compatriot Barbara Wall in March 1977.

The only players to wrest a game from the great Australian during her 16 years in the women's Open were Anna Craven-Smith in their 1963/4 semi-final and Sue Cogswell at the same stage in 1976/7. The most successful of her final opponents were Craven-Smith who gleaned 17 points in February 1967 – the only occasion on which McKay dropped six points or more in two games of a final – and Fran Marshall who won 15 and 11 in the Australian's first two finals. No one else reached double figures! In all McKay dropped just 101 points in 16 finals – an average of just over two per game.

When Mrs McKay retired from the event the title remained in Australian hands in the shape of Sue Newman (now Mrs King) and Barbara Wall before Vicki Hoffman ensured 22 years of Australian rule by winning four in a row – the last two as Mrs Cardwell. She, like Morgan and McKay, decided to resign her title undefeated.

Lisa Opie was the player expected to win in 1984 but her temperament let her down in the final against Sue Devoy, so much so that she earned herself a £1000 fine and a ban from competing in 1985.

The winner's Challenge Cup was presented by Queen's Club which hosted the event for the first 18 years while the runners-up trophy is in memory of first champion Joyce Cave. Total prize money has increased notably over the years and in 1983/4 the fund was £11 225, setting a world record for a women's event.

1921
Final: Miss J. Cave beat Miss N. Cave 11–15, 15–10, 15–9.
1922
Final: Miss S. Huntsman beat Miss N. Cave 6–15, 15–9, 17–15.
1923
Final: Miss N. Cave beat Miss J. Cave 15–8, 15–13.
1924
Final: Miss J. Cave beat Miss N. Cave 15–3, 6–15, 16–13.
1925
Final: Miss C. Fenwick beat Miss N. Cave 15–12, 15–11.
1926
Final: Miss C. Fenwick beat Miss N. Cave 4–9, 9–6, 9–2, 9–5.
1927
Final: Miss J. Cave beat Miss C. Fenwick 4–9, 9–5, 10–9, 9–6.

1928
Final: Miss N. Cave beat Miss J. Cave 9–6, 3–9, 9–2, 3–9, 9–6.

1929
Final: Miss N. Cave beat Miss C. Fenwick 10–8, 9–1, 7–9, 9–5.

1930
Final: Miss C. Fenwick beat Miss N. Cave 9–7, 10–8, 9–10, 9–1.

1931
Final: Miss S. Noel beat Miss J. Cave 9–5, 9–7, 9–1.

1932
Final: Miss S. Noel beat Miss S. Keith-Jones 9–4, 9–0, 9–2.

1933
Final: Miss S. Noel beat Miss M. Lumb 9–7, 9–0, 9–6.

1934
Final: Miss M. Lumb beat Hon. A. Lytton-Milbanke 9–4, 9–0, 9–1.

1935
Final: Miss M. Lumb beat Hon. A. Lytton-Milbanke 9–5, 9–5, 9–4.

1936
Final: Miss M. Lumb beat Mrs I. H. McKechnie 9–3, 9–2, 9–0.

1937
Final: Miss M. Lumb beat Mrs I. H. McKechnie 9–3, 9–2, 9–1.

1938
Final: Miss M. Lumb beat Miss S. Noel 9–6, 9–1, 9–7.

1939–45 No competition.

1946
Final: Miss J. Curry beat Mrs R. J. Teague 9–3, 10–9, 9–5.

1947
Quarter-finals: Miss J. Curry beat Miss F. B. Cooke 3–9, 9–1, 9–2, 9–3; Miss A. M. Carlisle beat Miss M. de Borman (Bel) 9–7, 9–3, 9–5; Mrs R. J. Teague beat Mrs H. Bleasby 9–5, 9–2, 9–1; Miss J. R. M. Morgan beat Mrs B. Hilton 9–1, 9–0, 7–9, 9–2.
Semi-finals: Curry beat Carlisle 9–2, 9–3, 9–4; Morgan beat Teague 9–1, 7–9, 9–6, 9–1.
Final: Curry beat Morgan 9–5, 9–0, 9–10, 6–9, 10–8.

1948
Quarter-finals: Miss J. Curry beat Miss M. de Borman (Bel) 9–1, 9–1, 9–7; Miss A. M. Carlisle beat Miss F. B. Cooke 9–0, 9–6, 9–2; Mrs B. Hilton beat Miss G. W. James 9–4, 9–4, 9–3; Miss J. R. M. Morgan beat Mrs W. H. Harris 9–0, 9–3, 9–2.
Semi-finals: Curry beat Carlisle 0–9, 9–2, 9–0, 9–0; Morgan beat Hilton 9–1, 9–3, 9–2.
Final: Curry beat Morgan 2–9, 9–3, 10–8, 9–0.

1949
Quarter-finals: Miss J. R. M. Morgan beat Miss P. Howe 9–4, 9–5, 9–7; Miss A. M. Carlisle beat Mrs W. H. Harris 1–9, 2–9, 9–4, 9–1, 9–0; Mrs B. Hilton beat Mrs W. H. Gordon 9–5, 9–8, 9–5; Miss J. Curry beat Miss A. V. M. Isaac 9–2, 9–5, 9–3.
Semi-finals: Morgan beat Carlisle 9–3, 9–2, 9–4; Curry beat Hilton 10–8, 9–5, 9–2.

Final: Morgan beat Curry 9–4, 9–3, 9–0.

1950
Quarter-finals: Miss J. R. M. Morgan beat Mrs H. R. Townsend 9–1, 9–0, 9–3; Miss S. Speight beat Mrs D. Cooper 9–5, 9–1, 9–0; Miss M. Gowthorpe beat Mrs P. Gotla 9–3, 9–1, 9–3; Miss J. Curry beat Miss A. V. M. Isaac 9–4, 9–6, 9–1.
Semi-finals: Morgan beat Speight 9–3, 9–1, 9–1; Curry beat Gowthorpe 9–3, 9–0, 9–2.
Final: Morgan beat Curry 9–1, 2–9, 9–3, 9–4.

1951
Quarter-finals: Miss J. R. M. Morgan beat Miss S. Speight 9–6, 9–6, 9–2; Miss A. V. M. Isaac beat Miss L. R. Byrne 9–0, 9–2, 9–3; Mrs G. R. Turner beat Mrs H. R. Townsend 9–6, 9–5, 5–9, 10–8; Miss J. Curry beat Miss M. Gowthorpe 9–1, 9–5, 6–9, 9–2.
Semi-finals: Morgan beat Isaac 9–2, 9–3, 3–9, 9–0; Curry beat Turner 9–3, 10–8, 7–9, 9–2.
Final: Morgan beat Curry 9–3, 9–1, 9–5.

1952
Quarter-finals: Mrs H. R. Townsend beat Mrs A. Teague 2–9, 8–10, 9–0, 9–5, 10–8; Miss R. Walsh beat Mrs W. H. Harris 9–1, 7–9, 9–5, 9–5; Miss S. Speight beat Miss A. G. Bates 9–4, 6–9, 9–1, 9–0; Miss J. R. M. Morgan beat Miss M. Gowthorpe 9–5, 9–1, 9–2.
Semi-finals: Townsend beat Walsh 9–4, 5–9, 9–6, 9–3; Morgan beat Speight 9–6, 9–1, 9–6.
Final: Morgan beat Townsend 9–4, 9–2, 9–4.

1953
Quarter-finals: Miss S. Speight beat Miss R. Walsh 9–2, 9–5, 9–3; Mrs A. Teague beat Mrs H. R. Townsend 9–4, 5–9, 9–1, 8–9, 9–4; Mrs G. R. Turner beat Miss M. Gowthorpe 9–6, 9–5, 9–2; Miss J. R. M. Morgan beat Miss L. R. Byrne 9–0, 9–1, 6–9, 9–2.
Semi-finals: Speight beat Teague 9–5, 9–1, 9–2; Morgan beat Turner 9–1, 9–3, 9–2.
Final: Morgan beat Speight 9–3, 9–1, 9–7.

1954
Quarter-finals: Mrs G. R. Turner beat Miss M. Gowthorpe 9–5, 9–2, 9–3; Miss L. R. Byrne beat Miss J. Tissot (Aus) 10–9, 4–9, 7–9, 9–5, 9–5; Miss R. Walsh beat Miss D. C. Herman 9–0, 9–2, 9–6; Miss J. R. M. Morgan beat Mrs H. R. Townsend 9–3, 9–0, 9–7.
Semi-finals: Turner beat Byrne 7–9, 9–4, 9–2, 10–9; Morgan beat Walsh 9–4, 9–2, 9–7.
Final: Morgan beat Turner 9–5, 9–3, 9–6.

1955
Quarter-finals: Miss S. Speight beat Miss M. Gowthorpe 9–1, 10–8, 9–7; Mrs H. R. Townsend beat Miss D. C. Herman 10–9, 9–4, 5–9, 9–6; Mrs G. R. Turner beat Mrs J. Deloford 1–9, 6–9, 9–2, 9–4, 9–5; Miss J. R. M. Morgan beat Mrs J. D. Campion 9–4, 9–6, 9–2.
Semi-finals: Speight beat Townsend 9–0, 9–3, 9–6; Morgan beat Turner 9–2, 9–2, 9–7.
Final: Morgan beat Speight 9–6, 9–4, 9–2.

1956
Quarter-finals: Miss S. Speight beat Miss M. E. Morgan 9–3, 9–3, 9–5; Mrs G. R. Turner beat Miss D. C. Herman 10–9, 9–0, 9–7; Mrs J. D. Campion beat Mrs H. R. Townsend 9–0, 5–9, 6–9, 9–4, 9–2; Miss

J. R. M. Morgan beat Mrs J. Deloford 9–2, 9–2, 7–9, 9–4.

Semi-finals: Speight beat Turner 9–6, 9–5, 9–7; Morgan beat Campion 9–5, 9–0, 9–3.

Final: Morgan beat Speight 4–9, 9–5, 9–1, 9–6.

1957

Quarter-finals: Mrs S. Macintosh (née Speight) beat Miss D. C. Herman 3–9, 9–3, 9–7, 9–4; Mrs J. Deloford beat Mrs H. R. Townsend 9–5, 2–9, 3–9, 10–9, 9–3; Miss M. Gowthorpe beat Mrs G. R. Turner 6–9, 9–6, 9–2, 9–5; Miss J. R. M. Morgan beat Mrs R. Cooper 9–2, 9–2, 9–6.

Semi-finals: Macintosh beat Deloford 9–7, 9–6, 9–6; Morgan beat Gowthorpe 9–5, 9–2, 9–6.

Final: Morgan beat Macintosh 9–2, 9–4, 9–2.

1958

Quarter-finals: Mrs S. Macintosh beat Mrs H. R. Townsend 9–7, 9–7, 9–1; Miss D. C. Herman beat Mrs R. Cooper 9–2, 9–3, 9–0; Mrs G. E. Marshall beat Mrs G. R. Turner 10–9, 9–10, 2–5 retd; Miss J. R. M. Morgan beat Miss M. Gowthorpe 9–7, 9–7, 9–2.

Semi-finals: Macintosh beat Herman 9–5, 9–6, 9–4; Morgan beat Marshall 4–9, 4–9, 9–2, 9–3, 9–0.

Final: Morgan beat Macintosh 9–4, 9–1, 9–5.

1959

Quarter-finals: Mrs S. Macintosh beat Miss P. Drew 9–0,

Anna Craven-Smith (*left*), winner of the 1960 Women's Junior Championship, and Mrs Sheila Macintosh, 1959 winner of the Women's Open. Later in the sixties Miss Craven-Smith reached the Open final three times only to lose to Heather McKay. She did however gain the distinction of being one of two players to claim a game off the great Australian. *Sport and General*

9–1, 9–4; Mrs J. Deloford beat Mrs J. D. Campion 9–2, 9–0, 9–7; Mrs F. R. D. Corbett (née Herman) beat Mrs J. Tomlin 9–1, 9–0, 9–1; Mrs G. E. Marshall beat Miss P. Gimson 9–2, 9–3, 9–2.

Semi-finals: Macintosh beat Deloford 9–3, 9–3, 9–4; Marshall beat Corbett 9–1, 9–3, 4–9, 9–0.

Final: Macintosh beat Marshall 4–9, 8–9, 9–5, 9–3, 9–6.

1960

Quarter-finals: Miss M. Gowthorpe beat Mrs R. Nagle 9–0, 9–6, 9–3; Mrs G. R. Turner beat Mrs B. J. Whitehead 10–8, 9–6, 9–7; Mrs F. R. D. Corbett beat Mrs J. Deloford 9–4, 10–9, 9–3; Mrs G. E. Marshall beat Mrs J. R. White 9–3, 9–0, 9–4.

Semi-finals: Turner beat Gowthorpe 7–9, 9–5, 9–2, 9–2; Marshall beat Corbett 9–5, 9–4, 9–4.

Final: Marshall beat Turner 9–3, 9–5, 9–1.

1961

Quarter-finals: Mrs G. E. Marshall beat Mrs B. J. Whitehead 9–1, 9–5, 9–3; Miss A. M. Price beat Mrs J. R. White w.o.; Miss E. C. Hargreaves beat Mrs M. N. Crane 9–3, 9–2, 10–8; Miss H. Blundell (Aus) beat Miss M. Muncaster 9–7, 9–4, 9–6.

Semi-finals: Marshall beat Price 9–0, 9–1, 9–0; Blundell beat Hargreaves 9–2, 9–2, 9–3.

Final: Blundell beat Marshall 9–6, 9–5, 9–4.

1962

Quarter-finals: Mrs G. E. Marshall beat Mrs J. R. White 9–3, 10–8, 9–1; Mrs S. Macintosh beat Mrs B. J. Whitehead 9–4, 9–7, 9–6; Miss M. Muncaster beat Miss E. C. Hargreaves 9–2, 9–5, 3–9, 7–9, 9–5; Miss H. Blundell (Aus) beat Miss A. Craven-Smith 9–4, 9–1, 9–2.

Semi-finals: Marshall beat Macintosh 9–5, 9–4, 9–5; Blundell beat Muncaster 9–3, 9–2, 9–6.

Final: Blundell beat Marshall 9–3, 9–2, 9–6.

1963

Quarter-finals: Miss H. Blundell (Aus) beat Mrs J. R. White 9–0, 9–2, 9–0; Miss A. Craven-Smith beat Miss P. McClenaughan (Aus) 2–9, 9–2, 9–7, 9–7; Miss M. Muncaster beat Mrs S. Macintosh 9–4, 6–9, 10–8, 9–5; Mrs G. E. Marshall beat Mrs J. Irving (Aus) 9–6, 9–3, 9–3.

Semi-finals: Blundell beat Craven-Smith 9–4, 7–9, 9–1, 9–3; Marshall beat Muncaster 9–4, 9–6, 9–5.

Final: Blundell beat Marshall 9–2, 9–2, 9–1.

1964

Quarter-finals: Miss H. Blundell (Aus) beat Miss A. M. Price 9–1, 9–0, 9–4; Mrs J. R. White beat Mrs R. Turner 9–6, 8–10, 9–4, 9–5; Miss A. Craven-Smith beat Miss K. Dempsey 9–0, 9–4, 9–0; Mrs G. E. Marshall beat Miss P. McClenaughan (Aus) 9–6, 9–5, 10–8.

Semi-finals: Blundell beat White 9–0, 9–1, 9J1–1; Craven-Smith beat Marshall 1–9, 6–9, 9–4, 10–8, 9–5.

Final: Blundell beat Craven-Smith 9–0, 9–1, 9–2.

1965

Quarter-finals: Mrs H. McKay (née Blundell) (Aus) beat Miss B. Johnson (Aus) 9–0, 9–1, 9–2; Mrs G. E. Marshall beat Miss M. Burke (Aus) 9–2, 5–9, 9–3, 9–0; Mrs B. Irving (Aus) beat Miss A. M. Price 9–1, 9–2,

The arrival of a certain Heather Blundell in England for the Women's Open in 1962 created mild interest in squash and the sporting press. It was enough to attract one Fleet Street photographer, however, who attended one of her practice sessions and captioned this picture of Heather tying up her shoe lace as 'the Australian champion being photographed in training'. *Central Press*

9–2; Miss A. Craven-Smith beat Mrs S. Macintosh 9–5, 8–10, 9–4, 9–0.

Semi-finals: McKay beat Marshall 9–6, 9–5, 9–1; Craven-Smith beat Irving 9–5, 9–4, 9–2.

Final: McKay beat Craven-Smith 9–0, 9–0, 10–8.

1966

Quarter-finals: Miss A. Craven-Smith beat Miss B. Johnson (Aus) 9–5, 9–5, 9–7; Mrs G. E. Marshall beat Miss B. Baxter (Aus) 9–4, 9–2, 9–7; Miss M. Hawcroft (Aus) beat Mrs M. Tierney (Aus) 9–7, 9–1, 9–2; Mrs H. McKay beat Mrs S. Macintosh 9–3, 9–1, 9–5.

Semi-finals: Craven-Smith beat Marshall 9–1, 8–10, 9–4, 9–3; McKay beat Hawcroft 9–1, 9–0, 9–3.

Final: McKay beat Craven-Smith 9–1, 10–8, 9–6.

1967

Quarter-finals: Mrs. H. McKay (Aus) beat Miss D. Holton (SA) 9–2, 9–0, 9–0; Mrs G. Erskine (SA) beat Miss M. Roche (SA) 9–5, 3–9, 9–6, 9–6; Miss E. Allnutt (SA) beat Mrs J. Eckstein (SA) 9–7, 9–6, 9–7; Miss B. Johnson (Aus) beat Miss C. van Veen (SA) 9–1, 9–0, 0–9, 9–2.

Semi-finals: McKay beat Erskine 9–0, 9–0, 9–0; Johnson beat Allnutt 9–10, 9–4, 9–2, 9–1.

Final: McKay beat Johnson 9–0, 9–0, 9–0.

1968

Quarter-finals: Mrs. H. McKay (Aus) beat Miss C. Fleming (NZ) 9–1, 9–0, 9–2; Mrs S. Macintosh beat Miss M. Burke (Aus) 9–6, 9–7, 9–7; Miss S. McClure (Sco) beat Mrs A. Chapman 9–3, 9–3, 2–9, 9–5; Mrs G. E. Marshall beat Miss A. M. Price 9–4, 9–2, 8–10, 9–6.

Semi-finals: McKay beat Macintosh 9–0, 9–0, 9–0; Marshall beat McClure 9–4, 4–9, 9–1, 9–4.

Final: McKay beat Marshall 9–2, 9–0, 9–0.

1969

Quarter-finals: Mrs. H. McKay (Aus) beat Mrs J. Claughton 9–0, 9–1, 9–1; Mrs A. Chapman beat Mrs V. Watson 9–3, 9–2, 9–1; Miss M. Roche (SA) beat Miss J. Wilson 9–7, 9–4, 9–4; Mrs G. E. Marshall beat Miss A. M. Price 9–4, 9–2, 8–10, 9–6.

Semi-finals: McKay beat Chapman 9–0, 9–1, 9–0; Roche beat Marshall 6–9, 10–8, 10–8, 9–5.

Final: McKay beat Roche 9–1, 9–1, 9–0.

1970

Quarter-finals: Mrs. H. McKay (Aus) beat Mrs P. Bleasdale 9–0, 9–0, 9–1; Mrs M. Jackman (Aus) beat Miss J. Wilson 9–7, 9–4, 9–5; Mrs J. Irving (SA) beat Mrs A. Chapman 9–0, 9–1, 9–0; Mrs G. E. Marshall beat Miss M. Baker (Aus) 9–7, 7–9, 4–9, 9–4, 9–4.

Semi-finals: McKay beat Jackman 9–7, 9–0, 9–4; Irving beat Marshall 9–7, 9–5, 9–6.

Final: McKay beat Irving 9–0, 9–3, 9–1.

1971

Quarter-finals: Miss K. Malan (SA) beat Mrs F. R. D. Corbett 9–7, 9–4, 9–1; Miss J. Wilson beat Miss J. Barham 4–9, 9–6, 9–7, 9–4; Mrs G. E. Marshall beat Mrs J. Wainwright 10–8, 9–4, 9–2; Mrs. H. McKay (Aus) beat Mrs A. Chapman 9–1, 9–0, 9–0.

Semi-finals: Malan beat Wilson 8–10, 9–6, 9–6, 9–6; McKay beat Marshall 9–1, 9–1, 9–3.

Final: McKay beat Malan 9–1, 9–1, 9–2.

1972

Quarter-finals: Mrs. H. McKay (Aus) beat Mrs G. E. Marshall 9–0, 9–1, 9–3; Mrs P. Buckingham (NZ) beat Miss J. Barham 9–6, 9–4, 8–10, 9–1; Miss C. Fleming (NZ) beat Mrs J. Webster (NZ) 9–2, 4–9, 1–9, 9–1, 9–3; Miss S. Newman (Aus) beat Miss I. Potgieter (SA) 9–10, 9–5, 9–1, 3–9, 9–2.

Semi-finals: McKay beat Buckingham 9–2, 9–0, 9–2; Fleming beat Newman 1–9, 7–9, 9–7, 9–2, 10–8.

Final: McKay beat Fleming 9–1, 9–0, 9–1.

1973

Quarter-finals: Mrs. H. McKay (Aus) beat Miss T. Veltman 9–2, 9–4, 9–4; Mrs G. E. Marshall beat Mrs J.

Pritchett 9–3, 9–2, 9–0; Miss S. Cogswell beat Miss J. Wilson 9–5, 9–1, 5–9, 7–9, 9–3; Miss J. Barham beat Mrs A. Chapman 9–0, 9–4, 8–10, 9–0.

Semi-finals: McKay beat Marshall 9–2, 9–1, 9–1; Cogswell beat Barham 9–4, 10–8, 9–5.

Final: McKay beat Cogswell 9–2, 9–1, 9–2.

1974

Quarter-finals: Mrs. H. McKay (Aus) beat Miss C. van Nierop (Aus) 9–1, 9–2, 9–0; Miss M. Zachariah (Aus) beat Miss S. Cogswell 9–1, 9–5, 9–3; Miss S. Newman (Aus) beat Miss L. Hubinger (Aus) 9–5, 9–1, 10–8; Mrs D. Jackman (Aus) beat Mrs I. Hewitt (Ire) 9–5, 9–2, 9–2.

Semi-finals: McKay beat Zachariah 9–1, 9–0, 9–1; Jackman beat Newman 7–9, 9–4, 9–10, 9–1, 9–6.

Final: McKay beat Jackman 9–3, 9–1, 9–5.

1975

Quarter-finals: Mrs. H. McKay (Aus) beat Miss K. Gardner 9–0, 9–0, 9–0; Miss T. Lawes beat Miss A. Smith 9–5, 9–3, 7–9, 5–9, 10–8; Miss S. Cogswell beat Miss I. Hewitt (Ire) 10–8, 9–0, 10–8; Miss S. Newman (Aus) beat Mrs B. Diggens 9–1, 9–2, 9–4.

Semi-finals: McKay beat Lawes 9–2, 9–2, 9–1; Newman beat Cogswell 9–0, 9–10, 9–6, 4–9, 9–6.

Final: McKay beat Newman 9–2, 9–4, 9–2.

1976

Quarter-finals: Mrs. H. McKay (Aus) beat Miss R. Shapland (Aus) 9–1, 9–1, 9–0; Miss S. Cogswell beat Miss K. Gardner 9–0, 9–3, 9–1; Miss A. Smith beat Miss T. Lawes 9–4, 9–0, 9–1; Miss B. Wall (Aus) beat Miss M. Zachariah (Aus) 3–9, 9–5, 10–8, 9–7.

Semi-finals: McKay beat Cogswell 9–5, 9–7, 5–9, 9–0; Wall beat Smith 9–4, 6–9, 4–9, 9–3, 9–6.

Final: McKay beat Wall 9–3, 9–1, 9–2.

1977

Quarter-finals: Miss S. Cogswell beat Miss L. Hubinger (Aus) 9–6, 9–5, 9–3; Miss V. Hoffman (Aus) beat Miss J. Ashton 9–1, 9–0, 9–4; Miss R. Shapland (Aus) beat Miss B. Wall (Aus) 9–3, 9–4, 10–8; Miss S. Newman (Aus) beat Miss A. Smith 9–2, 9–1, 9–7.

Semi-finals: Hoffman beat Cogswell 9–6, 9–5, 9–3; Newman beat Shapland 9–5, 6–9, 10–9, 9–4.

Final: Newman beat Hoffman 9–4, 9–7, 9–2.

1978

Quarter-finals: Miss B. Wall (Aus) beat Mrs S. King (née Newman) (Aus) 9–0, 9–6, 9–5; Miss Angela Smith beat Miss V. Bridgens (SA) 9–3, 9–4, 9–4; Miss S. Cogswell beat Miss L. Hubinger (Aus) 9–1, 9–5, 9–4; Miss V. Hoffman (Aus) beat Mrs Anne Smith (Aus) 9–7, 3–9, 3–9, 9–2, 9–7.

Semi-finals: Wall beat Smith 9–4, 9–4, 9–7; Cogswell beat Hoffman 9–5, 9–10, 9–0, 9–1.

Final: Wall beat Cogswell 8–10, 6–9, 9–4, 9–4, 9–3.

1979

Quarter-finals: Miss S. Cogswell beat Miss J. Ashton 10–8, 9–1, 9–1; Miss M. Zachariah (Aus) beat Miss L. Moore 10–8, 9–1, 9–4; Miss V. Hoffman (Aus) beat Mrs S. King (Aus) 7–9, 9–3, 9–2, 9–0; Miss A. Smith beat Mrs B. Diggens 9–0, 9–0, 9–3.

Semi-finals: Cogswell beat Zachariah 9–5, 9–6, 9–7;

Hoffman beat Smith 7–9, 9–2, 9–3, 9–4.

Final: Hoffman beat Cogswell 9–5, 9–5, 9–3.

1980

Quarter-finals: Miss V. Hoffman (Aus) beatMiss M. Le Moignan 9–2, 9–3, 0–9, 9–7; Miss R. Anderson (Aus) beat Mrs R. Thorne (née Shapland) (Aus) 9–4, 9–5, 10–8; Miss M. Zachariah (Aus) beat Miss A. Smith 5–9, 9–7, 10–9, 9–6; Miss L. Opie beat Miss S. Cogswell 9–5, 9–2, 9–4.

Semi-finals: Hoffman beat Anderson 9–3, 9–1, 6–9, 9–4; Zachariah beat Opie 9–6, 10–8, 9–6.

Final: Hoffman beat Zachariah 9–6, 9–4, 9–0.

1981

Quarter-finals: Miss B. Oldfield (Aus) beat Mrs R. Thorne (Aus) 3–9, 9–7, 8–10, 9–6, 9–0; Miss L. Opie beat Miss M. Le Moignan 9–4, 9–0, 10–8; Miss A. Smith beat Miss C. Clonda (Aus) 7–9, 9–4, 9–6, 9–6; Mrs V. Cardwell (née Hoffman) (Aus) beat Miss R. Blackwood (NZ) 9–5, 9–5, 9–2.

Semi-finals: Opie beat Oldfield 7–9, 9–0, 9–3, 10–9; Cardwell beat Smith 9–2, 10–8, 9–0.

Final: Cardwell beat Opie 9–4, 5–9, 9–4, 9–4.

1982

Quarter-finals: Mrs V. Cardwell (Aus) beat Miss S. Cogswell 9–1, 9–3, 9–2; Miss M. Le Moignan beat Miss S. Devoy (NZ) 9–6, 9–0, 3–9, 9–2; Miss A. Smith beat Mrs R. Thorne (Aus) 4–9, 9–7, 4–9, 9–6, 9–3; Miss L. Opie beat Miss R. Blackwood (NZ) 9–2, 9–1, 9–4.

Semi-finals: Cardwell beat Le Moignan 9–2, 9–2, 9–10, 9–3; Opie beat Smith 0–9, 9–5, 9–6, 9–7.

Final: Cardwell beat Opie 9–10, 9–6, 9–4, 9–4.

1983

Quarter-finals: Miss L. Opie beat Miss A. Smith 9–5, 9–1, 10–8; Miss M. Le Moignan beat Mrs J. Miller (Aus) 9–3, 9–1, 9–5; Miss S. Devoy (NZ) beat Miss R. Blackwood (NZ) 9–4, 9–3, 9–4; Mrs R. Thorne (Aus) beat Miss S. Cogswell 9–5, 9–4, 9–3.

Semi-finals: Opie beat Le Moignan 8–10, 9–5, 10–9, 9–3; Devoy beat Thorne 4–9, 9–4, 9–3, 9–0.

Final: Devoy beat Opie 5–9, 9–0, 9–7, 9–1.

Notes

1 In all the above championship results the 1921/2 season is indicated by the date 1921, and similarly throughout for all years.

2 Venues: Queen's Club, London 1921–38; Lansdowne and Royal Aero Clubs, London 1946–68; BP Club, Sydenham 1969–73; Wembley, London 1974–79; Brighton 1980; Bromley, Kent 1981; Derby 1982; Brighton and Wembley 1983.

The French Open Championship

1982 (Paris)

Quarter-finals: Jahangir Khan (Pak) beat A. Kaoud (Egy) 9–3, 9–0, 9–0; S. Qaiser (Pak) beat G. Brumby (Aus) 10–8, 9–5, 10–9; R. Norman (NZ) beat G. Briars (Eng) 9–7, 6–9, 9–5, 9–1; G. Awad (Egy) beat L. Kvant (Swe) 6–9, 9–1, 9–6, 9–6.

Semi-finals: Jahangir Khan beat Qaiser 7–9, 9–6, 10–8, 9–3; Awad beat Norman 9–3, 9–2, 9–5.

Final: Jahangir Khan beat Awad 6–9, 9–5, 9–4, 9–7.
1983 (Paris)
Quarter-finals: Jahangir Khan (Pak) beat G. Awad (Egy) 9–3, 9–7, 9–6; H. Jahan (Pak) beat S. Qaiser (Pak) 10–8, 6–9, 1–9, 9–6, 10–9; D. Williams (Aus) beat R. Thorne (Aus) 9–6, 9–4, 9–0; Q. Zaman (Pak) beat M. Saad (Egy) 9–4, 10–8, 9–2.
Semi-finals: Jahangir Khan beat Jahan 9–6, 9–2, 9–5; Zaman beat Williams 9–6, 9–4, 0–9, 9–0.
Final: Jahangir Khan beat Zaman 9–3, 7–9, 9–1, 10–8.
1984 (Paris)
Quarter-finals: D. Williams (Aus) beat H. Jahan (Eng) 9–2, 9–5, 9–3; Q. Zaman (Pak) beat P. Kenyon (Eng) 1–9, 9–4, 9–6, 10–8; R. Norman (NZ) beat S. Davenport (NZ) 9–5, 9–6, 9–7; Jahangir Khan (Pak) beat G. Briars (Eng) 9–3, 9–5, 9–7.
Semi-finals: Jahangir Khan beat Norman 9–1, 9–2, 9–0; Williams beat Zaman 8–10, 9–2, 9–2, 9–4.
Final: Jahangir Khan beat Williams 9–0, 9–0, 9–1.

The Pakistan Open Championship

1983 (Karachi)
Quarter-finals: Jahangir Khan (Pak) beat A. Aziz (Egy) 9–3, 9–1, 9–2; H. Jahan (Pak) beat F. Gul (Pak) 9–6, 9–7, 9–1; Q. Zaman (Pak) beat P. Kenyon (Eng) 9–6, 9–0, 9–3; G. Briars (Eng) beat G. Alauddin (Pak) 7–9, 6–9, 9–1, 9–1, 10–8.
Semi-finals: Jahangir Khan beat Zaman 9–4, 9–3, 9–4; Jahan beat Briars 6–9, 9–3, 10–8, 9–4.
Final: Jahangir Khan beat Jahan 9–1, 9–2, 8–10, 9–2.
1984 (Karachi)
Quarter-finals: Jahangir Khan (Pak) beat R. George (Aus) 9–0, 9–1, 9–1; M. Ahmed (Pak) beat M. Saad (Egy) 9–7, 9–3, 9–1; G. Alauddin (Pak) beat S. Bowditch (Aus) 10–8, 10–8, 9–6; Q. Zaman (Pak) beat S. Qaiser (Pak) 9–4, 9–6, 9–2.
Semi-finals: Jahangir Khan beat M. Ahmed 9–2, 9–5, 9–6; Zaman beat Alauddin 9–3, 9–4, 9–5.
Final: Jahangir Khan beat Zaman 9–7, 9–7, 6–9, 9–1.

Chichester International Squash Festival

The Chichester Club in Sussex has staged international squash since 1975 when it initiated men's and women's tournaments as part of a seven event festival of squash. The club had then recently acquired a new glass backed championship court and this was to provide the venue for all the championships until 1982 when the final stages of the event moved to the nearby Chichester Theatre. Chichester that year made squash history by running the first championship in Britain on a four wall demountable transparent court, using the Swedish Transwall system. This style of promotion was repeated in 1983 with the aid of the ICI Perspex Court and the championship was notable for the recording of the world's longest match – that of the final between Jahangir Khan of Pakistan and Gamal Awad of Egypt lasting two hours and 46 minutes.

The Festival has also been notable in the amount of television coverage it has attracted, particularly in a sport which gets so little attention. Southern Television and subsequently TVS have consistently screened highlights of play and this has often been put out on the national network. Unfortunately, lack of sponsorship led to the Festival's postponement from its usual date in Spring 1984.

MEN
1979
Quarter-finals: G. Hunt (Aus) beat G. Briars (Eng) 9–6, 9–3, 9–4; G. Alauddin (Pak) beat R. Watson (SA) 9–5, 9–4, 4–9, 9–2; H. Jahan (Pak) beat M. Ahmed (Pak) 3–9, 9–4, 9–0, 9–4; Q. Zaman (Pak) beat M. Lilley (NZ) 9–4, 9–6, 9–0.
Semi-finals: Hunt beat Alauddin 9–4, 9–2, 5–9, 10–8; Jahan beat Zaman 3–9, 9–5, 2–9, 9–6, 9–2.
Final: Hunt beat Jahan 9–7, 9–4, 9–6.
1980
Quarter-finals: G. Hunt (Aus) beat M. Ahmed (Pak) 9–7, 10–8, 9–5; H. Jahan (Pak) beat B. Brownlee (NZ) 9–3, 9–7, 9–4; Mohibullah Khan (Pak) beat G. Alauddin (Pak) 3–9, 10–9, 10–8, 9–1; Q. Zaman (Pak) beat J. Barrington (GB & Ire) 9–6, 9–6, 9–6.
Semi-finals: Jahan beat Hunt 3–9, 9–5, 9–0, 9–5; Zaman beat Mohibullah Khan 9–3, 9–2, 9–5.
Final: Zaman beat Jahan 7–9, 6–9, 9–4, 9–4, 9–1.
1981
Quarter-finals: Q. Zaman (Pak) beat B. Brownlee (NZ) 9–5, 9–4, 9–4; Jahangir Khan (Pak) beat G. Awad (Egy) 9–2, 9–3, 9–2; H. Jahan (Pak) beat M. Ahmed (Pak) 9–6, 9–2, 9–6; G. Hunt (Aus) beat G. Alauddin (Pak) 9–6, 9–3, 9–1.
Semi-finals: Jahangir Khan beat Zaman 9–0, 9–2, 9–2; Hunt beat Jahan 4–9, 9–5, 3–9, 9–6, 9–3.
Final: Jahangir Khan beat Hunt 6–9, 9–0, 4–9, 9–4, 9–6.
1982
Quarter-finals: Jahangir Khan (Pak) beat G. Awad (Egy) 9–6, 10–8, 9–4; Q. Zaman (Pak) beat M. Ahmed (Pak) 9–0, 9–7, 9–5; H. Jahan (Pak) beat R. Norman (NZ) 7–9, 9–4, 9–7, 9–1; G. Hunt (Aus) beat D. Williams (Aus) 9–7, 9–2, 9–7.
Semi-finals: Jahangir Khan beat Zaman 9–3, 9–0, 9–3; Hunt beat Jahan 9–7, 4–9, 7–9, 9–1, 9–5.
Final: Jahangir Khan beat Hunt 9–2, 9–2, 9–6.
1983
Quarter-finals: Jahangir Khan (Pak) beat R. Norman (NZ) 6–9, 9–1, 9–0, 9–3; Q. Zaman (Pak) beat M. Ahmed (Pak) 9–4, 9–3, 9–5; G. Awad (Egy) beat D. Williams (Aus) 6–9, 5–9, 9–5, 9–0, 9–3; G. Briars (Eng) beat S. Qaiser (Pak) 7–9, 10–9, 9–6, 10–8.
Semi-finals: Jahangir Khan beat Zaman 9–1, 9–7, 8–10, 9–2; Awad beat Briars 10–8, 9–6, 9–2.
Final: Jahangir Khan beat Awad 9–10, 9–5, 9–7, 9–2.

WOMEN
1980
Semi-finals: Miss S. Cogswell (Eng) beat Miss L. Moore

(Eng) 9–0, 9–2, 9–0; Miss V. Hoffman (Aus) beat Miss
A. Smith (Eng) 10–8, 9–6, 9–5.

Final: Hoffman beat Cogswell 9–4, 2–9, 9–6, 9–4.

1981

Semi-finals: Miss V. Hoffman (Aus) beat Miss A. Smith
(Eng) 9–5, 9–6, 9–1; Miss S. Cogswell (Eng) beat Miss
J. Ashton (Eng) 9–3, 6–9, 9–6, 9–6, 8–10, 9–4.

Final: Hoffman beat Cogswell 9–2, 9–3, 9–1.

1982

Semi-finals: Miss L. Opie (Eng) beat Miss R. Strauss
(Eng) 9–3, 9–4, 9–5; Mrs V. Cardwell (née Hoffman)
beat Miss S. Cogswell (Eng) 10–8, 4–9, 4–9, 9–0, 9–1.

Final: Opie beat Cardwell 7–9, 9–7, 9–5, 3–9, 9–7.

1983

Semi-finals: Mrs V. Cardwell (Aus) beat Miss M. Le
Moignan (Eng) 9–5, 10–9, 9–1; Miss S. Cogswell (Eng)
beat Miss R. Blackwood (NZ) 9–5, 10–9, 9–3.

Final: Cardwell beat Cogswell 9–5, 3–9, 9–1, 9–4.

International Squash Players Association Championship

The official championship of the ISPA is open to any
member of the Association and is played on a standard
knock-out basis with seedings based on the ISPA's
latest computer-produced listing.

The inaugural tournament was held in 1977/8 at the
Abbeydale Park Club in Sheffield under the sponsorship of York company Shepherd Building Services.
The major upset was in the semi-final when Hiddy
Jahan, seeded 5, recovered from two games and 1–6
behind to beat favourite Geoff Hunt. Jahan had
already defeated fourth seed Gogi Alauddin for the
loss of just eight points in the previous round but
could not maintain his splendid form in the final
where he lost 1–3 to Qamar Zaman.

In its second year the event was surprisingly
unsponsored but this did not deter the world's leading
players, all of whom returned to Sheffield. Hunt was
seeded second to Zaman but the Australian defeated
his great rival in the final. The strength of the Pakistani contingent at the time was indicated by the fact
that Hunt and New Zealand's Bruce Brownlee were
the only non-Pakistanis to reach the quarter-finals.
(Earlier, Hunt had needed to recover from two games
to one down to beat South African Roland Watson.)

The 1979/80 season produced a new sponsor and a
change of venue. Abbey Life presented the tournament on the stage of the Gaumont Theatre, Southampton – the first time a theatre had been used for a
squash event. Zaman won his second title as he fought
off a brave fightback by Mohibullah Khan to triumph
3–2 after one hour and 45 minutes. This tournament
was the first as a professional for young Jahangir
Khan who led 2–1 against Hiddy Jahan before going
down 9–7, 1–9, 9–4, 7–9, 0–9, a performance that
prompted his opponent to predict 'Jahangir will be

world champion in two years'. How right he was.
Jahangir won the World Open in November 1981.

In early 1981 the event crossed the sea to Northern
Ireland where it was sponsored by Smirnoff. Jahangir
continued to demonstrate his improvement by finishing runner-up to Hunt and within the next couple of
months the youngster was to defeat the Australian at
Chichester and finish runner-up to him in the British
Open.

Twelve months later the championship returned to
its original home at Abbeydale Park thanks to an
eleventh-hour sponsorship deal with Thorntons Con-
fectioners. The Sheffield crowd was treated to an
almost faultless display by Jahangir, who by then was
world champion, as he demolished world number 4
Maqsood Ahmed 9–0, 9–0, 9–0, the first 'whitewash'
in a major final since Heather McKay defeated Bev
Johnson in the women's British Open in February
1968.

In 1982/3 the event moved again, this time to
Munich, Germany with Jahangir retaining his title at
the expense of Zaman.

1978 (Sheffield)

Quarter-finals: G. B. Hunt (Aus) beat A. Safwat (Egy)
10–8, 9–7, 9–5; H. Jahan (Pak) beat G. Alauddin (Pak)
9–3, 9–3, 9–2; Mohibullah Khan (Pak) beat B.
Brownlee (NZ) 4–9, 9–0, 10–9, 9–5; Q. Zaman (Pak)
beat C. J. Nancarrow (Aus) 9–6, 9–4, 9–2.

Semi-finals: Jahan beat Hunt 9–10, 7–9, 9–5, 9–0, 9–5;
Zaman beat Mohibullah Khan 9–3, 9–1, 1–9, 9–2.

Final: Zaman beat Jahan 10–9, 9–4, 3–9, 9–4.

1979 (Sheffield)

Quarter-finals: Q. Zaman (Pak) beat B. Brownlee (NZ)
9–3, 9–5, 9–5; H. Jahan (Pak) beat G. Alauddin (Pak)
9–0, 9–2, 9–6; M. Ahmed (Pak) beat Mohibullah Khan
(Pak) w.o.; G. B. Hunt (Aus) beat Torsam Khan (Pak)
9–3, 9–2, 9–2.

Semi-finals: Hunt beat Jahan 9–5, 9–5, 1–9, 9–4; Zaman
beat Ahmed 9–7, 6–9, 9–3, 2–9, 9–2.

Final: Hunt beat Zaman 9–7, 9–4, 5–9, 9–5.

1980 (Southampton)

Quarter-finals: Q. Zaman (Pak) beat A. Aziz (Egy) 9–3,
9–5, 9–2; M. Ahmed (Pak) beat B. Brownlee (NZ) 9–4,
9–3, 9–1; G. Alauddin (Pak) beat H. Jahan (Pak) 5–9,
9–4, 9–7, 9–4; Mohibullah Khan (Pak) beat
J. Barrington (GB & Ire) 5–9, 9–1, 9–2, 9–7.

Semi-finals: Zaman beat Ahmed 10–9, 7–9, 9–0, 9–3;
Mohibullah Khan beat Alauddin 9–4, 9–3, 9–5.

Final: Zaman beat Mohibullah Khan 9–5, 9–1, 7–9, 2–9,
9–7.

1981 (Ireland)

Quarter-finals: G. B. Hunt (Aus) beat S. Bowditch (Aus)
9–3, 9–3, 9–6; M. Ahmed (Pak) beat Q. Zaman (Pak)
10–9, 9–0, 9–1; Jahangir Khan (Pak) beat D. Williams
(Aus) 9–4, 9–5, 9–3; G. Awad (Egy) beat R. Watson
(SA) 9–4, 9–7, 9–4.

Semi-finals: Jahangir Khan (Pak) beat Ahmed 9–3, 9–1,

9–3; Hunt beat Awad 9–2, 9–6, 9–6.
Final: Hunt beat Jahangir Khan 9–5, 9–2, 9–5.

1982 (Sheffield)

Quarter-finals: Jahangir Khan (Pak) beat D. Williams
(Aus) 9–6, 9–0, 9–0; G. Awad (Egy) beat R. Watson
(SA) 9–5, 9–5, 9–0; M. Ahmed (Pak) beat R. Norman
(NZ) 9–3, 9–2, 9–6; G. Briars (Eng) beat L. Kvant
(Swe) 9–4, 9–5, 9–1.

Semi-finals: Jahangir Khan beat Awad 9–2, 9–0, 9–4;
Ahmed beat Briars 10–8, 7–9, 9–1, 3–9, 9–7.

Final: Jahangir Khan beat Ahmed 9–0, 9–0, 9–0.

1983 (Munich)

Quarter-finals: Jahangir Khan (Pak) beat D. Williams
(Aus) 9–3, 9–0, 9–1; S. Davenport (NZ) beat A. Safwat
(Egy) 7–9, 9–7, 9–3, 9–7; Q. Zaman (Pak) beat R.
Norman (NZ) 9–7, 9–0, 10–8; H. Jahan (Pak) beat M.
Ahmed (Pak) 10–8, 10–8, 9–4.

Semi-finals: Jahangir Khan beat Davenport 9–0, 9–7,
9–2; Zaman beat Jahan 9–2, 9–5, 4–9, 9–5.

Final: Jahangir Khan beat Zaman 9–4, 7–9, 9–5, 9–7.

World Masters Championship

For the roots of the World Masters one has to go back
to the autumn of 1975 when there was a specially
staged sponsored match between Geoff Hunt and
Qamar Zaman on the championship court of the new
Wembley Squash Centre. The Pakistani won the
match in five games.

In 1976 the event was enlarged and the format
changed to include the top four Pakistanis, Mohibullah Khan, Qamar Zaman, Hiddy Jahan and Gogi

136

Being a tournament director means being prepared for
everything. David Wild proved this when he answered
the call for a mop during the 1979 final of the World
Masters at Wembley. Finalists, Zaman and Barrington
found the break in play an amusing interlude. *Robin Eley
Jones*

Alauddin who played off over two nights for the right
to meet Geoff Hunt in the final. Zaman came through
to play the Australian and looked set to win again as he
led 4–0 in the fifth, but Hunt rallied to win the title in
100 minutes and earn £700.

The event then disappeared from the calendar for
two years but, when BBC Television confirmed an
intention to film a tournament in addition to the
British Open, it was revived in 1979 and relaunched as
the World Masters. The invited entry was expanded
to eight men but restricted to the top players from the
leading squash nations. Northampton Development
Corporation provided sponsorship and the first prize
was raised to £1520. Zaman produced one of his best
performances as he destroyed surprise finalist Jonah
Barrington for the loss of one point.

The following year the draw was increased to 16
players and invitations were extended to players by
virtue of their country's representation in the world's
top 30 with a maximum of three participants per
nation. That event produced one of squash's
greatest-ever shocks as Egypt's Gamal Awad beat
world champion Hunt in the first round – only the

second time the Australian had been beaten in the opening round of a competition in 17 years. Awad reached the final but was beaten by Mohibullah Khan who won the first prize of £2200.

1981 saw a new venue and sponsor as Thorn-EMI Heating took the event to Newcastle where top seed was Jahangir Khan. It was a clear indication of the youngster's dramatic improvement as he had not been invited the previous year since he was not one of Pakistan's top three players. Jahangir beat Zaman in an all-Pakistani final and retained his title at Leicester in 1982. The Masters found another new home in 1983 as it moved, under the auspices of ICI Perspex, to Warrington in the north-west of England. The format was again altered with 16 players being divided

into four groups and a round-robin system being employed to decide the four semi-finalists. The new format certainly did not upset Jahangir Khan who successfully defended his title against his country-man, Zaman.

1979 (Wembley Squash Centre, London)
Quarter-finals: Q. Zaman (Pak) beat G. Briars (Eng) 9–6, 7–9, 5–9, 9–3, 9–5; D. Williams (Aus) beat H. Jahan (Pak) 4–9, 9–6, 9–2, 7–9, 10–9; R. Watson (SA) beat A. Safwat (Egy) 9–4, 9–3, 9–5; J. Barrington (GB & Ire) beat B. Brownlee (NZ) 3–9, 9–6, 4–9, 10–8, 9–3.
Semi-finals: Zaman beat Watson 3–9, 9–0, 9–2, 9–5; Barrington beat Williams 9–7, 9–6, 9–3.
Final: Zaman beat Barrington 9–1, 9–0, 9–0.

1980 (Wembley Squash Centre, London)
Quarter-finals: G. Awad (Egy) beat R. Watson (SA) 9–4, 9–3, 9–3; L. Kvant (Swe) beat M. Ahmed (Pak) 9–2, 9–2, 9–3; Mohibullah Khan (Pak) beat B. Brownlee (NZ) 4–9, 9–3, 9–7, 9–3; Q. Zaman (Pak) beat J. Barrington (GB & Ire) 9–5, 9–4, 2–9, 9–5.
Semi-finals: Awad beat Kvant 9–1, 6–9, 9–2, 9–0; Mohibullah Khan beat Zaman 10–9, 9–7, 9–5.
Final: Mohibullah Khan beat Awad 9–2, 6–9, 9–4, 10–8.

1981 (Kingstons Squash Centre, Newcastle)
Quarter-finals: Jahangir Khan (Pak) beat D. Williams (Aus) 9–4, 9–1, 9–1; H. Jahan (Pak) beat P. Kenyon (Eng) 10–8, 9–5, 9–1; G. Awad (Egy) beat G. Brumby (Aus) 10–8, 9–3, 0–9, 9–2; Q. Zaman (Pak) beat G. Briars (Eng) 9–0, 7–9, 9–2, 9–2.
Semi-finals: Jahangir Khan beat Jahan 9–1, 9–2, 9–0; Zaman beat Awad 4–9, 9–6, 9–4, 9–4.
Final: Jahangir Khan beat Zaman 4–9, 9–5, 9–2, 9–2.

1982 (Granby Halls, Leicester)
Quarter-finals: Q. Zaman (Pak) beat G. Briars (Eng) 2–9, 9–6, 4–9, 9–5, 9–0; H. Jahan (Pak) beat D. Williams (Aus) 7–9, 9–2, 8–10, 9–2, 10–8; G. Awad (Egy) beat R. Norman (NZ) 6–9, 9–6, 9–3, 9–5; Jahangir Khan (Pak) beat G. Brumby (Aus) 9–0, 9–5, 9–4.
Semi-finals: Jahangir Khan beat Zaman 9–1, 9–3, 10–8; Awad beat Jahan 8–10, 10–8, 10–9, 9–1.
Final: Jahangir Khan beat Awad 9–2, 9–4, 9–0.

1983 (The Spectrum, Warrington)
Round-robin format introduced – 4 groups of 4 players.
Semi-finals: Jahangir Khan (Pak) beat H. Jahan (Eng) 9–2, 9–0, 9–3; Q. Zaman (Pak) beat D. Williams (Aus) 9–6, 9–2, 9–4.
Final: Jahangir Khan beat Zaman 9–6, 8–10, 9–0, 9–3.

The European Championships

These championships are held annually and consist of team events for men's and women's sides representing countries who are members of the European Squash Rackets Federation (ESRF). Men's teams consist of five players and the women's three.

A player is qualified to play for the country of his/her birth, the country of his/her parents birth or a country in which he/she has resided for the previous three years and is still residing. (Residential qualifica-

Mohibullah Khan of Pakistan in triumphant mood after winning the 1980 World Masters. It was one of his last major successes because soon after he lost form and ranking through ill health. Then in 1982 he received a long prison sentence for drugs offences – a miserable end to a career which had seen him as one of the world's best players, in company with Hunt, Zaman, Jahan and Alauddin. *Robin Eley Jones*

tion cannot be obtained through a school or university unless the player's bona fide home is at that institution, e.g. he/she is a member of the permanent staff.) A player may not represent more than one country in one season.

The men's championship was first played in Edinburgh in 1973. England beat Scotland 5–0 in the final and Ireland, Wales, Sweden, Finland, Denmark, Netherlands, Greece and Monaco also competed. England continued to dominate until 1980 when Sweden surprisingly defeated them in Helsinki. The same result caused a further shock in Munich in 1983. The women's competition was introduced in Amsterdam in 1978 and to date England have been unbeaten, defeating Ireland in all six finals.

At the end of each championship the Finnish SRA Trophy and the Target Trophy are awarded respectively to the male and female players who, in the view of a 'select panel' formed by the host nation and the ESRF, have shown the greatest spirit of fair play, both on and off the court, and who have either demonstrated great perseverance or have won unexpectedly in a crucial match. The first winners were Denmark's Ken Watson in 1973 and Agneta Samuelsson of Sweden in 1980.

Up to 1981 competing countries were drawn in two separate groups with the winners playing off in the final and the runners-up meeting to decide third and fourth positions. In Cardiff in 1982 a new system was introduced in which the teams start off in a conventional knock-out line-up with the winners progressing to the next round and the losers moving 'backwards' to compete in a series of further knock-outs for the minor positions. In that year 19 men's and 16 women's teams took part.

The 1983 event in Munich saw England's men lose for only the second time in the history of the championship and as in Helsinki in 1980 it was Sweden who were their conquerors. England had to line up without two of their strongest players, Phil Kenyon and David Pearson, and the handicap proved too great for them. The tie was keenly balanced at two matches all when the Swedish number 1 Lars Kvant produced some of his best squash to beat British number 1 Gawain Briars 3–2 in the deciding rubber.

Wales improved two places from 1982 and there was a surprise as Ireland and Scotland finished in sixth and seventh place respectively – their lowest ever. Holland and Finland came in at number four and five to emphasise the growing strength of squash outside the UK.

It was a case of 'as you were' in the women's event. Since the event was inaugurated in 1978 England have beaten Ireland 3–0 in each final and Scotland and Wales have taken up the next two positions. The 1983

138

championship was no exception although Wales did edge Scotland out of third position.

1973 (Edinburgh, Scotland)
Pool A: England beat Sweden 5–0, Denmark 5–0, Monaco 5–0, Ireland 5–0. Ireland beat Monaco 5–0, Denmark 4–1, Sweden 4–1. Sweden beat Monaco 5–0, Denmark 4–1. Denmark beat Monaco 5–0.
Pool B: Scotland beat Netherlands 5–0, Greece 5–0, Wales 5–0, Finland 5–0. Wales beat Netherlands 5–0, Finland 5–0, Greece 5–0. Finland beat Greece 5–0, Netherlands 5–0. Netherlands beat Greece 5–0.
Final: England beat Scotland 5–0.

1974 (Stockholm, Sweden)
Pool A: England beat Finland 5–0, Denmark 5–0, Switzerland 5–0, Wales 5–0. Wales beat Denmark 5–0, Switzerland 5–0, Belgium 5–0. Finland beat Belgium 5–0, Switzerland 4–1. Denmark beat Finland 3–2, Belgium 5–0.
Pool B: Scotland beat Germany 5–0, Sweden 3–2, Greece 5–0, Netherlands 5–0. Ireland beat Netherlands 4–1, Greece 5–0, Germany 5–0, Sweden 3–2. Netherlands beat Germany 5–0. Greece beat Germany 5–0.
3/4 position: Ireland beat Wales 5–0.
Final: England beat Scotland 5–0.

1975 (Dublin, Ireland)
Pool A: England beat France 5–0, Sweden 5–0, Wales 5–0, Netherlands 5–0, Belgium 5–0. Sweden beat Belgium 5–0, Netherlands 5–0, France 5–0, Wales 3–2. Wales beat Netherlands 5–0, France 5–0, Belgium 5–0. Belgium beat Netherlands 3–2, France 3–2. Netherlands beat France 5–0.
Pool positions: 1 England, 2 Sweden, 3 Wales, 4 Belgium, 5 Netherlands, 6 France.
Pool B: Scotland beat Switzerland 5–0, Denmark 5–0, Germany 5–0, Finland 4–1, Ireland 5–0. Ireland beat Denmark 5–0, Finland 5–0, Switzerland 5–0, Germany 5–0. Finland beat Germany 5–0, Denmark 5–0, Switzerland 5–0. Denmark beat Switzerland 5–0, Germany 4–1. Switzerland beat Germany 3–2.
Pool positions: 1 Scotland, 2 Ireland, 3 Finland, 4 Denmark, 5 Switzerland, 6 Germany.
Playoffs: Germany beat France 3–2; Netherlands beat Switzerland 5–0; Denmark beat Belgium 5–0; Wales beat Finland 4–1.
3/4 position: Sweden beat Ireland 3–2.
Final: England beat Scotland 5–0.
Final positions: 1 England, 2 Scotland, 3 Sweden, 4 Ireland, 5 Wales, 6 Finland, 7 Denmark, 8 Belgium, 9 Netherlands, 10 Switzerland, 11 Germany, 12 France.

1976 (Brussels, Belgium)
Pool A: England beat France 5–0, Greece 5–0, Netherlands 5–0. Netherlands beat Greece 4–1, France 4–1. France beat Greece 4–1.
Pool positions: 1 England, 2 Netherlands, 3 France, 4 Greece.
Pool B: Scotland beat Belgium 5–0, Denmark 5–0, Monaco 5–0. Denmark beat Monaco 5–0, Belgium 5–0. Belgium beat Monaco 5–0.

Pool positions: 1 Scotland, 2 Denmark, 3 Belgium, 4 Monaco.

Pool C: Sweden beat Germany 5–0, Finland 4–1, Luxembourg 5–0. Finland beat Luxembourg 5–0, Germany 5–0. Germany beat Luxembourg 5–0.
Pool positions: 1 Sweden, 2 Finland, 3 Germany, 4 Luxembourg.

Pool D: Ireland beat Wales 4–1, Switzerland 5–0. Wales beat Switzerland 4–1.
Pool positions: 1 Ireland, 2 Wales, 3 Switzerland.

Playoffs: Positions 9/12: Belgium beat France 3–2, Switzerland beat Germany 3–2, France beat Germany 3–2, Belgium beat Switzerland 4–1; Positions 5/8: Denmark beat Finland 3–2, Wales beat Netherlands 3–2, Finland beat Netherlands 3–2, Wales beat Denmark 5–0.

Semi-finals: England beat Ireland 5–0. Scotland beat Sweden 4–1.

3/4 position: Sweden beat Ireland 5–0.

Final: England beat Scotland 5–0.

Final positions: 1 England, 2 Scotland, 3 Sweden, 4 Ireland, 5 Wales, 6 Denmark, 7 Finland, 8 Netherlands, 9 Belgium, 10 Switzerland, 11 France, 12 Germany, 13 Greece, 14 Luxembourg, 15 Monaco.

1977 (Sheffield, England)

Pool A: England beat Finland 5–0, Netherlands 5–0, Denmark 5–0, France 5–0. Finland beat France 5–0, Netherlands 4–1, Denmark 5–0. Netherlands beat Denmark 3–2, France 5–0. Denmark beat France 5–0.
Pool positions: 1 England, 2 Finland, 3 Netherlands, 4 Denmark, 5 France.

Pool B: Scotland beat Wales 4–1, Greece 5–0, Switzerland 5–0. Wales beat Switzerland 5–0, Greece 5–0. Switzerland beat Greece 3–2.
Pool positions: 1 Scotland, 2 Wales, 3 Switzerland, 4 Greece.

Pool C: Sweden beat Belgium 5–0, Ireland 3–2, Germany 5–0. Ireland beat Belgium 5–0, Germany 5–0. Belgium beat Germany 5–0.
Pool positions: 1 Sweden, 2 Ireland, 3 Belgium, 4 Germany.

Playoffs: Positions 10/13: Germany beat Greece 3–2, Denmark beat Germany 5–0, France beat Greece 5–0, France beat Germany 3–2; Positions 7/9: Belgium beat Switzerland 5–0, Netherlands beat Switzerland 5–0, Netherlands beat Belgium 5–0; Positions 4/6: Ireland beat Wales 4–1, Finland beat Wales 4–1, Ireland beat Finland 4–1; Positions 1/3: Sweden beat Scotland 3–2, England beat Scotland 5–0, England beat Sweden 5–0.

Final positions: 1 England, 2 Sweden, 3 Scotland, 4 Ireland, 5 Finland, 6 Wales, 7 Netherlands, 8 Belgium, 9 Switzerland, 10 Denmark, 11 France, 12 Germany, 13 Greece.

1978 (Amsterdam, Holland)

Pool A: England beat Luxembourg 5–0, Switzerland 5–0, Belgium 5–0. Belgium beat Switzerland 4–1, Luxembourg 4–1. Switzerland beat Luxembourg 5–0.
Pool positions: 1 England, 2 Belgium, 3 Switzerland, 4 Luxembourg.

Pool B: Sweden beat Italy 5–0, Denmark 5–0, Netherlands 5–0. Netherlands beat Denmark 5–0, Italy 5–0. Denmark beat Italy 5–0.
Pool positions: 1 Sweden, 2 Netherlands, 3 Denmark, 4 Italy.

Pool C: Scotland beat France 5–0, Wales 5–0. Wales beat France 5–0.
Pool positions: 1 Scotland, 2 Wales, 3 France.

Pool D: Finland beat Germany 5–0, Greece 5–0, Ireland 3–2. Ireland beat Greece 5–0, Germany 5–0. Germany beat Greece 4–1.
Pool positions: 1 Finland, 2 Ireland, 3 Germany, 4 Greece.

Playoffs: Positions 13/15: Italy beat Luxembourg 4–1, Greece beat Italy 3–2; Positions 9/12: Germany beat Switzerland 3–2, Denmark beat France 4–1, France beat Switzerland 3–2, Germany beat Denmark 3–2; Positions 5/8: Ireland beat Belgium 5–0, Netherlands beat Wales 3–2, Wales beat Belgium 5–0, Ireland beat Netherlands 4–1.

Semi-finals: Sweden beat Scotland 5–0, England beat Finland 5–0.

3/4 position: Scotland beat Finland 5–0.

Final: England beat Sweden 4–1.

Final positions: 1 England, 2 Sweden, 3 Scotland, 4 Finland, 5 Ireland, 6 Netherlands, 7 Wales, 8 Belgium, 9 Germany, 10 Denmark, 11 Switzerland, 12 France, 13 Greece, 14 Italy, 15 Luxembourg.

1979 (Hamburg, Germany)

Pool A: England beat Germany 5–0, Austria 5–0, Norway 5–0, Belgium 5–0. Germany beat Norway 5–0, Belgium 5–0, Austria 5–0. Belgium beat Austria 5–0, Norway 5–0. Norway beat Austria 4–1.
Pool positions: 1 England, 2 Germany, 3 Belgium, 4 Norway, 5 Austria.

Pool B: Scotland beat France 5–0, Italy 5–0, Spain 5–0, Netherlands 5–0. Netherlands beat Spain 5–0, France 5–0, Italy 5–0. France beat Spain 5–0, Italy 5–0. Italy beat Spain 3–2.
Pool positions: 1 Scotland, 2 Netherlands, 3 France, 4 Italy, 5 Spain.

Pool C: Ireland beat Greece 5–0, Switzerland 5–0, Finland 3–2. Finland beat Switzerland 5–0, Greece 5–0. Switzerland beat Greece 5–0.
Pool positions: 1 Ireland, 2 Finland, 3 Switzerland, 4 Greece.

Pool D: Sweden beat Denmark 5–0, Luxembourg 5–0, Monaco 5–0, Wales 5–0. Wales beat Monaco 5–0, Luxembourg 5–0, Denmark 4–1. Denmark beat Monaco 5–0, Luxembourg 5–0. Monaco beat Luxembourg 4–1.
Pool positions: 1 Sweden, 2 Wales, 3 Denmark, 4 Monaco, 5 Luxembourg.

Playoffs: Positions 17/19: Luxembourg beat Austria 4–1, Luxembourg beat Spain 3–2; Positions 13/16: Italy beat Monaco 3–2, Greece beat Norway 5–0, Greece beat Italy 5–0; Positions 9/12: Denmark beat France 4–1, Belgium beat Switzerland 4–1, Switzerland beat France 5–0, Denmark beat Belgium 4–1; Positions 5/8: Finland beat Germany 4–1, Wales beat Netherlands 3–2,

139

Netherlands beat Germany 5–0, Finland beat Wales 4–1.

Semi-finals: Sweden beat Scotland 3–2, England beat Ireland 5–0.

3/4 position: Scotland beat Ireland 4–1.

Final: England beat Sweden 5–0.

Final positions: 1 England, 2 Sweden, 3 Scotland, 4 Ireland, 5 Finland, 6 Wales, 7 Netherlands, 8 Germany, 9 Denmark, 10 Belgium, 11 Switzerland, 12 France, 13 Greece, 14 Norway, 15 Italy, 16 Monaco, 17 Luxembourg, 18 Spain, 19 Austria.

1980 (Helsinki, Finland)

Pool A: England beat Switzerland 5–0, Belgium 5–0, Norway 5–0, Germany 5–0. Germany beat Norway 5–0, Switzerland 4–1, Belgium 5–0. Belgium beat Norway 5–0, Switzerland 4–1. Switzerland beat Norway 5–0.
Pool positions: 1 England, 2 Germany, 3 Belgium, 4 Switzerland, 5 Norway.

Pool B: Sweden beat Denmark 5–0, Monaco 5–0, Spain 5–0, Netherlands 5–0. Netherlands beat Spain 5–0, Monaco 5–0, Denmark 4–1. Monaco beat Spain 4–1. Denmark beat Spain 5–0, Monaco 4–1.
Pool positions: 1 Sweden, 2 Netherlands, 3 Denmark, 4 Monaco, 5 Spain.

Pool C: Wales beat Greece 5–0, France 5–0, Italy 5–0, Scotland 3–2. Scotland beat Italy 5–0, Greece 5–0, France 5–0. France beat Italy 5–0, Greece 3–2. Greece beat Italy 5–0.
Pool positions: 1 Wales, 2 Scotland, 3 France, 4 Greece, 5 Italy.

Pool D: Finland beat Austria 5–0, Luxembourg 5–0, Ireland 4–1. Ireland beat Luxembourg 5–0, Austria 5–0. Luxembourg beat Austria 4–1.
Pool positions: 1 Finland, 2 Ireland, 3 Luxembourg, 4 Austria.

Playoffs: Positions 17/19: Italy beat Norway 4–1, Spain beat Italy 4–1; Positions 13/16: Switzerland beat Austria 4–1, Greece beat Monaco 4–1, Monaco beat Austria 3–2, Switzerland beat Greece 3–2; Positions 9/12: Belgium beat Luxembourg 5–0, Denmark beat France 4–1, France beat Luxembourg 5–0, Belgium beat Denmark 3–2; Positions 5/8: Ireland beat Germany 5–0, Scotland beat Netherlands 3–2, Netherlands beat Germany 4–1, Ireland beat Scotland 3–2.

Semi-finals: England beat Finland 5–0; Sweden beat Wales 5–0.

3/4 position: Finland beat Wales 4–1.

Final: Sweden beat England 3–2.

Final positions: 1 Sweden, 2 England, 3 Finland, 4 Wales, 5 Ireland, 6 Scotland, 7 Netherlands, 8 Germany, 9 Belgium, 10 Denmark, 11 France, 12 Luxembourg, 13 Switzerland, 14 Greece, 15 Monaco, 16 Austria, 17 Spain, 18 Italy, 19 Norway.

1981 (Amsterdam, Holland)

Pool A: Sweden beat Spain 5–0, Belgium 5–0, Austria 5–0, Germany 5–0. Belgium beat Austria 4–1, Spain 5–0. Germany beat Spain 5–0, Austria 5–0, Belgium 5–0. Austria beat Spain 3–2.
Pool positions: 1 Sweden, 2 Germany, 3 Belgium, 4 Austria, 5 Spain.

Pool B: England beat Italy 5–0, Denmark 5–0, Monaco 5–0, Netherlands 5–0. Netherlands beat Italy 5–0, Monaco 5–0, Denmark 5–0. Monaco beat Denmark w.o., Italy 5–0. Denmark beat Italy 5–0.
Pool positions: 1 England, 2 Netherlands, 3 Monaco, 4 Denmark, 5 Italy.

Pool C: Scotland beat Greece 5–0, France 5–0, Norway 5–0, Finland 4–1. Finland beat Norway 5–0, France 5–0, Greece 5–0. France beat Norway 5–0, Greece 3–2. Greece beat Norway 4–1.
Pool positions: 1 Scotland, 2 Finland, 3 France, 4 Greece, 5 Norway.

Pool D: Ireland beat Switzerland 5–0, Luxembourg 5–0, Wales 4–1. Wales beat Luxembourg 5–0, Switzerland 5–0. Switzerland beat Luxembourg 5–0.
Pool positions: 1 Ireland, 2 Wales, 3 Switzerland, 4 Luxembourg.

Playoffs: Positions 17/19: Norway beat Italy 3–2, Spain beat Norway 4–1; Positions 13/16: Denmark beat Greece 3–2, Austria beat Luxembourg 3–2, Greece beat Luxembourg 5–0, Denmark beat Austria 4–1; Positions 9/12: France beat Monaco 4–1, Belgium beat Switzerland 4–1, Switzerland beat Monaco 3–2, France beat Belgium 3–2; Positions 5/8: Wales beat Germany 5–0, Finland beat Netherlands 4–1, Netherlands beat Germany 5–0, Finland beat Wales 5–0.

Semi-finals: England beat Scotland 5–0, Sweden beat Ireland 4–1.

3/4 position: Ireland beat Scotland 3–2.

Final: England beat Sweden 3–2.

Final positions: 1 England, 2 Sweden, 3 Ireland, 4 Scotland, 5 Finland, 6 Wales, 7 Netherlands, 8 Germany, 9 France, 10 Belgium, 11 Switzerland, 12 Monaco, 13 Denmark, 14 Austria, 15 Greece, 16 Luxembourg, 17 Spain, 18 Norway, 19 Italy.

1982 (Cardiff, Wales)

Luxembourg beat Italy 3–2, Spain beat Austria 5–0, Greece beat Norway 4–1, England beat Luxembourg 4–1, Germany beat France 3–2, Scotland beat Monaco 5–0, Finland beat Switzerland 5–0, Wales beat Belgium 5–0, Ireland beat Spain 5–0, Netherlands beat Denmark 4–1, Sweden beat Greece 5–0, Monaco beat Italy 4–1, Switzerland beat Austria 5–0, Belgium beat Norway 4–1, France beat Luxembourg 5–0, Switzerland beat Monaco 5–0, Belgium beat Spain 3–2, Greece beat Denmark 5–0, Monaco beat Luxembourg 3–2, Spain beat Denmark 3–2, Switzerland beat France 3–2, Belgium beat Greece 3–2, England beat Germany 5–0, Finland beat Scotland 4–1, Ireland beat Wales 4–1, Sweden beat Netherlands 4–1, Scotland beat Germany 5–0, Wales beat Netherlands 3–2.

Playoffs: Positions 18/19: Austria beat Italy 5–0; 17/18: Norway beat Austria 3–2: 15/16: Denmark beat Luxembourg 4–1; 13/14: Spain beat Monaco 5–0; 11/12: Greece beat France 3–2; 9/10: Switzerland beat Belgium 3–2; 7/8: Netherlands beat Germany 4–1; 5/6: Wales beat Scotland 4–1.

Semi-finals: England beat Finland 5–0; Sweden beat Ireland 5–0.

3/4 position: Ireland beat Finland 3–2.

Final: England beat Sweden 5–0.

Final positions: 1 England, 2 Sweden, 3 Ireland,
4 Finland, 5 Wales, 6 Scotland, 7 Netherlands,
8 Germany, 9 Switzerland, 10 Belgium, 11 Greece,
12 France, 13 Spain, 14 Monaco, 15 Denmark,
16 Luxembourg, 17 Norway, 18 Austria, 19 Italy.

1983 (Munich, West Germany)

Section to decide positions 1–8.

Qualifying round: Spain beat Italy 4–1, Monaco beat
Austria 3–2, France beat Norway 5–0.

1st round: England beat France 5–0, Germany beat
Denmark 4–1, Finland beat Luxembourg 5–0, Wales
beat Switzerland 5–0, Holland beat Greece 3–2, Ireland
beat Monaco 5–0, Scotland beat Belgium 5–0, Sweden
beat Spain 5–0.

Quarter-finals: England beat Germany 5–0, Wales beat
Finland 3–2, Holland beat Ireland 3–2, Sweden beat
Scotland 5–0.

Semi-finals: England beat Wales 5–0, Sweden beat
Holland 5–0.

Final: Sweden beat England 3–2.

3/4 position: Wales beat Holland 5–0.

Positions 5–8: Finland beat Germany 5–0, Ireland beat
Scotland 3–2. 5/6: Finland beat Ireland 4–1. 7/8:
Scotland beat Germany 3–2.

Section to decide positions 9–19

1st round: Spain beat Norway 3–2, Austria beat
Switzerland 5–0, Italy beat Monaco 3–2.

2nd round: Greece beat Spain 4–1, Switzerland beat
Luxembourg 4–1, Belgium beat Italy 5–0, France beat
Denmark 4–1.

Semi-finals: Switzerland beat Greece 3–2, France beat
Belgium 4–1. 9/10: France beat Switzerland 3–2. 11/12:
Greece beat Belgium 5–0.

Positions 13–16: Spain beat Luxembourg 5–0, Denmark
beat Italy 5–0. 13/14: Spain beat Denmark 3–2. 15/16:
Luxembourg beat Italy 3–2.

Positions 17–19: Monaco beat Norway 3–2, Norway beat
Austria 3–2, Austria beat Monaco 3–2.

Positions: 17 Monaco, 18 Norway, 19 Austria.

1984 (Dublin, Ireland)

Qualifying round: Italy beat Monaco 4–1, Denmark beat
Austria 3–2, Norway beat Luxembourg 4–1.

1st round: Sweden beat Italy 4–1, Germany beat France
4–1, Netherlands beat Spain 5–0, Finland beat Belgium
5–0, Ireland beat Greece 5–0, Wales beat Denmark 3–2,
Scotland beat Switzerland 5–0, England beat Norway
5–0.

Quarter-finals: Sweden beat Germany 5–0, Finland beat
Netherlands 3–2, Ireland beat Wales 5–0, England beat
Scotland 5–0.

Semi-finals: Sweden beat Finland 4–1, England beat
Ireland 5–0.

Final: England beat Sweden 5–0.

3/4 position: Finland beat Ireland 4–1.

Positions 5–8: Netherlands beat Germany 4–1, Scotland
beat Wales 3–2. 5/6: Netherlands beat Scotland 3–2.
7/8: Wales beat Germany 3–2.

Section to decide positions 9–19:

1st round: Spain beat Monaco 5–0, Greece beat
Luxembourg 5–0, Austria beat Belgium 3–2.

2nd round: France beat Italy 3–2, Spain beat Austria 4–1,
Norway beat Switzerland 3–2.

Semi-finals: France beat Spain 3–2, Greece beat Norway
4–1.

9/10: France beat Greece 3–2. 11/12: Spain beat Norway
4–1.

Positions 13–16: Italy beat Austria 3–2, Switzerland beat
Denmark 3–2. 13/14: Switzerland beat Italy 3–2. 15/16:
Denmark beat Austria 3–2.

Positions 17–19: Belgium beat Luxembourg 4–1, Monaco
5–0, Luxembourg beat Monaco 4–1.

Positions: 17 Belgium, 18 Luxembourg, 19 Monaco.

European Junior Team Championship

This event was first run in Stuttgart, West Germany
in September 1983. Member countries of the European Squash Rackets Federation can each enter a
team of two boys and one girl who are under the age of
19 on 1 May of the year of the competition. In the
initial year some countries were allowed to enter two
teams. The 1984/5 championship will also be held in
Stuttgart and the 1985/6 event in Norway.

1983

Positions after pool matches: Group A: 1 Sweden,
2 Scotland, 3 Germany II, 4 Belgium. Group B:
1 England, 2 Germany, 3 France, 4 Switzerland II.
Group C: 1 Wales, 2 Netherlands, 3 Scotland II,
4 Norway. Group D: 1 Finland, 2 Ireland,
3 Switzerland, 4 Netherlands II.

Semi-finals: England beat Wales 3–0, Sweden beat
Finland 2–1.

Final: Sweden beat England 2–1: L. Soutter (Eng) beat T.
Backlund (Swe) 3–0; T. Svensson (Swe) beat N. Stiles
(Eng) 3–2; A. Wahlstedt (Swe) beat M. Roberts (Eng)
3–0.

3/4: Finland beat Wales 2–1. 5/6: Netherlands beat
Scotland 2–1. 7/8: Germany beat Ireland 2–1. 9/10:
France beat Germany II 2–1. 11/12: Scotland II beat
Switzerland 3–0. 13/14: Norway beat Netherlands 2–1.
15/16: Switzerland II beat Belgium 2–1.

WOMEN

1978 (Amsterdam, Holland)

Pool A: Wales beat Germany 3–0, Belgium 3–0, Sweden
2–1. Sweden beat Belgium 3–0, Germany 3–0. England
beat Germany 3–0, Belgium 3–0, Wales 3–0, Sweden
3–0. Germany beat Belgium 2–1.

Pool positions: 1 England, 2 Wales, 3 Sweden, 4 Germany,
5 Belgium.

Pool B: Ireland beat Netherlands 3–0, Switzerland 3–0,
Denmark 3–0, Scotland 3–0. Scotland beat Switzerland
3–0, Denmark 3–0, Netherlands 3–0. Netherlands beat
Denmark 3–0, Switzerland 2–1. Switzerland beat
Denmark 3–0.

Pool positions: 1 Ireland, 2 Scotland, 3 Netherlands,
4 Switzerland, 5 Denmark.

Playoffs: Positions 9/10: Denmark beat Belgium 3–0; 7/8: Germany beat Switzerland 2–1; 5/6: Sweden beat Netherlands 3–0; 3/4 Scotland beat Wales 3–0.

Final: England beat Ireland 3–0.

Final positions: 1 England, 2 Ireland, 3 Scotland, 4 Wales, 5 Sweden, 6 Netherlands, 7 Germany, 8 Switzerland, 9 Denmark, 10 Belgium.

1979 (Hamburg, Germany)

Pool A: Ireland beat Netherlands 3–0, Germany 3–0, Finland 3–0, Belgium 3–0, Scotland 3–0. Scotland beat Finland 3–0, Netherlands 3–0, Belgium 3–0, Germany 3–0. Finland beat Belgium 3–0, Netherlands 2–1, Germany 2–1. Germany beat Belgium 3–0, Netherlands 3–0. Netherlands beat Belgium 3–0.

Pool positions: 1 Ireland, 2 Scotland, 3 Finland, 4 Germany, 5 Netherlands, 6 Belgium.

Pool B: Wales beat Sweden 3–0, Denmark 3–0, Switzerland 3–0. England beat Switzerland 3–0, Sweden 3–0, Denmark 3–0, Wales 3–0. Sweden beat Switzerland 2–1, Denmark 3–0. Switzerland beat Denmark 3–0.

Pool positions: 1 England, 2 Wales, 3 Sweden, 4 Switzerland, 5 Denmark.

Playoffs: Positions 9/10: Netherlands beat Denmark 2–1; 7/8: Switzerland beat Germany 3–0; 5/6: Sweden beat Finland 3–0; 3/4: Scotland beat Wales 3–0.

Final: England beat Ireland 3–0.

Final positions: 1 England, 2 Ireland, 3 Scotland, 4 Wales, 5 Sweden, 6 Finland, 7 Switzerland, 8 Germany, 9 Netherlands, 10 Denmark, 11 Belgium.

1980 (Helsinki, Finland)

Pool A: England beat Germany 3–0, Belgium 3–0. Germany beat Belgium 3–0.

Pool positions: 1 England, 2 Germany, 3 Belgium.

Pool B: Ireland beat Austria 3–0, Netherlands 3–0. Netherlands beat Austria 3–0.

Pool positions: 1 Ireland, 2 Netherlands, 3 Austria.

Pool C: Scotland beat Finland 3–0, Denmark 3–0. Finland beat Denmark 3–0.

Pool positions: 1 Scotland, 2 Finland, 3 Denmark.

Pool D: Wales beat Sweden 2–1, Switzerland 3–0. Sweden beat Switzerland 3–0.

Pool positions: 1 Wales, 2 Sweden, 3 Switzerland.

Playoffs: Positions 9/12: Denmark beat Austria 3–0, Switzerland beat Belgium 2–1, Belgium beat Austria 3–0, Switzerland beat Denmark 3–0; 5/8: Sweden beat Germany 3–0, Finland beat Netherlands 3–0, Netherlands beat Germany 2–1, Sweden beat Finland 2–1.

Semi-finals: England beat Wales 3–0; Ireland beat Scotland 2–1.

3/4 position: Scotland beat Wales 2–1.

Final: England beat Ireland 3–0.

Final positions: 1 England, 2 Ireland, 3 Scotland, 4 Wales, 5 Sweden, 6 Finland, 7 Netherlands, 8 Germany, 9 Switzerland, 10 Denmark, 11 Belgium, 12 Austria.

1981 (Amsterdam, Holland)

Pool A: England beat Switzerland 3–0, Germany 3–0. Germany beat Switzerland 3–0.

Pool positions: 1 England, 2 Germany, 3 Switzerland.

Pool B: Ireland beat Luxembourg 3–0, Denmark 3–0, Netherlands 3–0. Netherlands beat Denmark 3–0, Luxembourg 3–0. Denmark beat Luxembourg 3–0.

Pool positions: 1 Ireland, 2 Netherlands, 3 Denmark, 4 Luxembourg.

Pool C: Scotland beat Belgium 3–0, Finland 3–0. Finland beat Belgium 3–0.

Pool positions: 1 Scotland, 2 Finland, 3 Belgium.

Pool D: Wales beat France 3–0, Austria 3–0, Sweden 3–0. Sweden beat Austria 3–0, France 3–0. France beat Austria 3–0.

Pool positions: 1 Wales, 2 Sweden, 3 France, 4 Austria.

Playoffs: Positions 13/14: Luxembourg beat Austria 2–1; 9/12: Belgium beat Denmark 2–1, Switzerland beat France 3–0, France beat Denmark 2–1, Switzerland beat Belgium 3–0; 5/8: Sweden beat Germany 3–0, Finland beat Netherlands 3–0, Netherlands beat Germany 2–1, Finland beat Sweden 2–1.

Semi-finals: England beat Wales 3–0, Ireland beat Scotland 2–1.

3/4 position: Wales beat Scotland 2–1.

Final: England beat Ireland 3–0.

Final positions: 1 England, 2 Ireland, 3 Wales, 4 Scotland, 5 Finland, 6 Sweden, 7 Netherlands, 8 Germany, 9 Switzerland, 10 Belgium, 11 France, 12 Denmark, 13 Luxembourg, 14 Austria.

1982 (Cardiff, Wales)

England beat Italy 3–0, Germany beat Switzerland 3–0, Scotland beat Luxembourg 3–0, Finland beat Denmark 3–0, Sweden beat France 2–1, Wales beat Monaco 3–0, Netherlands beat Belgium 3–0, Ireland beat Norway 3–0, Switzerland beat Italy 3–0, Denmark beat Luxembourg 3–0, France beat Monaco 3–0, Belgium beat Norway 3–0, Luxembourg beat Italy 3–0, Norway beat Monaco 3–0, Switzerland beat Denmark 3–0, Belgium beat France 2–1, England beat Germany 3–0, Scotland beat Finland 3–0, Wales beat Sweden 3–0, Ireland beat Netherlands 3–0, Finland beat Germany 2–1, Netherlands beat Sweden 2–1.

Playoffs: Positions 15/16: Monaco beat Italy 3–0; 13/14: Norway beat Luxembourg 3–0; 11/12: France beat Denmark 3–0; 9/10: Switzerland beat Belgium 3–0; 7/8: Sweden beat Germany 2–1; 5/6: Finland beat Netherlands 2–1.

Semi-finals: England beat Scotland 3–0; Ireland beat Wales 2–1.

3/4 position: Scotland beat Wales 2–1.

Final: England beat Ireland 3–0.

Final positions: 1 England, 2 Ireland, 3 Scotland, 4 Wales, 5 Finland, 6 Netherlands, 7 Sweden, 8 Germany, 9 Switzerland, 10 Belgium, 11 France, 12 Denmark, 13 Norway, 14 Luxembourg, 15 Monaco, 16 Italy.

1983 (Munich, West Germany)

Spain beat Austria 3–0, England beat Spain 3–0, Germany beat France 3–0, Wales beat Norway 3–0, Holland beat Switzerland 2–1; Sweden beat Italy 3–0, Scotland beat Monaco 3–0, Finland beat Belgium 3–0, Ireland beat Luxembourg 3–0, England beat Germany 3–0, Wales beat Holland 3–0, Scotland beat Sweden 2–1, Ireland

beat Finland 3–0, England beat Wales 3–0, Ireland beat
Scotland 2–1.

Final: England beat Ireland 3–0.

Play-offs (Places 3–8) Wales beat Scotland 2–1, Germany
beat Holland 3–0, Finland beat Sweden 3–0, Germany
beat Finland 2–1, Sweden beat Holland 2–1.

Positions: 3 Wales, 4 Scotland, 5 Germany, 6 Finland,
7 Sweden, 8 Holland.

Play-offs (Places 9–17) Spain beat Monaco 2–1, France
beat Austria 3–0, Switzerland beat Norway 3–0,
Belgium beat Luxembourg 3–0, Spain beat Italy 2–1,
Switzerland beat France 3–0, Belgium beat Spain 3–0,
Switzerland beat Belgium 3–0, France beat Spain 3–0,
Norway beat Luxembourg 2–1, Norway beat Monaco
2–1, Norway beat Austria 2–1, Luxembourg beat
Austria 3–0, Luxembourg beat Italy 2–1, Monaco beat
Luxembourg 2–1, Monaco beat Italy 2–1, Norway beat
Italy 3–0, Austria beat Monaco 2–1, Austria beat Italy
2–1.

Positions: 9 Switzerland, 10 Belgium, 11 France, 12 Spain,
13 Norway, 14 Luxembourg, 15 Monaco, 16 Austria,
17 Italy.

1984 (Dublin, Ireland)

England beat Scotland 3–0, beat Denmark 3–0, beat
Switzerland 3–0. Ireland beat Wales 2–1, beat Italy 3–0,
beat Netherlands 3–0. Scotland beat Monaco 3–0,
Wales beat Austria 3–0, Germany beat Norway 3–0,
Finland beat Spain 3–0, Netherlands beat France 3–0,
Switzerland beat Belgium 3–0, Belgium beat Denmark
3–0, France beat Italy 3–0.

Final: England beat Ireland 2–1.

Play-offs (Places 3–8) Scotland beat Germany 3–0, Wales
beat Finland 3–0, Germany beat Switzerland 3–0,
Finland beat Netherlands 2–1.

3/4: Scotland beat Wales 2–1. 5/6: Germany beat Finland
3–0.

7/8: Netherlands beat Switzerland 2–1.

Play-offs (Places 9–16) Belgium beat Norway 2–1, France
beat Spain 3–0, Denmark beat Monaco 2–1, Austria
beat Italy 3–0, Spain beat Austria 2–1, Norway beat
Monaco 3–0.

9/10: Belgium beat France 2–1. 11/12: Norway beat Spain
2–1.

13/14: Denmark beat Austria 2–1. 15/16: Monaco beat
Italy 2–1.

Asian Squash Rackets Federation Championship

1981 (Karachi)
TEAM (full results not available)
1–4 play-offs: Pakistan beat Malaysia 3–0, Singapore 3–0.
India beat Singapore 3–0, Malaysia 3–0.
Final: Pakistan beat India 3–0.
3/4 play-off: Singapore beat Malaysia 3–0.
Other placings: 5 Japan, 6 Philippines, 7 Kuwait,
8 Jordan, 9 Thailand, 10 Sri Lanka, 11 Dubai,
12 Bangladesh, 13 Lebanon, 14 Nepal.

INDIVIDUAL
Quarter-finals: M. Ahmed (Pak) beat O. Hyat (Pak) 2–9,
9–7, 9–0, 9–1; F. Gul (Pak) beat G. Alauddin (Pak)

9–6, 5–9, 9–3, 9–0; Q. Zaman (Pak) beat S. Qaiser
(Pak) 9–5, 9–4, 9–3; Jahangir Khan (Pak) beat Daulat
Khan (Pak) 9–2, 10–8, 9–6.
Semi-finals: Jahangir Khan beat Ahmed 9–1, 9–0, 9–4;
Zaman beat Gul 9–3, 9–10, 7–9, 9–1, 9–4.
Final: Jahangir Khan beat Zaman 10–8, 9–0, 9–0.

1984 (Amman, Jordan)
TEAM
Seven nations competing. Played on round-robin basis.
Pakistan beat Bahrain 3–0, Singapore 3–0, Jordan 3–0, Sri
Lanka 3–0, India 3–0, Malaysia 3–0. Singapore beat
Bahrain 3–0, Sri Lanka 3–0, Malaysia 3–0, Jordan 3–0,
India 2–1. India beat Sri Lanka 3–0, Malaysia 3–0,
Bahrain 3–0, Jordan 3–0. Malaysia beat Sri Lanka 3–0,
Bahrain 3–0, Jordan 3–0. Jordan beat Sri Lanka 3–0,
Bahrain 3–0. Sri Lanka beat Bahrain 3–0.
Final positions: 1 Pakistan, 2 Singapore, 3 India,
4 Malaysia, 5 Jordan, 6 Sri Lanka, 7 Bahrain.

INDIVIDUAL
Quarter-finals: M. Manchanda (Ind) beat K. Tan (Mal)
9–3, 9–1, 9–1; M. Ahmed (Pak) beat Z. Abidin (Sin)
9–0, 9–0, 9–5; F. Gul (Pak) beat G. Alauddin (Pak)
9–5, 6–9, 9–5, 9–5; Q. Zaman (Pak) beat P. Hill (Sin)
9–3, 9–0, 9–3.
Semi-finals: Ahmed beat Manchanda 9–1, 9–1, 9–1;
Zaman beat Gul 10–8, 9–2, 9–6.
Final: Zaman beat Ahmed 9–4, 9–2, 9–7. 3/4: Gul beat
Manchanda 9–1, 5–9, 9–1, 9–6.

Asian Junior Championship

1983 (Kuala Lumpur, Malaysia)
INDIVIDUAL
Semi-finals: U. Hayat (Pak) beat Jansher Khan (Pak) 9–2,
9–4, 9–1; A. Gul (Pak) beat A. Zaman (Pak) 9–4, 9–5,
9–4.
Final: Hyat beat Gul 8–10, 9–1, 9–5, 9–1.

1983 (Singapore)
TEAM
Semi-finals: Pakistan beat India 3–0, Malaysia beat
Singapore 2–1.
Final: Pakistan beat Malaysia 3–0: U. Hyat (Pak) beat R.
Hashim (Mal) 9–0, 9–5, 9–0; A. Gul (Pak) beat A. Lau
(Mal) 9–3, 9–2, 9–5; A. Zaman (Pak) beat A. Johnson
(Mal) 9–4, 9–5, 9–5.

Caribbean Squash Rackets Association (CASRA) Championships

1981 (Barbados)
Men
TEAM
Group A: Jamaica beat Cayman 4–1, Guyana 4–1, St.
Vincent 5–0. Guyana beat St. Vincent 5–0, Cayman
5–0. Cayman beat St. Vincent 5–0.
Group B: Bermuda beat Venezuela 5–0, Barbados 3–2,
Trinidad 5–0. Barbados beat Trinidad 5–0, Venezuela
5–0. Venezuela beat Trinidad 3–2.
Semi-finals: Jamaica beat Barbados 3–2; Bermuda beat
Guyana 3–2.

Final: Bermuda beat Jamaica 3–2: T. Boyce (Ber) beat O. Beck (Jam) 9–4, 9–2, 9–1; R. Thompson (Ber) beat J. Simmonds (Jam) 9–3, 9–6, 9–5; W. Burrowes (Jam) beat J. Jefferis (Ber) 3–9, 6–9, 9–7, 9–7, 10–8; D. Beckford (Jam) beat D. Evelegh (Ber) 9–10, 5–9, 9–7, 9–2, 9–3; R. Bartlett (Ber) beat S. Phillibert (Jam) 4–9, 9–0, 9–3, 9–6.

3/4: Guyana beat Barbados 3–2. 5/6: Venezuela beat Cayman 3–2.

INDIVIDUAL

Semi-finals: R. Thompson (Ber) beat J. Simmonds (Jam) 9–1, 9–6, 10–8; T. Boyce (Ber) beat R. Lee (Guy) 9–2, 9–5, 10–8.

Final: Thompson beat Boyce 9–7, 9–2, 1–9, 9–10, 9–6.

Women
TEAM

Group A: Bermuda beat Barbados 2–1, Cayman 3–0, St. Vincent 3–0. Barbados beat St. Vincent 3–0, Cayman 2–1. Cayman beat St. Vincent 3–0.

Group B: Guyana beat Jamaica 2–1, Trinidad 3–0, Venezuela 3–0. Jamaica beat Venezuela 3–0, Trinidad 3–0. Trinidad beat Venezuela 3–0.

Semi-finals: Jamaica beat Bermuda 3–0; Guyana beat Barbados 2–1.

Final: Jamaica beat Guyana 2–1: P. Manapol (Jam) beat J. Whithead (Guy) 9–3, 9–3, 9–6; S. Lawrence (Jam) beat I. Welingkar (Guy) 0–9, 9–6, 9–1, 9–1; C. Braithwaite (Guy) beat R. Stoddard (Jam) 2–9, 8–10, 9–4, 9–4, 9–4.

3/4: Barbados beat Bermuda 3–0. 5/6: Trinidad beat Cayman 3–0.

INDIVIDUAL

Semi-finals: P. Manapol (Jam) beat J. Whitehead (Guy) 9–2, 9–6, 9–4; S. Lawrence (Jam) beat A. Webber (Bar) 9–1, 9–6, 9–6.

Final: Manapol beat Lawrence 9–4, 9–3, 9–1.

1983 (Bermuda)
Men
TEAM

Jamaica 5 Venezuela 0, Bermuda 3 Bahamas 2, Barbados 4 St. Vincent 1, Bermuda 5 Trinidad & Tobago 0, Bahamas 3 Barbados 2, Bermuda 4 Jamaica 1, Trinidad & Tobago 4 Venezuela 1, Bermuda 5 St. Vincent 0, Jamaica 5 Barbados 0, Bahamas 4 Venezuela 1, Bahamas 4 Trinidad & Tobago 1, Bermuda 5 Venezuela 0, Barbados 5 Trinidad & Tobago 0, St. Vincent 3 Venezuela 2, Bahamas 5 St. Vincent 0, Jamaica 5 Trinidad & Tobago 0, Bermuda 4 Barbados 1, Jamaica 4 Bahamas 1.

Final: Jamaica 3 Bermuda 2: R. Thompson (Ber) beat W.

The Jamaican men and women's teams who contested the 1983 championship. From the left: John Simmonds, Lisa Stoddart, Wayne Burrowes, Graham McLeod (manager), Doug Beckford (captain), Otto Beck, Sue Lawrance, Scott McKay, Mary Schwier, Richard Lee, Ian Skinner, Sue Cornes, Angie Templar

Dugald McPherson (*left*), aged 79, and Jonny Leslie, aged 30, two players representing different ages of squash, pictured at the last British Amateur Championship in 1980. McPherson was an Amateur winner in 1924 and 1928 and a beaten finalist in 1931 while Jonny Leslie had the distinction of winning the last championship before squash went Open

Burrowes (Jam) 9–5, 10–8, 9–2; T. Boyce (Ber) beat R. Lee (Jam) 9–6, 9–2, 9–7; O. Beck (Jam) beat N. Cotter (Ber) 9–7, 10–8, 9–5; J. Simmons (Jam) beat J. Jefferis (Ber) 3–9, 9–5, 9–6, 6–9, 9–4; D. Beckford (Jam) beat R. Bartlett (Ber) 9–1, 9–6, 9–4.

INDIVIDUAL
Semi-finals: W. Burrowes (Jam) beat L. Cox (Bah) 4–9, 5–9, 9–7, 9–4, 9–2; R. Thompson (Ber) beat J. Wilson (Bah) 9–4, 9–2, 1–9, 5–9, 9–5.
Final: Burrowes beat Thompson 9–6, 9–7, 9–5.

Women
TEAM
Bermuda 2 Jamaica 1, Trinidad & Tobago 2 Venezuela 1, Bahamas 3 Barbados 0, Barbados 3 Trinidad & Tobago 0, Bermuda 3 Venezuela 0, Jamaica 3 Venezuela 0, Bermuda 3 Trinidad & Tobago 0, Bermuda 3 Bahamas 0, Barbados 2 Jamaica 1, Jamaica 3 Trinidad & Tobago 0, Bahamas 3 Venezuela 0, Barbados 3 Venezuela 0, Bahamas 3 Trinidad & Tobago 0, Jamaica 2 Bahamas 1, Bermuda 3 Barbados 0.
Final: Bermuda 2 Jamaica 1: S. Lawrence (Jam) beat J. Peake (Ber) 9–6, 9–0, 9–0; D. Kyme (Ber) beat S. Cornes (Jam) 9–3, 9–1, 9–0; E. Driscoll (Ber) beat A. Templar (Jam) 9–0, 9–4, 9–2.

INDIVIDUAL
Semi-finals: S. Lawrence (Jam) beat E. Driscoll (Ber) 9–4, 9–0, 9–4; J. Peake (Ber) beat D. Kyme (Ber) 4–9, 9–4, 9–4, 9–0.
Final: Lawrence beat Peake 9–4, 9–1, 9–4.

Girl's final: T. Newsam (Bar) beat L. Stoddard (Jam) 9–0, 9–5, 9–1.

Boy's final: S. McKay (Jam) beat P. Cyrus (St. Vin) 9–7, 9–10, 1–9, 9–5, 9–4.
Veteran's final: K. Parker (Bah) beat C. Donald (Ber) 9–5, 5–9, 9–6, 7–9, 9–4.

British Amateur Championship

The British Amateur was first played in April 1923 at Lord's, London and continued – apart from the war years – uninterrupted until, with squash having gone 'open', it was discontinued after the 1979 Championship.

The best amateur player during the early years was Jimmy Tomkinson but he was past his best when the tournament was introduced. He finished runner-up in three of the first four finals but finally won the title, at the age of 47, in 1926 – the first year in which the present-day scoring system was introduced.

Member of Parliament, Victor Cazalet beat Tomkinson to win in 1925 and went on to play in six consecutive finals, winning four. Later Egyptians Amr Bey and Ibrahim Amin also contested six each but Cazalet is the only player in the history of the tournament to do so in successive years. Amr followed Cazalet as champion and won the tournament six times between 1931 and 1937 – he did not compete in 1934. Five times during that period he completed 'the double' by also winning the British Open title – the only other man other than Jonah Barrington to achieve that feat. Current president of the SRA Norman Borrett re-established English supremacy by winning five consecutive titles immediately after the war before Gavin Hildick-Smith became the only ever South African champion in 1951.

The next 10 titles were split evenly between England's Alan Fairbairn, Roy Wilson and Nigel Broomfield, Michael Oddy of Scotland and Egyptian Amin. They also finished runner-up eight times between them – Amin four times, Wilson three times and Fairbairn once. In 1962 Ken Hiscoe became the first Australian winner when he beat Egypt's Tewfik Shafik in the final. Shafik was one of the unluckiest players ever to grace a squash court – he had been runner-up to Amin in the first all-Egyptian final in 1959, finished second again when Aftab Jawaid became the first Pakistani champion in 1963, and was a losing semi-finalist on three other occasions. (For good measure he was beaten twice in the semi-finals of the British Open and on two occasions was eliminated in the quarter-finals.)

Jawaid went on to complete a hat-trick of victories before Jonah Barrington arrived on the scene in 1966. Britain's greatest-ever player won three consecutive titles and completed the 'Amateur/Open double' in 1966 and 1967. When Barrington turned professional he was succeeded by Geoff Hunt who had lost their battle in the British Open final two months earlier.

Pakistanis won four of the next five championships – Gogi Alauddin and Mohibullah Khan took two each – while sandwiched in the middle was the first all-Australian final in which Cam Nancarrow defeated Bill Reedman. Kevin Shawcross brought the title back to Australia in 1975 before Bruce Brownlee became the only New Zealand winner a year later. In the final Brownlee beat England's Jonny Leslie – the first English finalist since Mike Corby lost to Barrington in 1968. However, after Gamal Awad of Egypt had won for two years, Leslie wrote his name in the record-books by winning the last championship at the expense of another New Zealander Ross Norman.

1922
Semi-finals: J. E. Tomkinson beat S. M. Toyne 15–7, 15–7; T. O. Jameson beat C. le C. Browning 15–6, 15–3.
Final: Jameson beat Tomkinson 17–12, 12–15, 15–0.

1923
Semi-finals: T. O. Jameson beat G. Robarts 15–6, 15–6; C. le C. Browning beat R. H. Wethered 15–5, 15–6.
Final: Jameson beat Browning 15–11, 16–14.

1924
Semi-finals: W. D. Macpherson beat R. G. de Quetteville 15–13, 18–13; J. E. Tomkinson beat F. W. Strawson 15–10, 15–5.
Final: Macpherson beat Tomkinson 17–14, 8–15, 15–7.

1925
Semi-finals: J. E. Tomkinson beat W. D. Macpherson 15–11, 12–15, 15–12; V. A. Cazalet beat H. W. Backhouse 15–4, 15–10.
Final: Cazalet beat Tomkinson 15–8, 12–15, 18–17.

1926
Semi-finals: J. E. Tomkinson beat H. W. Backhouse 9–6, 9–5, 9–10, 9–4; V. A. Cazalet beat W. L. Davis 9–2, 7–9, 9–0, 9–3.
Final: Tomkinson beat Cazalet 9–5, 9–7, 7–9, 9–6.

1927
Semi-finals: H. W. Backhouse beat P. V. F. Cazalet 9–2, 9–7, 4–9, 9–4; V. A. Cazalet beat P. Q. Reiss 9–4, 9–4, 2–9, 9–7.
Final: Cazalet beat Backhouse 4–9, 9–6, 3–9, 10–8, 9–4.

1928
Semi-finals: W. D. Macpherson beat R. S. Wright 9–2, 10–8, 5–9, 9–4; V. A. Cazalet beat G. d'O. Sheppard 9–0, 9–5, 9–5.
Final: Macpherson beat Cazalet 9–3, 9–1, 5–9, 1–9, 9–1.

1929
Semi-finals: W. F. Basset beat I. Akers-Douglas 5–9, 1–9, 10–8, 9–5, 9–2; V. A. Cazalet beat P. Q. Reiss 9–2, 8–10, 9–6, 9–5.
Final: Cazalet beat Basset 9–2, 9–5, 9–7.

1930
Semi-finals: K. C. Gandar Dower beat G. d'O. Sheppard 9–0, 9–3, 9–0; V. A. Cazalet beat F. D. Amr Bey (Egy) 6–9, 9–4, 7–9, 9–1, 9–0.

Final: Cazalet beat Gandar Dower 9–2, 6–9, 7–9, 9–6, 9–2.

1931
Semi-finals: W. D. Macpherson beat V. A. Cazalet 9–10, 9–7, 9–4, 9–0; F. D. Amr Bey (Egy) beat G. O. M. Jameson 4–9, 7–9, 9–3, 9–0, 9–1.
Final: Amr Bey beat Macpherson 9–7, 9–6, 4–9, 5–9, 9–0.

1932
Semi-finals: F. D. Amr Bey (Egy) beat P. Q. Reiss 9–0, 9–1, 9–5; E. Snell beat C. P. Hamilton 9–6, 9–1, 9–3.
Final: Amr Bey beat Snell 9–1, 9–0, 9–4.

1933
Semi-finals: F. D. Amr Bey (Egy) beat O. C. Browning 9–1, 9–3, 9–4; G. O. M. Jameson beat J. C. Gregory 0–9, 9–6, 9–4, 2–9, 9–5.
Final: Amr Bey beat Jameson 9–0, 9–2, 9–4.

1934
Semi-finals: C. P. Hamilton beat J. N. S. Ridgers 9–2, 9–0, 9–4; D. M. Backhouse beat J. A. Gillies 9–3, 10–8, 0–9, 8–10, 9–4.
Final: Hamilton beat Backhouse 9–7, 9–0, 9–4.

A much younger Dugald McPherson pictured with another Amateur winner of the 1920s, Victor Cazalet, who took the title in 1925, 1927, 1929 and 1930

1935

Semi-finals: E. Snell beat C. P. Hamilton 1–9, 3–9, 9–7, 10–8, 9–2; F. D. Amr Bey (Egy) beat N. W. D. Yardley 9–3, 9–3, 9–3.

Final: Amr Bey beat Snell 9–1, 9–0, 9–1.

1936

Semi-finals: F. D. Amr Bey (Egy) beat R. Pulbrook 9–3, 9–1, 9–0; E. Snell beat J. A. Gillies 9–2, 10–9, 9–5.

Final: Amr Bey beat Snell 9–4, 9–0, 9–2.

1937

Semi-finals: J. F. Stokes beat F. D. M. Flowerdew 9–7, 5–9, 9–7, 10–8; F. D. Amr Bey (Egy) beat J. W. C. More 9–4, 9–0, 9–0.

Final: Amr Bey beat Stokes 9–3, 9–4, 9–2.

1938

Semi-finals: K. C. Gandar Dower beat E. Snell 6–9, 9–5, 9–0, 1–9, 9–2; D. I. Burnett beat F. D. M. Flowerdew 9–3, 9–1, 9–1.

Final: Gandar Dower beat Burnett 2–9, 10–8, 9–6, 10–8.

1939–45 No competition.

1946

Semi-finals: N. F. Borrett beat B. C. Phillips 9–6, 9–5, 5–9, 9–4; J. A. Gillies beat G. O. M. Jameson 9–5, 3–9, 10–8, 0–9, 9–7.

Final: Borrett beat Gillies 9–3, 9–6, 9–3.

1947

Semi-finals: N. F. Borrett beat B. C. Phillips 9–6, 9–4, 9–6; J. R. Thompson beat A. A. T. Seymour-Haydon 7–9, 9–7, 9–1, 9–4.

Final: Borrett beat Thompson 9–2, 9–4, 9–4.

1948

Semi-finals: N. F. Borrett beat D. M. Bull 9–2, 9–1, 9–3; B. C. Phillips beat R. M. Boustead 6–9, 9–4, 9–3, 9–3.

Final: Borrett beat Phillips 9–2, 9–4, 9–2.

1949

Semi-finals: N. F. Borrett beat R. B. R. Wilson 9–1, 9–6, 9–6; J. A. Dagnall beat A. W. H. Mallett 5–9, 9–1, 8–10, 9–4, 9–6.

Final: Borrett beat Dagnall 9–4, 9–5, 10–8.

1950

Semi-finals: N. F. Borrett beat R. B. R. Wilson 1–9, 9–7, 1–9, 9–2, 9–4; G. Hildick-Smith w.o. B. C. Phillips.

Final: Borrett beat Hildick-Smith 9–6, 10–8, 9–1.

1951

Semi-finals: B. C. Phillips beat G. W. T. Atkins 9–5, 2–9, 9–3, 9–2; G. Hildick-Smith beat A. A. T. Seymour-Haydon 1–9, 9–1, 9–3, 6–9, 9–1.

Final: Hildick-Smith beat Phillips 9–3, 9–2, 9–2.

1952

Semi-finals: A. Fairbairn beat A. A. T. Seymour-Haydon 0–9, 9–7, 6–9, 9–6, 9–5; R. B. R. Wilson beat I. C. de Sales la Terriere 9–2, 9–3, 9–10, 9–7.

Final: Fairbairn beat Wilson 9–2, 9–2, 4–9, 9–1.

1953

Semi-finals: A. Fairbairn beat A. A. T. Seymour-Haydon 9–10, 9–5, 9–5, 9–2; R. B. R. Wilson beat D. B. Hughes 9–4, 9–3, 9–3.

Final: Fairbairn beat Wilson 7–9, 9–1, 7–9, 9–7, 9–7.

1954

Semi-finals: A. Fairbairn beat M. J. Perkins 9–2, 9–5,

9–2; R. B. R. Wilson beat A. A. T. Seymour-Haydon 9–10, 9–2, 9–0, 9–4.

Final: Wilson beat Fairbairn 9–7, 8–10, 9–6, 9–4.

1955

Semi-finals: R. B. R. Wilson beat N. Broomfield 9–1, 9–6, 9–7; I. Amin (Egy) beat M. F. Mohtadi 9–5, 9–3, 7–9, 9–7.

Final: Amin beat Wilson 4–9, 9–7, 3–9, 9–7, 10–8.

1956

Semi-finals: R. B. R. Wilson beat C. Kaplan 9–3, 7–9, 9–5, 2–9, 9–0; D. Callaghan beat N. Broomfield 9–7, 10–9, 9–1.

Final: Wilson beat Callaghan 7–9, 8–10, 9–1, 9–4, 9–6.

1957

Semi-finals: N. Broomfield beat M. A. Oddy 9–5, 9–0, 9–1; I. Amin (Egy) beat J. G. A. Lyon 6–9, 10–8, 9–3, 9–10, 9–5.

Final: Broomfield beat Amin 9–1, 9–7, 9–4.

1958

Semi-finals: N. Broomfield beat T. Shafik (Egy) 9–3, 9–7, 1–9, 9–7; I. Amin (Egy) beat M. A. Oddy 2–9, 9–5, 9–2, 9–7.

Final: Broomfield beat Amin 9–2, 9–6, 1–9, 9–7.

1959

Semi-finals: T. Shafik (Egy) beat M. A. Oddy 9–5, 10–9, 5–9, 9–2; I. Amin (Egy) beat D. B. Hughes 9–7, 7–9, 9–5, 9–3.

Final: Amin beat Shafik 9–7, 0–9, 9–6, 9–5.

1960

Semi-finals: I. Amin (Egy) beat D. B. Hughes 2–9, 9–6, 9–3, 10–9; M. A. Oddy beat T. Shafik (Egy) 9–3, 9–7, 9–6.

Final: Oddy beat Amin 9–2, 7–9, 10–8, 9–4.

1961

Semi-finals: M. A. Oddy beat T. Shafik (Egy) 9–3, 9–7, 9–6; I. Amin (Egy) beat K. J. Hiscoe (Aus) 6–9, 7–9, 9–3, 9–7, 9–3.

Final: Oddy beat Amin 9–5, 3–9, 10–8, 9–1.

1962

Semi-finals: T. Shafik (Egy) beat A. Jawaid (Pak) 7–9, 9–5, 9–7, 10–8; K. J. Hiscoe (Aus) beat R. Carter 7–9, 9–7, 9–7, 9–0.

Final: Hiscoe beat Shafik 9–3, 9–7, 5–9, 9–7.

1963

Semi-finals: A. Jawaid (Pak) beat K. J. Hiscoe (Aus) 2–9, 5–9, 9–5, 9–5, 9–6; T. Shafik (Egy) beat M. A. Oddy 4–9, 0–9, 9–1, 10–8, 9–7.

Final: Jawaid beat Shafik 7–9, 9–2, 5–9, 9–4, 9–5.

1964

Semi-finals: A. Jawaid (Pak) beat K. J. Hiscoe (Aus) 9–3, 9–1, 9–2; G. B. Hunt (Aus) beat J. G. A. Lyon 9–4, 9–1, 9–3.

Final: Jawaid beat Hunt 9–5, 8–10, 9–3, 10–9.

1965

Semi-finals: A. Jawaid (Pak) beat K. J. Hiscoe (Aus) 9–5, 5–9, 9–2, 6–9, 9–4; R. Carter beat G. B. Hunt (Aus) 6–9, 9–6, 9–2, 8–10, 9–5.

Final: Jawaid beat Carter 7–9, 9–2, 9–2, 9–10, 9–6.

1966

Semi-finals: R. Carter beat A. Jawaid (Pak) 9–1, 9–7, 9–5;

J. Barrington (GB & Ire) beat K. J. Hiscoe (Aus) 5–9, 2–9, 9–5, 9–5, 9–1.

Final: Barrington beat Carter 1–9, 9–6, 7–9, 9–7, 9–0.

1967

Semi-finals: J. Barrington (GB & Ire) beat A. M. H. Hill 9–1, 9–2, 9–0; M. W. Corby beat J. G. A. Lyon 5–9, 9–1, 9–7, 6–9, 9–7.

Final: Barrington beat Corby 9–3, 9–6, 2–9, 9–5.

1968

Semi-finals: J. Barrington (GB & Ire) beat P. E. Millman 9–4, 9–0, 9–0; M. W. Corby beat J. G. A. Lyon 9–2, 9–3, 5–9, 9–5.

Final: Barrington beat Corby 3–9, 9–1, 9–2, 9–3.

1969

Semi-finals: G. B. Hunt (Aus) w.o. D. Broom; A. Jawaid (Pak) beat M. W. Corby 10–8, 9–5, 9–7.

Final: Hunt beat Jawaid 9–7, 9–2, 9–0.

1970

Semi-finals: W. Reedman (Aus) beat S. Muneer (Pak) 9–7, 9–3, 9–2; G. Alauddin (Pak) beat J. N. C. Easter 9–5, 9–6, 9–3.

Final: Alauddin beat Reedman 9–3, 9–0, 9–5.

1971

Semi-finals: G. Alauddin (Pak) beat H. Jahan (Pak) 6–9, 9–1, 9–3, 9–4; M. Asran (Egy) beat P. E. Millman 9–5, 9–4, 9–1.

Final: Alauddin beat Asran 6–9, 9–3, 7–9, 9–6, 9–2.

1972

Semi-finals: C. J. Nancarrow (Aus) beat S. Muneer (Pak) 9–2, 10–9, 6–9, 9–5; W. Reedman (Aus) beat Q. Zaman (Pak) 9–3, 9–5, 7–9, 1–9, 10–9.

Final: Nancarrow beat Reedman 0–9, 9–2, 9–0, 9–7.

1973

Semi-finals: Q. Zaman (Pak) beat M. Saleem (Pak) 9–2, 9–3, 8–10, 9–2; Mohibullah Khan (Pak) beat H. Jahan (Pak) 5–9, 8–10, 9–7, 10–8, 9–6.

Final: Mohibullah Khan beat Zaman 9–5, 10–8, 6–9, 7–9, 10–8.

1974

Semi-finals: Mohibullah Khan (Pak) beat P. N. Ayton 9–10, 9–3, 9–6, 9–0; Q. Zaman (Pak) beat P. G. Verow 9–1, 9–5, 9–5.

Final: Mohibullah Khan beat Zaman 10–8, 9–5, 5–9, 9–5.

1975

Semi-finals: A. Aziz (Egy) beat S. H. Courtney 9–5, 9–5, 9–0; K. Shawcross (Aus) beat I. Holding (SA) 9–5, 9–4, 9–3.

Final: Shawcross beat Aziz 9–2, 9–7, 9–6.

1976

Semi-finals: B. Brownlee (NZ) beat M. Lilley (Aus) 7–9, 1–9, 9–0, 9–0, 9–5; J. C. A. Leslie beat L. Kvant (Swe) 9–0, 2–9, 8–10, 9–7, 9–6.

Final: Brownlee beat Leslie 9–3, 10–8, 8–10, 9–5.

1977

Semi-finals: G. Awad (Egy) beat D. Williams (Aus) 9–2, 4–9, 9–2, 9–8; M. Ahmed (Pak) beat J. C. A. Leslie 9–2, 9–2, 9–4.

Final: Awad beat Ahmed 3–9, 9–2, 4–9, 9–3, 9–5.

1978

Semi-finals: G. Awad (Egy) beat P. Kenyon 9–5, 9–7, 9–1; Atlas Khan (Pak) beat J. C. A. Leslie 9–4, 9–5, 7–9, 9–6.

Final: Awad beat Atlas Khan 9–5, 9–7, 2–9, 9–7.

1979

Semi-finals: R. Norman (NZ) beat R. Flynn (Aus) 9–5, 9–6, 4–9, 4–9, 9–1; J. C. A. Leslie beat M. Saad (Egy) 7–9, 2–9, 9–5, 9–3, 9–2.

Final: Leslie beat Norman 9–3, 9–3, 9–4.

Venues: Lords, London 1922; Bath Club, London 1923–38; Lansdowne and Royal Aero Clubs, London 1946–57, 1962; Royal Automobile Club, London 1958–61; Royal Automobile Club and Lansdowne, London 1963–71; Lambton Club, London 1972; Lambton and New Croydon, London 1973; Wembley, London 1974–79.

9 Facts and feats

The first recorded instance of court building specially for squash was in 1864 at Harrow when four squash courts were built.

The first national association to be formed was the United States SRA in 1907 and the Association also held the first national championship in the same year.

The first attempt to standardise the size of the international squash court was by the Tennis and Rackets Association in 1909 (*see* p. 19).

The first country conforming to the rules of the 'international' game (as played in Britain) to form a national association and inaugurate a national championship was South Africa in 1910.

The first attempt to standardise or approve an 'official' squash ball for the international game was by the Tennis and Rackets Association in 1923 (*see* p. 24).

The first attempt to standardise squash racket dimensions was by the Tennis and Rackets Association in 1925 (*see* p. 21).

The rules of squash were first standardised by the Tennis and Rackets Association in 1924.

The first radio commentary on a major squash championship was at the British Open on 7 April 1951. Max Robertson gave the commentary for the BBC Home Service from the Lansdowne Club where the semi-final match was taking place between M. A. Karim (Egy) and R. B. R. Wilson (Eng). Karim won 9–2, 8–10, 10–9, 9–5, and the second and third games were broadcast.

The first recorded televising of squash was at the Australian Men's Championship at Perth in 1962. This was achieved by removing the back door of the court and televising through the open doorway.

The first glass backwall to be installed was at the Abbeydale Club, Sheffield, England in October 1971 by Ellis Pearson Ltd.

The first use of a portable court for a major championship was in September 1978 in Kings Hall, Stock-holm, Sweden on the occasion of the Swedish leg of the PIA World Series. Perstorp Ltd erected a pre-fabricated court with a glass backwall in the arena. Approximately 600 people watched the final.

The first use of a four-wall transparent court for a major championship was the Transwall plexiglass court manufactured by Andren and Son, Stockholm. It was installed for the German Masters in Cologne in October 1981.

The largest recorded audience for a squash match was for the final of the British Open at Wembley Conference Centre on 10 April 1984 when the crowd was 2603. The court used for the event was the ICI perspex with four transparent walls. The previous largest was 1800 for the final of the French Open in March 1984 in Paris. The court used was the Pearson Twin-Vue with four glass walls.

Although rackets (US spelling racquets) with a soft ball was played in 1817 at Harrow School, Harrow, Greater London, there was no recognised champion of any country until John A. Miskey of Philadelphia won the American Amateur Singles Championship in 1907.

The most wins in the Amateur Championship is six by F. Amr Bey (b. Egypt, 14 February 1910), later appointed Ambassador in London, who won in 1931–33 and 1935–37. Norman Francis Borrett (b. 1 October 1917) of England won 5 times – 1946–50.

The longest recorded championship match was one of 2 hours 46 minutes when Jahangir Khan (Pak) beat Gamal Awad (Egy) 9–10, 9–5, 9–7, 9–2, the first game lasting a record 1 hour 11 minutes, in the final of the Chichester Festival, England, on 30 March 1983.

The shortest recorded match was when Deanna Murray beat Christine Rees in only 9½ min in a Ladies Welsh title match at Rhos-on-Sea, Clwyd, on 21 October 1979.

The first time two brothers contested a major international title – Hashim Khan and Azam Khan of Pakistan – was in the final of the 1953/4 British Open.

In 1977 in the final of the ISRF World Amateur Individual Championship in Toronto, Canada, Maqsood Ahmed of Pakistan beat his brother, Mohammed Saleem to become the first Pakistani player to take the title.

The first time that two sisters contested a major international title – Joyce Cave and Nancy Cave of Great Britain – was in the final of the spring 1922 inaugural British Open.

The first recorded instance of a player losing a first class match without serving was when Ian Wright played for Kent against Hampshire in the Premier Division of the Inter-County Championship on 1 November 1980 at Winchester Lawn Tennis and Squash Club. Wright lost 9–0, 9–0, 9–0 to Aubrey Waddy of Hampshire in 17 minutes. The match was played two days after Wright's 46th birthday and it was his first appearance for Kent.

The first man to win a major international professional title without conceding a point was Jahangir Khan (Pak) who beat Maqsood Ahmed (Pak) in the final of the 1982 ISPA Championship at the Abbeydale Club, Sheffield on 10 March. Jahangir won 9–0, 9–0, 9–0.

The first woman was Heather McKay (Aus) who beat Beverley Johnson (Aus) in the final of the 1968 British Open. Mrs McKay won 9–0, 9–0, 9–0.

The first players to be disqualified by a referee from a major international championship were Ali Aziz in the 1977 World Open in Australia – dismissed under the rule that play shall be continuous – and Hiddy Jahan of England dismissed from the Chichester Festival in 1983 for abuse and arguing with the referee.

The most international appearances:
Men: Christopher Wilson of Scotland. He retired from international squash after winning his 106th cap

A happy Chris Wilson having just been presented with a trophy cap to mark his 106th appearance for Scotland, a record number for any player, and achieved in a career stretching from 1969 to 1984

and playing for Scotland against England in Edinburgh in January 1984. He first played for his country in 1969.

Women: Geraldine Barniville of Ireland who has won 71 caps. She first played for Ireland against England in 1973 and retired from international squash in October 1983 after playing for Ireland against Wales in the WISRF Team Championship in Perth, Australia.

The longest span of internationals was achieved by Sheila Macintosh (née Speight), the 1960 British champion who played for England v. Wales in April 1949 and in December 1971 – a span of 22 years 8 months. Among men, Lawrence John Verney was only marginally less, representing Wales on 3 February 1950 and on 17 February 1972.

The most individual wins in the ISRF World Championships (amateurs and professionals) is three by Geoff Hunt of Australia – 1967, 1969, 1971.

The most team wins in the ISRF World Championships is four by Australia in 1967, 1969, 1971 and 1973.

The youngest player to win the ISRF World Individual Championships is Jahangir Khan of Pakistan, aged 15 years 10 months in the 1979 championship in Melbourne, Australia. He beat Phil Kenyon of Great Britain in the final. The 1979 event was the last for amateurs only.

The most individual wins in the WISRF World Championships is two by Heather McKay in 1976 and 1979.

The most team wins in the WISRF World Championships is two by Australia in 1981 and 1983.

The most wins in the British Open Championship (amateurs or professionals) is eight by Geoff Hunt of Australia in 1969, 1974 and 1976–81. Hashim Khan of Pakistan won seven times and Jonah Barrington of Great Britain and Ireland won six times.

The most appearances in the men's British Open finals is 10 by Geoff Hunt of Australia in 1968–69, 1971, 1973, 1975–80.

The most appearances in the women's British Open finals is 16 by Heather McKay of Australia, in 1962–77 inclusive.

The woman most times runner-up in the British Open is Nancy Cave (Eng) – 6 times in 1922 (spring), 1922 (December), 1924, 1925, 1926 and 1931.

The first woman to win the British Open final without conceding a point was Heather McKay of Australia who beat Beverley Johnson 9–0, 9–0, 9–0 in the 1968 final.

Prizemoney for the world's major events

MEN

	Sponsor	Venue	Total	First prize
British Open				
1983–84	Davies and Tate	Brighton/Wembley	£25 000	£4000
1982–83	Davies and Tate	Derby	£13 410	£2500
1981–82	Audi	Bromley	£25 000	£4000
1980–81	Audi	Bromley	£21 090	£3700
1979–80	Avis	Wembley	£15 835	£2750
1978–79	Avis	Wembley	£13 690	£2500
1977–78	Avis	Wembley	£11 520	£2000
1976–77	Lucas	Wembley	£10 500	£1800
1975–76	Lucas	Wembley	£ 9 400	£1650
1974–75	Benson and Hedges	Wembley	£ 4 385	£1250
1973–74	Benson and Hedges	Sheffield	£ 2 710	£1000
1972–73	Benson and Hedges	Sheffield	£ 1 700	£ 500
1971–72	Benson and Hedges	Sheffield	£ 1 000	£ 500
1970–71	Tudor Processing	Birmingham	Not Recorded	£ 100
ISPA World Open				
1975–76	Lucas	England	£ 9 400	£1650
1977	Uniroyal	Australia	A$40 000 including players expenses, sterling equivalent £25 477	A$8000 (£5095)
1979	McGuinness	Canada	C$50 000 including players expenses, sterling equivalent £19 455	C$8200 (£3190)
1980	Schweppes	Australia	A$50 000 including players expenses, sterling equivalent £24 248	A$8320 (£4034)
1981	McGuinness	Canada	C$50 000 (£22 222)	C$7500 (£3333)
1982	Audi	England	£27 500	£4400
1983	Canadian Club	Germany	DM160 000 including players expenses, sterling equivalent £40 302	DM25 600 (£6448)
ISRF World Individual Championship				
1983	Pilkington	New Zealand	NZ$68 400 £30 269	NZ$10 944 (£4842)

	Sponsor	Venue	Total	First prize
British Open				
1973–74		Sydenham	£ 150	£ 50
1974–75		Wembley	£ 250	£ 80
1975–76		Wembley	£ 300	£ 100
1976–77		Wembley	£ 375	£ 100
1977–78	Langham Life	Wembley	£ 950	£ 250
1978–79	Langham Life	Wembley	£ 1535	£ 500
1979–80	Pretty Polly	Brighton	£ 4956	£1200
1980–81	Pretty Polly	Wembley	£ 7220	£1500
1981–82	Audi	Bromley	£ 9180	£1700
1982–83	Davies and Tate	Derby	£ 9300	£1700
1983–84	Davies and Tate	Brighton/Wembley	£11 225	£2000
WISRF **World Open**				
1983	Town and Country	Australia	A$12 210 (Sterling equivalent £7445)	A$3000 (£1829)

The youngest player to win the men's British Open is Jahangir Khan of Pakistan, aged 18 years 119 days, in April 1982 when the event was held at the Churchill Theatre, Bromley, Kent. He beat Hiddy Jahan, then of Pakistan, now of England, in the final.

The youngest player to win the women's British Open is Susan Noel aged 19 years and 7 months in January 1932. She beat Joyce Cave 9–5, 9–7, 9–1. Joyce Cave was 19 years and 8 months when she won the first Open in 1922.

The largest prize money for the men's British Open is £25 000 for the 1981/2 and 1983/4 events sponsored by Audi and Davies & Tate, respectively.

The largest first prize for the men's British Open is £4000 won by Geoff Hunt of Australia competing in the 1981/2 championship sponsored by Audi, and Jahangir Khan (Pak) competing in the 1983/4 championship sponsored by Davies & Tate.

The largest prize money for the women's British Open is £11 225 for the 1983/4 championship, sponsored by Davies & Tate.

The largest first prize for the women's British Open is £2000 won by Sue Devoy (NZ) competing in the 1983/4 championship, sponsored by Davies & Tate.

The most wins in the British Open Vintage Championship (for players 55 and over) is by Hashim Khan who won it six times between 1978 and 1983.

The most wins in the World Open Championship is four by Geoff Hunt of Australia in 1976, 1977, 1979 and 1980.

Jahangir Khan of Pakistan has won three, in 1981, 1982 and 1983.

The most appearances in the men's World Open finals is 5, made by Geoff Hunt of Australia in 1975, 1977, 1979, 1980 and 1981.

The most appearances in the women's World Open finals is 2 made by Rhonda Thorne and Vicki Cardwell, both of Australia, in 1981 and 1983.

The youngest player to win the men's World Open is Jahangir Khan of Pakistan, aged 17 years 354 days, in November 1981 when the event was held in Toronto, Canada. He beat Geoff Hunt of Australia in the final.

The youngest player to win the women's World Open is Rhonda Thorne of Australia, aged 23 when the event was held in 1981 in Toronto, Canada. She beat Vicki Hoffman in the final.

The first man to win a World Open title without losing a game was Jahangir Khan in the 1983 championship held in Munich, West Germany. He played six matches, winning 18 games, conceding 39 points. In seven of the games he lost no points.

The first woman to win a World Open title without losing a game was Heather McKay (Aus) in the 1976 championship when the first event was held in Brisbane.

The first time two teenagers contested a World Open final was Tuesday 6 December 1983 in Munich, West Germany. Jahangir Khan of Pakistan, aged 19 years 11 months, met Chris Dittmar of Australia, aged 19 years and 10 months.

The largest first prize for the men's World Open is £6448 won by Jahangir Khan of Pakistan competing in the 1983 championship, sponsored by Canadian Club.

The largest first prize for the women's World Open is £1829, won by Vicki Cardwell of Australia competing in the 1983 championship held in Perth, Australia.

The first man to hold both the World Open and British Open titles (when two championships were held as separate events) was Geoff Hunt of Australia in 1977.

The first woman to hold both the World Open and British Open titles was Vicki Cardwell of Australia in 1983. (NB The first Women's World Championship in 1976 was an invitation event and was won by Heather McKay who at that time was also British Women's champion.)

The man most times runner-up in the World and British Open finals is Qamar Zaman of Pakistan with a total of seven. Three in the World Open (1977, 1979, 1980) and four in the British Open (1977, 1978, 1979, 1984).

The woman most times runner-up is Sue Cogswell of England with a total of four. Three in the British Open (1974, 1979, 1980) and once in the World Open (1979).

The most team wins in the European (ESRF) Championships (started in 1974) is nine by the England men's team.

In the women's competition (started in 1979) England have won every year.

The first woman to hold the British, Australian and American women's titles in the same season is Janet Shardlow (née Morgan) of England in 1954/5.

The most wins in the Women's Squash Rackets Association Championship (now generally known as the British Women's Open) is 16 by Heather McKay from 1961 to 1977.

The largest recorded fine imposed is £1000 on Lisa Opie (Eng) by the disciplinary committee of the English Women's Squash Rackets Association for bringing the game into disrepute while competing in the final of the 1983/4 British Open. Miss Opie was also banned from competing in the 1984/5 Open.

The longest running sponsorship is by Banbury Grandstands Ltd, manufacturers of the Banbury Squash Courts. In the 1969/70 season they launched a national club team championship (the Banbury Trophy) for men's teams of five players which was open to all clubs and affiliated to the English SRA. Prize money was £150 to the winning club and £50 to the runners-up. In 1976 a women's event was introduced.

At the end of the 1982/3 season the running of the tournament was taken over by the SRA and WSRA, although the event name was retained and the sponsoring company (now Banbury Squash Courts Ltd) continued to make a sizeable contribution towards running costs. By the end of the 1983/4 season the Banbury Trophy had been running for 15 seasons and prize money was £350 to the winning club and £175 to the runners-up.

Most appearances in major finals
Men (World Open, ISRF World Championship, British Open): Geoff Hunt (Aus) – 18 (World Open 5, ISRF 3, British Open 10); Jahangir Khan (Pak) – 9 (World Open 3, ISRF 2, British Open 4); Qamar Zaman (Pak) – 9 (World Open 3, ISRF 1, British Open 5); Hashim Khan (Pak) – 8 (British Open 8).

Vicki Cardwell (Aus), the first woman to hold both the World Open and British Open titles, pictured after winning the world event in Perth, Australia, in 1983.
Greg Wood

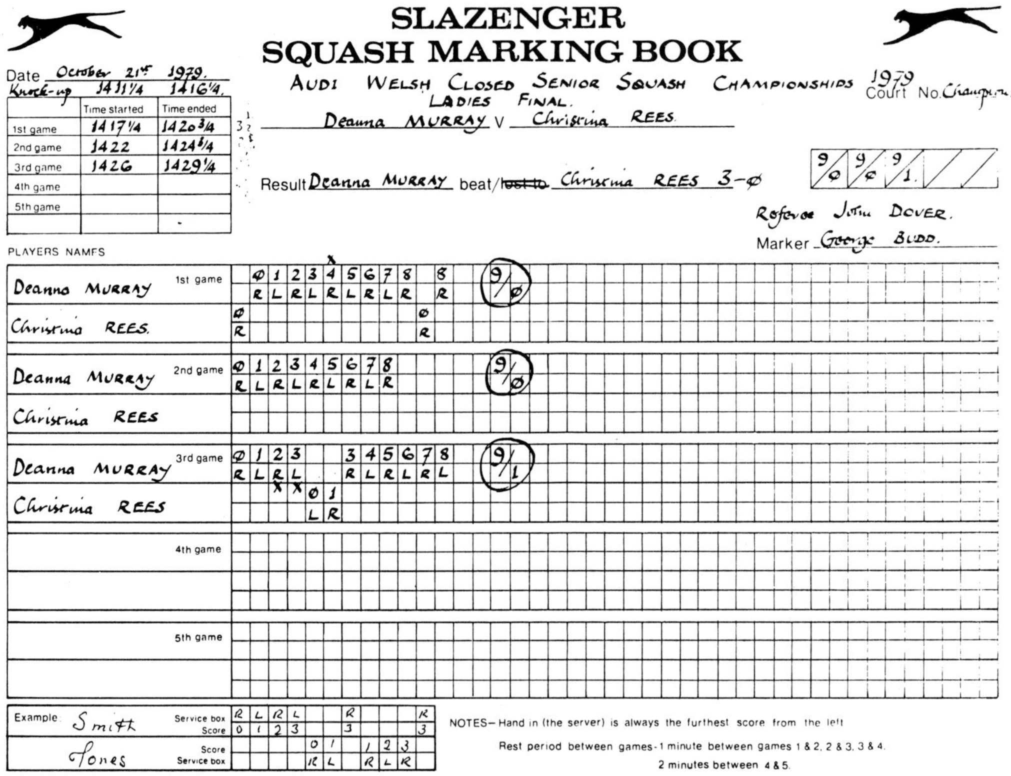

SLAZENGER
SQUASH MARKING BOOK

AUDI WELSH CLOSED SENIOR SQUASH CHAMPIONSHIPS 1979
LADIES FINAL.
Court No. *Championships*

Date *October 21st 1979.*
Knock-up *1411¼ 1416¼*

Deanna MURRAY v Christina REES.

Result *Deanna MURRAY* beat/~~lost to~~ *Christina REES 3–0*

	Time started	Time ended
1st game	1417¼	1420¾
2nd game	1422	1424¼
3rd game	1426	1429¼
4th game		
5th game		

Referee *John Dover.*
Marker *George Budd.*

9/0 9/0 9/1

PLAYERS NAMES

Deanna MURRAY — 1st game
Christina REES.

Deanna MURRAY — 2nd game
Christina REES

Deanna MURRAY — 3rd game
Christina REES

4th game

5th game

Example: Smith / Jones

NOTES— Hand in (the server) is always the furthest score from the left.
Rest period between games—1 minute between games 1 & 2, 2 & 3, 3 & 4.
2 minutes between 4 & 5.

The figures speak for themselves on the scoresheet recording Deanna Murray's 9½-minute win over Christina Rees in the final of the Welsh Women's Closed Championship in October 1979

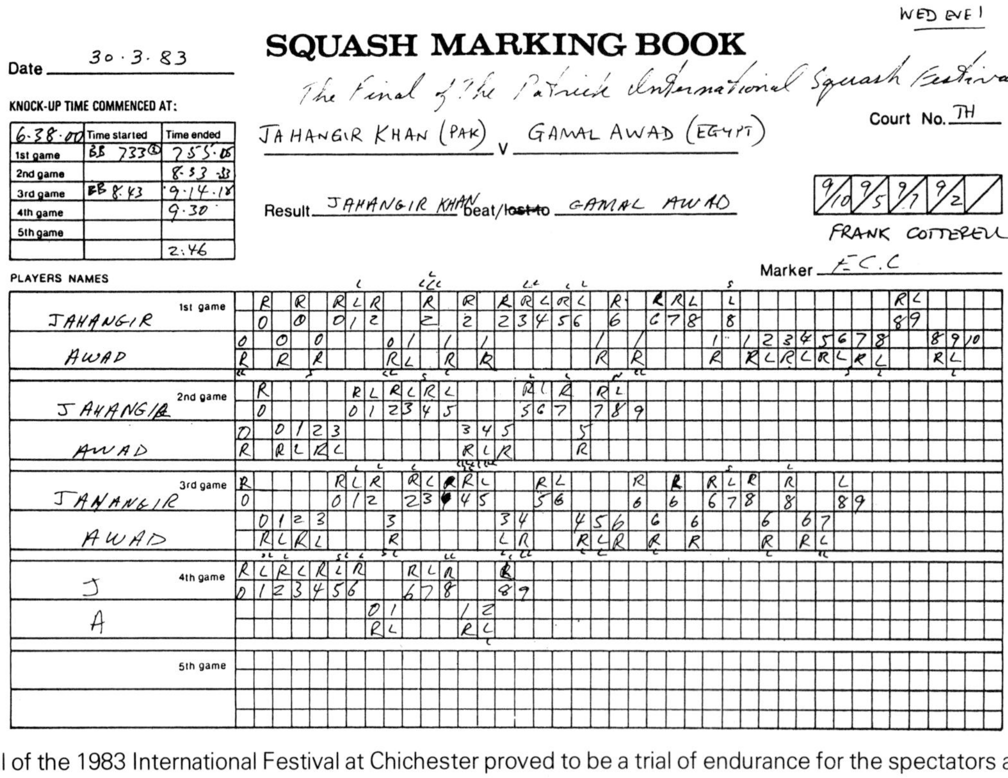

SQUASH MARKING BOOK

WED EVE 1

The Final of The Patrick International Squash Festival

Date *30.3.83*

JAHANGIR KHAN (PAK) v GAMAL AWAD (EGYPT)
Court No. *TH*

Result *JAHANGIR KHAN* beat/~~lost to~~ *GAMAL AWAD*

KNOCK-UP TIME COMMENCED AT:

	Time started	Time ended
6.38.00	BB 733	755.0
1st game		
2nd game		8.53.3
3rd game	BB 8.43	9.14.18
4th game		9.30
5th game		
		2:46

9/10 9/5 9/7 9/2

FRANK COTTERELL
Marker *E.C.C.*

PLAYERS NAMES

JAHANGIR — 1st game
AWAD

JAHANGIR — 2nd game
AWAD

JAHANGIR — 3rd game
AWAD

J — 4th game
A

5th game

The final of the 1983 International Festival at Chichester proved to be a trial of endurance for the spectators as well as the players with Pakistan's Jahangir Khan and Egypt's Gamal Awad occupying the court for a record 2 hours 46 minutes

154

Women (WISRF World Open, British Open): Heather McKay (née Blundell) (Aus) – 18 (WISRF 2, British Open 16). Janet Shardlow (née Morgan) (Eng) – 12 (British Open 12). Nancy Cave (Eng) – 9 (British Open 9). Vicki Cardwell (née Hoffman) (Aus) – 7 (WISRF 2, British Open 5).

Squash courts of the world

The 51 member nations of the International Squash Rackets Federation can boast a total of 31 322 squash courts, a figure that does not take into account courts belonging to such companies, private clubs, hotels, individuals not required to register or affiliate with national associations. There are six countries with more than 1000 courts, the list being headed by England (8419), Australia (6000), the USA (3500) and West Germany (2700) who made the jump from founding an association to being the fourth largest squash nation in less than 10 years.

England	8419	South Africa	1250
Australia	6000	Ireland	650
USA	3500	New Zealand	645
West Germany	2700	France	500
Canada	1400	Mexico	500

Scotland	500	Zambia	32
Finland	460	Israel	31
Sweden	450	Italy	30
India	450	Thailand	29
Netherlands	400	Papua New Guinea	25
Singapore	400	Philippines	25
Switzerland	400	Indonesia	23
Nigeria	350	Sri Lanka	17
Belgium	300	Bahamas	15
Wales	298	Jamaica	14
Argentina	250	Barbados	14
Brazil	200	Jordan	11
Malaysia	173	Bermuda	10
Zimbabwe	160	St. Vincent	8
Hong Kong	158	Monaco	6
Pakistan	120	Venezuela	5
Kuwait	80	Cayman Islands	2
Japan	80	Brunei and Taiwan are	
Egypt	72	also affiliated but	
Norway	60	details are not	
Spain	50	available	
Denmark	50		

The most courts in a club is 19 at Kingswood Squash Club, Basildon, Essex. The club opened in 1967 with six courts and extra courts have been added at various times up to 1978.

INDEX